# Israel's Palestinians

## *The Conflict Within*

**ILAN PELEG**

*Lafayette College, Easton, PA
and Middle East Institute, Washington DC*

**DOV WAXMAN**

*Baruch College and The Graduate Center,
City University of New York*

**CAMBRIDGE**
UNIVERSITY PRESS

CAMBRIDGE UNIVERSITY PRESS
Cambridge, New York, Melbourne, Madrid, Cape Town,
Singapore, São Paulo, Delhi, Tokyo, Mexico City

Cambridge University Press
32 Avenue of the Americas, New York, NY 10013-2473, USA

www.cambridge.org
Information on this title: www.cambridge.org/9780521157025

First published 2011

Printed in the United States of America

*A catalog record for this publication is available from the British Library.*

*Library of Congress Cataloging in Publication data*
Peleg, Ilan, 1944–
    Israel's Palestinians : the conflict within / Ilan Peleg, Dov Waxman.
        p.   cm.
    ISBN 978-0-521-15702-5 (pbk.)
    1. Palestinian Arabs.   2. Jewish-Arab relations.   3. Arab-Israeli conflict – 1993–
    I. Waxman, Dov.   II. Title.
    DS119.76.P464   2011
    305.8992'74–dc22          2010048889

ISBN 978-0-521-76683-8 Hardback
ISBN 978-0-521-15702-5 Paperback

# Contents

# Figures

# Preface and Acknowledgments

Our goal in writing this book is not only to provide a thorough scholarly analysis of Jewish-Arab relations in Israel but also to issue an urgent call for a major change in these relations. The book is intended to sound an alarm, to warn that, unless immediate and dramatic action is taken, the relationship between Israel's Jewish majority and its Palestinian-Arab minority will continue to deteriorate. This will put Arab-Jewish coexistence in Israel, the country's political stability, and the quality of its democracy seriously at risk. It will also undermine the prospects for a truly comprehensive and lasting solution to the Israeli-Palestinian conflict.

Some may think that we are being overly alarmist and that majority-minority relations in Israel are not nearly as bad, or as unstable, as we suggest. It might even be argued that whatever the complaints and frustrations of Israel's Palestinian minority, they have never really posed a threat to the state and have always remained firmly under its control. According to this view, the predicament of the Palestinian minority in Israel today and the relationship between it and the Jewish majority – though far from ideal – is not a pressing issue or major concern, certainly not for a country that faces a host of internal challenges and external threats. We strongly disagree with this perspective. For us, the divide between Jewish and Palestinian-Arab citizens of Israel is the deepest and most dangerous social and political divide within the country, and Israel's unequal treatment of its Palestinian minority is as problematic for the country's future as its continued occupation of Palestinian territories. Ignoring or minimizing this problem is to court disaster – possibly, the complete collapse of the two-state solution to the Israeli-Palestinian conflict and major civil unrest and large-scale violence inside Israel.

In recent years, we have observed with increasing dismay a series of events and developments in Israel that are straining Jewish-Arab relations in the country to the breaking point – most notably, the massive Arab protests and riots that occurred in October 2000, the publication in 2006–2007 of four "Vision documents" by members of the Arab intellectual elite, the rise in the number of Arab voters boycotting or abstaining from Israeli elections, the violent clashes between Arabs and Jews in "mixed cities," the growing public discussion of transferring densely populated Arab regions in Israel to a future Palestinian state (a proposal vehemently rejected by the Arab residents of those regions), the 2009 electoral success of Yisrael Beiteinu led by Avigdor Lieberman that campaigned on an explicitly anti-Arab political platform and Lieberman's elevation to the post of foreign minister in the government of Prime Minister Benjamin Netanyahu, and the introduction of a number of discriminatory and anti-Arab bills in the Israeli parliament. All of this indicates to us a real crisis in majority-minority relations in Israel. The fragile coexistence that has prevailed between Jews and Arabs for decades is now in jeopardy as the two groups are becoming more politically polarized, with extremists on both sides gaining ground, and socially more alienated as heightened fear and suspicion keeps them apart.

In tandem with this crisis in majority-minority relations, the state itself suffers from a legitimacy crisis vis-à-vis its Palestinian citizens. After years of suffering from government neglect and systematic discrimination (a fact recognized by official Israeli government bodies), growing numbers of Palestinians in Israel have concluded that the state is inherently biased against them. Most believe that they will never be treated fairly and gain equality with Jewish citizens as long as Israel defines itself as a Jewish state. Consequently, the redefinition of the state has become the central demand of the Palestinian minority; but it is a demand that the Jewish majority adamantly and almost universally opposes. As the state's Jewish identity has become a major point of contention domestically, it has also been inserted into the Israeli-Palestinian peace process by Prime Minister Netanyahu's insistence that the Palestinian Authority officially recognize Israel as a Jewish state in a final peace agreement. Such recognition, however, is unlikely to be granted against the objections of the Palestinian minority in Israel – underlining the connection that we emphasize in this book between Israel's external and internal Palestinian problems.

In addition to offering a thorough analysis of Jewish-Arab relations in Israel and warning of the dangers that the country faces if it fails to solve its internal Palestinian problem, we also present in this book our own proposals for improving majority-minority relations in Israel. Drawing on the examples of other countries that have successfully managed ethno-national conflicts within their borders, we make specific recommendations for improving the relationship between the Jewish majority and the Palestinian minority in Israel. We also suggest a redefinition of the state in a way that can satisfy both Jewish and Palestinian needs. Although we do not expect readers to accept all of our proposals, we hope that our proposals will at least stimulate new thinking and encourage creative and bold action to address an issue that has all-too-often been ignored.

Our thinking is fundamentally guided by the conviction we share that Israeli Jews and Palestinians (both citizens and non-citizens of Israel) do not have to be enemies. The conflict between them – inside and outside Israel's pre-1967 borders – is not metaphysically preordained or historically determined. Although it is certainly long-running and deeply rooted, it is not completely intractable and beyond repair. The establishment of a Palestinian state and a domestic transformation of Israel can greatly alleviate, if not entirely eliminate, this conflict. We also firmly believe that the State of Israel can become a place in which Jews and Palestinians can live together as equal citizens; and that it can be, indeed *should* be, a homeland for the Jewish people, a pluralistic democracy, and a state for all its citizens. This book essentially makes the case for why this is so necessary and how this could be achieved.

In the course of researching and writing the book, we were helped by many people. We are very grateful to all the people in Israel who shared their perspectives with us. They are, in alphabetical order, Ibrahim Abu-Shindi, Bashir Bashir, Adella Biadi-Shlon, Morad Elsana, Khaled Furani, Ali Haider, Hassan Jabareen, Yousef Jabareen, Amal Jamal, Ilana Kaufman, Dov Khanin, Mordechai Kremnitzer, Rania Laham-Grayeb, Anat Maor, Mike Prashker, Elie Rekhess, Ilan Saban, Sammy Smooha, and Oren Yiftachel. We are especially thankful to Alan Dowty for his comments on the manuscript and to the anonymous reviewers of the manuscript for Cambridge University Press. We would like to thank our research assistants, Matthew Goldstein, Michael Handzo, Muhammad Kabir, and Andrew Schroeder, as well as our supportive editor at Cambridge University Press, Eric Crahan. The research and writing of this book was made possible by the institutional support received from Baruch College of the City University of New York and from Lafayette College.

Finally, we would like to note that this book is truly the result of a joint and equal effort, and the order in which our names appear on the book's cover was determined alphabetically.

We dedicate the book to all the individuals and groups in Israel and beyond who are tirelessly working to promote Jewish-Arab coexistence, cooperation, and equality. They give us hope for a better future for a country we care about deeply.

Ilan Peleg & Dov Waxman
March 1, 2011

# Introduction

## *The Other Palestinian Problem*

> Israel is liable in the end to doom its Arab citizens to fulfill its fears of them. How long can a relatively large minority be assumed by the majority to be an enemy without in the end actually turning into one? How long can the state exist as a stable political framework if this is how it treats a sixth of its citizens? Slowly and steadily, as if slumbering, Israel is missing its chance to rescue itself from a horrible mistake. It is creating for itself the enemy it will run up against after its other enemies have made their peace with it.
>
> David Grossman, Israeli writer[1]

No conflict in the world today receives more attention, attracts more controversy, and elicits more emotion than the Israeli-Palestinian conflict. Yet, for all the diplomatic interest, news coverage, and political passion it generates, the conflict between Israel and the Palestinians is widely misunderstood. For some, the conflict is about the struggle of the Jewish state to survive in the Middle East and the unrelenting opposition it faces from Palestinians determined to prevent this. For others, the conflict is about the struggle of the Palestinians to end Israel's long-running occupation over them and achieve national self-determination. Both of these common and competing perspectives identify the two sides in the conflict as Jews in Israel and Palestinians in the West Bank, Gaza Strip, and East Jerusalem (territories seized by Israel in the 1967 Arab-Israeli war), and both ultimately lend themselves to the belief that the conflict between the two nations can be solved if Palestinians accept the existence of the State of Israel and Israel ends its occupation of Palestinian territories and

---

[1] David Grossman, *Sleeping on a Wire: Conversations with Palestinians in Israel* (New York: Picador, 2003), 308.

allows a Palestinian state to be established in them. In short, two states
for two peoples is the key to Israeli-Palestinian peace.

The "two-state solution" to the Israeli-Palestinian conflict has long
been advocated by the international community (ever since the United
Nations [UN] General Assembly passed Resolution 181 partitioning
Palestine into two states, one Jewish and one Arab, on November 29,
1947) and in recent years has been actively promoted by successive U.S.
administrations. President Barack Obama has made achieving the two-
state solution one of the top foreign policy goals of his administration.
As he declared in his address to the UN General Assembly in September
2009: "The time has come – the time has come to re-launch negotiations
without preconditions that address the permanent status issues: security
for Israelis and Palestinians, borders, refugees, and Jerusalem. And the
goal is clear: Two states living side by side in peace and security – a
Jewish state of Israel, with true security for all Israelis; and a viable, independent Palestinian state with contiguous territory that ends the occupation that began in 1967, and realizes the potential of the Palestinian
people."[2] President Obama then followed up on this by encouraging and
cajoling Israel's government led by Prime Minister Benjamin Netanyahu
and the Palestinian Authority under Mahmoud Abbas to engage peace
talks (first indirectly and then face to face).

Whether or not this latest attempt to broker an Israeli-Palestinian
peace agreement succeeds, it will not actually solve the conflict. It will
be, at best, an incomplete solution rather than a comprehensive one.
This is because a two-state solution, essential though it is, will only
address the needs of Palestinians in the West Bank, Gaza Strip, and East
Jerusalem, and possibly Palestinian refugees elsewhere if they emigrate
to the new Palestinian state or receive sufficient compensation (there is
little, if any, chance that they will be able to exercise a "right of return"
to Israel).[3] But Palestinians in the Occupied Territories and Palestinians
in the Diaspora are not the only Palestinians. There are also Palestinians
who live in Israel and are Israeli citizens. At present, there are approximately 1.3 million Palestinian citizens of Israel[4] – about 20 percent of

---

[2] "Remarks by the President to the United Nations General Assembly," Office of the Press
Secretary, The White House, September 23, 2009.

[3] There are roughly 4.6 million Palestinian refugees living outside the West Bank and Gaza
Strip (3.9 million inside); approximately 3 million of them live in Lebanon, Syria, and
Jordan. It is unlikely that most of these refugees will "return" to Palestine or Israel fol-
lowing a peace agreement.

[4] We use the term "Palestinian citizens of Israel" to refer to members of Israel's Arab minority, whom Israeli Jews generally call "Israeli Arabs." We avoid using the label "Israeli

Israel's total population[5] and about 12 percent of Palestinians worldwide.[6] This Palestinian population has been almost completely ignored by the international community. For decades, international discussion of what has become known as the "Palestinian problem" or "Palestinian question" has focused almost exclusively on the dire predicament of Palestinians living under Israeli occupation in the West Bank, Gaza Strip, and East Jerusalem. Whereas the situation of Palestinians in the Occupied Territories has received a great deal of international attention, the situation of the Palestinian minority in Israel has received little, if any, attention. Indeed, many international observers are barely even aware of the existence of such a minority. Nor is it just the international community that has ignored Israel's Palestinian minority; so too has the Arab world,[7] and even the official leadership of the Palestinian national movement (the Palestinian Liberation Organization [PLO] and the Palestinian Authority [PA]).[8]

The widespread and longstanding tendency to disregard, to forget about, or to simply be unaware of the Palestinian minority in Israel has been reflected in all of the accords, initiatives, conferences, and summits aimed at achieving Israeli-Palestinian peace over the years. None of the peace plans, neither official nor unofficial, that have been proposed have ever dealt with the situation of the Palestinian minority in Israel, especially its future status in a two-state solution.[9] The 1993 Oslo Agreement,

---

Arabs" in this book because it does not accurately convey the self-identity of Arabs in Israel. In numerous surveys conducted over many years, the majority of Arab citizens of Israel define themselves as Palestinian rather than as "Israeli Arab" (this will be discussed in more detail in Chapter 1). Throughout the book, therefore, we will use the terms "Arab citizens of Israel" and "Palestinian citizens of Israel" interchangeably, as well as the terms "Arab minority" and "Palestinian minority."

[5] This figure excludes Arab permanent residents of Israel who do not hold Israeli citizenship; specifically, Palestinians living in East Jerusalem and Druze living in the Golan Heights.

[6] Rhoda Ann Kanaaneh, *Surrounded: Palestinian Soldiers in the Israeli Military* (Stanford, CA: Stanford University Press, 2009), 2.

[7] There is widespread ignorance in the Arab world about Palestinian citizens of Israel. See, for instance, Zvi Barel, "What are Israeli Arabs? Are they Jewish?" *Ha'aretz*, May 25, 2004.

[8] The PA, like the PLO before it, has largely ignored Palestinian citizens of Israel, and the latter has no official representation in the PLO or the PA. Muhammad H. Amara, "Israeli Palestinians and the Palestinian Authority," *Middle East Review of International Affairs* 4, no. 1 (March 2000), 39.

[9] The Obama administration in its new National Security Strategy released in May 2010 did at least obliquely acknowledge the importance of ensuring equal rights for Palestinian citizens of Israel in the framework of a two-state solution to the Israeli-Palestinian conflict. In affirming the U.S. desire for a two-state solution, the document called for "a Jewish state of Israel, with true security, acceptance, and *rights for all Israelis*; and a

the 2001 Clinton Parameters, the 2002 Arab Peace Initiative, the 2003 Road Map, and the 2003 Geneva Accord all failed to address the issue of the Palestinian minority in Israel. Not only has the Palestinian minority consistently been ignored in the various peace plans, it has also always been excluded from participating in the peace process itself.[10] The specific interests and concerns of the Palestinian minority have therefore never been addressed in any of the numerous attempts at Israeli-Palestinian peace making.

The reason for this omission lies in the prevailing view of the "Palestinian problem" as one primarily concerning Palestinians in the Occupied Territories and, secondarily, those in the Diaspora. This view of the "Palestinian problem," however, is too narrow. More than ever before, the "Palestinian problem" goes beyond the demand for statehood by Palestinians in the territories, and it cannot simply be solved by estab- lishing a Palestinian state in the West Bank and Gaza. We believe that the basic conception of the Palestinian problem that has guided peacemaking efforts to date is too limited and hence flawed, and that it is necessary to have a broader understanding of the Palestinian problem, one that includes Palestinians in Israel. It is this belief that has led us to write this book. In it, we examine the status of the Palestinian minority in Israel and its relationship with the state and the Jewish majority. We argue that these relations have seriously deteriorated in recent years and that this poses a real threat to the stability of Israel, to the quality of Israeli democ- racy, and to the potential for peace in the Middle East.

## The Internal Conflict and the External Conflict

Our fundamental claim in the book is that the growing ethno-national conflict within Israel today between Israeli Jews and Palestinian Arabs should be viewed as part of the larger conflict between Israel and the Palestinians. The Palestinian minority in Israel now poses a challenge to the future of the Jewish state that is as significant and urgent as that

viable, independent Palestine with contiguous territory that ends the occupation began in 1967 and realizes the potential of the Palestinian people" (italics added). This is the first time that an American administration has noted the need for Israel as a Jewish state to safeguard the rights of all its citizens. Aluf Benn, "Obama's new vision of a Jewish state guarantees rights of Israeli Arabs," *Ha'aretz*, June 8, 2010.

[10] An Arab Knesset member, Mohammad Meiari, did attend the Madrid peace conference in 1991 in order to raise the concerns of the Palestinian minority in Israel, but he was completely ignored. "The Palestinian Arab Citizens of Israel: Status, Opportunities and Challenges for an Israeli-Palestinian Peace," Mossawa Center, Haifa, Israel, June 2006, 59.

posed to it by Palestinians in the territories. After enduring decades of discrimination, marginalization, and neglect, Israel's Palestinian citizens have become increasingly alienated from the state and from Israeli-Jewish society and increasingly frustrated with the status quo in Israel.[11] They have also grown more politically assertive, embracing Palestinian nationalism, demanding their collective rights as a national minority, and calling for the abolition of the definition of Israel as a Jewish state. Hence, the issue of the status and future of the Palestinian minority in Israel can no longer be ignored. To do so not only jeopardizes stability, coexistence, and democracy within Israel, but also any possibility of truly comprehensive Israeli-Palestinian peace.

A comprehensive, lasting, and stable solution to the Israeli-Palestinian conflict is ultimately dependent on a resolution of the Jewish-Palestinian conflict within Israel as much as it is dependent on resolving the conflict between Israel and Palestinians in the Occupied Territories. There is little chance of reaching an Israeli-Palestinian peace agreement without addressing the issue of the Palestinian minority in Israel. This is because recent Israeli governments (specifically, the Netanyahu government since 2009 and its predecessor, Ehud Olmert's government between 2005 and 2009) have repeatedly insisted that the PA explicitly recognize Israel as a Jewish state in the framework of any Israeli-Palestinian "final status" agreement.[12] Prime Minister Netanyahu, for instance, in a major foreign policy speech at Bar Ilan University on June 14, 2009, stipulated that he would accept a Palestinian state only if the Palestinians "truly recognize Israel as the state of the Jewish people."[13] By making Israel's acceptance of a Palestinian state conditional on Palestinian recognition of Israel as a Jewish state, Netanyahu has effectively established a direct linkage between the internal conflict involving Jewish and Palestinian citizens

---

[11] According to one survey of a representative cross-section of Palestinian citizens of Israel, the vast majority was opposed to a continuation of the status quo in Israel, with only 12 percent of respondents deeming this to be acceptable to them. Nadim N. Rouhana, ed., *Attitudes of Palestinians in Israel on Key Political and Social Issues: Survey Research Results* (Haifa, Israel: Mada al-Carmel, September 2007).

[12] The main reason for this Israeli demand seems to be that it is seen as a way of blocking a Palestinian demand for a "right of return" to Israel of millions of Palestinian refugees and their descendants.

[13] "Full text of Netanyahu's foreign policy speech at Bar Ilan," *Ha'aretz*, June 14, 2009. Ehud Olmert, Netanyahu's predecessor as prime minster, made this demand prior to the Annapolis summit meeting with President George W. Bush and PA President Mahmoud Abbas in November 2007, describing Palestinian recognition of Israel "as a Jewish state" as a "precondition" for peace. Aluf Benn, "Israel to release up to 400 Palestinian prisoners ahead of Summit," *Ha'aretz*, November 12, 2007.

of Israel over the Jewish character of the State of Israel and the external Israeli-Palestinian conflict over the future of the West Bank and Gaza. Resolving the latter conflict now necessitates resolving, or at least ameliorating, the former conflict, because as long as the majority of Palestinians within Israel oppose its exclusive Jewish identity, it is highly unlikely that the PA leadership in Ramallah will agree to recognize Israel as a Jewish state, as this would not only go against the wishes of most Palestinians in Israel,[14] but it would also be deeply unpopular among Palestinians in the territories.

Even if the PA leadership could somehow be persuaded to officially recognize Israel as a Jewish state in return for Palestinian statehood, this would not really end the Israeli-Palestinian conflict. Contrary to popular opinion in much of the world, this conflict cannot be resolved just by ending the Israeli occupation and establishing a Palestinian state. Although terminating the occupation is a necessary condition for settling the Israeli-Palestinian conflict, it is not a sufficient condition. While Palestinians in the territories might be satisfied with finally having their own state (and this is itself debatable), Palestinians in Israel will definitely not be satisfied with such an outcome if their own status inside Israel does not significantly improve (only a small number of them are likely to actually move to a Palestinian state[15]). Leaders of the Palestinian minority in Israel have already publicly stated this.[16] Thus, as Hillel Halkin puts it: "The problem of Israel's Arab citizens has been overshadowed by Israel's prolonged conflict with the Palestinians living in the territories occupied in the 1967 war. And yet just as the problem existed before 1967, so it will continue to exist, only in a more acute form, if and when the Israeli-Palestinian conflict is settled. Or rather, the Israeli-Palestinian conflict cannot be settled as long as Israeli Arabs remain an angry, alienated, and growing minority, for they will simply become its new focus."[17]

---

[14] In a survey conducted before the Annapolis summit in November 2007, 65.6 percent of Palestinian citizens of Israel thought that the PA did not have the right to recognize Israel as a Jewish state. Nadim Rouhana, "Israel's Palestinians Speak Out," http://www.mada-research.org, December, 2007.

[15] In an opinion poll, only a small minority of Palestinian citizens of Israel (11.9 percent) expressed a willingness to move to a future Palestinian state. Sammy Smooha, *Index of Arab-Jewish Relations in Israel 2004* (Haifa: The Jewish-Arab Center, University of Haifa, 2005), 49.

[16] See Yoav Stern, "Israeli Arab leaders: A Palestinian state is not the solution for us," *Ha'aretz*, December 4, 2007.

[17] Hillel Halkin, "The Jewish State and Its Arabs," *Commentary*, January 2009, 30–31.

Under the best circumstances, an agreement between Israel and the PA over the future of the West Bank, Gaza Strip, and East Jerusalem will only be a first step toward an overall settlement of the Israeli-Palestinian conflict. The establishment of a Palestinian state must be accompanied by a transformation of the relationship between Israel's Jewish majority and Palestinian minority. Ultimately, the Israeli-Palestinian conflict will not be over until the status and conditions of Palestinians in Israel are addressed in a way that is more or less satisfactory to both the Jewish majority and the Palestinian minority in Israel.

One of the main goals of this book is to present detailed ideas on how to do this. On the whole, the proposals we make are designed to strike a balance between what we consider the reasonable demands of the Jewish majority and the reasonable demands of the Palestinian minority. In trying to find this middle ground, we recognize that our proposals are unlikely to appeal to everyone. Some will be objectionable to Jews, others to Palestinians. We believe, however, that it is possible to meet the basic needs, if not completely satisfy all the desires, of most Jews and Palestinians in Israel. Guided by this belief, we put forward ideas for improving the status and conditions of Palestinians in Israel that we think are just and viable. That is, in formulating our proposals, we have both normative and practical considerations in mind. Normatively, we are concerned to ensure the right of the Jewish people to a homeland of its own, and at the same time guarantee the rights of Palestinians in Israel, as individuals and as an indigenous national minority. Practically, we want to offer ideas that can realistically be adopted by Jewish and Palestinian leaders in Israel and gain popular support within both the Jewish majority and Palestinian minority.

Our key proposals involve officially recognizing Palestinians in Israel as a national minority; increasing their collective rights to allow them to enjoy greater cultural autonomy within Israel (including self-management of their own educational, cultural, and religious institutions); enhancing their political representation (by formally recognizing the Palestinian minority's representative institutions, especially the High Follow-up Committee for Arab Citizens, and ensuring the inclusion of the Arab minority in the state's decision-making processes); and significantly raising their socio-economic status (through affirmative action programs and long-term development plans specifically for the Palestinian community). In short, we believe that major political and economic changes need to occur within Israel in order to meet the needs of the Palestinian minority. At the same time, we believe that it would be desirable for members of the Palestinian minority to render some kind of national service to the state (which does not involve serving in the Israeli army), because this could help to ease widespread Jewish concerns about their loyalty to the state and foster their identification with the state.

The status quo in Israel cannot continue. It is neither morally acceptable nor politically stable. We do not, however, think that it is realistic or justified for Israel to abandon its Jewish character and simply become "a state of all its citizens" as many Palestinians in Israel wish it to be.[18] We are equally opposed to the idea that Israel ought to become a bi-national state as some commentators have suggested.[19] Instead, we believe that Israel should redefine itself as both a "Jewish homeland and state of all its citizens." We think that Israel's primary mission should be to serve the interests of all its citizens (like all modern democracies) rather than the interests of the Jewish people, but that it should still serve as a place of refuge and cultural vitality for Jews worldwide because of its historic, religious, and contemporary significance for the Jewish people. We are in favor, therefore, of changing the definition of the State of Israel, but in a moderate and inclusive manner.

Israel stands to gain many benefits from making such changes. They will bolster Israeli democracy, social cohesion, political stability, national security, economic growth, and its international image and legitimacy. They will also move Israel nearer to achieving the lofty vision of its founders, as expressed most clearly in its May 1948 Declaration of Independence, which promised a state that would "foster the development of the country for the benefit of all its inhabitants [...]" and "ensure complete equality of social and political rights to all its inhabitants [...]."[20] Israel has so far failed to live up to this promise. Although Palestinian citizens of Israel have benefited from rising living standards and have enjoyed more democratic freedoms than most Arabs elsewhere, they have always been and still are economically and politically inferior to Jewish citizens of Israel. In the words of one scholar, "they are formally citizens, but inferior ones,

---

[18] In a survey taken in 2004, 88.6 percent of Palestinian citizens of Israel wanted Israel to become "a state of all its citizens." Smooha, *Index of Arab-Jewish Relations*.

[19] See, for instance, Tony Judt, "Israel: The Alternative," *The New York Review of Books*, October 23, 2003; Ali Abunimah, *One Country: A Bold Proposal to End the Israeli-Palestinian Impasse* (New York: Metropolitan Books, 2006).

[20] "The Declaration of the Establishment of the State of Israel May 14, 1948," Israel Ministry of Foreign Affairs, Jerusalem, Israel, http://www.mfa.gov.il/MFA/Peace%20Process/ Guide%20to%20the%20Peace%20Process/Declaration%20of%20Establishment%20 of%20State%20of%20Israel.

struggling, marginalized, feared by the state yet largely Hebrew-speaking, passport-carrying, and bureaucracy-engaging."[21]

Though the Palestinian minority is no longer the completely ghettoized community it was during Israel's formative era (1948–1967), it remains a distinct,[22] separate, largely unassimilated community on the margins of Israeli society (this is not to say that Palestinians in Israel have not undergone acculturation – adopting aspects of Israeli-Jewish culture – but they have not assimilated and have no desire to[23]). Moreover, the Palestinian minority continues to be widely perceived as a security threat, a potential "fifth column" in Israel's ongoing conflict with the Palestinian nation as a whole. Palestinians in Israel still have to live with the suspicion and at times outright hostility of members of the Jewish majority. As the Association for Civil Rights in Israel (ACRI), the country's leading civil rights organization, noted in its 2007 annual report: "Arab citizens are exposed to differential and humiliating treatment, and are often regarded with suspicion in Jewish towns, in the street, at the entrance to public recreation and commercial facilities, and at bus and train stations"[24]; or as Ahmad Tibi, a leading Palestinian politician in Israel more bluntly put it: "The problem is that they [the Israeli government and Israeli Jews] are dealing with us like enemies and not as citizens."[25]

Abiding Israeli-Jewish suspicion toward them is only one of the many problems facing Palestinians in Israel. They also have to contend with persistent poverty, relatively high levels of unemployment, inadequate educational resources, land confiscations, home demolitions, municipal under-funding, and discriminatory legislation. All of this has left many Palestinians in Israel angry and resentful. They feel highly deprived

---

[21] Kanaaneh, *Surrounded*, 3.

[22] Israeli sociologist Sammy Smooha notes that: "Arabs and Jews [in Israel] diverge on all core elements of culture. They have different languages, religions, nationalities, family patterns, and ways of life. Each of these cultural components contains many values, norms, symbols, beliefs, preferences, feelings, heritages, and memories, turning the Arab and Jewish cultures into genuinely distinct and separate cultures and making the ethnic boundaries between the two communities clear, rigid, and hardly passable." Sammy Smooha, "Arab-Jewish Relations in Israel: A Deeply Divided Society," in Anita Shapira, ed., *Israeli Identity in Transition* (New York: Praeger, 2004), 40.

[23] Smooha, "Arab-Jewish Relations in Israel," 43.

[24] The Association for Civil Rights in Israel, "The State of Human Rights in Israel and the Occupied Territories 2007 Report," 16.

[25] Quoted in Philip Weiss and Adam Horowitz, "Loyalty and Democracy in Lieberman's Israel: Interviews with Israeli Knesset Members Alex Miller and Ahmad Tibi," *TPM Café*, June 8, 2009, http://tpmcafe.talkingpointsmemo.com/2009/06/08/loyalty_and_democracy_in_liebermans_israel_intervi/.

compared to Israeli Jews, rejected by Israeli-Jewish society, and unfairly treated by the state.[26] Most have bitterly concluded that Israel is inherently biased against them, and that they will never be treated fairly and gain equality with Jewish citizens as long as Israel defines itself as a Jewish state.[27] Consequently, the re-definition of the state has become the central demand of the Palestinian minority. It is a demand that the Jewish majority adamantly and almost unanimously opposes.

## A Dangerous Divide

The growing and increasingly outspoken opposition of the Palestinian minority to Israel's identity as a Jewish state has provoked an angry backlash among Israeli Jews. Feeling isolated internationally and threatened regionally (especially by the rising power of Iran), Israeli Jews have become more rightwing, hawkish, and illiberal in recent years. This has aggravated long-running tensions between the two communities. Fear and mistrust are now very high on both sides.[28] Palestinians in Israel fear severe infringements of their civil rights, violence by the state and by Jewish citizens, the revocation of their citizenship, and even expulsion from the state (whether in the context of a territorial exchange with the Palestinian Authority or because of nationalist pressure to strengthen the Jewish nature of the state).[29] Jews in Israel, by contrast, see "Israeli Arabs" as both security and demographic threats. They fear the spread of radicalism within the Arab minority – whether in the form of growing Palestinian nationalism or Islamism – and the perceived security risk this poses to Israel, especially in the event of another Palestinian intifada or Arab-Israeli war. Israeli Jews also fear that Arab demographic growth will eventually swamp Israel's Jewish population and nullify the Jewish

---

[26] In 2004, more than half of Palestinians in Israel (53.4 percent) felt alien and rejected in Israel. Smooha, *Index of Arab-Jewish Relations*.

[27] Rouhana, ed., *Attitudes of Palestinians in Israel*.

[28] In a survey conducted in 2007, 54 percent of Palestinian citizens of Israel polled felt that it was "impossible to trust the Jewish majority." Cited in Elie Rekhess, "Israel and Its Arab Citizens – Taking Stock," Tel Aviv Notes, October 16, 2007. A poll taken in 2004 among Israeli Jews found that a large majority of them (80.8 percent) believed that "an Arab citizen who defines oneself as a 'Palestinian Arab in Israel' cannot be loyal to the state and its laws." Smooha, *Index of Arab-Jewish Relations*, 38.

[29] In a survey taken in 2004, 81 percent of Palestinian citizens of Israel said they feared severe infringements of their rights, 71.9 percent feared state violence, 70.6 percent feared violence by Jewish citizens, and 63.5 percent feared expulsion from Israel. Smooha, *Index of Arab-Jewish Relations*.

state.[30] Thus, in the words of the Israeli writer David Grossman: "Each is mortally afraid of the other. [...] Those fears now seem to be the only thing that connects them."[31]

Fuelling the fears on both sides of the Jewish-Palestinian divide in Israel are widespread prejudice and negative stereotypes. These attitudes are deeply rooted within both communities in large part as a result of the protracted Arab-Israeli conflict, but they are reinforced by a lack of "genuine integration and meaningful interaction between the two communities."[32] There is very little integration and a great deal of social separation between Jews and Palestinians in Israel[33] – they generally live apart, study apart, and interact only in the workplace, and even then usually as a boss and a worker (because Palestinians continue to be concentrated in blue-collar and unskilled positions within the Israeli labor market). Palestinians mostly live in their own villages, towns, and urban neighborhoods;[34] they attend their own elementary and high schools, and they do not perform military service (except for the Druze and some Bedouin). There is, therefore, little informal social contact between Palestinian and Jewish citizens of Israel. Intermarriage is extremely rare, and even personal friendships are uncommon.[35] In fact, most Israeli Jews do not personally know any Palestinians in Israel (only a quarter of Israeli Jews actually do).[36] Not only do Israeli Jews rarely encounter Palestinian citizens of Israel in their daily lives, but also they rarely read about them or hear about them in the media, and when they do it is often in negative ways.[37]

[30] In a 2004 survey, 83.9 percent of Israeli Jews said they feared the danger of Arab citizens of Israel supporting the Palestinian people, and 66.7 percent said they feared the danger of a high Arab birthrate. Smooha, *Index of Arab-Jewish Relations*.

[31] Grossman, *Sleeping on a Wire*, 334.

[32] "The Palestinian Arab Citizens of Israel," Mossawa Center, 66–67.

[33] There are very few places in Israel where Jews and Palestinians are integrated, most notably the "Oasis of Peace" community (Wahat al-Salaam/ Neve Shalom) and a few experimental Arabic-Hebrew bilingual schools.

[34] Palestinians mostly live in the Galilee (a rural area in northern Israel), the Triangle (an area bordering the "Green line" separating Israel from the northern part of the West Bank), and in the Negev desert (in the south). According to Smooha, nine-tenths live in exclusively Arab communities, and one-tenth live in separate Arab neighborhoods in Jewish towns. Smooha, "Arab-Jewish Relations in Israel," 42.

[35] Smooha, "Arab-Jewish Relations in Israel," 42.

[36] Public opinion research conducted through February and March 2010 by Dahlia Scheindlin on behalf of *Merchavim: The Institute for Shared Citizenship*.

[37] See Gadi Wolfsfeld, A. Avraham, and Issam Abu Rayah, "When Prophesy Always Fails: Israeli Press Coverage of the Arab Minority Land Day Protests," *Political Communication* 17, 2 (2000), 115–131; and Nechama Laor, Noa Alpent Leffler, and

Given the de facto segregation that exists between Jews and Palestinians in Israel, it is hardly surprising that the divide between them is the country's deepest social cleavage. There are many cleavages in Israeli society – between secular and religious Jews, between Ashkenazim and Mizrahim,[38] between natives and immigrants, and so forth – but the social and political divide between the Jewish majority and the Palestinian minority is by far the most problematic. Majority-minority relations in Israel have never been good. There has always been an undercurrent of wariness and tension, rather than outright hatred. As one observer has written: "Many Jews fear and distrust Arabs, but they are polite and respectful in their presence. Many Israeli Arabs feel anger at Jewish society, but they seldom express it in their contacts with individual Jews."[39] This state of relations has been accurately characterized as a "cold peace."[40] But even this "cold peace" is now at risk. The uneasy and fragile coexistence that currently prevails between Jews and Palestinians in Israel is in danger. It is our contention in this book that unless dramatic action is taken to remedy this, the Jewish majority and the Palestinian minority are on a collision course.

There has been a serious deterioration in Jewish-Palestinian relations in Israel over the past decade, specifically since the massive protests and rioting by Palestinians inside Israel that erupted in October 2000. Numerous events and developments since then have contributed to these worsening relations, among them the publication of four "Vision Documents" by members of the Palestinian intellectual elite in Israel in 2006–2007, inter-communal violence in Acre in October 2008 and in Umm al-Fahm in March 2009, the public discussion in Israel of transferring Palestinian-inhabited regions in Israel to a future Palestinian state (a proposal vehemently rejected by the Palestinian residents of those regions), the electoral success of Avigdor Lieberman's Yisrael Beiteinu party with its anti-Arab political platform, and the introduction of a number of parliamentary bills directed against members of the Palestinian minority. External events and developments have also played a part in the deterioration of Jewish-Palestinian relations in Israel – most notably the second Palestinian

---

Havi Inbar-Lankri, "The Absent and Present at Peak Viewing Time – Follow-up Study," http://www.rashut2.org.il/editor.

[38] Ashkenazim are Jews of European origin and Mizrahim are Jews of Middle Eastern and North African origin (also known as Sephardim).

[39] Halkin, "The Jewish State," 32.

[40] Yaakov Kop and Robert E. Litan, *Sticking Together: The Israeli Experiment in Pluralism* (Washington, DC: Brookings Institution Press, 2002), 97.

intifada, the war between Israel and Hezbollah in Lebanon in 2006, and the war between Israel and Hamas in Gaza in 2008–2009.

The deep and growing rift between the Jewish majority and the Palestinian minority is a subject of grave and widespread concern in Israel today. In a 2007 survey, for example, 87 percent of the Israeli public thought that Jewish-Arab relations in Israel were not good.[41] In another public opinion poll taken in 2010, the vast majority of Israeli citizens viewed the Jewish-Arab rift as an existential threat to Israel.[42] We share this view. The internal Jewish-Palestinian conflict has undoubtedly become Israel's biggest domestic threat. Indeed, a violent clash between Jews and Palestinians inside Israel may well pose as serious a threat to the country as the threat of conflict between Israel and Arabs outside the state's borders (including those in the Occupied Territories).

The Israeli public's awareness of the severity of the threat posed by the deterioration in Jewish-Palestinian relations in Israel provides at least some grounds for optimism. So does the fact that most Israeli citizens (Jews and Palestinians alike) support coexistence and believe there is an urgent need for improved Jewish-Palestinian coexistence in Israel.[43] Most also condemn discrimination and believe that fair treatment among citizens in the country is important.[44] These beliefs give us some hope that majority-minority relations in Israel can be improved and the Palestinian minority can eventually gain acceptance and equality in the country. It is with this hope in mind that we have written this book.

## Plan of the Book

The book is divided into two parts. In Part I, we examine in depth the conflict between the Jewish majority and the Palestinian minority in Israel. We begin in Chapter 1 by looking at the Palestinian minority itself, its internal composition, collective identity, and socio-economic status. We also look at how much inequality there really is between Palestinians and Jews in Israel. Chapter 2 focuses on the politics of the Palestinian minority, describing how Palestinian political behavior in Israel has changed

---

[41] Israel Democracy Institute, "2007 Israeli Democracy Index: Cohesiveness in a Divided Society," June, www.idi.org.il.
[42] Scheindlin, Public opinion research, 2010.
[43] Todd L. Pittinsky, Jennifer J. Ratcliff, and Laura A. Maruskin, *Coexistence in Israel: A National Study*, (Cambridge, MA: Center for Public Leadership, Harvard Kennedy School, Harvard University, 2008).
[44] Scheindlin, Public opinion research, 2010.

over time. We discuss the way in which Palestinians in Israel have gone from being politically repressed to being politically mobilized and asser-tive, even defiant. This discussion leads us to address in Chapter 3 the controversial question of whether the Palestinian minority is becoming radicalized, as many commentators in Israel claim. We dispute this claim in the chapter, but argue that the Palestinian minority has become more militant in its political attitudes and behavior in recent years. Having concentrated on the Palestinian minority in Chapters 1–3, in Chapter 4 we turn our attention to the Jewish majority. We discuss its views and attitudes toward the Palestinian minority both historically and more recently, and point to some alarming current trends and developments in Israeli politics. In doing so, we show how dramatically Jewish-Palestinian relations in Israel have deteriorated in the last decade.

Once the nature and magnitude of the conflict within Israel between Jews and Palestinians is clear to the reader, in Part II of the book we consider how to better manage the conflict. In Chapter 5 we go back to Israel's formative years to show how the new state became what we call a "Jewish Republic." We emphasize the critical decisions made at the outset of statehood by the leadership of the state that affected majority-minority relations in Israel for decades to come. In doing so, we challenge the commonly held belief that Israel's problems really started with the occu-pation of the West Bank and Gaza Strip beginning in 1967. To gain a wider perspective on the Jewish-Palestinian conflict within Israel, in Chapter 6 we examine ethno-national conflicts through a theoretical and compar-ative lens. It is important to realize that the Jewish-Palestinian conflict in Israel is not exceptional and that other ethno-national conflicts can provide useful insights and ideas, especially concerning methods of con-flict management. We particularly look at "accommodationist" models of conflict management and group-based approaches that involve granting collective rights to minorities. Chapter 7 contains our ideas for improving the status, rights, and conditions of Palestinians in Israel and transform-ing the relationship between the Jewish majority and Palestinian minor-ity. At the heart of this chapter is our call for re-defining Israel as both a "Jewish homeland and state of all its citizens." Looking ahead to the future, Chapter 8 assesses the prospects for a transformation of Israel in the manner that we proposed. To do so, it begins by examining how other states dominated by ethno-national majorities have been transformed. It then discusses the political forces and social groups within Israel that are likely to support or resist a transformation of Israel into a more egalitar-ian and inclusive democracy. The chapter ends by outlining some possible scenarios for the future, especially the future dangers that Israel faces if the ongoing deterioration in Jewish-Palestinian relations in the country is not reversed. Finally, in the book's conclusion, we summarize our overall argument and then return to the linkage between the internal and external Jewish-Palestinian conflicts that is a central theme of our book, addressing the question of how an Israeli-Palestinian peace agreement and the establishment of a Palestinian state might affect the internal conflict between Jews and Palestinians in Israel.

PART I

THE CONFLICT WITHIN

# Palestinians in Israel

## Separate and Unequal

> In our state there will be non-Jews as well – and all of them will be equal citizens; equal in everything without exception; that is: the state will be their state as well.
>
> David Ben-Gurion, December 1947[1]

For most people, in Israel and around the world, "Israelis" are Jews or, more precisely, Jews who live in Israel. Israel – the Jewish state – according to this widespread perception is populated by Jews who have resurrected Jewish sovereignty in their ancestral homeland after millennia of dispersal and statelessness. Whether or not one celebrates or condemns this historical development, the Jewishness of the country's population (however secular some may be) is generally taken for granted. The equation of Israeli with Jew is constantly repeated in the media and by politicians and activists, "pro-Israel" and "anti-Israel" alike.

This common discourse has given rise to a great deal of popular confusion. All too often, people are completely unaware of the large number of non-Jewish citizens of Israel – around 1.8 million people – who make up a quarter of the country's total population of 7.5 million. One in four Israelis, in other words, are not Jewish. The vast majority of this significant non-Jewish population are Arabs, who at the end of 2009 numbered 1,526,000, a little more than 20 percent of Israel's population.[2] This basic

---

[1] Quoted in Dan Urian and Efraim Karsh (eds.), *In Search of Identity: Jewish Aspects in Israeli Culture* (Portland, OR: Frank Cass, 1999), 1.

[2] Ruth Eglash, "Israel's population at 2010 is 7.5m," *The Jerusalem Post*, December 30, 2009. This figure includes roughly 250,000 Arabs living in annexed East Jerusalem who are permanent residents of Israel but not citizens (because Israel's Central Bureau of

demographic fact about the country is crucial for understanding its politics and considering its future development. Ignorance of Israel's Arab population, then, is a common and serious mistake. Demographically, Israel is a bi-national country, and although Jews form a large majority, Arabs are a significant, and growing, minority.[3] Israel's Arab population is currently growing at a faster rate than its Jewish population.[4] This is due to a higher Arab fertility rate (the average number of births per woman), which according to Israel's Central Bureau of Statistics is now about 3.8 for Arabs, compared with only 2.8 for Jews. Although the Arab fertility rate has substantially declined over the years – it was more than eight children per woman in the 1960s[5] – even if this decline continues and the Arab birthrate drops to the same level as the Jewish birthrate, the Arab share of Israel's population looks set to steadily increase in the years to come because of generational lag. Thus, in the future, Arabs are likely to constitute a larger percentage of the total Israeli population, probably around 30 percent, or even 35 percent by 2050.[6]

This demographic trend will change the face of the next generation of Israelis. A growing proportion of younger Israelis will be Arabs.[7] Already, a quarter of school-age children in Israel are Arab. In ten years time (by 2020), the majority of primary-school students are likely to be either Arabs or the children of ultra-Orthodox Jews (*Haredim*), and it is projected that by 2030 Arabs and will make up almost half of all 18- and 19-year-olds in Israel.[8] What will this mean for the country's future? How will Israel deal with its burgeoning Arab population? Can they be accommodated and satisfied within a self-declared Jewish state?

Statistics includes them in its calculations of the total Arab population in Israel). Our study, however, excludes the Arab population of East Jerusalem as well as the smaller Druze population in the Golan Heights, because we are concerned only with Arab citizens of Israel. Arabs in East Jerusalem and Druze in the Golan Heights are permanent residents of Israel but, with few exceptions, not Israeli citizens (although they are entitled to Israeli citizenship because Israel annexed East Jerusalem and the Golan Heights, very few East Jerusalem Arabs and Golan Druze have applied for citizenship).

[3] Yair Sheleg, "The demographics point to a binational state," *Ha'aretz*, May 27, 2004.
[4] In 2007, for instance, the Arab population grew by 2.6 percent, whereas the Jewish population grew by 1.6 percent, see http://www.cbs.gov.il
[5] Richard Cincotta and Eric Kaufmann, "The Changing Face of Israel," *Foreign Policy*, June 2009.
[6] Yaakov Kop and Robert E. Litan, *Sticking Together: The Israeli Experiment in Pluralism* (Washington, DC: Brookings Institution Press, 2002), 62–63.
[7] Currently, 30.4 percent of Arabs in Israel are under the age of 25, compared to 20.8 percent of Jews. Jack Habib et al., "Labour Market and Socio-Economic Outcomes of the Arab-Israeli Population," *OECD Social, Employment and Migration Working Papers No. 102* (March 18, 2010), 14.
[8] Cincotta and Kaufmann, "The Changing Face of Israel."

To begin to answer these questions, it is first necessary to better understand the Arabs in Israel – who they are, how they live, and what they want. This chapter attempts to do this. In it, we examine two issues that are paramount to the future of Arabs in Israel and their relations with Israeli Jews and the state – the issues of identity and equality. We start out by addressing the complex issue of Arab identity, asking how Arabs define themselves and what changes have occurred in their sense of collective identity. We consider the question of whether Arabs in Israel really constitute a single minority, and we discuss their internal differences. We then tackle the debate over the "Israelization" versus the "Palestinization" of the Arab minority and argue that both processes have in fact taken place. Based on the results of numerous surveys, we claim that the most accurate collective identity for Arabs in Israel today is "Palestinian Arab citizens of Israel."

After defining the collective identity of Arabs in Israel, we move on to address the critical issue of equality and try to assess how much equality there really is in Israel between Arabs and Jews. Our cursory review of the status of Arabs in different areas clearly shows that there is a great deal of inequality between Jews and Arabs in almost every respect. Put simply, Arabs are second-class citizens in Israel. Moreover, Arab-Jewish inequality is actually getting worse in recent years. Although this inequality has many causes, we argue that discriminatory state policies and persistent government neglect are mostly to blame. Finally, in the conclusion to this chapter, we note how Arabs themselves feel about the discrimination and inequality they suffer from. This brief discussion of current Arab attitudes and views leads into the next chapter's analysis of Arab political behavior since Israel's establishment until the present day.

## A Minority or Minorities?

In this book, we depict Arabs in Israel as a single group, a distinct minority, and we examine the politics of this group, its demands vis-à-vis the state, and its relations with the Jewish majority. But is this depiction really appropriate? Should we think of Arabs in Israel as a single minority, or is it best to disaggregate them into various sub-groups? That is, do Arabs belong to one group, or are they instead a collection of disparate religious and ethnic groups? The latter view has historically been how the Israeli authorities have seen Arabs in Israel. Rather than conceiving of them and treating them as a single minority, the state has traditionally differentiated between different religious and ethnic groups among the

Arabs and pursued somewhat different approaches toward them. It has even avoided using the term "Arab minority" in official state documents, generally preferring instead to use the terms "non-Jewish population," "Arab sector," or "minorities" when referring to Arabs in Israel.

There is good reason to be careful about depicting Arabs in Israel as a single group. They are divided along family, religious, ethnic, and regional lines. The many divisions and differences among Arabs in Israel have made it difficult for them to share a collective identity, let alone a common political agenda. As Baruch Kimmerling and Joel Migdal noted in their groundbreaking study of the Palestinian people: "A unifying Palestinian national identity [for Arabs in Israel] has been slow to emerge, party due to sectarian and cultural differences among them [...]. These differences have affected Arabs' ability to construct a unified community and constituency in the Jewish state."[9] The Arab community is certainly heterogeneous. It is made up of different religious and ethnic groups – principally, Muslims, Christians, Druze, and Bedouins[10] – each of which has its own distinct sense of identity. Muslims, mostly Sunnis, are the largest group, making up more than three-quarters of the Palestinian community (about 82 percent of the entire Arab population). Bedouins (once nomadic shepherds) are a subgroup within the Muslim population, numbering around 170,000 and mostly residing in the southern Negev (Naqab) desert region of the country and the northern Galilee. This creates a division among the Bedouins, between those in the north and those in the south (who are poorer). The Bedouin are also divided by their tribal affiliations. The Christian Arab population, about 9 percent of the total Arab population, are themselves divided into many different sects, and a number of these, especially the Greek Orthodox and Roman Catholic Churches, have a long history of quarreling and mutual hostility. Christian Arabs in general have also at times had a tense relationship and bitter disputes with Muslim Arabs (especially in the major Arab town of Nazareth[11]). Finally, the Druze (around 104,000 in Israel, roughly 9 percent of the Arab population[12]) are the most distinct group

---

[9] Baruch Kimmerling and Joel S. Migdal, *The Palestinian People: A History* (Cambridge, MA: Harvard University Press, 2003), 180.

[10] There are also about 5,000 Circassians, who live in two villages in the Galilee region, who are Sunni Muslims but not Arabs.

[11] The conflict between Muslim and Christian Arabs in Nazareth focused on the Muslim shrine of Shihab al-Din, which is adjacent to the Basilica of the Annunciation.

[12] This figure includes the 18,000 Druze who live in the Israeli-occupied Golan Heights, most of whom still consider themselves citizens of Syria.

within the Arab population, so much so in fact that many Druzes do not even consider themselves Arabs at all.[13] Druzes generally have quite different attitudes from the rest of the Arab minority. Unlike other Arabs, Druzes perform compulsory military service, something that has created a rift between the Druze community and other Arabs in Israel.[14] As a result of this, the Druze are something of a special case in terms of their status in Israeli society compared with other Arabs.[15]

The example of the Druze is indicative of the way in which the Israeli state has attempted to develop different relationships with Druze, Bedouin, Christian, and Muslim Arabs. Rather than treating the Arabs as a single community, Israeli authorities have adopted different approaches toward each group, favoring some over others. As Rhoda Kanaaneh writes: "the state has created a hierarchy within the Arab community: Druze are at the top, followed by Bedouins, and then Christians, with the remaining majority of non-Druze, non-Bedouin Muslims at the bottom as the least-favored type of citizen."[16] In doing so, the state has sought to exploit internal differences within the Arab population for its own purposes.[17] In the words of Kanaaneh: "Israeli authorities attempted to consolidate their power by [...] exacerbating inter-group tensions, disputes, and rivalries [within the Arab community]."[18] Sowing and strengthening intra-Arab divisions in order to prevent Arab unity was one way in which Israeli authorities have tried to control the state's Arab population, which they have always viewed as an actual or potential security threat. This policy was explicitly stated in a top-secret official memo about government policy toward the Arabs in the early years of the state. According to the memo: "The government's policy [...] has sought to divide the Arab population into diverse communities and regions [...]. The municipal status of the Arab villages, and the competitive spirit of local elections,

---

[13] Thus, one scholar notes that Druze in Israel have been "Druzified and de-Arabized." Rhoda Ann Kanaaneh, *Surrounded: Palestinian Soldiers in the Israeli Military* (Stanford, CA: Stanford University Press, 2009), 10.

[14] Kimmerling and Migdal, *The Palestinian People*, 182. Druzes are drafted into the Israeli army; although other Arabs may serve voluntarily, only a very small number choose to do so (almost all of them are Bedouins).

[15] Israeli-Jewish journalist Avirama Golan has observed that Israeli-Jewish society has traditionally regarded the Druze as "Arab-lite." Avirama Golan, "Where the 'alliance of blood' has led," *Ha'aretz*, February 17, 2005.

[16] Kanaaneh, *Surrounded*, 10.

[17] The state authorities, for example, have tried to exploit differences between Christian Arabs and Muslim Arabs. Laurence Louer, *To Be an Arab in Israel* (New York: Columbia University Press, 2007), 14–16.

[18] Kanaaneh, *Surrounded*, 10.

deepened the divisions inside the villages themselves. The communal policy and the clan divisions in the villages prevented Arab unity [...]."[19]

Thus, the Israeli state's policy toward the Arab minority was basically one of "divide and rule."[20] According to Laurence Louer:

> In order to preclude Israel's Arab citizens from constituting themselves into a community, and thus to maintain their loyalty, it was necessary either to develop their cultural affinities with the Jewish population, or to fragment them by bringing to the fore their internal social divisions. In the event, the authorities opted for the alternative of fragmentation. Seeking to transform Arab ethnic identities into basic political factions, the various experts involved therefore began with the claim that rather than a single Arab minority in Israel, there were multiple Arab minorities: not a community, but a number of ethnic groups, each motivated by different interests and each with its specific relationship with the State.[21]

Louer argues that in pursuing this "divide and rule" policy, the Israeli state has purposefully tried to politicize Druze, Bedouin, and Christian identities, whereas it has tried to depoliticize Muslim identity.[22] If so, it has only really been effective in the case of the Druze population.[23] The Israeli authorities, with the help of a co-opted Druze elite, have been largely successful in getting the Druze to regard themselves as a separate community, even a nation.[24] As a result of systematic efforts by Israeli authorities from the 1948 war onward to separate the Druze from the rest of the Arab community in Israel and create a distinct Druze collective identity, most Druzes in Israel have now adopted this collective identity.[25] These efforts included the imposition of mandatory military service, the recognition by the state of the Druze as an autonomous religious community, and the creation of a separate educational stream for Druze (within the Arabic educational system). The state also officially classifies the Druze as a separate ethnic group.

Although the Druze are generally regarded by Israeli authorities and Israeli-Jewish society as more "loyal" to the Jewish state than other

---

[19] Quoted in Tom Segev, *1949: The First Israelis* (New York: Free Press, 1986), 65.
[20] Louer, *To Be an Arab in Israel*, 11–14.
[21] Louer, *To Be an Arab in Israel*, 12.
[22] Louer, *To Be an Arab in Israel*, 17.
[23] Ilana Kaufman, "Ethnic Affirmation or Ethnic Manipulation: The Case of the Druze in Israel," *Nationalism and Ethnic Politics* 9, no. 4 (2004), 53–82. Kaufman argues that the Israeli state successfully manipulated the religious identity of the Druze.
[24] Kais Firro, "Reshaping Druze Particularism in Israel," *Journal of Palestine Studies* 30, no. 3 (Spring 2001), 51.
[25] Hence, Firro describes the Druze collective identity in Israel as an "imposed collective identity." Firro, "Reshaping Druze Particularism in Israel," 51.

Arabs because of their participation in military service and in the state's security establishment,[26] this has not meant that they receive the same treatment as Israeli Jews. According to Ramzi Halabi, the former mayor of Dalyat Karmel, the largest Druze town in Israel: "Compared to the rest of the Arabs, the Druze are better off – but not that much better. The Druze have been better integrated [into Israeli society] through military service and financial assistance – a result of their historic loyalty to the state. But although we fulfill the same duties as Jews, we are not granted the same rights or privileges."[27] Similarly, Israeli journalist Avirama Golan observes that: "the Druze have been pushed aside into a situation of neglect that is reserved for minorities in general, and Arabs in particular."[28] Consequently, the loyalty to and identification with the state that Israeli Druzes have historically demonstrated is now under threat as a rift is emerging between the Druze and the state.[29] Indeed, a recent survey showed a marked decline in patriotism within the Druze community in Israel.[30]

If the Israeli state's "special relationship" with the Druze is faltering, then they have long since disappeared with the Bedouins and Christian Arabs, both of whom the state also tried to cultivate such relationships with.[31] Together with their Muslim counterparts, Bedouin and Christian Arabs, as well as some Druze, are increasingly uniting as one community. In doing so, they are reacting against the Israeli state's traditional approach of segmenting the Arab community into different

---

[26] About 25 percent of Druze workers in Israel are employed in the military, police, and other security services. This is more than double the percentage of Israeli Jews employed in the security forces. Dominic Moran, "Israel's state-Druze rift," *International Relations and Security Network*, November 6, 2007, http://www.isn.ethz. ch/isn/Current-Affairs/Security-Watch/Detail/?ots591=4888CAA0-B3DB-1461–98B9-E20E7B9C13D4&lng=en&id=53699.

[27] Quoted in International Crisis Group, "Identity Crisis: Israel and its Arab Citizens," *Middle East Report* 25, 1 (March 2004), 2.

[28] Golan, "Where the 'alliance of blood' has led." This point is also made by Kanaaneh, who notes that: "Despite the special benefits Druze receive as a loyal minority, they continue to be treated as Arabs in most of their interactions with the state. For Druze villagers, inequalities with Jews in terms of land confiscation, municipal budgets, education, and employment, as well as discrimination in the army are constant reminders of their immutable Arabness in the eyes of the state." Kanaaneh, *Surrounded*, 12.

[29] Moran, "Israel's state-Druze rift." Vivid evidence of this was the rioting that occurred in the Druze village of Peki'in on October 30, 2007. See also, Oren Yiftachel and Michaly D. Segal, "Jews and Druze in Israel: State Control and Ethnic Resistance," *Ethnic and Racial Studies* 21, no. 3 (1998), 476–506.

[30] Sharon Roffe-Ofir, "Rift between Israel, Druze growing," *Ynet*, January 18, 2008.

[31] Kanaaneh, *Surrounded*, 12–13.

"minorities." They are rejecting the politics of division and instead are trying to articulate a common collective identity, set of interests, and political agenda.

To be sure, even if Arabs in Israel are able to overcome their sectarian and ethnic divisions, their political and ideological differences still undermine Arab solidarity and cohesion.[32] However, such differences are certainly no greater, and may well be less, than those that divide Israeli Jews. Just as it is appropriate, therefore, to think of Israeli Jews as a single, albeit not monolithic, community, so too is it appropriate to think of Arabs in Israel in this way. Treating the Arabs in Israel as a disparate collection of different groups not only serves to reify divisions within the Arab community but also obscures the many commonalities among them. For all their differences, what Arabs in Israel have in common is far more important than what divides them.

### The Collective Identity of Arabs in Israel: "Palestinians in Israel"

If, as the previous section argued, Arabs in Israel do constitute a single minority, then how should this minority be described? That is, what label should be attached to them? Much more than merely semantics is at stake. How one chooses to identify the Arab minority in Israel is often indicative of one's politics. Supporters of Israel generally refer to the Arab community in Israel as "Israeli Arabs" or "Arab Israelis" – using the terms commonly used by Israeli governments, the Hebrew-language media in Israel, and most Israeli Jews. Critics of Israel, by contrast, tend to describe Israel's Arab citizens simply as Palestinians or Palestinian Arabs. In doing so, they emphasize the Palestinian national identity of the Arab population in Israel and clearly reject the Israeli state's longstanding avoidance of that label.[33] Which, if any, of these names is correct? Are Arabs in Israel "Israeli Arabs" or "Palestinian Arabs"? Are they Israelis or Palestinians? In this section, we will argue that the answer is that they are both, and neither.

To understand this admittedly confusing claim, it is first necessary to recognize that the collective identity of Arabs in Israel is complex,

---

[32] Kimmerling and Migdal, *The Palestinian People*, 183.

[33] The category of Palestinian citizens is absent from the discourse of the Israeli state. Kanaaneh claims that the reason "the state of Israel has historically avoided the term 'Palestinian' [is] because of the implied recognition of the existence of such a national group and its rights." Kanaaneh, *Surrounded*, 10.

multifaceted, and fluid (just like the collective identity of Jews in Israel[34]). Arab identity is not singular or fixed. Hence, it is futile and fallacious to try to "pin down" one specific dimension of Arab collective identity and claim that it is always the sole or even the most important Arab identity. Instead, Arab collective identity in Israel, like all collective identities, should be understood as something that is changeable and multi-dimensional, composed of different elements whose importance (or salience) fluctuates over time and varies from individual to individual, group to group.

The collective identity of Arabs in Israel has changed over time in response to numerous internal (community based) and external developments (these developments will be discussed more fully in the next chapter).[35] Undoubtedly, the most significant change has been the shift from an Israeli-Arab identity to a Palestinian identity. During the early years of Israel's existence from 1948 to 1967, an Israeli-Arab identity prevailed and very few Arabs in Israel publicly identified themselves as Palestinians.[36] Although the apparent weakness of Palestinian identity among Arabs in Israel before the 1970s may have been based partly on a fear of openly identifying as a Palestinian (given the repressive measures the state authorities exercised vis-à-vis Arab citizens in the 1950s and much of the 1960s), it is indisputable that Palestinian nationalism has gained strength among Arabs in Israel in the decades following the 1967 war and Israel's conquest of East Jerusalem, the West Bank, and Gaza Strip.[37] As a national consciousness has spread among Arabs in Israel, growing numbers of them have rejected the Israeli-Arab identity that the state has tried to cultivate[38] and instead have increasingly come to adopt a Palestinian national identity.

---

[34] On the collective identity of Israeli Jews, the changes it has undergone, and the debate over its definition see, Dov Waxman, *The Pursuit of Peace and the Crisis of Israeli Identity: Defending/Defining the Nation* (New York: Palgrave Macmillan, 2006).

[35] Muhammad Amara, "The Collective Identity of the Arabs in Israel in an Era of Peace," *Israel Affairs* 9, 1–2 (Autumn/Winter 2003), 249–262.

[36] Kimmerling and Migdal, *The Palestinian People*, 186.

[37] Elie Rekhess, "The Evolvement of an Arab-Palestinian National Minority in Israel," *Israel Studies* 12, 3 (2007), 21. The Oslo peace process also reinforced Arabs' sense of Palestinian national identity and strengthened their Palestinian nationalism.

[38] The Israeli state authorities deliberately promoted an apolitical, de-nationalized Arab identity through the state-controlled Arabic education system, thereby suppressing the emergence of Palestinian national identity among Arab youth. See Ismael Abu-Saad, "State-Controlled Education and Identity Formation Among the Palestinian Arab Minority in Israel," *American Behavioral Scientist* 49, 8 (April 2006), 1085–1100;

Hence, after 1967, Palestinian identity has strengthened and become more salient among Arabs in Israel, a process that has been termed "Palestinization."[39] Whereas there is no question that over time the Arab community in Israel has undergone "Palestinization," what is more questionable is whether it is also undergoing a process of "Israelization." This question has been the subject of much scholarly debate. Sammy Smooha, an Israeli sociologist and a leading expert of Arab-Jewish relations, has long argued that Arabs in Israel are being "Israelized."[40] In his words: "They are getting used to, and finding numerous advantages in, life in Israel: modern lifestyles, welfare state benefits, rule of law, democracy. They dearly cherish Israeli citizenship."[41] Contrary to this view, Nadim Rouhana, a political psychologist who grew up as a Palestinian in Israel, argues that Israelization has not really taken place, or is at most only superficial. Unlike Smooha, Rouhana sees Arab involvement in Israeli society and politics as merely a pragmatic adjustment to the necessities of living in Israel. It is purely instrumental behavior and implies no emotional attachment to the country and no real sense of Israeli identity. As he puts it: "A new language [Hebrew] and lifestyle do not in themselves reflect a subjective experience of being an Israeli."[42]

The question of Arab collective identity in Israel, however, should not be framed in terms of Israelization versus Palestinization because this implies a false dichotomy between the two processes. Palestinization and Israelization are not necessarily contradictory. Both can take place simultaneously and even reinforce one another. This is, in fact, exactly what has happened. Arabs in Israel, especially younger generations, have become more Palestinian in their self-identity, and at the same time they have been deeply influenced by Israeli culture – a process of acculturation. They have not assimilated into Israeli society, but they have clearly adopted many aspects of Israeli culture. Thus, Laurence Louer has

and Yousef T. Jabareen, "Law and Education: Critical Perspectives on Arab Palestinian Education in Israel," *American Behavioral Scientist* 49, no.8 (April 2006).

[39] Jacob M. Landau, *The Arab Minority in Israel, 1967–1991: Political Aspects* (Oxford: Clarendon Press, 1993), 167–170.

[40] See, Sammy Smooha, *Arabs and Jews in Israel Vol.1: Conflicting and Shared Attitudes in a Divided Society* (Boulder, CO: Westview Press, 1989); Sammy Smooha, *Arabs and Jews in Israel Vol. 2: Change and Continuity in Mutual Intolerance* (Boulder, CO: Westview Press, 1992).

[41] Sammy Smooha, "Are the Palestinian Arabs in Israel Radicalizing?," *Bitterlemons* 24, 2 (June 24, 2004), http://www.bitterlemons-international.org/previous.php?opt=1&id=45#182.

[42] Nadim Rouhana, *Palestinian Citizens in an Ethnic Jewish State: Identities in Conflict* (New Haven, CT: Yale University Press, 1997), 119.

observed that: "[...] to identify oneself as Palestinian is neither to reject Israeli citizenship nor to close oneself off culturally from Israel."[43]

At issue, then, is whether this cultural influence actually entails the adoption of an Israeli identity. There is at least some evidence that the process of acculturation into Israeli society has engendered an emotional attachment to Israel among Arabs. In a survey carried out in 2007, for instance, a large majority of Arab citizens (75 percent) said that they felt some kind of belonging to Israel (ranging from a small to high degree of belonging), whereas only a quarter of respondents had no sense of belonging to Israel.[44] However, this sense of belonging does not mean that Arabs are willing to identify themselves as Israelis. In fact, few do, as survey after survey reveals. In a survey conducted by the Israel Democracy Institute in 2008, 45 percent of Arab citizens identified themselves as Arab, 24 percent as Palestinians, 19 percent identified themselves by their religious affiliation, and only 12 percent said they were Israelis.[45] Similarly, in a 2001 survey by The Institute for Peace Research, 33 percent of Arab respondents said the label "Israeli" accurately described their identity;[46] and in another poll conducted in 2000, only 15 percent of Arabs considered themselves Israeli, whereas 70 percent considered themselves Palestinian.[47]

Most Arab citizens of Israel, therefore, do not think of themselves as Israelis. It is important to stress that this should not simply be construed as a rejection of Israeli identity and an embrace of Palestinian identity instead. Israeli and Palestinian identities are not necessarily mutually exclusive. The relationship between them is not zero-sum, whereby it is impossible for Arab citizens of Israel to hold both Israeli and Palestinian identities. It is possible, at least in theory, to be both Israeli and Palestinian.[48] In practice, however, having both identities is immensely challenging (to say the least) in a highly politicized and polarized society where Palestinian nationalism is widely feared and often strongly resented and even despised by Israeli Jews. Hence, for many Arabs in Israel, Israeliness and Palestinianness are indeed in conflict. Furthermore, when considering the

---

[43] Louer, *To Be an Arab in Israel*, 199.
[44] Nadim Rouhana, ed., *Attitudes of Palestinians in Israel on Key Political and Social Issues: Survey Research Results* (Haifa: Mada al-Carmel, 2007).
[45] Kobi Nahshoni, "Poll: Most Israelis see themselves as Jewish first, Israeli second," *Ynet*, May 8, 2008.
[46] Ori Nir, "Israeli Arab alienation intensifies," *Ha'aretz*, May 21, 2001.
[47] Louer, *To Be an Arab in Israel*, 35.
[48] Just as it is possible to be Scottish and British or Quebecois and Canadian.

question of collective identity it is important not to assume more freedom of choice for Arabs in Israel than they actually enjoy.[49] To put it simply, Arab citizens of Israel cannot freely choose whether to be Israelis or Palestinians. In reality, a full-fledged Israeli identity is actually closed off to them, at least in so far as it is widely understood – by Jewish and Arab citizens alike – to have an ethno-religious dimension. That is, Jewishness is for many a defining element of Israeliness, so much so in fact that the terms "Israeli" and "Jew" are frequently used interchangeably in Israel. As long as Israeli identity is bound up with Jewishness, therefore, Arabs in Israel cannot fully identify themselves as Israelis, even if they might wish to. Hence, although Israelization is occurring on an objective level, at least in terms of changing Arab cultural habits and lifestyles, Arabs in Israel cannot really become Israelis on a subjective level.

Nevertheless, most Arab citizens of Israel do have some sense of Israeli identity, albeit a fairly weak and marginal one. Instead of a unitary conception of identity, according to which people have only one identity, it is important to recognize that identities are multiple and often overlapping. Thus, Arabs in Israel have more than just a Palestinian national identity. The rise of Palestinian nationalism has not displaced other identities and loyalties. Rather, Arabs have a complex identity with a Palestinian component, a pan-Arab component, a religious component, and a civic Israeli component.[50] The multiple identities of Arabs in Israel is clearly demonstrated in a survey conducted in 2000, which showed that most Arabs are attached to more than one identity (in the survey, 77 percent of Arab men and women assigned high salience to at least three different identities).[51] In general, of the multiple identities held by Arabs, their Arab identity was the most important identity, then their religious identities (Muslim, Christian, or Druze), followed by their Palestinian and Israeli identities.[52] These different identities varied in salience, however, for different groups within the Arab community. Palestinian identity, for instance, was the most important identity for the vast majority of Muslims; but although it was also important to Christians, it was not as important to them as

[49] Rebecca Kook, *The Logic of Democratic Exclusion: African Americans in the United States and Palestinian Citizens in Israel* (Lanham, MD: Lexington Books, 2002), 99.
[50] Sammy Smooha, *Index of Arab-Jewish Relations in Israel 2004* (Haifa: The Jewish-Arab Center, University of Haifa, 2005), 45.
[51] Muhammad Amara and Izhak Schnell, "Identity Repertoires Among Arabs in Israel," *Journal of Ethnic and Migration Studies* 30, 1 (January 2004), 183.
[52] Amara and Schnell, "Identity Repertoires Among Arabs in Israel," 182–183.

their Arab identity.[53] Most Druzes, by contrast, strongly emphasized their religious identity and their civic Israeli identity, whereas a Palestinian identity was not at all relevant to the vast majority of them.[54]

Hence, one must be careful about making generalizations about the collective identity of Arabs in Israel. Not all Arabs identify themselves as Palestinian,[55] and even those that do may value other identities more highly. With this caveat in mind, what conclusions can be reached about Arab collective identity? First, both Palestinian nationalism and Israeli citizenship shapes the collective identity of the Arab community; and second, that a new collective identity has emerged among Arab citizens in Israel, distinct from that of Palestinians elsewhere. This identity is that of "Palestinians in Israel."[56] As Smooha writes: "The hybrid identity that is slowly emerging and spreading among them [Arabs] is the self-identification as 'Palestinians in Israel.' It properly conveys the primacy of Palestinian affiliation and orientation without renouncing Israeli connections."[57] This is supported by Rouhana's extensive social-psychological study of the collective identity of Arabs in Israel based on his survey data and primary interviews with Arab political leaders.[58] Thus, according to Oren Yiftachel: "[...] with the possible exception of the Druze, the Arabs in Israel are carving a separate but increasingly unified political identity, which occupies the space between their Palestinian nation and the Israeli state."[59]

In sum, what has taken place since 1967 is the gradual emergence of a self-identified and distinct Palestinian national minority in Israel. The Arab community in Israel now perceives itself as a national minority and increasingly demands to be recognized as such. The Israeli state, however, refuses to define its Palestinian Arab citizens as a national minority and continues to treat them instead as "a fractured collection of ethnic

---

53 Amara and Schnell, "Identity Repertoires Among Arabs in Israel," 183.
54 Druzes are overwhelmingly united in their rejection of a Palestinian identity. In the survey, only 13 percent of them said a Palestinian identity was salient or very salient to them. Amara and Schnell, "Identity Repertoires Among Arabs in Israel," 182–183.
55 In Sammy Smooha's survey carried out in 2003, only about half of Arabs identified themselves as Palestinian. Smooha, *Index of Arab-Jewish Relations in Israel 2004*, 48.
56 The most popular identity selected by Arabs in the survey conducted by Smooha in 2003 was "Palestinian Arab in Israel." Smooha, *Index of Arab-Jewish Relations in Israel 2004*.
57 Sammy Smooha, "Arab-Jewish Relations in Israel: A Deeply Divided Society," in Anita Shapira, ed., *Israeli Identity in Transition* (Westport, MA: Praeger Publishers, 2004), 44.
58 Rouhana, *Palestinian Arabs in an Ethnic Jewish State*.
59 Oren Yiftachel, *Ethnocracy: Land and Identity Politics in Israel/Palestine* (Philadelphia: University of Pennsylvania Press, 2006), 177.

and religious groups."[60] The denial of official recognition of their status as a national minority has therefore become one of the grievances of Arab citizens vis-à-vis the state of Israel. Yet it is only one of many such grievances and by no means the most important (except perhaps to some Arab intellectuals). Far more pressing for most Arabs in Israel is the inequality and discrimination that continues to mar their lives and put numerous obstacles in the way of their community's social and economic development and their personal advancement and well-being. The next section of this chapter will briefly review this inequality and discrimination.

## The Status of Arabs in Israel: Second-Class Citizens

On the 14th of May 1948, when David Ben-Gurion, Israel's first prime minster, announced the establishment of the State of Israel, he read aloud the words of the new state's Declaration of Independence. After proclaiming "the establishment of a Jewish state in the land of Israel," the declaration went on to promise that Israel "will foster the development of the country for the benefit of all its inhabitants," and "will ensure complete equality of social and political rights to all its inhabitants irrespective of religion, race or sex."[61] Has the Jewish state lived up to this promise? Has this explicit commitment to equality for all Israeli citizens – Jewish and Arab – been kept? The answer is surely no. Now, more than sixty years after the state's establishment, the idealistic aspirations of Israel's Declaration of Independence remains far from being fulfilled. Much like the soaring rhetoric of the United States of America's Declaration of Independence that the American reality has always fallen far short of (most glaringly during the decades of slavery and denial of civil rights to African Americans), the reality of life in the Jewish state for its non-Jewish citizens, especially Arabs, has been one of persistent inequality and discrimination.

To be sure, Arab citizens of Israel have never experienced the formal discrimination, disenfranchisement, and systematic exclusion that African Americans once endured in the United States (although they did live under strict military rule until 1966). As individual citizens, Arabs have formal equality and enjoy the right to vote and be elected

---

[60] Kanaaneh, *Surrounded*, 3.
[61] See Knesset, "The Declaration of the Establishment of the State of Israel," (May 14, 1948). Tellingly, the Declaration promised equality "irrespective of religion, race, or sex," but not of nationality.

to parliament, as well as many other political, social, and cultural free-doms; as a minority, however, Arabs do not have any collective political rights).[62] They certainly have many more rights and protections than their fellow Palestinians in the West Bank and Gaza Strip. Yet, when compared with Israel's Jewish citizens, Arabs are decidedly unequal. They suffer from numerous inequities, tacit discrimination, government neglect, and social prejudice. They are largely excluded from the coun-try's public life,[63] they have not been integrated socially or economically, and they are generally treated with suspicion by the state and by Israeli-Jewish society. As such, collectively, Arabs are very much second-class citizens in Israel.

It would be wrong, however, to ignore the significant socio-economic development that Arabs in Israel have achieved since 1948. Over the years, the Arab community has undergone a process of modernization and has been transformed from an impoverished mostly rural and feudal society dependent on subsistence agriculture to a more modern, indus-trialized, individualistic, and mobile society. Arab living standards have substantially improved, as their levels of education, employment, health, housing, and income have all steadily risen.[64] One clear indication of the gains that have been achieved is the increase in life expectancy for Arabs – life expectancy for Arab women increased from an average of 71.9 years in the period 1970–1974 to 77.4 years in the period 1994–1998; and for Arab men from an average of 68.5 years in the period 1970–1974 to 74.2 years in the period 1994–1998.[65] Another indication is the dramatic decline in infant mortality in the Arab community – from 24.2 deaths per 1,000 births in 1980 to 8.2 deaths per 1,000 births in 2003. These statistics are unambiguous proof of the progress that the Arab community has made since Israel's establishment. But while they tell a story of progress on the one hand, on the other hand they also tell a story of inequality. In 2003, Arabs in Israel had a lower life expectancy

---

[62] Despite this formal equality, Israeli law does distinguish between Jews and non-Jews in regard to immigration – the Law of Return grants automatic immigration and citizenship rights to any Jew in the world, in accordance with a central ideological goal of Zionism. Palestinian Arabs have no such rights. On the legal discrimination against Arabs in Israel, see for instance, David Kretzmer, *The Legal Status of Arabs in Israel* (Boulder, CO: Westview Press, 1990); Yoav Peled, "Citizenship Betrayed: Israel's Emerging Immigration and Citizenship Regime," *Theoretical Inquiries in Law* 8, no. 2 (2007), 333–358.

[63] Yoav Peled, "Ethnic Democracy and the Legal Construction of Citizenship: Arabs Citizens of the Jewish State," *American Political Science Review* 86, no. 2 (1992), 432–443.

[64] Smooha, "Arab-Jewish Relations in Israel," 45.

[65] Kop and Litan, *Sticking Together*, 54.

than Jews (3.3 years lower for Arab men, and 3.8 years lower for Arab women compared to their Jewish male and female counterparts); and the infant mortality rate of Israel's Arab population was twice as high as that of its Jewish population.[66]

Much the same story is true in the area of education. The continuous rise in Arab educational levels has been one of the biggest changes the community has undergone since 1948. In that year, 80 percent of Arabs in Israel were illiterate; forty years later, in 1988, only 15 percent were illiterate.[67] The average Arab child in Israel now receives much more schooling that their parents and grandparents ever did. In 1961, the average number of years of schooling for Arabs was just 1.2 years;[68] in 2007, it had reached 10.2 years.[69] Yet, this was still less than the 12.6 years of schooling that Jews in Israel received. Similarly, the number of Arab university students has skyrocketed over the years, increasing from only 46 in 1956–1957 (0.6 percent of the Arab population) to 7,903 in 1998–1999 (7.1 percent of the Arab population).[70] However, Arabs are still vastly under-represented among university students in Israel – making up only 8.1 percent of all university students in 2003, less than half their share of the country's population.[71]

The disparities between Israel's Arab and Jewish citizens in health and education reflect the broader socio-economic chasm that divides the two communities. The extreme socio-economic inequality between Jews and Arabs is one of the biggest, if not the biggest, problems that affect majority-minority relations in Israel. It is essential, therefore, to appreciate the magnitude of this problem. A wide range of socio-economic measures testify to this inequality; especially telling are poverty levels, unemployment rates, average incomes, and occupational structure and types of professions.

---

[66] These figures were provided by Israel's Central Bureau of Statistics and its Ministry of Health, respectively, and were reported in "The Palestinian Arab Citizens of Israel: Status, Opportunities and Challenges for an Israeli-Palestinian Peace" (The Mossawa Center, Haifa, Israel, June, 2006), 34. See also, Dov Chernichovsky and Jon Anson, "The Jewish–Arab Divide in Life Expectancy in Israel," *Economics & Human Biology* 3, 1 (March 2005), 123–137.

[67] Gershon Shafir and Yoav Peled, *Being Israeli: The Dynamics of Multiple Citizenship* (Cambridge: Cambridge University Press, 2002), 120.

[68] Shafir and Peled, *Being Israeli*, 120.

[69] Habib et al., "Labour Market and Socio-Economic Outcomes of the Arab-Israeli Population," 15.

[70] Amal Jamal, "Strategies of Minority Struggle for Equality in Ethnic States: Arab Politics in Israel," *Citizenship Studies* 11, 3 (July 2007), 269.

[71] This figure was provided by Israel's Central Bureau of Statistics, http://www.cbs.gov.il/.

Poverty is undoubtedly the greatest hardship that Arabs in Israel endure. According to the Organisation for Economic Co-operation and Development (OECD), around 50 percent of the Arab population lives in poverty (which means that they earn less than half of the median income in Israel).[72] While Israel has enjoyed strong economic growth over much of the past two decades, Arab citizens have reaped few of the benefits.[73] On the contrary, the poverty rate among Arab families has significantly increased since the 1990s, rising from a level of 35 percent in 1990 to 45 percent in 2002 (based on net income).[74] Arab children have been particularly hard-hit by this increase in poverty – in 2003, nearly 60 percent of them lived below the poverty line.[75] In recent years, the poverty rate for Arab families has fluctuated between around 50–55 percent, compared to around 15 percent for Jewish families.[76] In other words, Arab families in Israel are more than three times as likely to be poor than Jewish families.

Arabs, therefore, are one of the poorest groups in Israeli society (along with *Haredim* and Ethiopian Jews).[77] It must be noted that persistently high Arab poverty rates in Israel are partly due to large Arab families, which reduces per capita income, and the low workforce participation rate of Arab mothers, which reduces per family income (in both respects,

---

[72] The OECD conducted an extensive review of Israel's economy and its labor market and social policies in considering Israel's application to join the organization. See OECD, *Labour Market and Social Policy Review of Israel – 2010* (Organization for Economic Cooperation and Development, Paris, France, 2010), available at http://www.oecd.org/els/israel2010.

[73] OECD, *Labour Market and Social Policy Review of Israel.*

[74] Figures provided in Mtanes Shihadeh, *Poverty as Policy* (Haifa: Mada al-Carmel – the Arab Center for Applied Social Research, July 2004). Thus, the OECD report on Israel observes that "[...] the socio-economic chasm between the general Jewish population and the two large minority groups [Arabs and Haredim] is widening. Since 2000, employment has increased and poverty declined among the majority population (albeit only slightly). By contrast, poverty rates for the Arab and Haredi populations have increased by nearly 20 percentage points." OECD, *Labour Market and Social Policy Review of Israel,* 2. There has, however, been a slight reduction in the level of Arab poverty in recent years (from 54 percent poverty among Arab families in 2006 to 49.4 percent in 2008). For these latest figures, see Sikkuy's 2008 Equality Index at http://www.sikkuy.org.il/english/home.html

[75] The exact figure was 57.5 percent. See, "The Palestinian Arab Citizens of Israel," Mossawa Center, 32.

[76] See the report by Israel's National Insurance Institute: Miri Endeweld, Alex Fruman, Netanela Barkali, Daniel Gottlieb, *2008 Poverty and Social Gaps Annual Report* (National Insurance Institute, Research and Planning Administration, Jerusalem, October 2009), 18. Available at http://www.btl.gov.il

[77] Within the Arab population, Bedouin Arabs are by far the most disadvantaged, with four out of five Bedouin living beneath the poverty line. OECD, *Labour Market and Social Policy Review of Israel,* 5.

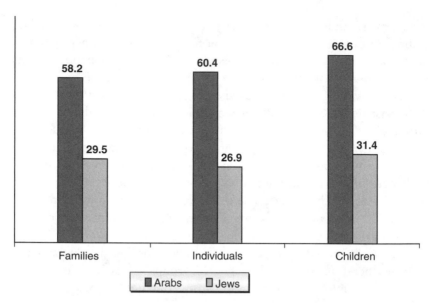

FIGURE 1.1. Arab and Jewish poverty rates.
*Source*: The Equality Index of Jewish and Arab Citizens in Israel, 2008.

Arabs are very similar to Haredim in Israel).[78] Nevertheless, the major causes of Arab poverty are high levels of unemployment and low levels of income. Unemployment among Arabs is rife – in 2003, for example, out of forty-seven towns in Israel with higher than average unemployment rates (more than 10.3 percent in that particular year), forty-six were Arab towns, and the twenty-five towns with the highest unemployment rates in the country (ranging between 13.9 and 24.8 percent) were all Arab towns.[79] In terms of income, the average per capita income of Arabs in Israel in 2007 was $7,700, compared with $19,000 for Israelis as a whole.[80] On average, Arab men earn just 60 percent of the national average wage, and Arab women earn 70 percent of the average wage.[81]

---

[78] In 2007, only 18.6 percent of Arab women in Israel were employed, compared with 63.1 percent of Jewish women. Habib et al., "Labour Market and Socio-Economic Outcomes of the Arab-Israeli Population," 21.

[79] Adalah Web site, http://www.adalah.org

[80] Mossawa Centre, *The Human Rights Status of the Palestinian Arab Minority, Citizens of Israel* (Haifa, October 2008). Under-reporting of income is widespread among Arabs, so their real income level might be slightly higher than official economic data. Hillel Halkin, "The Jewish State & Its Arabs," *Commentary* 30, 127 (2009): 32.

[81] OECD, *Labour Market and Social Policy Review of Israel.*

The large income gap between Arab and Jewish workers in Israel has long been a defining feature of the country's economy.[82] Arabs have generally held the low-wage jobs in Israel's highly segmented labor market.[83] Although, over the years, Arabs have gone from being farmers and unskilled laborers to becoming industrial workers, small business owners, and professionals (especially teachers, lawyers, doctors, and pharmacists),[84] they still mostly occupy the lower rungs of the occupational ladder.[85] In 2003, for instance, a quarter of all employed Arab men worked in construction.[86] The majority of Arabs work in Jewish-owned businesses and under Jewish bosses (which means that the Arab minority is economically dependent on the Jewish majority and hence vulnerable[87]); and only a small number of Arabs work in the top occupational categories of managerial, professional, and scientific/academic occupations.[88] Arabs are particularly under-represented in Israel's booming high-tech industry – a recent study found that only 4 percent of Israeli workers in the high-tech sector were Arabs.[89] Nor is this only an issue in the private sector. Arabs make up a little more than 6 percent of Israeli government employees (admittedly, a significant improvement from just 2.1 percent of civil servants in 1992).[90]

---

[82] For instance, the average gross income of a Palestinian adult was 54 percent of that of a Jewish adult in 1980 and about 56 percent in 1990 (after-tax figures were 58 percent and 60 percent, respectively). Shafir and Peled, *Being Israeli*, 119.

[83] Elia T. Zureik, *The Palestinians in Israel: A Study in Internal Colonialism* (London: Routledge and Kegan Paul, 1979), 131–141; Michael Shalev, "Jewish Organized Labor and the Palestinians: A Study of State/Society Relations in Israel," in Baruch Kimmerling, ed., *The Israeli State and Society: Boundaries and Frontiers* (Albany: State University of New York Press, 1989), 93–134; and Joel S. Migdal, *Through the Lens of Israel: Explorations in State and Society* (Albany: State University of New York Press, 2001), 176.

[84] The percentage of Arabs employed in the professions nearly tripled between 1960 to 1990, increasing from 4.2 percent to 12.2 percent of all working Arabs, while the percentage of Arabs working in agriculture plummeted from 46.8 percent in 1960 to only 7 percent in 1990. Alan Dowty, *The Jewish State: A Century Later* (Berkeley: University of California Press, 1998), 200.

[85] The most menial and lowest-paid jobs in Israel are now taken by foreign workers, legal and illegal, who currently number approximately 300,000 people. They have been brought in over the years to replace Palestinian workers from the West Bank and Gaza. See Evan R. Goldstein, "Does Israel have an Immigrant Problem?" *Foreign Policy*, 25 January 2010.

[86] This figure was provided by Israel's Central Bureau of Statistics, http://www.cbs.gov.il/.

[87] Sammy Smooha, "Control of Minorities in Israel and Northern Ireland," *Comparative Studies in Society and History* 22, 2 (1980), 271.

[88] Shafir and Peled, *Being Israeli*, 117.

[89] Sharon Roffe-Ofir, "Peres acknowledges discrimination in employment of Arabs," *Ynet*, 13 January 2010.

[90] According to Sikkuy's 2008 Equality Index, 6.7 percent of civil service employees in Israel were Arab citizens, an increase from 5 percent in 2003.

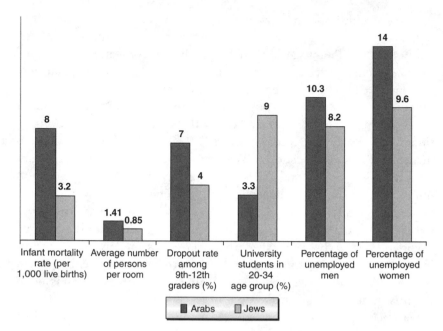

FIGURE I.2. Selected indicators of Arab-Jewish inequality.

*Source*: The Equality Index of Jewish and Arab Citizens in Israel, 2008.

Although the low-status occupations held by Arabs compared to Jews in Israel is partly a consequence of a generally lower level of skills and education, other factors are also responsible, as one scholar notes: "Both as individuals and as a collectivity, the Arabs cannot compete equally and fairly with Jews for opportunities because of untrustworthy status, incomplete command of Hebrew, exclusion from powerful Jewish social networks, and interpersonal and institutional discrimination."[91] Security considerations (or claims thereof), lack of social networks, and discrimination have particularly affected the employment opportunities for Arab university graduates.[92] Many are unemployed – one out of two was out of work in 2009[93] – and many others are under-employed. Very few Arab

[91] Smooha, "Arab-Jewish Relations in Israel," 45.

[92] Ron Friedman, "Employers reluctant to hire Ethiopians, Haredim and Arabs, study shows," *The Jerusalem Post*, November 9, 2009.

[93] Figure provided in Gershom Gorenberg, "Is Israel a Democracy?" *The American Prospect*, December 4, 2009.

university graduates get jobs in high-paying, high-status occupations in the Jewish labor market.[94] In fact, the gap between the educational attainment and occupational attainment of Arabs in Israel is actually increasing.[95] The consequences of this are not hard to fathom, as Irit Tamir, chairwoman of an Israeli employers' coalition that promotes equality for Arab university graduates, recently spelled out: "We are cultivating another talented, educated, frustrated and bitter generation."[96]

In sum, all the evidence presented in this brief review of the economic circumstances of Arabs in Israel points to the continuing socio-economic inequality between the Arab minority and the Jewish majority. There can be no question that although the overall material conditions of Arab life in Israel have greatly improved over the years, the material disparities between Arabs and Jews remain large. The significant socio-economic gaps between the Jewish majority and the Arab minority in many different areas cannot be attributed to a single cause. They are the result of multiple factors, some of which have already been mentioned (notably, large Arab families, the low participation rate of Arab women in the labor force, the overall lower skill level of the Arab workforce, and discrimination in the labor market). The State of Israel, therefore, cannot be totally blamed for all Arab-Jewish inequalities. But it does bear a significant amount of responsibility. Discriminatory state policies and practices dating back decades and neglect by many Israeli governments are both major causes of the general socio-economic gap between Arabs and Jews. Long-term discrimination and neglect by the state have perpetuated and even exacerbated Arab-Jewish inequalities (Arab agriculture and industry has long been underfunded and underdeveloped, for example, compared to the extensive state effort made to develop Jewish agriculture and industry). This is particularly apparent in two critically important areas – access to land and housing, and government budget allocations.

No issue better encapsulates the discrimination, de jure and de facto, that Arabs in Israel have experienced since the state's founding than that of land. The State of Israel's Jewish identity and Zionist mission is perhaps most clearly expressed in the preference that it has persistently demonstrated for its Jewish citizens over its Arab citizens in access to land,

---

[94] The average salary of an Arab college graduate is 35 percent lower than that of a Jewish graduate. Ora Coren, "3,000 Arab graduates looked for jobs: Only 170 found one," *Ha'aretz*, March 10, 2010. See also, Ora Coren, "Survey: Managers support hiring Arabs, but don't act on it," *Ha'aretz*, March 10, 2010.

[95] Shafir and Peled, *Being Israeli*, 120.

[96] Quoted in Roffe-Ofir, "Peres acknowledges discrimination in employment of Arabs."

land planning, rural and urban development, and provision of housing. The most egregious examples of official discrimination against Arabs can be found in these areas. This is hardly surprising when one considers the centrality of control over land in the whole Arab-Jewish conflict. Since Zionist settlers first arrived in Ottoman Palestine at the end of the nineteenth century, through the years of the British Mandate, and throughout the existence of the State of Israel, the struggle for control over land has been at the very heart of the conflict between Jews and Palestinians. Territory, more than any other resource, has been continually fought over and has often aroused the most intense passions on both sides. For Jews, the success of the entire Zionist project has depended on Jewish territorial control (although the desired borders of this territory have long been the subject of much debate within the Zionist movement).[97] Hence, the Zionist movement in the pre-state period and subsequently the State of Israel has continually tried to expand Jewish control over the land (whether acquiring land by purchasing it, forcibly seizing it, or legally appropriating it), generally at the expense of the indigenous Palestinian population.

The Palestinians, for their part, have also prized possession of land, not only because of its economic value in a traditionally rural society, but also because of the social status and even sense of identity and self-esteem they derive from it. Consequently, Palestinians have always fiercely resisted, at times violently, Jewish efforts to gain control over land – a resistance expressed through the concept/strategy of *sumud* (steadfastness). This has also been true in the decades after 1948, when the most common cause of protest by Israel's Palestinian Arab citizens has been land issues. Arguably more than anything else, Israel's appropriations of Arab land and its bureaucratic and legal restrictions on Arab access to and use of land have angered and embittered its Arab citizens.[98]

Since its inception in 1948 until today, Israel has embarked on a program of "Judaizing" the country through a variety of laws and bureaucratic rules and regulations.[99] This has entailed the systematic transfer of land from Arab to Jewish hands, so that Jews went from controlling only

---

[97] Baruch Kimmerling, *Zionism and Territory: The Socioterritorial Dimensions of Zionist Politics* (Berkeley: University of California Press, 1983).

[98] Professor Sammy Smooha, an expert on the attitudes and views of Arabs in Israel, has noted that Arabs whose families have lost land tend to be significantly more negative toward Jews and toward the State of Israel than other Arab citizens. Interview with the Authors, June 8, 2009.

[99] See Oren Yiftachel and Alexander Kedar, "Landed Power: The Making of the Israeli Land Regime," *Theory and Criticism* 16 (2000), 67–100. [Hebrew].

13.5 percent of the land in 1949 to 93 percent by the 1960s.[100] As part of this Judaization of the land, between 50 and 60 percent of Arab-held land in Israel was expropriated by the state.[101] "In the process," writes Israeli scholar Oren Yiftachel, "Arabs have not only lost individual property but have also been dispossessed of much of their collective territorial assets and interests, because nearly all land transferred to the state (ostensibly for public purposes) was earmarked for Jewish use."[102]

As a result of the state's Judaization policies, while Israel's Arab population has increased by at least sevenfold since 1948, the land reserves available to them have shrunk. Although they now constitute nearly 20 percent of Israel's population, Arabs own only 3.5 percent of the state's land.[103] Even less state land (no more than 2.5 percent) is under the jurisdiction of Arab local authorities.[104] In parts of the country where Arabs reside in great numbers, the lack of Arab control over the land is especially acute. In the Galilee region, where around 70 percent of the population is Arab, Arab-run municipalities have jurisdiction over merely 16.1 percent of the land; and in the northern Negev region where Arabs comprise about 25 percent of the population, Arab municipalities have jurisdiction over only 1.9 percent of the land.[105]

Arabs have also been prevented from establishing new settlements in the country. Whereas more than 700 Jewish settlements have been established by the state (within Israel's pre-1967 borders), the only Arab settlements that the state has ever established were aimed at coercively urbanizing and geographically concentrating the Bedouin of the Negev and the northern Galilee.[106] These Bedouin townships are the poorest towns in Israel. About half of the Negev Bedouin population now reside in the new townships established by the state, while the other half of the Bedouin population in the Negev (approximately 80,000 people) live in extreme poverty in thirty-six "unrecognized" villages (settlements that the state refuses to recognize despite the fact that most of them have been in existence for decades) and nine recently recognized villages. These

[100] Yiftachel and Kedar, "Landed Power," 4.
[101] Yiftachel, *Ethnocracy*, 166.
[102] Yiftachel, *Ethnocracy*, 166.
[103] Oren Yiftachel, Rassem Khamaissi, and Sandy Kedar, "Land and Planning," in Dan Rabinowitz, As'ad Ghanem, and Oren Yiftachel, eds., *After the Rift: New Directions for Government Policy towards the Arab Population in Israel* (November 2000), 17.
[104] Yiftachel, Khamaissi, and Kedar, "Land and Planning," 17.
[105] Ilan Peleg, "Jewish-Palestinian Relations in Israel: From Hegemony to Equality?" *International Journal of Politics, Culture, and Society* 17, 3 (2004), 422.
[106] Yiftachel, Khamaissi, and Kedar, "Land and Planning," 17.

villages lack basic services such as water, sewage, and electricity (it is against the law for state utilities to supply these basic services), and there are no schools, health clinics, or access roads. As if all this were not bad enough, their inhabitants have to live with the constant threat of having their homes demolished because the state deems them to be illegal.

The massive loss of Arab-owned land and the lack of land under Arab municipal control have had a dire impact on Arab development and housing, as there is not enough available land, especially land for residential construction. This scarcity of land directly influences Arab living conditions. Arab towns and villages have a high population density, and a severe shortage of housing means overcrowding in Arab homes. The state has done very little to provide housing for a growing Arab population – between 1975 and 2000, public housing units built for the Arab population were just 0.3 percent of the total (fewer than 1,000 housing units out of a total of 337,000).[107] Furthermore, government restrictions on residential construction in Arab areas means that residential building in Arab towns and villages is often illegal because of the difficulty of obtaining building permits (such permits require approved outline plans, and approval for these plans by local and regional planning authorities has often been very slow). The large amount of unauthorized construction of Arab homes results in occasional house demolitions by the authorities, which then lead to confrontations between the authorities and the Arab residents. This obviously antagonizes the Arab community vis-à-vis the state.

In addition to an acute shortage of housing in their own communities, Arabs also encounter various barriers (formal and informal) that limit their ability to live in Jewish communities.[108] They are effectively unable to acquire or lease land in some 80 percent of Israel's territory (that is, in areas controlled by Jewish rural regional councils).[109] Moreover, Arabs are excluded from state agencies in charge of land allocation and urban planning. In fact, many decisions about the allocation and use of state land are made by the Jewish National Fund (JNF) and the Jewish Agency, quasi-state agencies that are exclusively run by Jews and, legally, solely geared toward serving Jews.

---

[107] International Crisis Group, *Identity Crisis*, 12.
[108] This is still the case despite the Israeli Supreme Court's historic ruling in March 2000 (*Qaadan v. Katzir*) that the Qaadans, an Arab family, could not be denied the right to move into Katzir, a Jewish *moshav* (a cooperative settlement). This ruling meant that Arab citizens of Israel could no longer be legally prevented from purchasing property or building on state-owned lands.
[109] Yiftachel, Khamaissi, and Kedar, "Land and Planning," 17.

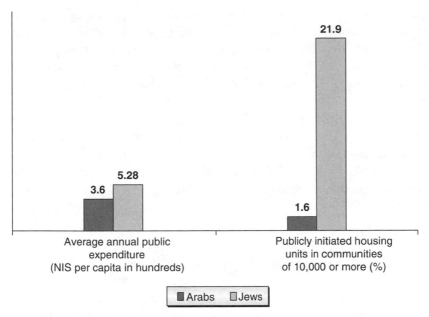

FIGURE 1.3. Inequality in public spending.
*Source*: The Equality Index of Jewish and Arab Citizens in Israel, 2008.

While official discrimination against the Arab minority is most glaringly apparent in the case of the state's land policies and practices, it is also clearly evident in the unequal provision of government funding to Arab municipalities compared with funding provided to Jewish municipalities. Year after year, numerous Israeli non-governmental organizations have demonstrated that Arab municipalities received significantly less money from the government for the development of their physical infrastructure (that is, roads, electricity, sewage, water, etc.) than their Jewish counterparts.[110] In fact, Arab towns in Israel even receive less money for development than Jewish settlements in the Occupied Territories.[111]

---

[110] See, in particular, the annual reports on Arab-Jewish equality produced by the Israeli non-governmental organization *Sikkuy: The Association for the Advancement of Civic Equality in Israel*, all of which are based solely on official Israeli government data. http://www.sikkuy.org.il/english/home.html

[111] The Adva Center reported that in 2004 the Israeli government spent much more money on development in Jewish settlements in the West Bank than it did on Arab towns in Israel. The average per capita infrastructure grant from the government in 2004 was

Persistent inequality in government funding has particularly affected the Arab educational system. Public spending on education per child in Arab localities is about one-third lower than in predominantly Jewish municipalities.[112] The Arab school system, therefore, has always suffered from a lack of resources compared with the Jewish school system.[113] This has resulted in larger class sizes and a worse student–per-teacher ratio,[114] poor physical facilities (especially a shortage of classrooms[115]), and a lack of other educational services (such as extra-curricular activities, psychological counseling, and health services).[116] The fact that Arab school students have the highest dropout rates and lowest achievement levels in the country is no doubt related to this underfunding.[117]

## Conclusion

The inequality, neglect, and discrimination, described in this chapter, that Arab citizens of Israel face has generated intense frustration and deep resentment among them. They are acutely aware of the socio-economic gap between them and Israeli Jews, and they are very conscious of being discriminated against. Indeed, a recent survey of a representative cross-section

---

1,241 shekels (NIS) in West Bank settlements, compared to only NIS 738 in Arab towns; the per capita grant for social, educational, health, and welfare services was NIS 1,949 in settlements, compared to NIS 1,346 in Arab towns. Motti Basok, "The state gave more to settlements, less to development towns and the least to Arab towns," *The Marker* supplement, *Ha'aretz*, February 13, 2006.

[112] OECD, *Labour Market and Social Policy Review of Israel*, 4.

[113] Shafir and Peled, *Being Israeli*, 123.

[114] The *Statistical Abstract of Israel*, an official government publication, reported in 2001 that the average number of students per class in Jewish schools was 25, whereas it was 30 students per class in Arab schools. Central Bureau of Statistics, *Statistical Abstract of Israel, 2001* (Jerusalem: Government of Israel, 2001), table 8.8.

[115] Israel's state comptroller, for instance, found that the Arab sector lacked 1,082 classrooms at the beginning of the 2007–2008 school year. Yousef T. Jabareen, "Who's afraid of educated Arabs?" *Ha'aretz*, July 24, 2009.

[116] Shafir and Peled, *Being Israeli*, 123.

[117] According to a study by Israel's Education Ministry study, in 2008 only 32 percent of Arab students passed their high school matriculation exams, compared to 60 percent of Jewish students who passed the exam. Moreover, Arab students who passed the exam scored lower than the national average both on the exam and the psychometric tests that are required for university or college admission. As a result, 45 percent of Arab applicants are not accepted to higher education programs. In addition to unequal government budget allocations, socio-economic disadvantages and cultural biases in the standardized curricula also help account for the poor performance of Arab students compared with their Jewish peers. Jabareen, "Who's afraid of educated Arabs?"

of the Arab community (Muslims, Christians, Bedouin, and Druze) found that the vast majority believed that they face discrimination by the state in land allocation, allocation of budgets for local government, allocation of budgets for education, and the provision of housing support for young couples. In fact, most of the Arab respondents in the survey believed that they are treated unequally in almost every aspect of life in Israel, especially in treatment by the police, employment opportunities in Jewish-owned companies and government offices, resource allocation by the state, and influence on important state decisions.[118] Thus, Nadim Rouhana and Ahmad Saabneh, the authors of the study, concluded that: "[T]here is not one single area [of life] in which a majority of Arab citizens think that the state treats them the same as it treats the Jewish citizens."[119]

It is not only Arab citizens of Israel, however, who are aware of this discrimination. Awareness is also gradually increasing within the Israeli-Jewish public. An opinion poll taken by the Israel Democracy Institute in 2007, for instance, showed that 55 percent of Israeli Jews thought that Arabs in Israel were discriminated against. The same poll showed growing support among Israeli Jews for equality between Arabs and Jews – 56 percent of Israeli Jews supported this, up from 47 percent in 2003.[120] These figures indicate after a long time of being ignored by successive Israeli governments and the Israeli-Jewish public, the serious problems of the Arab minority in Israel are finally beginning to be recognized. The issue of Arab-Jewish inequality in Israel can no longer be easily suppressed or simply dismissed. Instead, in recent years it has become a topic of much public discourse in Israel and has slowly risen up the national agenda.[121] As a result, there is now widespread agreement in Israel that the socio-economic gap between Arabs and Jews is a critical issue that should be addressed as soon as possible, and most Israeli Jews believe that the government should urgently take great measures in order to close this gap.[122]

---

[118] For example, 35 percent thought that there is legal equality between Arabs and Jews; 23 percent thought there is equality in education; 20 percent thought that there is equality of opportunities for success in life; and only 7 percent believed that there is equality in the level of influence on important state decisions. Rouhana, ed., *Attitudes of Palestinians in Israel on Key Political and Social Issues*, 2.

[119] Rouhana, ed., *Attitudes of Palestinians in Israel on Key Political and Social Issues*, 4–5.

[120] Israel Democratic Institute, *The 2007 Israel Democracy Index*, 2007.

[121] See, for instance, The Reut Institute, "Integrating Israel's Arab citizens into the ISRAEL 15 Vision," February 2009.

[122] In a survey carried out in 2004, 67.4 percent of Israeli Jews thought this. Smooha, *Index of Arab-Jewish Relations in Israel 2004*, 105.

This is undoubtedly a welcome, albeit very belated, development. Nevertheless, this greater awareness of inequality and discrimination and Israeli-Jewish support for government measures to lessen Arab-Jewish inequality have not yet been translated into much concrete governmental action. Many fine speeches have been made and some new initiatives announced,[123] but little has actually changed on the ground. In fact, despite the new attention given to the issue of Arab-Jewish inequality in Israel, the socio-economic gaps between Jews and Arabs have actually widened in many respects in recent years, as Sikkuy's Equality Index from 2008 reveals.[124]

There is a very long way to go, therefore, before there is any kind of Arab-Jewish equality in Israel. As far as most Arab citizens of Israel are concerned, this will never happen as long as Israel remains a Jewish state. Thus, their demand for a re-definition of the State of Israel has become a central element of their long political struggle for equality, as the next chapter will explain.

[123] In February 2007, the Olmert government established a special bureau within the Prime Minister's Office to promote economic development within the Arab community. This bureau has established a private investment fund to invest in projects within the Arab sector, which the government allocated 80 million shekels to (the goal was to also raise at least this much from the private sector). In March 2010, the Netanyahu government announced a five-year plan to spend 800 million shekels (around $200 million) to promote economic development in a dozen Arab towns (the plan actually originated under the previous Olmert government). The plan aims at increasing employment opportunities, improving public transportation, and building more housing units in the towns of Maghar, Nazareth, Sakhnin, Shfaram, Umm el-Fahm, Kalansawa, Tamra, Tira, Kafr Qassem, Rahat, Daliat al-Carmel, and Usfiya. More than 300,000 Arabs live in these towns, roughly a quarter of Israel's Arab population. Ron Friedman, "Equal opportunity for all Israelis," *The Jerusalem Post*, March 22, 2010.

[124] According to the 2008 Equality Index (an aggregate index, based on official government data, of the gaps between Jewish and Arab citizens of Israel in the areas of health, housing, education, employment, and social welfare), between 2006 and 2008 the gaps between Arabs and Jews increased in the fields of welfare, health, employment, and housing. The only exception was in education, but the slight improvement in this area was due more to a decline in the Jews' achievements than a rise in the achievements of Arabs.

# Palestinian Politics in a Jewish State

> We are moving towards a new era of self-recognition, where it is necessary
> to create our future path, crystallize our collective identity and draw up our
> social and political agenda.
>
> The Future Vision of the Palestinian Arabs in Israel, 2006[1]

In the previous chapter we discussed the collective identity and socio-
economic status of the Arab minority in Israel. We argued that despite
the heterogeneity of Arab society, Arabs in Israel are a singular minority
with a shared collective identity that differs from that of Israeli Jews as
well as from that of Palestinians outside Israel – they are "Palestinians
in Israel." Thus, a self-identified Palestinian minority has come into existence since 1948, as Palestinians in Israel have reconstituted themselves
from being part of a national majority in Mandatory Palestine to being
a distinct national minority in Israel. Compared with Israel's Jewish
majority, the Palestinian minority has always been and remains to this
day inferior in many important respects. Although Palestinians in Israel
have achieved a great deal of progress over the years, as a group they still
lag far behind Israeli Jews and suffer from a lot of material hardship.

In this chapter we will examine the political behavior of the Palestinian
minority, especially its major political demands. Dramatic and important shifts have taken place in Palestinian politics in Israel over the years,
as Palestinians have adjusted to new circumstances, opportunities, and
challenges. It is essential to understand that the political orientation of
Palestinians in Israel is not fixed or predetermined; instead it is highly

[1] The National Committee for the Heads of Arab Local Authorities in Israel, *The Future
Vision of the Palestinian Arabs in Israel* (Nazareth: Al Woroud, 2006), 5–6.

susceptible to changes within the Palestinian community in Israel, within Israel itself, and within the wider Middle East region. Recognizing this fact helps us avoid making sweeping generalizations about Palestinian political behavior. It also counteracts the image that is often propagated of Palestinians in Israel as passive victims who are acted upon (by the Israeli state and the Jewish majority) rather than acting.[2] By focusing on the political behavior of Palestinians in Israel, therefore, we hope to emphasize Palestinian political agency, albeit within a structural context that severely limits their political opportunities.

This chapter, therefore, will analyze the changing dynamics of Palestinian politics in Israel. Rather than try to provide a comprehensive review of Palestinian politics in Israel, this chapter will only focus on the most important political developments and the most significant long-term political trends.[3] For analytical purposes, the course of Palestinian politics in Israel will be divided into three distinct periods: (1) the period from Israel's establishment in 1948 until the 1967 war; (2) the period from the end of the 1967 war until the early 1990s; (3) the period from the beginning of the Oslo peace process in 1993 until the present day. Each of these periods features significant differences in Palestinian political activity, and seminal events in the history of the Palestinian minority have occurred during each of them. Although we will examine the political behavior of the Palestinian minority in each of these periods, we will pay much greater attention to the latest period. In discussing this period, we will analyze in detail the contents of the recent "Vision Documents" because we are most concerned with understanding what these documents could mean for the future of Palestinian-Jewish relations in Israel.

## The 1950s and 1960s: Repression and Resistance

The first two decades of Israel's existence, from 1948 to 1967, was basically a period of political "quietism" for the Palestinian minority.[4] There

---

[2] Ahmad Sa'di, "Minority Resistance to State Control: Towards a Re-analysis of Palestinian Political Activity in Israel," *Social Identities* 2, 3 (1996), 395–412. Palestinians in Israel are commonly depicted as the objects of history rather than as agents of their history. Emphasis is placed on the state and the Jewish majority, not the actions and behavior of the Palestinians themselves. Sa'di criticizes this approach and stresses the need to incorporate the Palestinians as an active agent in the shaping of their history.

[3] A more detailed and thorough history of Palestinian politics in Israel is provided by As'ad Ghanem, *The Palestinian-Arab minority in Israel, 1948–2000* (Albany: State University of New York Press, 2001); see also Jacob M. Landau, *The Arab Minority in Israel, 1967–1991: Political Aspects* (Oxford: Clarendon Press, 1993).

[4] Alan Dowty, *The Jewish State a Century Later* (Berkeley: University of California Press, 1998), 194.

was little independent political activity among Palestinians in Israel and a very low level of political mobilization. For the most part, the Palestinian minority avoided politics and did not challenge the new Jewish state that had arisen in their homeland. Indeed, during this period Palestinians in Israel did not even identify themselves as such, adopting instead the "Israeli Arab" label assigned to them by the state.

It is not hard to understand why the Palestinian minority in Israel was not very politically active during this time given the collective disaster that had just occurred to the Palestinian nation as a whole in the war of 1947–1949 (initially a civil war between Jews and Palestinians in Mandatory Palestine, it then became an interstate war between Israel and five Arab states). This war and its cataclysmic consequences for Palestinians – their decisive defeat in battle, the expulsion and flight from Palestine of roughly 700,000–750,000 Palestinians,[5] the destruction of more than 400 Palestinian villages, and the total collapse of Palestinian society – is simply termed the *al-Nakba* (the Catastrophe) by Palestinians. It is by far the most seminal event in Palestinian history and collective memory.[6] Those Palestinians who were still in Israel when the armistice agreements were signed between Israel and its Arab neighbors in 1949 (as well as some who managed to return in the years immediately following the war[7]) were left as a defeated minority. The mass exodus (forced and voluntary) of Palestinians between 1947 and 1949 suddenly transformed the Palestinians from being a national majority in their own homeland to a small and vulnerable minority in a Jewish state. Before the war, the Palestinian population of Mandatory Palestine was double the Jewish population; after the war, only about 156,000 Palestinians remained in Israel, around 12.5 percent of the new state's population.[8] These Palestinians were also now a small minority (slightly more than 10 percent) among Palestinians in general, most of whom became refugees in neighboring countries. Thus, in the words of Baruch Kimmerling and Joel Migdal: "What remained under Israeli control after the 1948 war was a remnant – a crumbling part of Palestinian Arab society."[9]

5  On the mass expulsions and flight of Palestinians during the war of 1947–1949, see Benny Morris, *The Birth of the Palestinian Refugee Problem, 1947–1949* (New York: Cambridge University Press, 2004).

6  Ahmad Sa'di, "Catastrophe, Memory and Identity: Al-Nakbah as a Component of Palestinian Identity," *Israel Studies* 7, 2 (2002), 175–198.

7  From 1948 to 1953, more than twenty thousand Arab refugees (defined by the state as "infiltrators") entered Israel. They were hidden in Arab towns and villages and were eventually granted Israeli citizenship.

8  Baruch Kimmerling and Joel S. Migdal, *The Palestinian People: A History* (Cambridge, MA: Harvard University Press, 2003), 175.

9  Kimmerling and Migdal, *The Palestinian People*, 172.

    This "remnant" of Palestinian society was geographically dispersed in
small villages (the Palestinian urban centers of Haifa and Jaffa had been
de-populated of Palestinians in the course of the war, leaving Nazareth as
the only major Arab city in Israel), and had no national political leadership (because the political elite had become refugees). It was also utterly
demoralized and deeply traumatized, living with the constant fear that
they too might be expelled by the state, especially if they openly challenged it.[10] Thus, left leaderless, weak, fragmented, and fearful after 1948,
therefore, the Palestinian minority was in no state to engage in much
political activity. Furthermore, the leadership that did come to dominate Palestinian politics during the early years of the state were heads
of *hamulas* (clans), and their rivalries prevented any unified Palestinian
leadership from emerging and allowed the state to manipulate these clan
rivalries to its own advantage.[11]

    The political quietism of the Palestinian minority in the 1950s and
1960s was not solely due to the devastating impact of the *Nakba*. Another
major reason for this quiescence was the fact that the vast majority of
Palestinians in Israel were placed under military rule from 1948 to 1966
(the Military Government was applied to all Palestinians living in the
Galilee and in the "triangle" region along the Israeli-Jordanian 1949
armistice line as well as to the Bedouin in the Negev).[12] In effect, they
lived under an authoritarian regime that severely restricted their political freedom and many aspects of their daily lives (such as their ability to
travel out of their towns and villages and to open businesses). This regime
also closely monitored their behavior and speech through the extensive
use of informers and collaborators.[13] In short, the Military Government
permeated every aspect of Palestinian life in Israel, thereby effectively
controlling the Palestinian minority and ensuring its obedience to the
state (although on occasion, the state authorities needed to resort to
harsh measures such as deportations and administrative detentions in
order to neutralize political opposition).[14]

---

[10] Dowty, *The Jewish State*, 194–195.

[11] Kimmerling and Migdal, *The Palestinian People*, 176.

[12] By the time the Military Government ended, a short time before the 1967 war, it covered
     around 220,000 people of a total Arab population of about 260,000.

[13] See Hillel Cohen, *Good Arabs: The Israeli Security Agencies and the Israeli Arabs, 1948–
     1967* (Berkeley: University of California Press, 2010).

[14] See Ian S. Lustick, *Arabs in the Jewish State: Israel's Control of a National Minority*
     (Austin: University of Texas Press, 1980); and Elia Zureik, *The Palestinians in Israel: A
     Study in Internal Colonialism* (London: Routledge and Kegan Paul, 1979).

Although the combined impact of the Nakba and the Military Government on the Palestinian minority greatly limited their political activism during Israel's first two decades,[15] it was never a completely submissive minority. In fact, as Hillel Cohen has demonstrated, the depiction of a passive and docile Arab minority during Israel's early decades, common in many accounts of this period, is not entirely accurate. According to Cohen, "The extent of active opposition by Arab citizens to the state's actions was much greater than is generally thought."[16] Drawing on previously classified documents, especially police files, Cohen has revealed that during this time "lively nationalist activity took place in many Palestinian population centers in Israel."[17] Despite the repression they faced from the military authorities and the state security's agencies, Arab nationalist groups and individuals were active throughout the 1950s and 1960s, especially in trying to strengthen Arab national identity among the Palestinian minority.

The most notable of these groups was *Al-Ard* ("the Land" in Arabic), a nationalist movement established in 1958 that promoted pan-Arabism and a distinct Palestinian identity.[18] Although it was only a very small movement (with 200 members at most),[19] it is nevertheless significant because it was the first Arab nationalist movement in Israel to publicly call for equal rights for all citizens and an end to discrimination against Arabs. In 1965, it organized the Arab Socialist List to run in the Knesset elections that year, but the Supreme Court disqualified the party on the grounds that it rejected the Jewish nature of the state and identified with Arab enemy states.[20]

The most important venue for Arab political activism during this time, however, was within Israel's Arab-Jewish Communist party (Maki).[21] The Communist Party was basically the only permitted vehicle of Arab

---

[15] Another factor, which should be noted, was the belief or hope among many Palestinians in Israel that their predicament was only temporary and that the Arab states, led by Egypt's charismatic President Gamal Abdel Nasser, would eventually come to their rescue (as the constant barrage of propaganda from the Arab world promised).

[16] Cohen, *Good Arabs*, 6.

[17] Cohen, *Good Arabs*, 4.

[18] Adham Saouli, "Arab Political Organizations Within the Israeli State," *The Journal of Social, Political and Economic Studies* 26, 2 (2001), 449.

[19] Kimmerling and Migdal, *The Palestinian People*, 197.

[20] *Al-Ard*'s Arab nationalist political platform was later espoused by the Balad party, which, unlike Al-Ard, has not been banned (despite some attempts to do so). This indicates a degree of liberalization in the state's treatment of the Palestinian minority.

[21] Ilana Kaufman, *Arab National Communism in the Jewish State* (Gainesville: University Press of Florida, 1997).

protest. Unlike *Al-Ard*, it was able to stay within the bounds of acceptable political discourse in Israel while expressing Arab nationalist and
anti-Zionist sentiment.[22] Thus, during the first two decades of statehood,
Arab protest in Israel was largely channeled through the Communist
Party.[23] Although the Communist Party provided an important means for
Arabs to express their discontent, it was always on the margins of Israeli
politics and considered beyond the pale as a potential coalition partner
in any Israeli government (as Ben-Gurion famously put it "*bli Herut ve
Maki*," which means "without Herut and Maki"; Herut was the right-
wing revisionist party led by Menachem Begin).

Ultimately, the Palestinian minority in the early years of the state
was politically repressed and marginalized. It was under the control of
the state and completely at its mercy. This was made tragically clear on
October 29, 1956, when Arab citizens from the village of Kfar Qassem
who had been out working in the fields returned to their village at sun-
down after a military curfew had been declared that they were unaware
of (it was the eve of the 1956 Suez War). On their return to the village,
Israeli Border Police lined them up and shot them, killing 48 villagers,
including many women and children.[24] For Palestinians in Israel, the
Kafr Qassem massacre, as it became known, now stands in their collective memory as the first bloody milestone in the history of the Palestinian
minority in Israel.

### The 1970s and 1980s: The Palestinian Awakening

While the Palestinian minority in Israel was politically repressed and
marginalized by the Israeli state and ignored and forgotten about by the
Arab world in its first two decades of existence, in its next two decades
it slowly but surely made its presence known, both within Israel and in
the Arab world. It was in this period of the 1970s and 1980s that the
Palestinian minority really emerged and started to become politicized.
In essence, it went from being a defeated and downtrodden minority to
becoming a more confident and politically assertive one.

There were many reasons for this transformation. These can be identified at the communal, national, and regional levels. Communally,

---

[22] Kimmerling and Migdal, *The Palestinian People*, 185.
[23] Kaufman, *Arab National Communism in the Jewish State*.
[24] Kimmerling and Migdal, *The Palestinian People*, 195. Those responsible for the Kfar
    Qassem massacre were later tried and convicted by the state.

Palestinian society in Israel changed a great deal as it experienced socio-economic development (especially due to the post-1967 economic boom in Israel). The rapid decline of Arab agriculture in Israel led to the de-peasantification and proletarianization of much of Palestinian society. At the same time, Palestinians in Israel enjoyed rising living standards and higher levels of education, including more and more university graduates.[25] As an increasing number of Palestinians became small business owners and professionals (especially teachers, lawyers, doctors, and pharmacists),[26] a new middle class grew quickly. Consequently, Palestinian society in Israel ceased to be the poor, rural, traditional society it once was, dominated by a *mukhtar* leadership. Instead, it became a more modern, more affluent, and better-educated society with a new political and intellectual elite. This new elite started to set the Arab public agenda, articulating the community's goals and organizing the means to achieve them. In doing so, it gradually took over the national leadership from the *mukhtars*.

The end of the Military Government in 1966 facilitated this transition in Arab leadership and alleviated the restrictions on Arab political activity. Instead of living under an authoritarian regime, Palestinians in Israel were finally able to take greater advantage of Israeli democracy. Another change in Israel that they benefited from in this respect was the end of the political hegemony of the Mapai party, which in one guise or another had ruled Israel without interruption for thirty years. The historic victory of Menachem Begin's Likud party over Labor (Mapai's successor) in the 1977 election signaled the emergence of a competitive two-party system. This effectively increased the political importance of Arab voters and Knesset members for both major parties, but especially for the Labor party which could no longer take this support for granted (as Mapai once did when it ran affiliated Arab lists headed by co-opted Arab leaders that garnered virtually all the Arab vote in elections).

Perhaps the biggest change that affected the Palestinian minority in the 1970s and 1980s occurred as a result of the 1967 "Six-Day" War and its repercussions across the Middle East. Israel's stunning military victory over Egypt, Syria, and Jordan in the war and its conquest of the heavily Palestinian-populated areas of the West Bank, Gaza Strip, and East Jerusalem brought the Palestinian issue back to the forefront of the

---

[25] Kimmerling and Migdal, *The Palestinian People*, 191–192.

[26] While the percentage of Arabs working in agriculture plummeted from 46.8 percent in 1960 to only 7 percent in 1990, the percentage of Arabs employed in the professions nearly tripled between 1960 to 1990, increasing from 4.2 percent to 12.2 percent of all working Arabs. Dowty, *The Jewish State*, 200.

Arab-Israeli conflict. Between 1948 and 1967, Palestinian nationalism had been in retreat, and pan-Arabism was ascendant. The Arab states' humiliating defeat in the 1967 war, however, discredited pan-Arabism and gradually led to a revival of Palestinian nationalism, championed by Yasser Arafat's Palestinian Liberation Organization (the PLO, formed in 1964). The affect this had on Palestinians in Israel was profound, especially because for the first time since 1948 they were able after the 1967 War to renew social, cultural, economic, and political contacts with their fellow Palestinians in the West Bank, Gaza Strip, and East Jerusalem as a result of Israel's occupation of those territories. The rise of the Palestinian national movement in Middle East politics after 1967 and the renewed contact with other Palestinians spurred growing numbers of Palestinians in Israel to openly embrace their own Palestinian national identity. Hence, the national consciousness of the Palestinian minority significantly increased after 1967 (a process described in the previous chapter as Palestinization).[27]

Together, these communal, national, and regional developments from the mid-1960s onward galvanized the Palestinian minority. Less traumatized and timid, Palestinians in Israel became more self-confident and assertive and thus more willing to challenge the state and the Jewish majority.[28] Consequently, Palestinians in Israel became increasingly politically active. In contrast to their relative political passivity in the 1950s and 1960s, the 1970s and 1980s was a period of intense political activism.[29] The increasing politicization of Palestinian citizens in Israel led to the formation of numerous national organizations, political parties, and social and political movements. Hence, the Palestinian minority became both politically mobilized and, equally important, organized.

Beginning in the 1970s, national institutions to represent the Palestinian minority were established, most notably the National Committee of the Arab Councils and Mayors (founded in 1974), the National Committee for the Defense of Arab Land (set up in 1975), and the Supreme Follow-Up Committee on the Affairs of Arab Citizens (formed in 1982), which has become the de facto (though not de jure) recognized representative of the Arab community in Israel.[30] In the 1980s and 1990s, Arab political

---

[27] Elie Rekhess, "The Evolvement of an Arab-Palestinian National Minority in Israel," *Israel Studies* 12, 3 (2007), 3.

[28] Ghanem, *The Palestinian-Arab Minority in Israel, 1948–2000*, 22.

[29] Rekhess, "The Evolvement of an Arab-Palestinian National Minority in Israel," 9.

[30] The High Follow-Up Committee is made up of the leaders of the Arab community in Israel, including its elected representatives (Arab Knesset members, Arab mayors, and heads of

parties were also established. In 1977, *Hadash* (the Democratic Front for Peace and Equality, known as *al-Jabha* in Arabic) was formed as the successor to *Rakah*, which had earlier split from Maki (the Communist Party). Although an Arab-Jewish party, Hadash appealed primarily to Arab voters, calling for Israel's complete withdrawal from all the territories occupied in the 1967 war, Israeli recognition of the PLO, the establishment of a Palestinian state alongside Israel, and full and equal rights for all Israeli citizens. Hadash won about 50 percent of the Arab vote in the elections of 1977 and 1981.[31] This represented a major change in Arab voting patterns, as Arab voters shifted their electoral support away from Mapai/Labor and their affiliated Arab lists after decades of voting for them.[32] In 1984 the Progressive List for Peace (PLP) was established, another joint Arab-Jewish party; but unlike Hadash, the PLP emphasized Palestinian national identity. Then in 1988, the first all-Arab political party (that was not affiliated with Labor or its predecessors) – the Arab Democratic Party – was founded by Abdul Wahab Darawshe, a former Labor Party Knesset member. The Arab Democratic Party also called for Israeli recognition of the PLO, for the establishment of a Palestinian state, and for equality for Arab citizens.

In addition to national organizations and political parties, Arab social and political movements also emerged during the 1970s and 1980s. The secular nationalist movement *Abna Al-Balad* (Sons of the Village) sprang up in the 1970s and was especially active on university campuses.[33] Echoing the PLO, it called for the establishment of a secular Palestinian state on the whole territory of historic Palestine. The 1980s saw the rise of the Islamic movement (founded in 1983), driven by the general rise of Islamism in the Middle East (particularly after the 1978–1979 Iranian Revolution) and by contacts with Islamic institutions, scholars, and clerics in the West Bank and Gaza. Especially active at the local level, the Islamic movement built mosques, schools, free health clinics, drug and alcohol rehabilitation centers, and other local social institutions. In doing

---

local councils) and the secretaries and leaders of all Arab political parties and movements. Although the state does not officially recognize the High Follow-Up Committee, Israeli governments do consult with it and take its views and decisions into account.

[31] *Hadash*' share of the Arab vote gradually declined after the 1981 elections as new, avowedly nationalist Palestinian parties emerged. Gershon Shafir and Yoav Peled, *Being Israeli: The Dynamics of Multiple Citizenship* (Cambridge: Cambridge University Press, 2002), 130.

[32] This change began in the mid-1960s when Rakah received 24 percent of the Arab vote in 1965, rising to 37 percent in 1973. Shafir and Peled, *Being Israeli*, 130.

[33] Kimmerling and Migdal, *The Palestinian People*, 198.

so, it tried to establish a separate, self-sufficient "Islamic society" that was independent of the Israeli state.[34] By the 1990s, the Islamic movement also became very influential in municipal politics, gaining control, for instance, over the large Arab town of Umm al-Fahim.

The decades of the 1970s and 1980s were not only a time of growing political organization within the Palestinian community in Israel but also an era of increasing political protests by them. The seminal event in this respect occurred on March 30, 1976, a day when the National Committee for the Defense of Arab Land had called for a general strike by the Arab community to protest the confiscation of Arab land in the Galilee as part of the state's planned "Judaization of the Galilee." Massive demonstrations were held, in the course of which Israeli police killed six Arab protestors, dozens were injured, and 260 people were arrested. The day became known as "Land Day," and from then on it became an annual day of Palestinian protest in Israel – one of the most important occasions on the calendar for Palestinian citizens of Israel.[35]

Land Day inaugurated a new period of intense Palestinian protest that continued throughout the 1980s.[36] Many of these protests were displays of solidarity with Palestinians in the West Bank and Gaza, as well as with those in the Diaspora (in 1982, for instance, a general strike was called to protest the massacre of Palestinians in the refugee camps of Sabra and Shatila in Lebanon). These expressions of solidarity with Palestinians in the West Bank and Gaza reached their peak during the first intifada (1987–1993). Although the intifada did not spread within the "Green Line" (the 1949 armistice boundary), Palestinians in Israel nevertheless showed a high degree of solidarity with Palestinians in the Occupied Territories by regularly holding strikes, rallies, and demonstrations. They also provided material support to Palestinians in the territories in the form of food, clothes, and money.[37]

---

[34] Although religiously oriented, the Islamic movement is also a nationalist movement. As Rebecca Kook notes, "[T]he Islamic identity promulgated by the [Islamic] movement merely serves to underscore and reinforce, and not diminish Palestinian national identity." Kook, *The Logic of Democratic Exclusion: African Americans in the United States and Palestinian Citizens in Israel* (Lanham, MD: Lexington Books, 2003), 172.

[35] A Palestinian newspaper editor and journalist in Israel has accurately described Land Day as "the 'national day' of the Palestinians in Israel." Hisham Naffa', "The Palestinians in Israel and Operation Cast Lead: A View from Haifa," *Journal of Palestine Studies* 38, no. 3 (2009), 61.

[36] Arab protest activity in Israel declined after the 1980s. Oren Yiftachel, *Ethnocracy: Land & Identity Politics in Israel/Palestine* (Philadelphia: University of Pennsylvania Press, 2006), 172.

[37] Shafir and Peled, *Being Israeli*, 128.

But if the first intifada highlighted the solidarity between Palestinians in Israel and those in the Occupied Territories, it also underscored their differences. While Palestinians in the territories staunchly resisted Israel's occupation, both peacefully and violently, and suffered greatly in the process, Palestinian citizens of Israel went on with their lives and continued to enjoy material progress. Despite their frequent displays of solidarity, the fact remained that they were merely observers of, not participants in, the Intifada. They did not bear its costs or suffer its consequences, nor could they take credit for its accomplishments, especially in helping to restore Palestinian pride. Hence, the years of the first intifada were both the culmination of the renewal of the bonds between two formerly severed parts of the Palestinian nation – Palestinians in Israel and those in the West Bank and Gaza – and the beginning of a new period of disconnection between them. Ironically, this disconnection really became apparent when the Palestinian people seemed on the verge of finally achieving their long-cherished goal of national self-determination.

## The 1990s and 2000s: A New Agenda

The Declaration of Principles (DOP)[38] agreement signed with much fanfare on the White House lawn by Israel's Prime Minister Yitzhak Rabin and PLO leader Yasser Arafat on September 13, 1993, was a watershed moment in Palestinian history. After decades of official denial,[39] the government of Israel finally acknowledged the existence of a Palestinian people and recognized the PLO as its legitimate representative (the PLO, in turn, recognized the right of the state of Israel to exist and renounced terrorism). Even more importantly, this landmark agreement between Israel and the PLO – which became known as the "Oslo Accords" after the Norwegian capital where the agreement was hammered out after months of secret meetings – set out a process of incremental Israeli withdrawals from the Gaza Strip (except for the Jewish settlements there) and from much of the West Bank, starting with the city of Jericho; and as Israel

---

[38] The full name of the DOP agreement was the "Declaration of Principles on Interim Self-Government Arrangements."

[39] This denial was most famously expressed by Israeli Prime Minister Golda Meir in 1969 when she stated: "There was no such thing as Palestinians. When was there an independent Palestinian people with a Palestinian state? [ ... ] It was not as though there was a Palestinian people and we came and threw them out and took their country from them. They did not exist." Quoted in Dov Waxman, *The Pursuit of Peace and the Crisis of Israeli Identity: Defending/Defining the Nation* (New York: Palgrave Macmillan, 2006), 50.

withdrew, a newly established Palestinian Authority (PA) would take full or partial control over these areas. Thus, although the Oslo Accords deferred the start of negotiations toward a comprehensive peace treaty (during which the thorniest issues of permanent borders, Palestinian refugees, Jewish settlements, and Jerusalem would be taken up) to a later date on the grounds that both parties needed to first develop trust in one another, it was generally assumed that such a treaty would eventually come about, and with it a Palestinian state would be established.

For Palestinian citizens of Israel, the Oslo Accords and the ensuing Israeli-Palestinian peace process was bittersweet. On the one hand, it seemed to herald the accomplishment of the central goal of the Palestinian national movement – national self-determination. This was a goal that was cherished by the Palestinian minority in Israel, just as it was by Palestinians elsewhere. On the other hand, the Oslo Accords and the peace process did not address the question of the Palestinian minority in Israel. Despite the fact that the PLO claimed to represent the entire Palestinian nation, its leadership ignored the Palestinian population in Israel. Their interests, concerns, and future were not raised in the negotiations between Israel and the PLO, which basically only dealt with the West Bank and Gaza Strip. Not only did the leadership of the PLO not raise the issue of the Palestinian population in Israel in their negotiations with Israeli officials, but also they excluded the political leadership of the Palestinian minority itself from the peace process.[40] It was as if the Palestinian minority in Israel simply didn't exist. The failure of the Oslo peace process to address the question of the Palestinian minority in Israel, or even to acknowledge its existence, was particularly problematic considering the possible implications of the peace process for Palestinians in Israel. Would they be expected to move to a future Palestinian state? If they didn't, what status would they have in such a Palestinian state? What national rights, if any, might they eventually be able to enjoy in Israel? These fundamental questions, critical to the future of Palestinians in Israel, were not discussed at all in the peace process.

Despite its limitations and omissions from their perspective, the Oslo peace process still received enthusiastic support from the vast majority of Palestinians in Israel. This was primarily because it promised to deliver an independent Palestinian state, something they had long demanded (this demand featured prominently in Palestinian protests in Israel throughout the

[40] Elie Rekhess, "The Arabs of Israel After Oslo: Localization of the National Struggle," *Israel Studies* 7, 3 (2002), 3.

1970s and 1980s). It was also because most Palestinians in Israel believed, at least at the beginning of the peace process, that it would also bring about an improvement in their status within Israel.[41] They confidently expected that once the Israeli-Palestinian conflict was solved, their demands for equality in Israel would finally be addressed. As Elie Rekhess writes: "Peace on the horizon was widely perceived as engendering the first realistic chance since 1948 to eliminate discrimination against the Arabs and to attain equal status with the Jewish majority and full rights as citizens of the state."[42] This was not an unreasonable expectation. After all, the predicament of Palestinians in Israel since 1948 had often been summed up in the phrase "their nation was at war with their state." Ending this "war," and with it bringing about reconciliation between their nation and state, seemed to offer Palestinians in Israel an end to this difficult predicament. Other benefits would come once peace was achieved – discrimination against them would no longer be read-ily justified on the grounds of security, social prejudice toward them would lessen, and government funds that had previously gone to the settlements or to the military would be channeled to domestic needs. In short, hopes were initially high among Palestinians in Israel that they would be among the beneficiaries of a new era of peace.

This hope did not last long, however. As the peace process dragged on, Palestinians in Israel became disillusioned with it and its implications for their lives. In the words of Rekhess: "On the one hand, it became increas-ingly clear that the solution to the national dilemma of the Arab minor-ity was not to be found in the PA. The Authority continued to disregard Israel's Arabs as a factor in the final settlement, and focused all its energy on realizing the primary goal of establishing a Palestinian state. On the other hand, there was a growing awareness that integration in Israeli life as a fulfillment of the principle of equality was inestimably problematic and, in practice, doubtful."[43]

Overlooked by the peace process and excluded from it, and increas-ingly thinking that Israeli-Palestinian peace and a future Palestinian state would not necessarily solve their problems and fulfill their national aspirations, members of the Palestinian intellectual and political elite in Israel began to re-evaluate their political priorities. Instead of focusing on ending Israel's occupation of the territories, they gradually shifted their

[41] In a survey taken in 1995, 58 percent of Arab citizens of Israel stated that they believed that they would attain greater equality following a comprehensive peace agreement between Israel and the Palestinians. Cited in Rekhess, "The Arabs of Israel After Oslo," 6.
[42] Rekhess, "The Arabs of Israel After Oslo," 6.
[43] Rekhess, "The Arabs of Israel After Oslo," 7.

focus to improving the status of the Palestinian minority within Israel.[44] Instead of emphasizing the Palestinian struggle for self-determination, the Palestinian intellectual and political elite in Israel now emphasized the struggle for equal rights within Israel, a re-orientation that Rekhess terms "the localization of the national struggle."[45] Thus, the Oslo peace process led to a major change in the political agenda of the Palestinian minority in Israel. As Oren Yiftachel noted: "Although the solidarity with the Palestinians [in the occupied territories] and their struggle continues to be strong, a new agenda is developing that reflects the long-term goals of an increasingly assertive Palestinian-Arab community within Israel."[46]

The change in the Palestinian political agenda within Israel did not simply involve a greater concentration of the issues facing Palestinian citizens of Israel, as opposed to those facing Palestinians in the Occupied Territories. It also involved a change in how these issues were understood and what their solutions should be. That is, as the diagnoses of the problems of the Palestinian minority in Israel changed, so too did their proposed remedies. As long-standing demands were re-conceptualized and re-framed, a new political agenda slowly emerged beginning in the mid-1990s, taking shape and gaining clarity over the next decade. This re-formulated agenda went well beyond that of the past. It proposed far-reaching changes to the relationship between the state and the Palestinian minority; indeed, it sought a transformation in the nature of the state itself. As such, many Israeli-Jewish observers have regarded this new political agenda as disturbingly radical. It is certainly revolutionary in so far as it adamantly rejects the continued subordination of the Palestinian minority to the Jewish majority and seeks complete equality between the two national groups in Israel and the dismantling of the Jewish state.

Though revolutionary in some respects, the new, post-Oslo, Palestinian political agenda in Israel was also built on grievances that the Palestinian minority had for decades. Throughout the period after 1967, Palestinians in Israel had protested over the issues of land, especially the expropriation of Arab lands by the state, and their socio-economic conditions, demanding equal government funding and a reduction of socio-economic gaps between Arabs and Jews. These complaints of the Palestinians in Israel vis-à-vis their treatment by the state did not disappear, but instead they became part of a broader critique. Rather than just focusing on these resource distribution issues, Palestinian citizens now focused their

---

[44] Rekhess, "The Arabs of Israel After Oslo," 11.
[45] Rekhess, "The Arabs of Israel After Oslo."
[46] Yiftachel, *Ethnocracy*, 177.

attention on the nature of the Israeli state as the source of their "dispossession, deprivation, and marginalization."[47] Hence, Palestinians in Israel went from protesting unequal resource allocations (of land, government funds, etc.) by the state to protesting the nature of the state itself. Amal Jamal (a Palestinian scholar and Israeli citizen) writes: "In recent years, members of the Arab political and intellectual elite have begun pointing out that the lack of equal allocation mechanisms in Israel is not a temporary flaw in the bureaucratic system, but is intrinsically related to the identity of the state as Jewish. [...] Therefore, many claim that there can be no equality between Arabs and Jews as long as the state is defined in ethnic Jewish terms."[48]

Palestinian opposition to official discrimination against them, therefore, turned into opposition to Israel as a Jewish state. It was the state's Jewishness, not temporary security considerations or anything else, which was held to be responsible for the persistent government discrimination against Palestinian citizens. The fact that Israel is, in the words of Palestinian Israeli scholar Nadim Rouhana, a "constitutionally exclusive ethnic state,"[49] means that discrimination against Arab citizens is built into its very fabric and manifested in a host of laws and regulations that are designed to promote the interests of Jews alone (in areas such as immigration and land rights). Thus, Rouhana contended that: "[...] the state's constitutional ethnic exclusivity is the single most important factor in delineating the contours of the relationship between the state and its Arab minority and determining the future of this relationship."[50] As Palestinian intellectuals in Israel claimed that Israel as a Jewish state was geared toward maintaining Jewish superiority in all fields and granting preference to its Jewish citizens (and even non-citizens) over its Palestinian citizens (and applying policies of exclusion and discrimination against the latter), they also argued that this meant that, contrary to its own self-image, Israel was not really a democracy.[51] To claim to be a "Jewish and democratic state" as Israel did was, they contended, essentially a contradiction in terms.

---

[47] Amal Jamal, "Nationalizing States and the Constitution of 'Hollow Citizenship': Israel and its Palestinian Citizens," *Ethnopolitics* 6, 4 (2007), 472.
[48] Amal Jamal, "Strategies of Minority Struggle for Equality in Ethnic States: Arab Politics in Israel," *Citizenship Studies* 11, 3 (2007), 271.
[49] Nadim Rouhana, "Israel and its Arab Citizens: Predicaments in the Relationship between Ethnic States and Ethnonational Minorities," *Third World Quarterly* 19, no. 2 (1998), 280.
[50] Rouhana, "Israel and its Arab Citizens," 281.
[51] For this argument, see for instance As'ad Ghanem, "State and Minority in Israel: The Case of Ethnic State and the Predicament of its Minority," *Ethnic and Racial Studies* 21, 3 (1998), 428–448.

Over the course of the 1990s, this critique of Israel's claim to be a Jewish democracy became a central part of the political discourse of Palestinians in Israel. Increasingly, Palestinian political leaders in Israel openly challenged Israel's self-identity as a Jewish and democratic state.[52] As Ahmed Tibi (a Knesset member and the head of the Arab nationalist party Ta'al [the Arab Movement for Renewal]) succinctly put it: "Israel is democratic for its Jewish citizens and Jewish for its Arab citizens."[53] Nor was this just the view of members of the Palestinian intellectual and political elite in Israel. It also became the conventional wisdom within the Palestinian community in Israel. In a survey of a representative cross-section of Palestinian society (Muslims, Christians, Bedouin, and Druze) carried out in 2007, for instance, the vast majority of Palestinian citizens surveyed (81 percent) believed that there is a contradiction between Israel's definition of itself as both Jewish and democratic.[54] In the same survey, most of the respondents said that they wanted Israel to become "a state for all its citizens" (78 percent favored this).[55]

The slogan "a state for all its citizens" was coined by Azmi Bishara, a prominent Palestinian intellectual and politician in Israel who established the Arab nationalist party *Balad* (the National Democratic Assembly, also known as *Tajamu*) in 1996 and then ran for prime minister in Israel's elections in 1999 – the first time a Palestinian citizen had ever done so (Bishara eventually withdrew from the race). The demand for Israel to become a "state for all it citizens" was the centerpiece of Balad's platform.[56] Although the party has only been moderately successful in elections – it received 16 percent of the Arab vote in the 1999 election (giving it two Knesset seats), 21 percent of the Arab vote in the 2003 election (three Knesset seats), and 20 percent in the 2006 election (three Knesset seats) – its demand for Israel to become a "state for all its citizens," though vague, has been widely adopted by the Palestinian public in Israel.[57] It has become the most popular political slogan among Palestinians in Israel, and one that has also entered the political consciousness and discourse of Israeli Jews (albeit generally with negative connotations for the latter).

---

[52] Rekhess, "The Arabs of Israel After Oslo," 10.
[53] International Crisis Group Report, *Identity Crisis*, 11.
[54] Nadim Rouhana, ed., *Attitudes of Palestinians in Israel on Key Political and Social Issues: Survey Research Results* (Haifa: Mada al-Carmel, 2007).
[55] Rouhana, *Attitudes of Palestinians in Israel on Key Political and Social Issues*.
[56] Balad also called for the official recognition of the Palestinian minority as a national minority and cultural autonomy. See Balad's Web site: http://www.balad.org.
[57] Rekhess, "The Arabs of Israel After Oslo," 12.

Animating the Palestinian demand for a transformation of the Israeli state into a "state for all its citizens" was both a belief that government discrimination against them would only end once Israel ceased to be a Jewish state and a desire for a greater role in Israeli society and politics. Rather than being socially and politically marginalized as earlier generations of Palestinians in Israel had been, a new generation of Palestinian citizens of Israel wanted to be able to fully participate in the country's public life and feel a real sense of belonging to the state. In the words of one young Palestinian citizen of Israel: "Budgets are important, but that's not enough. I have to feel that I belong to this country. When I hear the national anthem now – what does it have to do with me? When I see the flag – what does it have to do with me?"[58] Labeled by two Israeli scholars (a Palestinian and a Jew) the "Stand-Tall generation," this more confident and assertive generation of Palestinians was "no longer interested in being marginal hangers-on of the Zionist project."[59] They did not just want to stop discrimination against them and attain more civil rights and funding from the Jewish state. They wanted to transform the state so that they could become fully equal with Israel's Jewish citizens. This implied a different conceptualization of equality to that prevalent in Israel – it did not simply mean equal treatment by the state, it also meant equal participation in the state. As Amal Jamal explains:

[Arab] Political leaders and intellectuals have begun criticizing the dominant conception of equality interpreted by the state as mere non-discrimination in the allocation of state resources, and as equality before the law. Equality [...] has been conceived of in Arab political discourse to mean positive equality; namely, the full right to participate in defining the main characteristics of the state, including its most fundamental symbols, and the right to power-sharing, especially in crucial decision-making.[60]

Together with a shift from defining equality solely in negative terms (as non-discrimination) to a positive, more substantive conception of equality (equal participation in public life), members of the Palestinian political and intellectual elite in Israel also articulated equality in less liberal, individualistic terms and in more collectivist terms. As Haneen Zoubi, an Arab Knesset Member (MK) from the Balad party (who was elected

---

[58] Quoted in Uriya Shavit, "Talk is cheap," *Ha'aretz*, October 20, 2000.

[59] Dan Rabinowitz and Khawla Abu-Baker, *Coffins on Our Shoulders: The Experience of the Palestinian Citizens of Israel* (Berkeley: The University of California Press, 2005), 3. The authors label the first generation of Palestinians in Israel "the generation of Survivors" and the second generation as "the Worn-Out generation."

[60] Jamal, "Strategies of Minority Struggle for Equality in Ethnic States," 270–271.

to the Knesset in the 2009 election, becoming the first woman to do so on an Arab party's list), put it: "The struggle solely for equality treats me as a number, it reduces me to part of a mathematical formula. It ignores my history, identity and narrative as a Palestinian. I want to be a full Israeli citizen, but it must not come at the expense of my people's collective rights to an identity and a past."[61] Thus, individual equality (i.e., the equality of all Israeli citizens *qua* citizens) was now deemed to be insufficient. National equality was also necessary (i.e., equality between the two national groups in Israel, Jewish and Palestinian).

Many Palestinian intellectuals, political activists, and leaders in Israel came to believe that "equality can only be reached if the state recognizes the Arab minority as a legitimate national collective and relinquishes the exclusive Jewish hegemony on the state as informed by Zionist ideology."[62] Although they still called for equal rights for Palestinians as individual citizens of Israel, they also demanded equality for Palestinians as members of a distinct, separate nation in Israel. "Arab politicians and intellectuals claim that individual rights are a good goal to struggle for," Amal Jamal writes, "but individual rights alone cannot fully satisfy the need of the Arab community for equality."[63] They want a state, therefore, in which Palestinians in Israel can exercise their full rights as citizens, as well as one that recognizes them as a national minority and grants them collective rights, not just individual rights.

In demanding recognition as a national minority, and the collective rights that go along with that, the leadership of the Palestinian minority was essentially engaging in the "politics of recognition,"[64] or in other words, the "politics of identity."[65] By presenting the Arab population in Israel as a national minority with collective rights, the Palestinian political and intellectual elite was rejecting the view of Arabs in Israel as "[...] an unconsolidated, disunited and fractured group of individuals," and instead depicting them as "a national collective with distinctive linguistic, cultural and historic attributes [...]."[66] Moreover, not only did they assert that Arabs in Israel constituted a national minority, but also that

[61] Jonathan Cook, "I want to be a full Israeli citizen," *The National*, February 24, 2000.
[62] Jamal, "Strategies of Minority Struggle for Equality in Ethnic States," 271.
[63] Jamal, "Strategies of Minority Struggle for Equality in Ethnic States," 273.
[64] Charles Taylor, in Amy Gutman, ed., *Multiculturalism: Examining the Politics of Recognition* (Princeton, NJ: Princeton University Press, 1994).
[65] Laurence Louer, *To be an Arab in Israel* (New York: Columbia University Press, 2007), 88.
[66] Rekhess, "The Arabs of Israel After Oslo," 19–20.

this minority was indigenous. The description of the Palestinian minority as "natives" became common in the intellectual and political discourse of Palestinians in Israel.[67] As Amal Jamal notes: "[Arab] Political leaders and intellectuals increasingly emphasize the historical fact that the Arab population in Israel is an indigenous minority and an integral part of the native people of the land of Palestine, a position that establishes entitlement to special rights [...]."[68] In doing so, the Palestinian elite has undoubtedly been influenced by the rising profile of national minorities and indigenous groups in international politics (such as the Native Americans in the United States, the First Nations in Canada, the Aborigines in Australia, the Maoris in New Zealand) and the increasing global legitimacy being given to minority and indigenous rights (the clearest evidence of this is the 1992 UN Declaration of the Rights of Persons belonging to National or Ethnic Religious and Linguistic Minorities and the 2007 UN Declaration on the Rights of Indigenous Peoples).[69]

Like other national minorities (such as Kurds in Turkey), Palestinians in Israel increasingly wanted cultural autonomy. Autonomy for the Palestinian minority in Israel was first proposed by a few Arab academics (notably Majid al-Hajj, Azmi Bishara, and Sa'id Zaydani) in the late 1980s, although at the time it was unclear whether this autonomy would be territorial or non-territorial.[70] By the latter half of the 1990s, many Arab politicians in Israel also voiced the demand for cultural autonomy.[71] This would involve Arab control over their own cultural and educational affairs. Control over their own educational system was a particularly popular idea among Arabs because the state was accused of trying to use its control over their school system to undermine the Palestinian identity of Arab pupils and instill loyalty to the Israeli state.[72] Though separate from the Jewish school system, the Arab educational system is not autonomous and is in fact tightly controlled by Israel's Ministry of Education (and even within the ministry, Jews rather than Arabs fill the top decision-making positions).[73]

[67] Rekhess, "The Arabs of Israel After Oslo," 22.
[68] Jamal, "Strategies of Minority Struggle for Equality in Ethnic States," 273.
[69] See Will Kymlicka, "The Internationalization of Minority Rights," *International Journal of Constitutional Law* 6, 1 (2008).
[70] Rekhess, "The Arabs of Israel After Oslo," 12.
[71] Rekhess, "The Arabs of Israel After Oslo," 13.
[72] Rekhess, "The Arabs of Israel After Oslo," 13–14.
[73] It is interesting to note in this context that the Jewish religious schools in Israel, in contrast to the Arab schools, are controlled by the religious community and its political representatives.

The state exercises tight control over Arab education in Israel in two main ways. First, the Ministry of Education determines the curriculum taught in Arab schools (as well as in all other schools under its control). Unlike the Zionist and nationalistic curriculum taught in Jewish schools that is designed to promote "Jewish" values, identity, and culture, however, the curriculum in Arab schools is aimed at preventing nationalism and the development of a Palestinian national identity among Arab students.[74] Hence, since the early years of the state, the Palestinian minority has not been able to cultivate its national identity and heritage through its educational system.[75] Second, the state decides who is allowed to teach in the Arab school system. This decision is ultimately in the hands of Israel's General Security Service (*Shin Bet*), which checks the background of potential teachers and can veto them from getting teaching positions.[76] "This security check," according to Ismael Abu-Saad, "is used to eliminate Palestinian educators who openly express a Palestinian national identity from the school system."[77] Thus, Arab intellectuals and politicians regarded educational autonomy as a critical means for developing the cultural and national identity of the Palestinian minority in Israel.

One other demand that attained prominence on the Palestinian political agenda in Israel in the 1990s was for the state to finally allow those Arab citizens who had fled or been driven out of their villages during the 1948 War (those who found refuge during the course of the war in other Arab towns or villages in Israel) to return to their villages of origin.[78] These internally displaced persons (IDPs, known in Israel as "present absentees" following the passage of the Law of Absentee Property in the Knesset in 1950) resettled (with the state's help) in other Arab towns and villages in Israel but never fully integrated into them and always sought to return to their abandoned villages. The state, however, barred them from returning to these villages, and even from being housed or employed in the

---

[74] Yousef Jabareen, "Law and Education: Critical Perspectives on Arab Palestinian Education in Israel," *American Behavioral Scientist* 49, no. 8 (2006), 1061.

[75] Ismael Abu-Saad, "State-Controlled Education and Identity Formation Among the Palestinian Minority in Israel," *American Behavioral Scientist* 49, 8 (2006), 1085–1100.

[76] Daphna Golan-Agnon, "Separate but Not Equal: Discrimination Against Palestinian Arab Students in Israel," *American Behavioral Scientist* 49, no. 8 (2006), 1080.

[77] Abu-Saad, "State-Controlled Education and Identity Formation Among the Palestinian Minority in Israel," 1093.

[78] According to official Israeli statistics, they numbered around 25,000 Arabs. This number increased in the years after the 1948 war as some Palestinian refugees managed to return Israel (labeled Arab "infiltrators" by the state) and subsequently received Israeli citizenship. Today, they constitute 15–20 percent of the total population of Palestinian citizens of Israel – about 200,000–300,000 people. Hillel Cohen, "The Internal Refugees

areas of their former villages.[79] Although some groups of IDPs had long campaigned to be allowed to return to their villages, this issue received much greater public attention in Israel following the start of the Oslo peace process in the early 1990s.[80] The Association for the Defense of the Rights of the Internally Displaced in Israel (ADRID) was established in 1995, after it became clear that the issue of Palestinian citizens of Israel who were internally displaced would not be addressed in the context of Israeli-Palestinian peace negotiations.[81] The organization demanded that Israel permit the return of the IDPs to their villages and declared that any Israel-PLO agreement dealing with Palestinian refugees and displaced persons that did not give the "internal refugees" the right to return to their villages of origin would be illegitimate.[82] In doing so, it tried to raise political awareness about the IDP issue among Palestinians in Israel and elsewhere, and it connected the issue of the IDPs to the wider issue of Palestinian refugees and their right of return.[83] As part of its attempt to raise political awareness of the IDP issue, the group organized marches to the sites of destroyed Arab villages, particularly on Israel's Independence Day and on Nakba Day (May 15 – the date of Israel's establishment according to the Western calendar).

The first Nakba Day memorial ceremony was held in 1997 at the ruins of the village of Ghabasiyya. The following year, on the fiftieth anniversary of the Nakba, bigger ceremonies were held at a number of sites of destroyed Arab villages in Israel. Since then, every year on Nakba Day, memorial ceremonies are held and many Palestinians in Israel take trips to the sites of former Arab villages. Thus, Nakba Day has become widely commemorated by the Palestinian community in Israel and has played an important

---

in the State of Israel: Israeli Citizens, Palestinian Refugees," *Palestine-Israel Journal* 9, no. 2 (2002).

[79] Hillel Cohen suggests three reasons for the state's refusal to allow Arab IDPs to return to their former villages. First, the state's desire to increase the land available for Jewish settlement, especially land for Jewish immigrants, resulted in Jewish immigrants being settled in abandoned Arab villages during the 1948 war and throughout the 1950s. Second, the state viewed Arab citizens as potential security threats, so it evacuated Arab villages along the border (such as the villages of Iqrit and Bir'im). Third, there was a desire to punish the Arabs for starting the 1948 war (in which about 6,000 Jews were killed). Cohen, "The Internal Refugees in the State of Israel."

[80] Rekhess, "The Arabs of Israel After Oslo," 26–27.

[81] Israel refused to allow the issue of IDPs to be included in the Oslo peace process between itself and the PLO on the grounds that it was an internal Israeli issue that should not therefore be dealt with in bilateral Israeli-Palestinian peace negotiations.

[82] Rekhess, "The Arabs of Israel After Oslo," 27.

[83] Cohen, "The Internal Refugees in the State of Israel."

role in the "restoration of the collective historic memory of the 'Nakba.'"[84]
To be sure, the Nakba has always been a central component of the collective memory of the Palestinian minority in Israel, but until quite recently this memory was mainly expressed in literature and in private emotions. As Rekhess writes: "[T]he memory of 1948 was never eradicated from the emotional world of the individual Arab [in Israel], yet the collective public expression of it has been minimal, and in this respect the phenomenon of a revival is difficult to deny."[85] Not only has Nakba Day given a new public expression to the collective memory of the Nakba held by the Palestinian minority in Israel, but also it has helped to strengthen the emotional and psychological connection of Palestinians inside Israel with Palestinians elsewhere. In the words of the Palestinian scholar Nur Masalha: "The Nakba Day connects the relatively isolated Palestinian community inside the Green Line with other Palestinian communities inside and outside historic Palestine. Collective memory helps to consolidate national bonds, mutual solidarity and shared history and memories."[86]

In sum, the unresolved and bitter legacy of the 1948 war, together with the demand for recognition as a national minority and collective rights, have steadily risen to the top of the Palestinian political agenda in Israel. Over the last two decades, therefore, the political demands of the Palestinian minority have significantly changed. They have become bigger, bolder, and more far-reaching. Palestinians in Israel are no longer simply seeking to be accepted as equal citizens, entitled to the same rights and opportunities as Jews in Israel. Most now also want to be accepted as members of a national minority, entitled to collective rights, and as members of a larger Palestinian nation who are entitled to some kind of redress by Israel for the wrongs it has allegedly committed against them.

### The Vision Documents

The new political agenda of the Palestinian minority in Israel was most clearly – and controversially – put forward in a series of documents published in 2006–2007 titled: "The Future Vision of the Palestinian Arabs

---

[84] Rekhess, "The Arabs of Israel After Oslo," 29.
[85] Rekhess, "The Arabs of Israel After Oslo," 29.
[86] Nur Masalha, "Collective Memory, Indigenous Resistance and the Struggle for Return: Palestinians inside Israel Six Decades after the Nakba," *Jadal*, no. 3, 1 (May 2009), http://www.mada-research.org/publications/PDF/Jadal_May09_Eng.pdf.

in Israel,"[87] "An Equal Constitution for All: On the Constitution and the Collective Rights of Arabs Citizens in Israel,"[88] "The Democratic Constitution,"[89] and "The Haifa Declaration."[90] Produced by different Palestinian organizations in Israel and written by prominent Palestinian academics, intellectuals, and political activists (all Israeli citizens), these four documents represented the most public, direct, sweeping, and substantive challenge ever posed by Palestinian citizens to their status within the Jewish state. In the words of Elie Rekhess: "These documents [...] constitute a watershed in the history of Jewish-Arab relations in Israel."[91] For the first time, leaders of the Palestinian minority openly expressed, not only their opposition to the status quo, but also their vision of Israel's future and the place of Palestinians within it. Hence, these documents have collectively become known as the "Vision documents." They provide a Palestinian narrative of Israeli history, present a harsh critique of Israel's treatment of its Palestinian minority, and make numerous demands, including proposing some far-reaching changes to the Israeli state and political system, most notably calling on Israel to abandon its exclusively Jewish identity and recognize its Palestinian citizens as an indigenous national minority with collective rights. These Vision documents, therefore, offer the most authoritative expression of the sentiments, criticisms, demands, and aspirations of the Palestinian minority in Israel. For this reason, it is important to examine the contents of these seminal documents in some detail.[92]

---

[87] The National Committee for the Heads of Arab Local Authorities in Israel, *The Future Vision of the Palestinian Arabs in Israel*.

[88] Yousef Jabareen, "An Equal Constitution for All? On a Constitution and Collective Rights for Arab Citizens in Israel," (Haifa: Mossawa Center: The Advocacy Center for Arab Citizens in Israel, 2007), http://www.mossawacenter.org/files/files/File/An%20 Equal%20Constitution%20For%20All.pdf.

[89] Adalah: The Legal Center for Arab Minority Rights in Israel, "The Democratic Constitution" (2007), http://www.adalah.org/eng/democratic_constitution-e.pdf.

[90] Mada al-Carmel: The Center for Applied Social Research, "The Haifa Declaration," (2007), http://www.mada-research.org/archive/haifaenglish.pdf.

[91] Elie Rekhess, "No Balm in Galilee," *The Jerusalem Post*, November 27, 2007.

[92] Although the various Vision documents are not identical in their approaches, claims, and demands, the similarities between these documents are much greater and more significant than their differences (in fact, some of the same individuals were involved in writing the different documents). It is, therefore, appropriate to examine these documents together, although in the following discussion greater attention will be paid to "The Future Vision of the Palestinian Arabs in Israel" because it has generated the most attention since its publication and because it expresses the broadest spectrum of opinion within the Palestinian community in Israel (because it was authored by thirty-eight Palestinian

"We are the Palestinian Arabs in Israel, the indigenous peoples, the residents of the States of Israel, and an integral part of the Palestinian People and the Arab and Muslim and human Nation."[93] Thus begins the "Future Vision" document, clearly defining the collective identity of the Palestinian minority in Israel. The "Haifa Declaration" goes further, stating:

> Despite the setback to our national project and our relative isolation from the rest of our Palestinian people and our Arab nation since the *Nakba*; despite all the attempts made to keep us in ignorance of our Palestinian and Arab history; despite attempts to splinter us into sectarian groups and to truncate our identity into a misshapen "Israeli Arab" one, we have spared no effort to preserve our Palestinian identity and national dignity and to fortify it. In this regard, we reaffirm our attachment to our Palestinian homeland and people, to our Arab nation, with its language, history, and culture, as we reaffirm also our right to remain in our homeland and to safeguard it.[94]

These statements of identity are significant because they are assertions of Palestinian national identity in defiance of the long-standing tendency of the state and Israeli-Jewish society to avoid recognizing the Palestinian national identity of Arab citizens of Israel. In rejecting an "Israeli Arab" identity and declaring the attachment of Arabs in Israel to their Palestinian national identity, the documents underscore the "Palestinization" of the Arab community in Israel (a process discussed in the previous chapter). The proud and defiant assertions of Palestinian identity in these documents are not only aimed externally at an Israeli-Jewish audience long accustomed to ignoring or denying this identity but also internally at their own Arab constituency. They remind Arabs in Israel of their Palestinian identity, and they reinforce this identity. In this respect, the documents provide a clear and unequivocal answer to the vexing question of identity that Arabs in Israel have long grappled with: "Who are we?"

Furthermore, the documents actually help construct this Palestinian identity by providing a collective historical narrative for Arabs in Israel. Such a narrative provides the heterogeneous Arab community in Israel

---

academics, legal experts, and community activists and officially endorsed by the committee composed of the heads of Arab local councils and the Supreme Follow-Up Committee on the Affairs of Arab Citizens). Conversely, the document "An Equal Constitution for All: On the Constitution and the Collective Rights of Arabs Citizens in Israel" will not be discussed because it is the work of only one author (Yousef Jabareen) who is also a contributor to the "Future Vision" document.

93 The National Committee for the Heads of Arab Local Authorities in Israel, *The Future Vision of the Palestinian Arabs in Israel*, 5.

94 Mada al-Carmel, "The Haifa Declaration."

with a common, single biography and hence bolsters a collective sense of
Palestinian identity. The historical narrative presented in the documents
is essentially a Palestinian nationalist one, according to which Zionism
is a European colonialist enterprise. In the first chapter of the "Future
Vision" document, Israel is described as "the outcome of a settlement
process initiated by the Zionist-Jewish elite in Europe and the west and
realized by colonial countries contributing to it [...]."⁹⁵ This description
is far removed from the dominant Israeli-Jewish perception of Israel as
the product of the return of the Jewish people from exile to their ancient
homeland. Indeed, the historical connection of the Jewish people to the
land of Israel is completely ignored in the document, as is the partition
vote by the United Nations General Assembly calling for a Jewish state to
be established alongside an Arab one. By omitting these facts, which provide crucial legitimacy to the existence of a Jewish state, this chapter of
the "Future Vision" document basically portrays Israel as an illegitimate
creation. Likewise, the "Haifa Declaration" depicts Israel as the product
of a "colonial-settler project" that was carried out "in concert with world
imperialism and with the collusion of the Arab reactionary powers."⁹⁶

The historical narrative presented in the Vision documents is starkly at
odds with the traditional Zionist version of Israeli history in which Israel
appears the innocent, virtuous party, constantly victimized and attacked
by anti-Semitic Arab enemies. All the documents refer to the Nakba of
1948 as a formative event for the Palestinian minority. They pointedly
note that it is precisely because of the Nakba that they are a minority
"against their will," in the words of the "Democratic Constitution."⁹⁷
In the "Future Vision," "Haifa Declaration," and the "Democratic
Constitution,"⁹⁸ Israel is solely blamed for the creation of the Palestinian
refugee problem.⁹⁹ The "Haifa Declaration," for example, states that in
1948, "the Zionist movement committed massacres against our people,
turned most of us into refugees, totally erased our villages, and drove out
most inhabitants out of our cities."¹⁰⁰

---

⁹⁵ As'ad Ghanem, "The Palestinian Arabs in Israel and their Relation to the State of Israel,"
  in *The Future Vision of the Palestinian Arabs in Israel*, 9.
⁹⁶ Mada al-Carmel, "The Haifa Declaration," 11–12.
⁹⁷ Adalah, "The Democratic Constitution," 4.
⁹⁸ The "Democratic Constitution" refers to the "injustice" of the *Nakba* perpetrated by
  Israel. Adalah, "The Democratic Constitution," 4.
⁹⁹ No mention is made anywhere of the attack against the fledgling Jewish state by five
  Arab armies (Egypt, Syria, Transjordan, Lebanon and Iraq).
¹⁰⁰ Mada al-Carmel, "The Haifa Declaration," 12.

The subsequent history presented in the documents is equally damning of Israel's actions as Israel is accused of uprooting, repressing, abusing, and even killing its Palestinian citizens.[101] The "Future Vision" document sums up this history in the following manner: "Since the Al-Nakba of 1948 (the Palestinian tragedy), we have been suffering from extreme structural discrimination policies, national oppression, military rule that lasted till 1966, land confiscation policy, unequal budget and resources allocation, rights discrimination and threats of transfer. The State has also abused and killed its own Arab citizens, as in the Kufr Qassem massacre, the land day in 1976 and Al-Aqsa Intifada back in 2000."[102] Unlike the other documents, the "Haifa Declaration" also describes Israel's occupation of the Palestinian territories following the 1967 war. Here too, the description of Israel's behavior in the territories is highly negative: "Israel carried out policies of subjugation and oppression in excess of those of the apartheid regime in South Africa. [...] Israel has perpetrated war crimes against Palestinians, killed and expelled thousands, assassinated leaders, jailed tens of thousands ... inflicted physical and psychological torture, and bulldozed thousands of houses [...]."[103]

The Vision documents are also scathing in their portrayals of the state's discriminatory treatment of its Palestinian citizens. In the words of the "Haifa Declaration": "The State of Israel enacted racist land, immigration, and citizenship laws, and other laws that have allowed for the confiscation of our land and the property of the refugees and internally displaced persons. [...] It has spread an atmosphere of fear through the Arab educational system, which is supervised by the security services. The state has exercised against us institutional discrimination in various fields of life such as housing, employment, education, development, and allocation of resources." Similarly, in the section of the "Future Vision" document titled "The legal status of the Palestinian Arabs in Israel," the author states: "Since the establishment of the State back in 1948, Israel has taken a discriminating policy towards the Palestinian Arab citizens, through implementing discriminatory laws and legislations (canonized discrimination)."[104] The author of this section goes on to write that "official discrimination on a national basis is the core of all forms of

101  "View," in *The Future Vision of the Palestinian Arabs in Israel*, 5; Mada al-Carmel, "The Haifa Declaration," 12; Adalah, "The Democratic Constitution," 5.
102  "View," in *The Future Vision of the Palestinian Arabs in Israel*, 5.
103  Mada al-Carmel, "The Haifa Declaration," 13.
104  Yousef Jabareen, "The legal status of the Palestinian Arabs in Israel," in *The Future Vision of the Palestinian Arabs in Israel*, 12.

discrimination against the Palestinian Arabs in Israel. It is the root cause from which Palestinians in Israel suffer, individually and collectively."[105]

Israel, therefore, is accused of systematically discriminating against its Palestinian citizens. All of the Vision documents squarely place the blame for this discrimination on Israel's identity as a Jewish state. As the "Future Vision" document puts it: "[T]he official definition of Israel as a Jewish State created a fortified ideological barrier in the face of the possibility of obtaining full equality for the Palestinian Arab citizens of Israel."[106] In other words, discrimination against Palestinians in Israel is not an aberration; rather it is an inevitable by-product of Israel's definition as a Jewish state. Hence, as long as Israel identifies itself as a Jewish state, its Palestinians citizens will suffer unequal treatment.

Not only do the documents attribute the discrimination against Palestinian citizens to Israel's official identity as a Jewish state, but also they claim that this means that Israel is not fully democratic. "Israel can not be defined as a democratic State. It can be defined as an ethnocratic state [...]," writes Asaad Ghanem in the "Future Vision" document.[107] Indeed, according to the Vision documents, it is precisely the fact that the Israeli state is undemocratic that constitutes the primary rationale for why it should be fundamentally transformed, and many of the documents' proposals are explicitly justified on the grounds that they are necessary in order for Israel to be fully democratic. Although each of the documents describe this desired transformation of the Israeli state in slightly different ways – the "Future Vision" document talks of establishing a "consensual democracy,"[108] the "Haifa Declaration" espouses a bi-national state,[109] and the "Democratic Constitution" proposes a "democratic, bilingual, multicultural state"[110] – they all essentially involve the abolition of the Jewish state.

At the heart of all the Vision documents is an extensive set of demands and proposals for changing the relationship between the Palestinian minority and the state and addressing the basic needs of Palestinians in Israel. The main demands issued in the Vision documents can be grouped into three broad categories: (1) historical redress; (2) equity; and (3) political governance.

---

[105] Jabareen, "The Legal Status of the Palestinian Arabs in Israel," 13.
[106] Jabareen, "The Legal Status of the Palestinian Arabs in Israel," 13.
[107] Ghanem, "The Palestinian Arabs in Israel and Their Relation to the State of Israel," 9.
[108] Ghanem, "The Palestinian Arabs in Israel and Their Relation to the State of Israel," 10.
[109] Mada al-Carmel, "The Haifa Declaration," 16.
[110] Adalah, "The Democratic Constitution," 3.

First, all the documents demand that Israel take measures to redress the historic injustices it is accused of. Above all, the documents call on Israel to acknowledge its responsibility for the Nakba. According to the "Haifa Declaration," Israeli recognition of the Palestinian narrative is essential for reconciliation between the "Jewish Israeli people" and the "Arab Palestinian people."[111] In addition, the "Haifa Declaration" and the "Democratic Constitution" demand that Israel recognize the right of return of Palestinian refugees (in accordance with UN Resolution 194); whereas the "Future Vision" document only suggests that Israel pay compensation to its Palestinian citizens and allow the "present absentees" to return to their villages in Israel.[112] Israel is also called on to redress other wrongs it has committed in the past against its Palestinian citizens. In particular, Israel must return Palestinian land and property it has appropriated over the years.[113] Moreover, the "Future Vision" document recommends that Israel "adopt policies of corrective justice in all aspects of life in order to compensate for the damage inflicted on the Palestinian Arabs due to the ethnic favoritism policies of the Jews."[114] Likewise, the "Democratic Constitution" calls for "affirmative action based on the principles of distributive justice in the allocation of land and water and in planning."[115]

Second, equality is also high on the list of demands in the Vision documents. Because all the documents condemn the lack of equality between Jews and Palestinians in Israel and the discrimination that Palestinians endure, they are unanimous in demanding equal treatment for Palestinians and Jews and equal distribution of resources (e.g., budgets, land, and housing). Thus, the "Future Vision" states: "Israel should refrain from adopting policies and schemes in favor of the majority. Israel must remove all forms of ethnic superiority, be that executive, structural, legal or symbolic."[116] In line with this, therefore, the "Law of Return" that gives Jews the automatic right of citizenship in Israel would be annulled and Israel's national symbols, such as the flag and anthem, would be changed. In a similar vein, the "Haifa Declaration" declares: "Our vision for the future relations between Palestinian Arabs and Israeli Jews in this

---

[111] Mada al-Carmel, "The Haifa Declaration," 14.
[112] "The Democratic Constitution" also calls for allowing the return of the "present absentees" to their villages and for them to receive compensation from the state. Adalah, "The Democratic Constitution," 14.
[113] See, for instance, Adalah, "The Democratic Constitution," 5, 14.
[114] Ghanem, "The Palestinian Arabs in Israel and Their Relation to the State of Israel," 11.
[115] Adalah, "The Democratic Constitution," 14.
[116] Ghanem, "The Palestinian Arabs in Israel and Their relation to the State of Israel," 11.

country is to create a democratic state founded on equality between the two national groups. [...] In practice, this means annulling all laws that discriminate directly or indirectly on the basis of nationality, ethnicity, or religion – first and foremost the laws of immigration and citizenship – and enacting laws rooted in the principles of justice and equality."[117] In other words, according to the Vision documents, in order to ensure Jewish-Palestinian equality in Israel, all the laws and symbols associated with Israel's Jewish identity must be abolished.

Third, the Vision documents propose various changes in the political structure of the state to allow for power sharing in the central government between Jews and Palestinians and greater self-governance by the Palestinian community. The "consensual democracy" that the "Future Vision" document advocates involves implementing what is essentially a consociational system of government. Such a system would guarantee the Palestinian community formal representation in governmental decision making and a veto on certain issues of direct concern to them. It would be a major departure from Israel's existing system of government in which Arab parties have always been excluded from government coalitions and have little or no ability to prevent the passage of legislation that affects the Palestinian community.

Although the "Future Vision" document is vague on how consociationalism would actually function in Israel, the "Democratic Constitution" provides two different models for how this could work. The first model involves the creation of a "Parliamentary Committee for Bilingual and Multicultural Affairs" with half of its members drawn from Arab or Arab-Jewish parties. All government legislation and statutes would have to be approved by this committee (unless two-thirds of the Knesset voted to override the committee's decision).[118] The second model would give Arab or Arab-Jewish parties in the Knesset veto power over proposed legislation if 75 percent of their members voted against the legislation on the grounds that it violated the fundamental rights of the Palestinian minority.

The other major demand in the area of political governance made by the Vision documents concerns granting the Palestinian community non-territorial autonomy in education, culture, and religious affairs. Self-rule in these areas would give the Palestinian minority a measure of self-determination within Israel, which these documents claim they are

---

[117] Mada al-Carmel, "The Haifa Declaration," 16.
[118] Adalah, "The Democratic Constitution," 9–10.

entitled to as an indigenous national minority. Indeed, it is the Palestinian community's status as an indigenous national minority that underpins the Vision documents' demands for restructuring the Israeli political system. Unlike other minority groups in Israel, Palestinians are, according to the documents, entitled to power sharing and greater autonomy because they are members of a distinct nation living in their homeland (as opposed to immigrant minority groups, for example).

## Conclusion

Taken together, the Vision documents demonstrate that the issue Israel now faces with regard to its Palestinian minority is not just a material issue that can be remedied through increased government spending and providing Palestinians with equal opportunities. Ending discrimination against Palestinians and providing them with full equality as individual citizens is no longer enough (if it ever was). The Palestinian minority also wants collective rights. They want both individual equality and national equality with Jews.[119] Furthermore, they are not prepared to wait until the Israeli-Palestinian conflict is over for these demands to be met. If in the past the Palestinian minority in Israel hoped that their predicament would improve with the coming of Israeli-Palestinian peace – that is, when their state would no longer be at war with their nation – this hope has now faded along with the hope for Israeli-Palestinian peace. Instead, increasingly impatient for an end to their second-class status in Israel, there is a greater sense of urgency to the demands made by the Palestinian minority. "Equality now" is the unequivocal message of the Vision documents, and, as far as most Palestinians in Israel are concerned, this equality can only be achieved by completely transforming Israel and abolishing its Jewish character.

For Israeli Jews, the vast majority of whom are staunchly committed to maintaining Israel's Jewish identity (notwithstanding their own

---

[119] According to a public opinion poll conducted among the Arab public in December 2006-January 2007 by the Yafa Institute (commissioned by the Konrad Adenauer Program for Jewish-Arab Cooperation), a majority of the Arab public agreed with the demands of the "Future Vision" document, although only 16 percent of respondents had actually heard of it. Only 14 percent of respondents said they thought Israel should remain a Jewish and democratic state in its current format; 25 percent wanted a Jewish and democratic state that guarantees full equality to its Arab citizens; and 57 percent said they wanted a change in the character and definition of the state. Elie Rekhess, ed., *"The Arabs in Israel" Update Series*, The Konrad Adenauer Program for Jewish-Arab Cooperation (February 7, 2007), 7–9.

disagreements over what this means in practice), the message of the Vision documents is alarming and deeply disconcerting. Indeed, the reactions to them in the Hebrew press in Israel were overwhelmingly negative and hostile.[120] Israeli-Jewish critics of the Vision documents were especially incensed by the documents' refusal to accept the legitimacy of Zionism and the Jewish state,[121] and they strongly objected to the documents' demand for Israel to cease being a Jewish state. Instead of promoting a long-overdue and much-needed dialogue between Jews and Palestinians in Israel over their future together (as some of the authors of the Vision documents claimed was their intention), the Vision documents provoked angry denunciations by Israeli-Jewish politicians and media pundits and further fuelled a growing anxiety among many Israeli Jews over what they perceived as the "radicalization" of Arabs in Israel.

Thus, rather than addressing the substance of the Vision documents themselves, public discussion in Israel increasingly focused on the growing "danger" of the "radicalization" of Arab citizens of Israel. This discussion – which at times seemed to border on the hysterical – in turn, contributed to an ethno-nationalist anti-Arab backlash within the Israeli-Jewish population. In Chapter 4, this backlash will be fully analyzed, but before doing so it is first necessary to tackle head-on the contentious question of whether, in fact, the Palestinian minority is really becoming radicalized. This will be the subject of the next chapter.

---

[120] See, for example, Yossef Lapid, "A State within a State," *Ma'ariv*, December 6 2006; Avraham Tal, "This means war," *Ha'aretz*, December 9, 2006; Amnon Rubinstein, "And the Left is Silent," *Ma'ariv*, January 5, 2007; Ze'ev Schiff, "Self-Inflicted Injury," *Ha'aretz*, January 26, 2007; Uzi Benziman, "Azmi Bishara as an Example," *Ha'aretz*, April 11, 2007; Evelyn Gordon, "'Kassaming' Coexistence," *The Jerusalem Post*, May 23, 2007.

[121] See, for instance, Asher Susser's comments in his exchange with As'ad Ghanem, one of the authors of the Future Vision document. "Dialogue no. 6, March 2007, between As'ad Ghanem and Asher Susser," *Bitterlemons*, http://www.bitterlemons-dialogue.org/dialogue6.html

# 3

# A Radicalized Minority?

> This state came here and was enforced on the ruins of my nation. I accepted citizenship to be able to live here, and I will not do anything, security-wise, against the state. I am not going to conspire against the state, but you cannot ask me every day if I am loyal to the state. Citizenship demands from me to be loyal to the law, but not to the values or ideologies of the state. It is enough to be loyal to the law.
>
> Azmi Bishara, Palestinian Arab leader[1]

The Palestinian Arab minority in Israel today is highly politicized. This was not always the case. It has undergone a gradual process of politicization over time, which has reached its zenith in recent years. As the previous chapter demonstrated, over the last six decades there has been a clear trend of greater political activism and self-assertion among Palestinian citizens of Israel. In stark contrast to their political quiescence during Israel's early years (1948–1967), members of the Palestinian minority (especially its younger members) have become increasingly mobilized and vocal in expressing their dissatisfaction with their "second-class" status within Israel. During the last four decades or so, they have staged countless protests, rallies, strikes, and demonstrations. They have cast off the co-opted, acquiescent, traditional leadership that once represented them in favor of younger, bolder leaders who are willing to openly challenge the Israeli-Jewish establishment. No longer content with just demanding equality (in government budget allocations, bureaucratic appointments, etc.), the leadership of the Palestinian minority now demands that Israel cease to define itself as a Jewish state, and in doing so they

---

[1] Quoted in Suzanne Goldenberg, "Hated and Feted," *The Guardian*, March 23, 2002.

strongly denounce Zionism and stridently reject Israel's claim to be a democracy.[2] All this has prompted claims by Israeli-Jewish observers that the Palestinian minority is becoming radicalized. This chapter assesses what truth, if any, there is to this common claim. Given its profound implications for the future of majority-minority relations in Israel, the question of whether Palestinians in Israel are radicalizing is one that must be directly addressed.

The belief that the Palestinian minority is becoming increasingly radicalized is now held by many Israeli policy makers and by much of the Israeli-Jewish public. It is regularly expressed in the Israeli media, often in a very alarmist tone.[3] Arab citizens of Israel are frequently depicted in the press and on television as political extremists and even terrorists.[4] Indeed, they mostly appear in Hebrew-language media when they are involved in a crime, a terrorist attack, or a violent protest.[5] But it is not just the media that is responsible for the popular belief that Arabs in Israel are radicalizing. Numerous developments have given rise to and reinforced this belief. The ascendancy of Palestinian nationalism within the Arab community in Israel over the past few decades (reflected in the self-identification of Arabs in Israel as Palestinians and demonstrations of solidarity with Palestinians in the Occupied Territories), the increase in voting for Arab nationalist parties (rather than Jewish-Zionist ones), the growing support for the Islamic Movement and especially for its militant Northern wing, the strident rhetoric of prominent Arab Knesset members, the public opposition to the Jewish-Zionist character of the

---

[2] For instance, Azmi Bishara, the leader of the Palestinian nationalist political party Balad, ran for prime minister in the 1999 election, the first-ever Palestinian candidate to do so (he withdrew his candidacy just before the election). The centerpiece of his election campaign was his demand that Israel become a "state for all its citizens" rather than a Jewish state.

[3] See, for instance, Sharon Roffe-Ofir, "Breach of Trust: Where are Israeli Arabs headed?" *Ynet*, November 3, 2008.

[4] An op-ed in *The Jerusalem Post*, for example, described Arab MKs as "raving, angry extremists." Seth Frantzman, "The failure of Israel's Arab MKs," *The Jerusalem Post*, February 16, 2010.

[5] According to a recent study by the Israeli Center for Strategic Communications, what little attention Arab citizens of Israel receive in the Hebrew-language media (in 2008 they appeared in less than 1 percent of the items in current affairs programs on television and radio and in the press) mostly occurs when they are involved in a crime, a terrorist attack, or a violent protest. The study also found that if the Jewish public reads about "Arab-Israelis" or watches or listens to an Arab, it is most likely to be framed in the context of how that person is a security threat to the Jewish majority. Anat Rosilio, "Absent from the discourse," *Common Ground News Service* – Middle East, English Edition, July 9, 2009.

state, the popularity of Nakba commemorations, and the Vision documents' depiction of Israel as an illegitimate colonial enterprise and their demands for autonomy have all been widely perceived by Israeli Jews as signaling the radicalization of the Arab community.[6]

This has stirred a great deal of anxiety among Israeli Jews, fuelling their fears over the loyalty of Arabs in Israel[7] and the security threat they pose.[8] Nor is this concern limited to the general public. In fact, in the wake of the publication of the "Future Vision" document (discussed in Chapter 2), Israel's domestic intelligence agency – the General Security Service (GSS, known in Hebrew as *Shabak* or *Shin Bet*) – was reported to have warned then Prime Minister Ehud Olmert that Israel's Arab population was rapidly becoming a "strategic threat" and a "genuine long-range danger to the Jewish character and very existence of the State of Israel." The GSS report went so far as to declare that the internal threat of Arab irredentism exceeded that of any external danger, even including the threat from Iran.[9] In the minds of many in Israel, therefore, the perceived radicalization of the Arab minority means that there is a growing danger of it becoming an unruly, violent, and potentially secessionist minority. Hence, according to this view, the chances for a violent Arab-Jewish conflict occurring within Israel are very high. Indeed, for some, the question is not whether a conflict will occur, but when. As Likud Knesset member Michael Eitan, then chairman of the Knesset's Constitution, Law and Justice Committee, bluntly stated in 2004: "Nobody has any hopes or expectations for Jewish-Arab relations in Israel. I don't see a positive scenario [...] the clash [inside Israel] is unavoidable."[10]

---

[6] Whereas recent developments (such as the publication of the Vision documents) have focused public and political attention on the purported radicalization of the Palestinian minority, some scholars in Israel (most notably Elie Rekhess and Jacob Landau) have been suggesting for a long time that Arabs in Israel were becoming radicalized and that this process began with Israel's occupation of the Palestinian territories in 1967. For a critical discussion of this scholarly argument, see Sammy Smooha, "The Arab Minority in Israel: Radicalization or Politicization?" *Studies in Contemporary Jewry* 5 (1989), 59–88.

[7] In a 2003 public opinion poll, for instance, two-thirds of Israeli Jews believed that Arab citizens of Israel are disloyal to the state. Asher Arian, *Israeli Public Opinion on National Security Memorandum no. 67* (Tel Aviv: Jaffee Center for Strategic Studies, 2004), 34.

[8] An opinion poll conducted in 2007 revealed that 68 percent of Israeli Jews feared the possibility of civil unrest among Israeli Arabs. "28% of Israel's Arabs deny Holocaust," *The Jerusalem Post*, March 18, 2007.

[9] Hillel Fendel, "GSS: Israeli Arabs Are Existential Danger to Israel," *Israel National News*, November 12, 2007.

[10] International Crisis Group, "Identity Crisis: Israel and its Arab Citizens," *Middle East Report* 25, 1 (March 2004), 20.

Are these fears and dire warnings well grounded? How serious is the risk of mass violence? Is the Palestinian minority really radicalizing? This chapter seeks to answer these critical questions. In it, we will argue that the "radicalization thesis" is flawed for three main reasons: first, it is too sweeping; second, it is too vague; and third, it is too deterministic. But, it is not entirely false. Along with the general politicization of the Palestinian minority, there has been an increase in militancy, particularly since the collapse of the Oslo peace process, the outbreak of the second intifada, and the "events" of October 2000. Since 2000, and especially in recent years, the attitudes of some Palestinians in Israel have become more radical. The steadily declining Palestinian turnout in Israeli elections is also a worrying trend, underscoring the increasing alienation of the Palestinian minority from the state and the Jewish majority. More and more Arab citizens are losing the desire to belong to an Israeli society that they feel has repeatedly rejected them. The growing sense of frustration and even despair among Palestinians in Israel does indeed raise the danger of an outburst of violence in the future. Nevertheless, to simply describe the Palestinian minority as undergoing radicalization does not do justice to the complexity of the political views of Palestinians in Israel or to the multifaceted nature of Palestinian political activity in Israel. Nor does it adequately capture the shifts in Palestinian attitudes over time. In short, the radicalization thesis is simplistic and misleading.

## The Case against Radicalization

The most obvious problem with the radicalization thesis is that it makes a sweeping generalization about more than a million Palestinian citizens of Israel, suggesting that most of them are politically radical or are in the process of being radicalized. In this respect, the radicalization thesis reflects a common tendency in Israeli-Jewish discourse about "Israeli Arabs," treating them as a monolithic group about which huge generalizations are made. In doing so, it completely ignores the significant political divisions within the Palestinian minority. Israeli sociologist Sammy Smooha has systematically studied these divisions for many years and has produced a useful typology of the different political perspectives of Palestinians in Israel.[11] He divides Arabs in Israel into four main political

[11] Sammy Smooha, *Arabs and Jews in Israel Vol. 2: Change and Continuity in Mutual Intolerance*, (Boulder, CO: Westview Press, 1992), 174–178. See also Sammy Smooha, "The Arab Minority in Israel: Radicalization or Politicization?" *Studies in Contemporary Jewry* 5 (1989), 59–88.

groups: (1) "accommodationists" who essentially accept the status quo and seek to obtain concessions through the political system; (2) "reservationists" who are critical of the status quo and would like to change some elements of the existing system but are willing to cooperate with the state authorities; (3) "oppositionists" who accept Israel as a state but not its Jewish-Zionist character and thus support radical change; and (4) "rejectionists" who oppose the existence of the State of Israel and want to replace it with a Palestinian state, if necessary by extralegal or even violent means. Smooha's extensive surveys of Arab attitudes (regularly conducted since 1976) indicate that this division has been fairly stable over time, albeit with a slight growth in the number of "reservationists" and "oppositionists,"[12] while the proportion of "rejectionists" among Arabs in Israel has fluctuated.[13]

Although the political agenda of the Palestinian minority has changed over the past decade or so and has become more far-reaching and ambitious, as the previous chapter discussed, it is not really radical by international standards. The political demands of the Palestinian minority are by no means extreme. Most want some kind of autonomy within Israel, not secession from it. Most want a two-state solution to the Israeli-Palestinian conflict, not a bi-national state or a Palestinian state in place of Israel. Nor do most Palestinians in Israel want to live in a future Palestinian state alongside Israel – for this reason, they strongly oppose proposals to cede Palestinian populated parts of Israel west of the green line to a Palestinian state. In other words, the vast majority of Palestinian citizens of Israel accept Israel's right to exist, support its continued existence, and want to live in it. This seems to count for little, however, in the eyes of many Israeli Jews. As Smooha notes: "Jews do not appreciate the growing acceptance of Israel as a state by Israeli Arabs and expect them to accept it as a Jewish-Zionist state as well."[14]

The growing assertiveness of the Palestinian minority in Israel has unnerved the Jewish majority and led many Israeli Jews to view all sorts of manifestations of this assertiveness as indicative of radicalization. Indeed, for many Israeli Jews even the act of identifying oneself as a Palestinian is seen as radical. The fact that most Arabs in Israel have now embraced their Palestinian identity and are much less reticent than earlier

[12] Smooha, *Arabs and Jews in Israel Vol. 2*, 201–205.
[13] For instance, the proportion of Arabs denying Israel's right to exist dropped from 20.5 percent in 1976 to 11 percent in 1980 and rose to 18 percent in 1985. Smooha, "The Arab Minority in Israel," 66.
[14] Smooha, "The Arab Minority in Israel," 86.

generations in expressing solidarity with Palestinians elsewhere, especially those in the Occupied Territories, is thus widely perceived by Israeli Jews as a sign of their radicalization. But this perception is mistaken. There is nothing specifically radical about identifying as a Palestinian and supporting other Palestinians (at least not unless it is also radical for Jews in Israel to identify as Jews and support other Jews).

Another supposed indication of radicalization is the popular support for the Islamic Movement among Palestinians in Israel. Whether this really implies radicalization is also doubtful. The popularity of the Islamic Movement does not necessarily mean that Palestinians in Israel want to live in an Islamic, *Sharia*-ruled state. In fact, unlike most other Islamist movements, the Islamic Movement in Israel does not seek to transform Israel into an Islamic state.[15] Its more modest and pragmatic goals are to strengthen "an Islamic way of life" for Palestinian Muslims in Israel, maintain the Palestinian presence on their land, and preserve Islamic holy sites (although the Northern wing of the Islamic Movement can be regarded as radical in so far as it refuses to recognize Israel's existence and seeks to create an autonomous Islamic society within the country[16]).

What many Israeli Jews perceive as radical, then, is not really radical at all. Of course, this begs the question of what we mean by "radical."

---

[15] In the words of Ibrahim Sarsour, the head of the "Southern wing" of the Islamic movement since 1999: "[...] it is a naïve idea to think about creating an Islamic state or looking forward to having an Islamic state inside Israel. Because we are aware of the limitations – we are aware of the realities on the ground. We are aware of the fact that we are a part of the Israeli Jewish state." Quoted in Tilde Rosmer, "The Islamic Movement in the Jewish State," in Khaled Hroub, ed., *Political Islam: Context versus Ideology* (London: Saqi Books, 2010), 16.

[16] The Islamic movement split in 1996 over the issue of participation in Knesset elections. The split resulted in two branches, one led by Sheikh Abdallah Nimr Darwish and the other by Sheikh Ra'ed Salah. The Islamic Movement of Ra'ed Salah is often referred to as the "Northern wing," and the Islamic Movement of Abdallah Nimr Darwish is referred to as the "Southern wing." This division refers to the localities of the towns from which these two leaders live in the so-called Triangle and does not represent a real geographical division. The two branches of the Islamic Movement share the same religious goals – to protect Muslim holy sites and to revive the observance of Islam among Palestinian Muslims – but their politics differ as the Northern wing is more rejectionist and advocates autonomy, or a self-reliant Islamic society, whereas the Southern wing is more integrationist and advocates participation in the state and the advancement of a multicultural society. Since 1996, the Southern wing of the Islamic movement has participated in Knesset elections in 1999, 2003, and 2006 in a coalition with the Arab Democratic Party and three other smaller Arab parties called the United Arab List (UAL). The UAL gained 5 seats, 2 seats, and 4 seats in those elections respectively. Rosmer, "The Islamic Movement in the Jewish State," 17.

For most Israeli Jews, it seems that anyone who rejects Zionism and
Israel's identity as a Jewish state is a radical. By this criterion, the majority of Palestinians in Israel would certainly be radicals – after all, they are
definitely not Zionists.[17] According to a narrower and less ideological
definition of radical, however, most Palestinians are not radical. Smooha
defines Arab radicalism as rejection of "coexistence between the Arab
national minority and the Jewish national majority in Israel as a democratic state within its pre-1967 borders."[18] Employing this definition,
Smooha elaborates on what counts and does not count as radical:

> It would be radical for an Arab to reject Israel's right to exist as a state within the
> Green Line or to have it replaced by a Palestinian state. It would not be radical
> for an Arab to reject Israel as a Jewish-Zionist state or as a Greater Israel or to
> have it replaced by a bi-national state. It would be radical for an Arab to reject
> any minority status in Israel, but it would not be radical for an Arab to pursue a
> national minority status for the Arabs. It would be radical for an Arab to endorse
> or use illegal or violent means of struggle, to boycott Jewish persons or institu-
> tions, to define one's collective identity without reference to Israel, to seek seces-
> sion from the state, and to see the future of the Arabs dissociated from Israel. It
> would not be radical for an Arab to endorse or use extra-parliamentary means
> of struggle, to define one's collective identity in Palestinian terms, to favor sepa-
> rate communities, to seek autonomy, or to support and promote non-rejectionist
> causes of Palestinian nationalism (nation-building, end of occupation, formation
> of a Palestinian state in the West Bank and Gaza Strip, and recognition of the
> PLO as a legitimate representative of the Palestinian people).[19]

Ultimately, then, whether one views the political demands of Palestinians
in Israel as being radical or not depends on one's definition of "radical."
What is much more clear-cut and less open to interpretation is the nature
of their political methods. These methods are not radical but peaceful,
lawful, and democratic. In the words of Amal Jamal: "Although the Arab
demand for collective national rights and power-sharing as well as the
instrumentalization of its indigenous status may sound like radical claims,
the struggle to achieve them is through legal means and from within the
Israeli system."[20] There is very little support among Palestinians in Israel

---

[17] In a 2007 survey, the vast majority of Palestinians in Israel (92 percent of respondents)
thought that the Zionist movement is racist, that Israel's establishment in 1948 was
unjust (83 percent of respondents), and that Jews had no right to establish a Jewish state
in Palestine (85 percent of respondents). Nadim Rouhana, ed., *Attitudes of Palestinians
in Israel on Key Political and Social Issues: Survey Research Results* (Haifa: Mada al-
Carmel, 2007).

[18] Smooha, *Arabs and Jews in Israel Vol. 2*, 20.

[19] Smooha, *Arabs and Jews in Israel Vol. 2*, 21.

[20] Jamal, "Strategies of Minority Struggle for Equality in Ethnic States," 278.

for the use of violence to achieve their objectives.[21] Hence, for the most part, they have not engaged in terrorism or mass violence against the state – with few exceptions, Palestinian citizens of Israel did not participate in the first or the second intifada.[22] Rather than use violence or other illegal methods, the Palestinian minority has consistently relied on parliamentary and extra-parliamentary politics to advance their agenda.[23]

In parliamentary politics, Palestinian citizens of Israel have expressed their discontent with the status quo by increasingly voting for non-Zionist parties.[24] Beginning in the 1980s and continuing to this day, the Palestinian public has steadily shifted its electoral support away from Zionist parties (notably the Labor party) to Arab-Jewish (Hadash[25]) and Arab political parties – these parties received 69 percent of the Arab vote in the 2003 Knesset elections, 72 percent in the 2006 elections, and 83 percent in the 2009 election.[26] Hence, according to Oren Yiftachel, "The increasing non-Zionist vote obviously indicates growing opposition to Israel's character as a Zionist Jewish state."[27] While this is certainly true, it is also worth stressing that this opposition, though radical from an Israeli-Jewish perspective, is still being expressed at the ballot box.

[21] Support among Palestinians in Israel for the use of violence has actually substantially declined over the years. In 1976, 17.9 percent supported the use of violence; this dropped to 8.0 percent in 1988 (during the first intifada), 6.0 percent in 1995 (during the Oslo peace process), and 5.4 percent in 2002 (at the height of the second intifada). Sammy Smooha, "Arab-Jewish Relations in Israel: A Deeply Divided Society," in Anita Shapira, ed., *Israeli Identity in Transition*, (Westport, MA: Praeger Publishers, 2004), 55.

[22] Although only a small number of Palestinian citizens of Israel were involved in terrorist activities during the second intifada, there was a significant increase compared to the number involved in terrorism before the second intifada. In 1999, only two Palestinian citizens were found to be involved in terrorist activity; in 2001, the number had increased to thirty and the next year to seventy-seven. Figures provided in International Crisis Group, *Identity Crisis*, 25.

[23] Smooha, "Arab-Jewish Relations in Israel," 52.

[24] This includes the Druze and Bedouin who are also turning away from Zionist parties. Between 1992 and 2003, the number of votes for non-Zionist parties more than doubled among these two groups. Yiftachel, *Ethnocracy*, 177. Druze voting patterns, however, remain distinct and differ considerably from that of other Arabs.

[25] Hadash (the Democratic Front for Peace and Equality) is the only joint Arab-Jewish party. Unlike the Zionist left parties (e.g., Meretz), Hadash is opposed to defining Israel as a Jewish state (see its official Web site: http://hadash2009.org.il/). Its support comes mostly from Arabs. In the 2009 election, Hadash received about 30 percent of the Arab vote, making it the most popular party among Arabs in that election. Less than one in ten voters for Hadash in the 2009 election were Jews. The Mossawa Center, "The Palestinian Arab Minority and the 2009 Israeli Elections," The Mossawa Center (Haifa, Israel, March 2009), 32.

[26] The Mossawa Center, "The Palestinian Arab Minority and the 2009 Israeli Elections."

[27] Yiftachel, *Ethnocracy*, 174.

Although Arab Knesset members have been very vocal in protesting government policies and actions, and they have certainly brought attention to the concerns of the Palestinian minority (albeit, sometimes negative and hostile attention), they have not succeeded in bringing about any major improvements for their constituents, and they have had little, if any, impact on policy making in Israel in general. Part of the blame for this lies with the Arab parties themselves who have been unable to unite and thus increase their collective influence, but the biggest reason for the ineffectiveness of Arab parties is the fact that they are effectively barred from becoming a member of any government coalition. Because they are never invited to participate in a government coalition, Arab parties cannot extract the kinds of concessions for their voters that other smaller, sectoral parties (including non-Zionist ultra-Orthodox Jewish parties) are routinely able to do, nor can they exert any real influence on the government's decision-making process.

In light of the meager results that their engagement in parliamentary politics has brought them, the Palestinian minority has pursued additional means to advance their interests and goals. Foremost among these has been the use of a legal strategy to promote their rights. Just as African Americans used the American legal system in their civil rights struggle in the 1950s and 1960s, Palestinians in Israel have turned to the Israeli courts to overturn discrimination against them. This legal activism has resulted in the Supreme Court issuing a number of groundbreaking rulings in support of equality for Arab citizens, most significantly the landmark decision in March 2000 in the case of *Qaadan v. Katzir* that removed the ban on the purchase of JNF-owned land by Arab citizens (a decision whose significance has been compared to that of *Brown v. Board of Education* in the United States). These legal achievements, however, have only been partially translated into practice.[28]

As the limits of using the Israeli legal system to overturn discrimination and ensure individual and collective equality has become apparent, in the last few years there has been a growing effort by Palestinian

---

[28] The actual impact of the *Qaadan v. Katzir* ruling, for instance, has been very limited, as various ways have been found to circumvent it. Recently, for example, selection committees of some rural communities in the north of the country (specifically, in the Misgav Administrative District) have introduced rules requiring anyone applying to join their community to declare their allegiance to Zionism and to Israel as Jewish and democratic state. These rules are basically a means of excluding Arabs from moving into their communities, without violating the Supreme Court's ruling.

non-governmental organizations (NGOs) in Israel to raise international awareness about the issues affecting the Palestinian minority.[29] In trying to bring their issues to international attention, Palestinian NGOs like *Adalah* ("Justice") and *Mossawa* ("Equality") have lobbied international organizations (e.g., UN committees for the protection of minority and human rights) and regional groups (most notably the European Union[30]) and reached out to foreign embassies and foreign media. This international outreach has met with some success as the Palestinian minority has gained greater visibility in the international arena. For instance, the UN has recognized Adalah as an advisory organization that can participate in the UN's Socio-Economic Council, and in May 2005 the European Parliament held a discussion on the topic of the Arab minority in Israel.[31]

The international outreach of organizations like Adalah and Mossawa are one example of the political activism of Palestinian NGOs in Israel. Many other Palestinian NGOs also engage in advocacy and protest activities.[32] In fact, since the 1980s and especially in the 1990s there has been a rapid proliferation of Palestinian NGOs in Israel,[33] and they have come to play an important role in the empowerment and development of Palestinian society in Israel.[34] The mushrooming of Palestinian NGOs in Israel, therefore, represents another way in which Palestinian citizens of Israel are attempting to change the status quo. Although the goals of some of these NGOs (such as those involved in drafting the Vision

[29] Interview with Hassan Jabareen, General Director of Adalah – The Legal Center for Arab Minority Rights in Israel, June 24, 2009, Haifa. Adalah, an Arab civil rights organization founded in 1997, has been at the forefront of promoting and defending Arab civil rights in Israel.

[30] In pursuing its "European strategy," Mossawa – The Advocacy Center for Arab Citizens in Israel – established an office in Brussels in 2008. Author interview with Rania Laham-Grayeb and Adella Biadi-Shlon, Deputy Directors of Mossawa, June 24, 2009, Haifa.

[31] Reut Institute, "Internationalization of the Issue of Israeli Arabs," June 14, 2005, http://reut-institute.org/Publication.aspx?PublicationId=535.

[32] For example, the Arab Association for Human Rights (HRA), the Follow-up Committee on Arab Education, the Arab Center for Alternative Planning, the Association of Forty (which strives for formal recognition of unrecognized Arab villages), Mada al-Carmel (the Arab Center for Applied Social Research), WAVO (Women against Violence), and Kayan Feminist Organization.

[33] According to one recent study, there are more than 1,500 Palestinian NGOs in Israel (1,385 that are service providers – providing welfare, educational, and cultural services, among other things – and 132 advocacy organizations). Amal Jamal, "The Counter-Hegemonic Role of Civil Society: Palestinian-Arab NGOs in Israel," *Citizenship Studies*, 12, 3 (2008), 289.

[34] Jamal, "The Counter-Hegemonic Role of Civil Society," 283–306.

documents) may seem radical to many Israeli Jews, their methods are certainly not.

It should be clear by now that the radicalization thesis is seriously flawed. In addition to the reasons we have already discussed, a further major problem with the radicalization thesis must also be noted – it is overly deterministic in its prediction of the political direction in which Palestinians in Israel are heading. That is, according to the radicalization thesis, it seems as if the Palestinian minority is bound to become ever more restive and rebellious, eventually even violent. Thus, it gives rise to a kind of fatalistic attitude about Jewish-Palestinian relations in Israel as a conflict, potentially a violent one, between the two groups appears all but inevitable. Such an attitude is unwarranted because, contrary to the radicalization thesis, there is no linear trend in Arab attitudes from political moderation to extremism. In fact, Arab attitudes fluctuate, becoming more radical or more moderate in accordance with changing circumstances and new events. They are particularly responsive to developments inside Israel as well as between Israel and Palestinians in the West Bank and Gaza.

The war in Gaza between Israel and Hamas from December 2008 to January 2009, for example, had a radicalizing effect on Palestinians in Israel.[35] Marches and demonstrations against the war took place in many Arab towns and villages throughout Israel,[36] and the police arrested

---

[35] According Ibrahim Abu-Shindi, a longtime Arab activist for Arab-Jewish coexistence in Israel, Arab attitudes toward Jews in Israel changed as a result of the war in Gaza because of the enthusiastic support for the war by Israeli Jews, which deeply dismayed the Arab community. Consequently, Arabs started to hate Israeli Jews and not just the government. Interview with Ibrahim Abu-Shindi, Director of the Arab-Jewish Community Center in Jaffa, June 28, 2009, Jaffa. Similarly, in a report published shortly after the Gaza war, the Arab advocacy organization the Mossawa Center warned that: "The emotional fallout from the solidarity between Palestinian citizens of Israel and Palestinians inside Gaza has created resentment and frustration from the Arab community towards the state of Israel. These feelings could have the effect of shifting the community away from dialogue and engagement with their neighbors within Israel, resulting in further hostility or even violence." The Mossawa Center, "The Palestinian Arab Minority and the 2009 Israeli Elections."

[36] After Israel launched its military offensive in Gaza, the Supreme Follow-Up Committee for Arab Citizens of Israel immediately declared a "Day of Wrath and Mourning for the Martyrs among our Compatriots in the Gaza Strip," announced a general strike, and called for demonstrations and protest marches throughout the country. It also issued a statement denouncing Israel as "a criminal state in all its constituent parts, including its political leaders and those entrusted with its security," and declaring that the state was "committing genocidal actions, war crimes, and crimes against humanity directed against our compatriots in the Gaza Strip." Hisham Naffaʿ, "The Palestinians in Israel

hundreds of Arab demonstrators.[37] What has been described as the largest Arab demonstration ever held in Israel took place in the Arab town of Sakhnin on January 3, 2009, when an estimated crowd of more than 100,000 Arab citizens from all over Israel attended a rally to protest Israel's military offensive.[38] The protestors carried Palestinian flags and banners and held placards adorned with slogans declaring solidarity with the residents of Gaza.[39] Whereas the vast majority of Palestinians in Israel were staunchly opposed to the Gaza war, Israeli Jews were overwhelmingly supportive of the war. Hence, the war polarized the two communities and worsened the relations between them.[40]

In general, the actions and policies of Israeli governments can strongly influence the political beliefs and attitudes of the Palestinian minority. A government that is perceived to be hostile or unsympathetic to them (and to Palestinians elsewhere) will engender greater antagonism and encourage radicalism among the Palestinian minority; conversely, a government that is regarded as supportive and sympathetic will elicit more positive feelings and less adversarial political views. In short, the better they are treated by the state, the more moderate the Palestinian minority becomes.

This was most clearly the case from 1992 to 1995 during the period of the Labor-led government under Prime Minister Rabin, a time that Smooha describes as "a golden age for the Arabs."[41] During this time, Arab political parties enjoyed the most power and influence that they have ever had because the survival of Rabin's government depended on Arab parliamentary support (the three Knesset votes of Hadash and the two Knesset votes of the Arab Democratic Party). Although Rabin did not invite Hadash or the Arab Democratic Party to join his government,[42]

---

and Operation Cast Lead: A View from Haifa," *Journal of Palestine Studies* 38, no. 3 (2009), 55.

[37] Jonathan Lis, "Israel arrests 700 people, mostly Arabs, in protests against IDF Gaza op," *Ha'aretz*, January 12, 2009, http://www.Ha'aretz.com/hasen/spages/1054763.html.

[38] Naffa', "The Palestinians in Israel and Operation Cast Lead," 57–58.

[39] In addition to staging regular protests, Palestinians in Israel also donated money, clothing, supplies, and medicines to Palestinians in Gaza. The Arab town of Umm al-Fahm, for example, collected 6 million shekels (about $1.5 million) to give to the United Nations Relief and Works Agency for Palestine Refugees in the Near East (UNRWA) for delivery in Gaza. Naffa', "The Palestinians in Israel and Operation Cast Lead," 59.

[40] There were even fights between Jewish and Arab students over the Gaza War at universities across the country.

[41] Smooha, "Arab-Jewish Relations in Israel," 38.

[42] Officially including these parties in his government coalition would have violated an informal rule against having Arab parties in government, something that Rabin (like all other Israeli prime ministers) dared not challenge.

both parties were in an informal coalition with Rabin's government and had a quasi coalition agreement with it that guaranteed their support in the Knesset in exchange for various policies designed to benefit the Palestinian minority and promote greater Arab-Jewish equality.[43]

Consequently, numerous significant improvements for the Palestinian minority occurred under the Rabin government. After decades of under-funding, state resources allocated to the Arab sector were substantially increased, especially in the areas of education, health, and welfare benefits – most notably, the Rabin government ensured equal access to health care for Arab and Jewish citizens and equal child benefit allowances (by removing the extra benefits for families of those who had served in the Israel Defense Forces). The Rabin government also established forty-eight new family health clinics in Arab localities; increased the recruitment of Arab university graduates into the higher ranks of the civil service; and granted construction permits and stopped demolishing unauthorized buildings in Arab towns.[44]

In addition to these practical measures by the Rabin government aimed at improving the lives of Israel's Arab citizens, Prime Minister Rabin also made a number of significant gestures indicating his desire to fully integrate the Arab community. He appointed two Arabs as deputy ministers and abolished the position of advisor to the prime minister on Arab affairs, which had effectively marked Arab citizens out from other citizens. He also staunchly defended his government's dependence on the votes of Arab Knesset members in the face of strong criticism from his political opponents on the right, bluntly stating on one occasion for instance: "It is time, once and for all, to decide whether the Israeli-Arab public is an integral part of Israel. Those who claim that it is not should come out and apologize to those Arabs whose votes they had solicited."[45]

---

[43] In discussing the period of the Rabin government and its dependence on the support of Arab parties in the Knesset, Shafir and Peled write: "In evaluating this episode one could consider the glass as half-full or half-empty. It could be argued that for the first time Palestinians had real influence at cabinet level, albeit from the outside, and that they used this influence to promote both the peace process and the material interests of their community. On the other hand, it could be pointed out that the Labor government was attacked viciously for its dependence on Arab votes and that both Rabin and Shimon Peres [...] made frantic efforts to enlarge their coalitions, so that they would not have to depend on these votes." Gershon Shafir and Yoav Peled, *Being Israeli: The Dynamics of Multiple Citizenship* (Cambridge: Cambridge University Press, 2002), 131.

[44] Laurence Louer, *To be an Arab in Israel* (New York: Columbia University Press, 2007), 62.

[45] Quoted in Myron J. Aronoff and Pierre M. Atlas, "The Peace Process and Competing Challenges to the Dominant Zionist Discourse," in Ilan Peleg ed., *The Middle East Peace*

All of this had a moderating affect on the attitudes of Palestinians in Israel. This is clearly discernible in Smooha's survey of Arab attitudes carried out in 1995 (shortly before Rabin's assassination) in which the percentage of Arab citizens who denied Israel's right to exist was halved from 13.5 percent in 1988 to 6.8 percent in 1995, and the percentage of Arabs who supported the establishment of a Palestinian state in all of historic Palestine instead of Israel dropped from 29.5 percent in 1988 to 16.6 percent in 1995. Another indication of moderation was the decline in Arab support for illegal demonstrations, which dropped from 13.1 percent in 1988 to 6.0 percent in 1995. Even the self-identification of Arabs in Israel changed considerably under the positive influence of the Rabin government – those Arabs who defined themselves as a (non-Israeli) Palestinian dropped from 27.1 percent in 1988 to only 10.3 percent in 1995.[46]

During the period of the Rabin government, therefore, the attitudes of Palestinians in Israel became more moderate rather than more radical. This challenges the radicalization thesis because it clearly demonstrates that there is no long-term linear trend in Arab attitudes. Instead, these attitudes are influenced by Israeli government policies, among other things, and can change for the better as well as for the worse. While it is critically important to recognize this, it also necessary to acknowledge that since the Rabin government, and especially over the last decade or so, the moderation in Arab attitudes that occurred under the Rabin government has been reversed. In recent years, much of the Arab public in Israel and its political leadership have become more militant and elements of it have become more radical.

## Growing Alienation, Militancy, and Radicalism

If the early 1990s during the period of the Rabin government was a "golden age" for Israel's Palestinian citizens, a time when they appeared to be on the verge of finally being treated as equal members of Israeli society and allowed to be full participants in Israeli politics, the years since then have been a dark age. As their hopes for Arab-Jewish equality and Israeli-Palestinian peace have receded, Palestinians in Israel have become increasingly frustrated, disillusioned, and disaffected, and consequently

---

*Process: Interdisciplinary Perspectives* (Albany, NY: State University of New York Press, 1998), 45.
[46] Smooha, "Arab-Jewish Relations in Israel," 55.

more militant in their political behavior and more radical in their political views and goals.

This is apparent on both the elite and popular levels. The rhetoric of Arab leaders (such as Azmi Bishara, Ahmad Tibi, Ibrahim Sarsur, and Ra'ed Salah) has become more extreme, defiant, and combative.[47] Similarly, the discourse of Arab intellectuals in Israel is more strident and uncompromising – for example, in the calls for a bi-national state in Israel/Palestine.[48] Arab public opinion has also become more radical, as shown in Smooha's surveys of Arab attitudes. In the 2001 survey, for instance, 29.1 percent of Arab citizens supported the establishment of a Palestinian state in all of historic Palestine instead of Israel, a significant increase from 16.6 percent in 1995.[49] Even stronger evidence of growing radicalism within the Arab public were the results of the 2008 survey in which only 53.7 percent of Arab citizens recognized Israel's right to exist, a huge decline from 81.1 percent who recognized this right in the 2003 survey.[50] Even fewer Arabs – just 41 percent – recognized Israel's right to exist as a Jewish and democratic state, down from 65.6 percent who did so in 2003. The survey also revealed a large increase in the percentage of Arabs who said that they had participated in protests in the past year (41.4 percent in 2008 compared with 28.7 percent in 2003) and an increase in Arab support for violence (in 2008, 12.6 percent of Arab respondents supported the use of all means, including violence, in the struggle to improve their situation, compared with 5.4 percent who supported this in 2003). The statistic that received by far the most media attention in Israel was the 40.5 percent of Arabs who said that the Holocaust never happened.[51] Although this is certainly a disturbingly high figure and indicates an alarming increase in Holocaust denial among Arabs in Israel (a 12.5 percent increase from the 2006 survey), arguably even more disconcerting, at least in terms of the prospects for Arab-Jewish coexistence in Israel, was the big increase in the proportion of Arabs who said that they objected to having a Jewish neighbor – 47.3 percent of Arab respondents in 2008 compared with 27.2 percent in 2003.

[47]  Yiftachel, *Ethnocracy*, 181.
[48]  Yiftachel, *Ethnocracy*, 182.
[49]  Smooha, "Arab-Jewish Relations in Israel," 55.
[50]  Sammy Smooha, *Index of Arab-Jewish Relations in Israel 2008* (Haifa: The Jewish-Arab Center, University of Haifa, 2009. The survey was conducted before the Gaza War in December-January 2008–2009, which hardened Arab attitudes even more.
[51]  See, for instance, Sharon Roffe-Ofir, "40% of Israeli Arabs: Holocaust never happened," *Ynet*, May 17, 2009.

Underlying this dramatic change in popular Arab attitudes since the time of the Rabin government has been a growing sense of alienation. To be sure, many Palestinians in Israel have always felt alienated to some degree from the state and Israeli-Jewish society, but this feeling of alienation has been reinforced and has grown since Rabin's assassination in November 1995. Palestinians in Israel felt anger and sadness over the assassination as Rabin, just as most Israeli Jews did,[52] but their reaction was largely ignored by the media in Israel and by the Jewish public, for whom Rabin's assassination was "an internal Jewish affair."[53] The fact that Palestinian citizens were mostly excluded from the rituals of national mourning and remembrance in the wake of Rabin's assassination served to underline their exclusion from Israeli society. Moreover, in the years that followed this tragic and traumatic event, the efforts to ease the political and cultural tensions and divisions among Israeli Jews – which were widely held to have been an underlying cause of the assassination – only further marginalized and alienated Palestinian citizens. To make matters worse, the narrow right-wing government led by Likud leader Benjamin Netanyahu that came to power in 1996 disregarded the Arab sector in Israel and stymied the Oslo peace process. The negative impact that the aftermath of Rabin's assassination and the policies of the Netanyahu government (which remained in power until 1999) had on the attitudes of Palestinians in Israel is evident in the increase in the percentage of those who rejected Israel's right to exist, which jumped from 6.8 percent in 1995 to 18.6 percent in 1999.[54]

While Arab alienation increased in the late 1990s, it was the collapse of the Oslo peace process and the outbreak of the second intifada that really brought it to the surface in an explosive manner in what has become known as the "events of October 2000." These events were "the closest the Arab citizens of the state ever came to civil revolt."[55] In the first ten days of October 2000 as the so-called Al Aqsa Intifada got underway in the territories (following Ariel Sharon's provocative visit to the *Haram*

---

[52] Majid Al-Haj, "An Illusion of Belonging: Reactions of the Arab Population to Rabin's Assassination," in Yoram Peri ed., *The Assassination of Yitzhak Rabin* (Stanford, CA: Stanford University Press, 2000), 167–170.

[53] Al-Haj, "An Illusion of Belonging," 173.

[54] Sammy Smooha, *Index of Arab-Jewish Relations in Israel 2004* (Haifa: The Jewish-Arab Center, University of Haifa; Jerusalem: The Citizens' Accord Forum between Jews and Arabs in Israel; Tel Aviv: Friedrich Ebert Stiftung, 2005), 92.

[55] Baruch Kimmerling and Joel S. Migdal, *The Palestinian People: A History* (Cambridge, MA: Harvard University Press, 2003), 209.

*al-Sharif* [Noble Sanctuary]/Temple Mount on September 28, 2000), massive demonstrations were held in Arab-populated areas throughout Israel. In the course of these demonstrations, Arab protesters blocked roads (including major highways and junctions), burned tires, and set fire to buildings such as post offices, banks, and gas stations. Some Arab youth threw stones (and in a few cases, firebombs) at cars, police vehicles, and policemen, as well as at some Jewish civilians (one Jewish driver was even killed). In trying to quell the demonstrations, police officers (including police snipers) fired tear gas, rubber-coated steel bullets, and even live ammunition. Thirteen Arab protesters (including a Palestinian from Gaza) were shot and killed by the police, and many more were injured. This was the single bloodiest event for Palestinian citizens of Israel since the Kfar Qassem massacre in 1956.

The violence was not restricted to clashes between the police and Arab demonstrators. In reaction to Arab rioting, in some "mixed" cities (i.e., cities with a large population of Jews and Arabs) Jewish mobs attacked Arabs and Arab property, and violent clashes occurred between Jewish and Arab rioters. The worst instance of Arab-Jewish violence took place in the town of Upper Nazareth. Jewish mobs responded to Arab rioting in the adjacent Arab town of Nazareth by throwing stones and Molotov cocktails at Arab neighborhoods and damaging Arab-owned property in (predominantly) Jewish Upper Nazareth; and on October 8, 2000, hundreds of Jewish rioters faced off against about a hundred Arabs on two sides of the road separating Nazareth from Upper Nazareth. The mobs exchanged insults and threw stones at one another. In the melee, two Arabs were killed and many injured. Never before in the state's history had there been such inter-communal violence,[56] and for a moment the country seemed to tilter on the edge of civil war.

The eruption of the second intifada triggered the huge demonstrations and widespread rioting by Arabs that occurred in October 2000, but this was only the most immediate or proximate cause; the underlying cause was the persistent discrimination and neglect by the state that the Palestinian minority had endured for decades. The anger that Palestinians in Israel expressed in October 2000 was an anger born out of frustration and resentment over their own predicament in Israel as much as it was over Israel's forceful response to the second intifada. Palestinians in Israel were not only protesting in solidarity with Palestinians in the territories,

---

[56] There had of course been far worse inter-communal violence between Jews and Arabs in 1947–1948.

but also against the inequality and hardships they themselves faced.[57] In particular, they were bitterly disappointed with the Labor-led government of Prime Minister Ehud Barak. Despite campaigning in the run-up to the 1999 election with the slogan "A State for All" – echoing the popular slogan coined by Azmi Bishara of a "State for All its Citizens" – and receiving an overwhelming 95 percent of the Arab vote in the election, Barak didn't invite any Arab party to join his coalition government, didn't appoint any Arab ministers, and didn't pay much attention to the Arab public in Israel once he became prime minister.[58] Thus, Elie Rekhess writes that: "The October 2000 riots reflected the disappointment of the Arabs in Israel with Prime Minister Ehud Barak personally and with his government's policies toward the Arab sector generally." More fundamentally, according to Rekhess: "The uprising [in October 2000] represented the culmination of a process of growing alienation and discontent over unfulfilled expectations to attain equality, especially by the younger generation."[59]

The disaffection of the Palestinian minority only increased in the aftermath of the October 2000 events. The Palestinian community was shocked and outraged by the police's aggressive and heavy-handed reaction to the protests. The fact that the police fired live ammunition at Arab protestors was a brutal demonstration to them of their inferior status in Israeli society. As Ahmed Tibi put it, "We were regarded not as demonstrators but as enemies and treated as such. Before seeing us as citizens, they saw us as Arabs. Jewish citizens demonstrate, but none of them [are] killed."[60] The hostile and highly critical reaction of much of Israeli-Jewish society to the Arab demonstrations and riots of October 2000 also deeply dismayed the Palestinian community. Particularly disappointing was the lack of an outcry among Israeli Jews, especially among left-wing Jews, over the police's killing of Arab demonstrators. It seemed as if the welfare and lives of Palestinian citizens of Israel were of little, if any concern, to Israeli-Jewish society (just as Israeli Jews seemed to care little for Palestinians in the Occupied Territories). To

[57] In a survey carried out in January 2000, 53 percent of Arab citizens identified discrimination as the main reason for the October 2000 protests and riots, while 34 percent identified solidarity with the Palestinian struggle. Michal Shamir and Tammy Sagiv-Schifter, "Conflict, Identity, and Tolerance: Israel in the Al-Aqsa Intifada," *Political Psychology* 27, no. 4 (2006), 571.

[58] Louer, *To be an Arab in Israel*, 96.

[59] Elie Rekhess, "In the Shadow of National Conflict: Inter-group Attitudes and Images of Arab and Jews in Israel," *TriQuarterly* 131 (Winter 2007), 212.

[60] International Crisis Group, *Identity Crisis*, 9.

make matters worse, many Palestinians in Israel now felt that they had become the objects of outright suspicion by Israeli Jews who regarded them as disloyal and potentially dangerous. This exacerbated their sense of alienation from Israeli-Jewish society and from the state itself.[61] One measure of the extent of this alienation was a survey taken in 2004 in which a majority (53.4 percent) of Palestinian citizens said that they felt alien and rejected in Israel.[62]

The October 2000 events were a wake-up call for Israel. The Arab minority could no longer be ignored as it had been for so long by Israeli governments (with the notable exception of the Rabin government) and Israeli-Jewish society. Alarmed by the risk of an internal intifada and under pressure from an Arab public outraged over the police's killing of thirteen Arab demonstrators, the Barak government established a state commission of inquiry to investigate "the clashes between security forces and Israeli civilians."[63] The commission, known as the Orr Commission because it was headed by Justice Theodor Orr, worked for more than two years, during which time thousands of documents were submitted and testimonies from hundreds of witnesses were heard.

On September 1, 2003, the Orr Commission submitted its final report to the government. In its report, the Commission explicitly noted the frustration and alienation felt by Arabs in Israel. Even more importantly, the report identified the discrimination faced by Arab citizens as one of the fundamental causes of the October Events (along with the behavior of the police and incitement by Arab leaders). The report categorically stated: "Government handling of the Arab sector has been primarily neglectful and discriminatory. The establishment did not show sufficient sensitivity to the needs of the Arab population, and did not take enough action in order to allocate state resources in an equal manner. The state did not do enough or try hard enough to create equality for its Arab citizens or to uproot discriminatory

---

[61] The impact of the events of October 2000 on the sense of alienation felt by the Palestinian minority is evident in the results of a survey that showed that in February 2001 only 21 percent of Palestinian citizens felt proud to be an Israeli, whereas the year before (in April 2000) this number was 55 percent. Asher Arian, Shlomit Barnea, and Parzit Ben-Nun, *The 2004 Israeli Democracy Index* (The Israel Democracy Institute: Jerusalem, 2004), 30.

[62] Smooha, *Index of Arab-Jewish Relations in Israel 2004.*

[63] The Barak government initially proposed a public commission of inquiry but was forced to appoint a state commission of inquiry because the Supreme Arab Follow-Up Committee, following pressure from the families of those killed in the October Events, refused to cooperate with a public commission of inquiry.

or unjust phenomenon."[64] This was the first time there had been any public recognition by a government body of the discrimination that Arab citizens of Israel have suffered from since the establishment of the state. Not only did the Orr Commission report make an unprecedented official acknowledgment of decades of state discrimination against Arab citizens, it discussed this discrimination in detail in many different areas of life and called for the state to end it. Among its recommendations was for the government to "initiate, develop and activate plans to resolve the disparities [between Jewish and Arab citizens], with an emphasis on budgetary items related to all aspects of education, housing, industrial development, employment and public services." The report also called for greater Arab representation in government institutions and in the public sector.

The Orr Commission's report turned out to be a missed opportunity. Instead of quickly acting on the report's recommendations in order to assuage the anger of the Arab minority and improve its relations with the state, the government (then led by Prime Minister Sharon) merely established a Ministerial Commission to study the report (the Lapid Commission), which ended up completely disregarding its major recommendations. The fact that most of the Orr Commission's recommendations were not implemented only further alienated and angered the Arab community (as did the fact that no policemen were indicted for killing Arab demonstrators in October 2000).[65]

To this day, the events of October 2000 stand out as the most visible and violent manifestation of the alienation, frustration, and discontent felt by many Palestinian citizens of Israel. They demonstrate the dangers of what can happen when the pent-up anger of a marginalized minority finally explodes. The fact that there has been no repetition of these events since then (at least on a similar scale) does not mean that the Palestinian minority is any less alienated. If anything, it has become even more alienated in the years since October 2000, and its relations with the state and the Jewish majority have deteriorated even further.

A major way in which this alienation has been expressed over the last decade has been through the growing trend of boycotting or at least not participating in Israeli elections. Although the Arab voting rate has been declining for decades (see the graph depicting the turnout rate of Arab

---

[64] "The official summation of the Or Commission report," *Ha'aretz*, September 1, 2003, available at http://www.Ha'aretz.com/hasen/pages/ShArt.jhtml?itemNo=335594.

[65] Personal interview with Ali Haider, Co-Executive Director of Sikkuy, June 29, 2009, Ramat Aviv, Israel.

voters since the first Knesset election in 1949) and has long been lower than the national average,[66] the election for prime minister in February 2001 was a turning point in Arab voting behavior. There was an organized boycott of the election in protest over Prime Minister Barak's unfulfilled promises to the Arab public, the events of October 2000, and Israel's response to the second intifada. The boycott was widely supported in the Arab community, including by all the Arab political parties, and resulted in more than 80 percent of the Arab electorate in Israel not voting in the election.[67] Only 18 percent of Arab citizens voted for prime minister in 2001, a historic low for the community (most of these voters were reportedly Druze, and one-third cast a blank ballot).[68] The Arab boycott of the February 2001 election was not just a one-off protest. Instead, it marked the beginning of a new trend of abstention and boycotts that continued in subsequent elections.[69] Thus, 62 percent of the Arab electorate voted in the 2003 parliamentary elections; this dropped to 56 percent in the 2006 elections and further declined to a mere 54 percent in the 2009 elections – this was the lowest Arab turnout ever in a parliamentary election, and it amounted to a decline of 22 percent compared to the Arab turnout ten years earlier in the 1999 election.[70]

It is impossible to really know how much of the dramatic decline in the participation rate of Arab voters is due to an active boycott or people simply not bothering to vote.[71] There has certainly been an increase in recent years in efforts to encourage Arab citizens to boycott Knesset elections. The secular nationalist movement *Abna al-Balad* ("Sons of the Village") and the northern branch of the Islamic Movement have long opposed participating in Israeli elections on ideological grounds, and in recent years they have been joined in their calls for boycotting elections

[66] Smooha, "The Arab Minority in Israel," 78.
[67] This helped Ariel Sharon secure a landslide victory over Barak in the election as he won 62.3 percent of the votes cast.
[68] The Mossawa Center, "The Palestinian Arab Minority and the 2009 Israeli Elections," 10.
[69] As'ad Ghanem, and Muhannad Mustafa, "The Palestinians in Israel and the 2006 Knesset Elections: Political and Ideological Implications of Election Boycott," *Holy Land Studies* 6, 1 (2007), 51–73.
[70] The Mossawa Center, "The Palestinian Arab Minority and the 2009 Israeli Elections," 30. The Arab turnout in 2009 would probably have been even lower were it not for the fact that opposition to Avigdor Lieberman's Yisrael Beiteinu party helped mobilize Arab voters.
[71] It should be noted that voter turnout in Israeli elections is declining in general. In 2003, only 67.8 percent of Israeli Jews voted, and in 2006 that dropped to 63 percent.

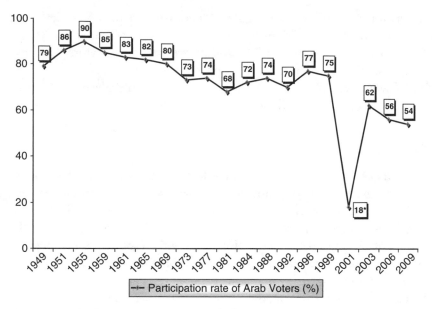

FIGURE 3.1. Arab voter turnout in Israeli elections, 1949–2009.

*Note*: *The 2001 election was for Prime Minister only.

by various Arab groups, activists, and intellectuals. One of the arguments made by boycott proponents is that if Arab citizens do note vote in Knesset elections, then eventually they can establish their own Arab parliament as an alternative to the Knesset.[72]

While ideological opposition to participating in Israeli elections is no doubt partly responsible for the low Arab voter turnout, it is unlikely to account for most of it. A bigger reason for the steady decline in voting is a sense of futility.[73] Simply put, many Palestinian citizens no longer believe that their vote can bring about any improvement in their lives. Frustrated by the lack of effectiveness of Arab parties, the Palestinian public has begun to lose faith in the ability of their Knesset representatives to bring about any real change.[74] There is now widespread skepticism among Palestinians in Israel about the efficacy of parliamentary politics as a

---

[72] Yair Ettinger, "To boycott or not to boycott," *Ha'aretz*, January 26, 2003.

[73] Ghanem and Mustafa, "The Palestinians in Israel and the 2006 Knesset Elections," 68.

[74] In a survey in 2007, only 35 percent of Palestinian citizens thought that Arab Knesset members were effective. Rouhana, ed., *Attitudes of Palestinians in Israel on Key Political and Social Issues*, 9.

means for them to achieve equality.[75] Because they do not believe that they can exercise any serious influence within the Israeli political system, Palestinian citizens are essentially withdrawing from it.[76] More than anything else, therefore, it is their feeling of being politically marginalized and disempowered that has led growing numbers of Palestinian citizens not to vote in Israeli elections.

## Conclusion

Contrary to the belief of many Israeli Jews, on the whole the Palestinian minority in Israel today is not radical. The vast majority of Palestinians in Israel want to coexist with Israeli Jews, remain citizens of the State of Israel, and overwhelmingly prefer peaceful protest over violence as the means of change. Nevertheless, Israel cannot afford to be complacent. Although radicalism remains rare, it is undoubtedly on the rise within the Palestinian minority, fuelled by a growing sense of alienation and despair. Since Rabin's assassination, the Palestinian minority has become increasingly politically frustrated. Over the past decade this has manifested itself in the steadily declining participation of Arab voters in Israeli elections. If this trend continues, as is likely, the Arab participation rate will soon fall below 50 percent – meaning that the majority of the Arab public will not take part in Israeli elections. This withdrawal from parliamentary politics in Israel is potentially very dangerous.[77] As Palestinian citizens "exit" the Israeli political system,[78] the risk of civil disobedience and/or large-scale

[75] In a 2002 survey, 83 percent of Palestinian respondents expressed dissatisfaction with their ability to influence Israeli governments, and 33.4 percent of respondents agreed with the statement "no one represents their interests in the state of Israel." Aas Atrash and Sarah Ozacky-Lazar, "A Survey of Political and National Attitudes of the Arabs in Israel," October–November 2002 (Givat Haviva: The Institute for Peace Research), cited in The Mossawa Center, "The Palestinian Arab Minority and the 2009 Israeli Elections," 10.

[76] According to the 2009 Israeli Democracy Index conducted by the Israel Democracy Institute, Arab citizens of Israel were the most detached from Israeli politics, with only 39 percent of them expressing any political interest. Israel Democracy Institute, "2009 Israeli Democracy Index," August 2009. Reported in Dana Weiler-Polak, "Poll: Half of Israelis feel those born elsewhere can't be 'true Israelis'," *Ha'aretz*, August 3, 2009.

[77] In a similar vein, Ja'far Farah, the director of Mossawa, notes that: "there is a dangerous situation whereby the avenues for venting popular communal frustration are gradually being discredited or blocked – with the perceived lack of efficacy of Knesset representation or voting, failures of local government and closure of Islamic movement institutions." International Crisis Group, *Identity Crisis*, 10.

[78] Albert O. Hirschman, *Exit, Voice, and Loyalty: Responses to Decline in Firms, Organizations, and States* (Cambridge, MA: Harvard University Press, 1970).

violent protest increases. This risk is exacerbated by the emergence of a younger generation of Palestinians in Israel. These youth, many of whom are socially deprived and marginalized, could well be less reluctant than earlier generations to use illegal and even violent measures to protest their second-class status in Israel. As a report by the *International Crisis Group* notes: "Increased urbanisation, combined with a lack of educational and employment opportunities, has created a large pool of disaffected youth at a time when traditional, rural- and tribal-based control mechanisms have weakened."[79]

This raises the danger of an "internal intifada" by Palestinians in Israel. According to some observers, this danger is a very real one.[80] Others, however, are less pessimistic, pointing out that Palestinians in Israel have too much to lose, especially economically (they already paid a severe economic price for the protests and riots of October 2000 as Israeli Jews stopped visiting Arab towns and villages to shop and eat). Moreover, they fear that any violent protests will be met with a very strong police response, as occurred in October 2000. They also fear other repercussions from the state if they engage in mass violence, above all – deportation (in this respect, the traumatic impact of the Nakba on the Palestinian minority continues to this day). In short, the Palestinian minority is too risk-averse to carry out an internal intifada.[81] Another factor that could militate against the likelihood of an internal intifada is better handling of Arab demonstrations by the Israeli police and better relations in general between the police and the Arab community.[82] By avoiding the kind of heavy-handed and aggressive response to Arab demonstrations that the police employed in October 2000 – which only escalated the protests and heightened tensions – the police can help ensure that such demonstrations remain peaceful and do not spread elsewhere.

---

[79] International Crisis Group, *Identity Crisis*, 26.
[80] For example, Binyamin Ben-Eliezer, former Labor party leader and then minister for infrastructure in Prime Minister Olmert's government, publicly warned of this danger in September 2007. Yoav Stern, "Ben-Eliezer: Continued Neglect of Israeli Arabs May Spark 'Internal Intifada,'" *Ha'aretz*, 9 September 2007. Mordechai Kremnitzer, a prominent Israeli legal scholar and senior fellow at the Israel Democracy Institute, also believes that there is a "significant risk" of an internal intifada in the future. Interview with Mordechai Kremnitzer, Jerusalem, June 7, 2009.
[81] Interview with Amal Jamal, Professor of Political Science, Tel Aviv University, Ramat Aviv, June 10, 2009.
[82] This is the goal of an ongoing project that was launched in 2002 by the Abraham Fund Initiatives, an Israeli NGO that promotes Arab-Jewish coexistence and equality. For information about this project, see http://www.abrahamfund.org.

Although an internal intifada may be unlikely, the consequences for Israel of having an alienated and angry minority in its midst are impossible to safely predict. Ultimately, whether the Palestinian minority becomes more radical depends in part on how it is treated by the state and Israeli-Jewish society – put simply, the worse it is treated, the more radical it is likely to become. In other words, the behavior of the Palestinian minority will be heavily influenced by the behavior of the Jewish majority. The beliefs and attitudes of Palestinians in Israel are shaped by the beliefs and attitudes of Jews in Israel, and vice versa.[83] This has clearly been the case since the events of October 2000, which led to a hardening of opinion on both sides and more militancy and radicalism among Palestinians and Jews in Israel.[84] It is to the Jewish side that we now turn as the next chapter looks at the behavior and attitudes of the Jewish majority toward the Palestinian minority.

---

[83] Thus, Rekhess notes that: "Polarization of Jewish-Israeli attitudes towards Arab Israelis evokes a similar process among Arab Israelis and their attitudes toward Jewish-Israelis." Rekhess, "In the Shadow of National Conflict," 236.

[84] Oren Yiftachel argues that since the "October Events," a "process of negative dialectics" has developed between Jews and Arabs in Israel "in which the growing hostility of one side exacerbates a similar discourse among the other (although this dialectical process is, of course, uneven, with the Israeli state and the Jewish public being more powerful." Yiftachel, *Ethnocracy*, 178–179.

# 4

## The Jewish Majority and the Arab "Other"

> For the first time we shall be the majority living with a minority, and we
> shall be called upon to provide an example and prove how Jews live with
> a minority.
>
> Pinhas Lavon, Israel's defense minister, 1954–1955[1]

Up until this point in the book, we have focused our attention on the
Palestinian minority in Israel. We have done so because it is essential to
understand the developments that have taken place within the Arab community over the past few decades and especially in recent years in order
to accurately assess the current state and likely future of Jewish-Arab
relations in Israel. In particular, we believe that the growing political
assertiveness of the Palestinian minority and its increasing demands for
recognition as a national minority and for collective rights, including cultural autonomy, represent a major challenge for Jewish-Arab relations.

In this chapter, we examine the other side of the majority-minority
divide in Israel – Israeli-Jewish society. We will first discuss the perceptions, beliefs, and views of Israeli Jews concerning Arab citizens of Israel
and explain what gives rise to them. We will then discuss the attitudinal
and political trends among Israeli Jews since the events of October 2000,
which we regard as a significant turning point in Israeli-Jewish attitudes.
This chapter will argue that although the Jewish majority in Israel has
always been wary and suspicious of the Arab minority, this attitude has
greatly intensified over the past decade as many Israeli Jews have come
to perceive the Arab minority as an enemy – a threat to Israeli national

---

[1] Tom Segev, *1949: The First Israelis* (New York: Free Press), 45.

security and to the continued existence of Israel as a Jewish state. This perception has contributed to a rightward shift in Israeli politics with serious repercussions for the political freedom of Palestinians in Israel and potentially even for the future of Israeli democracy itself.

Before proceeding, a brief caveat is in order. Although we refer to the Jewish majority as a whole in this chapter (and indeed throughout the book), we recognize that this majority is by no means homogenous and monolithic. On the contrary, Israeli-Jewish society contains many divisions (above all, between religious and secular Jews) and sub-groups (Ashkenazim, Mizrahim, Russians, Ethiopians, natives, immigrants, etc.). The divisions and debates among Israeli Jews have sometimes been almost as deep and as bitter as those between Jews and Arabs. This was certainly the case during the early years of the Oslo peace process when the animosity between Israeli-Jewish supporters and opponents of the Oslo Accords reached such heights that there were even fears of a civil war breaking out between them.[2] Nevertheless, for all its fractiousness, when it comes to the Arab minority, Israeli-Jewish society is surprisingly united. Although there are some differences of opinion among Israeli Jews, there are broad areas of agreement and widely held attitudes (as revealed in numerous surveys of Israeli-Jewish public opinion conducted over many years). Hence, in this chapter we focus on Israeli-Jewish society in general rather than on the internal divisions within it.

## Israeli-Jewish Attitudes toward Arab Citizens: Between Ambivalence and Antipathy

Having described in previous chapters the discrimination, neglect, and exclusion that Palestinian citizens of Israel suffer from, the reader might well conclude from this that widespread racism must be the underlying cause of this ill treatment. Indeed, this is certainly the belief of many Palestinians in Israel,[3] as well as many of Israel's critics around the world. Although there are undoubtedly racists within Israeli-Jewish society – as there are in every society – and there are some signs of an increase in racism in recent years, it would be wrong to simply characterize the attitude of Jews in Israel toward Arab citizens as racist. Most Israeli Jews believe

---

[2] On the division between Israeli Jews over the Oslo peace process, see Dov Waxman, *The Pursuit of Peace and the Crisis of Israeli Identity: Defending/Defining the Nation* (New York: Palgrave Macmillan, 2006).

[3] In the 2007 Democracy Index Survey, 51 percent of Arab citizens surveyed believed that Israeli Jews were racist.

in Jewish-Arab coexistence in Israel, support equality between Arabs and Jews (at least in principle), and favor reducing the socio-economic gaps between the two communities.[4] Clearly these are not the typical attitudes of racists.

Nevertheless, while supporting equality in theory, the vast majority of Israeli Jews also want to maintain Jewish supremacy in Israel. Most Israeli Jews are committed to democracy and civil rights for all Israeli citizens, yet they are opposed to Arab citizens having an equal say in major national decisions regarding the character of the state and its borders.[5] Similarly, most Jews are willing to allow Arabs to become integrated in certain spheres, but they do not want them to live in Jewish neighborhoods or their children to attend Jewish schools.[6] Such views underscore the ambivalence in the attitude of Israeli Jews toward Arab citizens.

Although it is important to appreciate this ambivalence, the fact is that Jews in Israel do exhibit high levels of xenophobia toward Arab citizens.[7] Numerous studies conducted over many years have revealed the hostile attitudes held by Israeli Jews toward Arab citizens.[8] In a study of Israeli-Jewish public opinion carried out shortly before the 1967 war, for instance, 80 percent of Israeli Jews agreed with the statement "It would be better if there were fewer Arabs [in Israel]"; a year later in 1968, 91 percent of respondents agreed with this statement.[9] In another study of Israeli-Jewish opinion conducted from 1967 to 1971, between 35 percent and 47 percent of Israeli Jews were not willing under any circumstances to be friends with an Arab citizen.[10] These anti-Arab attitudes have changed remarkably little over time. In Sammy Smooha's 2004 *Index of*

---

[4] Israel Democratic Institute, "2007 Israeli Democracy Index: Cohesiveness in a Divided Society" (June), http://www.idi.org.il.

[5] Sammy Smooha, *Index of Arab-Jewish Relations in Israel 2004* (Haifa: The Jewish-Arab Center, University of Haifa; Jerusalem: The Citizens' Accord Forum between Jews and Arabs in Israel; Tel Aviv: Friedrich Ebert Stiftung, 2005), 103.

[6] Smooha, *Index of Arab-Jewish Relations in Israel 2004*, 30

[7] See Ami Pedahzur and Yael Yishai, "Hatred by Hated People: Xenophobia in Israel." *Studies in Conflict & Terrorism* 22 (1999), 101–117.

[8] See Yochanan Peres, "Ethnic Relations in Israel," *The American Journal of Sociology* 76, no. 6 (1971), 1021–1047; see also Elie Rekhess, "In the Shadow of National Conflict: Inter-Group Attitudes and Images of Arab and Jews in Israel," *TriQuarterly* 131, 1 (Winter 2007), 225–226.

[9] Rekhess, "In the Shadow of National Conflict," 225–226.

[10] Abel Jacob, "Trends in Israel's Public Opinion on Issues Related to the Arab-Israeli Conflict, 1967–1972," *The Jewish Journal of Sociology* 16 (December 1974), 187–208, cited in Rekhess, "In the Shadow of National Conflict," 227.

*Arab-Jewish Relations in Israel,* a little more than half of the Jews polled (52 percent) were not willing to have an Arab neighbor.[11] The persistence of anti-Arab attitudes among Israeli Jews is clearly apparent in all of Smooha's surveys carried out since 1980. In that year, for instance, 50 percent of Jews thought that the state should encourage Arab citizens to leave the country; in 1988, the figure was 40 percent; and in 2004, it was 44 percent – relatively little change over the years.[12]

Not only do many Israeli Jews hold anti-Arab attitudes, they also carry with them negative stereotypes of Arabs (which reinforce their anti-Arab attitudes).[13] Arabs are widely perceived as primitive, violent, and even dirty.[14] These negative stereotypes can be traced back to when Zionist settlers first arrived in Palestine at the end of the nineteenth and the beginning of the twentieth century. Even before Arabs started actively opposing the Zionist movement, the attitude of most of the Jewish immigrants from Europe to the local Arabs was patronizing at best, if not downright disdainful (a small minority of Zionist settlers admired the Arabs). Influenced by a feeling of cultural superiority toward non-European people and cultures prevalent in Europe at the time,[15] European Jewish immigrants to Palestine perceived the Arabs as backward and uncivilized. Over time, this Eurocentric perception has become deeply rooted in Israeli-Jewish culture.[16] Derogatory stereotypes of Arabs have been widely disseminated through the mass media, educational materials, and cultural products.[17] As a result, generations of Israeli Jews have essentially been socialized to view Arabs in a very negative manner.

---

[11] Smooha, *Index of Arab-Jewish Relations in Israel 2004,* 23.

[12] Smooha, *Index of Arab-Jewish Relations in Israel 2004,* 99.

[13] Daniel Bar-Tal and Yonah Teichman, *Stereotypes and Prejudice in Conflict: Representation of Palestinians in Israeli Jewish Society* (Cambridge: Cambridge University Press, 2005), 222–225.

[14] In an extensive survey of Israeli-Jewish perceptions of the Arab minority carried out in 1980, 43.8 percent of Israeli Jews perceived the Arab minority as primitive (22.1 percent perceived them as developed), 38.7 percent as violent (21.7 percent as non-violent), and 31.7 percent as dirty (18.7 percent as clean). Sammy Smooha, "Jewish and Arab ethnocentrism in Israel," *Ethnic and Racial Studies* 10, 1 (1987), 1–26. A more recent survey conducted in 2007 revealed that 75 percent of Israeli Jews thought Arabs have a tendency toward violence. Democracy Index Survey, 2007, cited in Elie Rekhess, "Israel and its Arab Citizens – Taking Stock," Tel Aviv Notes, October 16, 2007.

[15] Edward Said, *Orientalism* (London: Penguin, 1995).

[16] This is evident in the fact that in 2007, 55 percent of Israeli Jews still believed that Arabs do not have the ability to reach the same level of cultural development as Jews. Democracy Index Survey, 2007, cited in Rekhess, "Israel and its Arab Citizens."

[17] Bar-Tal and Teichman, *Stereotypes and Prejudice in Conflict.*

Although a negative perception of Arabs predates the Arab-Jewish conflict over Israel/Palestine (and may have even helped fuel it), the conflict itself has been by far the most important cause of the negative attitudes and views of Israeli Jews toward Arab citizens. The Arab-Jewish conflict that began in Ottoman-controlled Palestine, escalated in British Mandatory Palestine, and continued since Israel's establishment (becoming the Arab-Israeli conflict after 1948) has profoundly shaped Israeli-Jewish attitudes toward Arabs. During the course of more than a century of bitter and often violent conflict, Israeli Jews have come to view Arabs as unyielding competitors for the control of the land (as indeed they were). Arabs were, in short, the enemy. Although Israeli Jews have gradually learned to differentiate between different groups of Arabs (e.g., "Israeli Arabs," Palestinians, Egyptians, Syrians), they still generally view all Arabs as actual or potential enemies simply because they are Arabs. This also applies to Israel's own Arab citizens. Hence, Israeli Jews harbor a deep and abiding suspicion of Arab citizens. To this day, many within the Jewish majority perceive the Arab minority as a threat, a potential fifth column that could and probably will join Israel's enemies in the event of a future war or support terrorism against Israel. In fact, in a 2009 survey an astonishingly large number of Israeli Jews (37.4 percent) actually believe that at least half of the population of Israel's Arab citizens have "planned or taken part in terrorist activities against Israel" since 1948![18]

What exacerbates the sense of threat felt by Israeli Jews is the fact that they are a minority in the region, and an unwelcome one at that. Despite their own majority status within Israel, Israeli Jews perceive themselves as an embattled minority pitted against the unrelenting hostility of the Arab world, and even of the entire Islamic world. This directly affects how they view Arab citizens of Israel. In Sammy Smooha's words: "The Jews perceive Arab citizens not as a small and vulnerable minority, but rather as a part of the Palestinian people, the Arab states and the Islamic world, who are considered strong and hostile towards the rights of the Jews and their very presence in the region."[19] Such a perception surely influences the way in which Israeli-Jewish society treats the Arab minority, as the Israeli novelist David Grossman writes: "We face the minority as if we are a minority in our land – in the struggle for survival that we still wage

---

[18] Only 17 percent of Israeli Jews surveyed believed that "an insignificant minority" of Arab citizens had been involved in terrorism. Rafi Nets-Zehngut and Daniel Bar-Tal, *The Israeli-Jewish Collective Memory of the Israeli-Arab/Palestinian Conflict* (manuscript in preparation).

[19] Smooha, *Index of Arab-Jewish Relations in Israel 2004*, 28.

in our hearts against it, in the battle for all kinds of 'territories' in the country, in the difficulty in being generous and sure of ourselves."[20]

Although the long-running Arab-Jewish/Arab-Israeli conflict is primarily responsible for instilling the deep-seated fear and enmity that many Israeli Jews harbor toward Arabs, including Arab citizens of Israel, it is by no means the only factor that shapes Israeli-Jewish attitudes and views. Another critically important factor is Zionist ideology. The vast majority of Israeli Jews are Zionists,[21] and this ideological commitment essentially determines how they view the state and its purpose as well as non-Jews within it. According to Zionism, the State of Israel was established to be a Jewish nation-state. That is, it is the homeland of the Jewish people (wherever they may be – inside or outside the country), and its purpose is to serve their interests. As David Ben-Gurion wrote in a diary entry in August 1937: "The state which will arise will be a Jewish one; Jewish in terms of its function, goal and purpose [...]. It will not be merely a state of Jews who happen to reside in the land but a country for the Jews, for the Jewish people [...]."[22] Israel, then, is not simply a Jewish state because it has a majority of Jews living within it; it is a Jewish state because it is concerned with securing Jewish interests. Although this perspective is not necessarily hostile to the Arab citizens living in Israel, it amounts to, at the least, the relegation of their collective interests to a secondary status. The overwhelming Zionist consensus among Israeli Jews, therefore, is that Israel must be a Jewish state and must ensure Jewish dominance – numerically, politically, culturally, and economically. "For most Jews," Smooha notes, "the idea of a Jewish state is not limited to a Jewish majority, Jewish symbols, the Hebrew language, and ties with Diaspora Jewry but extends to a favored Jewish status."[23] Hence, a consistently large majority of Israeli Jews believes that the state should give preferential treatment to Jews over Arabs.[24]

[20] David Grossman, *Sleeping on a Wire: Conversations with Palestinians in Israel* (New York: Picador, 2003), 260.

[21] Eighty percent of Israeli Jews defined themselves as Zionist in 2004. Smooha, *Index of Arab-Jewish Relations in Israel 2004*, 46.

[22] Quoted in Yossi Katz, "Status and rights of the Arab minority in the Nascent Jewish state," *Middle Eastern Studies* 33, no. 3 (1997), 568, note 108.

[23] Sammy Smooha, "Arab-Jewish Relations in Israel: A Deeply Divided Society," in Anita Shapira, ed., *Israeli Identity in Transition* (Westport, CT: Praeger Publishers, 2004), 47.

[24] In public opinion surveys carried out in 1988 and in 1995, almost three-quarters of Israeli Jews believed this. As'ad Ghanem, "Zionism, Post-Zionism and Anti-Zionism in Israel: Jews and Arabs in Conflict over the Nature of the State," in Ephraim Nimni, *The Challenge of Post-Zionism: Alternatives to Israeli Fundamentalist Politics* (London: Zed, 2003), 106.

The Jewish majority in Israel has remained remarkably steadfast in its adherence to the basic tenets of Zionism. This is borne out in surveys of Israeli-Jewish opinion over the years. For example, in 1980, 95.4 percent of Israeli Jews believed that Israel's Jewish-Zionist character should either be strengthened or kept the same; five years later in 1985, 94 percent of Israeli Jews felt this way; and fifteen years later in 1995, 94.7 percent of Israeli Jews felt this way.[25] Thus, despite a great deal of discussion and speculation during the years of the Oslo peace process in the 1990s about the declining attachment of Israeli Jews to Zionism and the rise of post-Zionism, even during this heady period of time most Israeli Jews were still strongly committed to Israel as a Jewish state and its Zionist objectives.[26]

Although Israeli Jews did become somewhat more liberal, open, and tolerant toward Arab citizens in the early 1990s, the extent of this attitudinal change should not be exaggerated. Thus, while the percentage of Israeli Jews who opposed the Arabs' right to vote in Knesset elections dropped from 42.8 percent to 30.9 percent between 1988 and 1995, the percentage of Jews who thought that Israel should encourage Arab citizens to leave the country changed much less (from 39.9 percent in 1988 to 36.7 percent in 1995).[27] The Oslo peace process and the emergence of post-Zionism in the early 1990s, therefore, did not fundamentally change the attitudes of Israeli Jews toward the Arab minority. In fact, in a poll conducted in 1995 by the Tami Steinmetz Center for Peace Research at Tel Aviv University, a majority of Jews believed that Israel's Arab citizens would be more loyal to a Palestinian state if one were to be established, and that Arab citizens should move to a future Palestinian state.[28]

The long-standing prevalence of Zionist ideology among Israeli Jews affects not just how they view the Israeli state and the status of Arabs within it but also how they define Israeli national identity. Despite Zionism's ambivalent stance on the relationship between Jewish identity and Israeli national identity, it always regarded the latter as ultimately inseparable from the former. However much Zionism disdained Judaism and Diaspora Jewry, for Zionists Jewishness is still an integral component of Israeli national identity.[29] Consequently, rather than defining Israeli

[25] Ghanem, "Zionism, Post-Zionism and Anti-Zionism in Israel," 105.
[26] Ghanem, "Zionism, Post-Zionism and Anti-Zionism in Israel," 104.
[27] Smooha, "Arab-Jewish Relations in Israel," 56.
[28] Cited in Rekhess, "In the Shadow of National Conflict," 230.
[29] The Jewish dimension of Israeli national identity has become more important since 1967. For a discussion of the reasons for this, see Waxman, *The Pursuit of Peace and the Crisis of Israeli Identity*.

national identity in civic terms, such that any Israeli citizen is a member of the Israeli nation (just as any American citizen, for instance, is a member of the American nation), Israeli Jews, in accordance with Zionism, define Israeli national identity in ethno-religious terms, restricting it to those deemed to be Jewish (the definition of who is a Jew is, of course, itself a contentious issue). In other words, Jewishness is a condition of membership in the Israeli nation, not citizenship.[30]

The exclusion of non-Jews, Arabs in particular, from the national community means that they are always regarded as outsiders by most Israeli Jews,[31] and as such their participation in the collective affairs of the nation and in national decision making is suspect at best, if not illegitimate by definition. This exclusion has an even more profound impact on Israeli-Jewish attitudes toward Arab citizens because it casts them as the "Other" – the group against which Israeli national identity defines itself.[32] The Other, or the "out-group" in the language of social psychology, is instrumental in defining all national identities (as well as other collective identities) because a nation is defined partly in terms of whom it excludes or opposes.[33] Thus, as the collective Other of Israeli Jews, Arabs help to provide Israeli Jews with a collective sense of "Self."[34] This makes it even harder for Israeli Jews to significantly change their

---

[30] Baruch Kimmerling, "Between the Primordial and the Civil Definitions of the Collective Identity: *Eretz Israel* or the State of Israel?" in Erik Cohen, Moshe Lissak, and Uri Almagor, eds., *Comparative Social Dynamics: Essays in Honor of S.N. Eisenstadt* (Boulder, CO: Westview, 1985), 262–283; Yoav Peled, "Ethnic Democracy and the Legal Construction of Citizenship: Arab Citizens of the Jewish State," *The American Political Science Review* 86, 1 (1992), 435.

[31] In a poll taken in 1995, for example, 51.7 percent of Israeli Jews believed that the label "Israeli" could only be applied to Jews and not to Arabs. Ghanem, "Zionism, Post-Zionism and Anti-Zionism in Israel," 109.

[32] Ilan Peleg, "Otherness and Israel's Arab Dilemma," in Laurence J. Silberstein and Robert L. Cohn, eds., *The Other in Jewish Thought and History: Constructions of Jewish Culture and Identity* (New York: New York University Press, 1994), 258–280. See also, Kook, *The Logic of Democratic Exclusion: African Americans in the United States and Palestinian Citizens in Israel* (Lanham, MA: Lexington Books, 2003), 57–73.

[33] Iver B. Neumann, "Self and Other in International Relations," *European Journal of International Relations* 2, no. 2 (1996), 166; Iver B. Neumann, Jennifer M. Welsh, "The Other in European Self-definition: An Addendum to the Literature on International Society," *Review of International Studies* 17, no. 4 (1991), 327–348.

[34] As the Israeli social psychologist, Dan Bar-On, has written: "part of the Israeli identity constructions [...] was defined negatively, through hatred of the enemy, rather than positively, through what Israelis are in their own right, irrespective of the definition of the Other." Dan Bar-On, "Israeli Society between the Culture of Death and the Culture of Life," *Israel Studies* 2, no. 2 (2003), 97.

attitudes toward Arabs citizens, since doing so risks undermining their own sense of national identity.

In addition to the protracted Arab-Jewish/Arab-Israeli conflict and Zionist ideology, ethnocentrism is another important factor that shapes Israeli-Jewish attitudes and views toward Arab citizens of Israel. Ethnocentrism is one of the central elements in the Israeli-Jewish ethos.[35] To be sure, this is hardly unique to Israeli Jews. Ethnocentrism – the tendency toward in-group favoritism and/or out-group hostility – is almost universal.[36] It is especially pronounced, however, among Jews in Israel due to the fact that Jewish communities have typically been insular and self-enclosed. As Alan Dowty notes: "Historically, Jewish communities reacted to threat by closing off from the outside world, building the best possible barriers to maintain separation and minimize outside intervention. [...] The protective embrace of one's own group was the primary defense against a hostile environment."[37] Jewish communities in the Diaspora fostered both a strong sense of community and a strong wariness toward the outside, non-Jewish world (needless to say, this was a wariness born of persistent discrimination and frequent persecution). Such attitudes have become deeply ingrained in Jewish culture and have persisted in Israeli-Jewish culture (reflected, for instance, in the prevailing "siege mentality" in Israel – the widespread belief among Israeli Jews that Israel is alone in a hostile world[38]).

The fact that Jews in the Diaspora have always been a minority wherever they lived also means that they have no historical experience of ruling over others, and hence have not developed cultural, political, or legal rules and norms that deal with how Jewish communities should treat non-Jews living in their midst. Jewish culture and religion offer little clear guidance on issues concerning the treatment and rights of non-Jewish minorities.[39] This only encourages the ethnocentric tendency among many Israeli Jews, especially among religious Jews in Israel (a growing portion of Israel's Jewish population). According to Charles S. Liebman,

---

[35] Smooha, *Arabs and Jews in Israel Vol. 1: Conflicting and Shared Attitudes in a Divided Society* (Boulder, CO: Westview Press, 1989), 130; see also Rekhess, "In the Shadow of National Conflict," 216.

[36] William G. Sumner, *Folkways* (Boston, MA: Ginn, 1906); Robert A. LeVine and Donald T. Campbell, *Ethnocentrism* (New York: Wiley, 1972).

[37] Dowty, *The Jewish State*, 25.

[38] On this belief, see Asher Arian, *Security Threatened: Surveying Israeli Opinion on Peace and War* (Cambridge: Cambridge University Press, 1995).

[39] Dowty, *The Jewish State*, 31–32.

a leading expert on religion and politics in Israel, "Judaism in Israel has become increasingly particularistic and ethnocentric. It promotes little tolerance for the individual rights of non-Jewish citizens, and even less for groups rights of minorities."[40] As a result, the dominant tendency among religious Israeli Jews is "one that grudgingly acknowledges the rights of non-Jews to live in Israel, to live their private lives in accordance with their religious or cultural norms, but only in so far as doing so has no influence on other Jews or on the public life of the state."[41]

### The Rise of Intolerance: A Jewish Backlash

For all the reasons just outlined, Israeli Jews in general have always been somewhat wary of the country's Arab citizens. Although they have come to accept, albeit grudgingly, the presence of an Arab minority in Israel and recognize the need to peacefully coexist with it, they have never fundamentally accepted Arabs as completely equal citizens and certainly not as members of the national community. For the most part, Israeli Jews have tolerated Arab citizens (and have proudly contrasted this tolerance with the treatment of minorities in Arab countries), but this tolerance has been weak and partial. It allows Arabs to remain in Israel with civil rights and freedom to engage in their own cultural and religious practices, but it rejects their full inclusion within Israeli society and politics. Segregation, rather than integration, is the long-standing preference of Israeli Jews; so Israeli Jews tolerate Arabs as long as they live within their own communities, attend their own schools, and largely keep to themselves. Israeli-Jewish toleration ends, however, when Arab citizens of Israel identify themselves as Palestinians or when they oppose the Jewish character of the state and its Zionist goals.[42] Thus, in a survey of Israeli-Jewish opinion conducted in 2004, a large majority of Jews (75.4 percent) believed that "Arab citizens have the right to live in the state as a minority with full civil rights,"[43] but only a minority (31.7 percent) agreed that "Arab citizens have the right to live in the state as a minority with full civil

---

[40] Charles S. Liebman, "Religion and Democracy in Israel," in Shlomo A. Deshen, Charles S. Liebman, Moshe Shokeid, eds., *Israeli Judaism: the sociology of religion in Israel* (New Brunswick, NJ: Transaction Publishers, 1995), 350.

[41] Liebman, "Religion and Democracy in Israel," 350.

[42] Smooha, *Index of Arab-Jewish Relations in Israel 2004*, 38. For instance, a large majority of Israeli Jews (80.8 percent in 2004) believed that "an Arab citizen who defines oneself as a 'Palestinian Arab in Israel' cannot be loyal to the state and its laws."

[43] Smooha, *Index of Arab-Jewish Relations in Israel 2004*, 35.

rights, whether they accept or do not accept the right of Israel to be a Jewish state."[44]

The limited and conditional nature of Israeli-Jewish tolerance of the Arab minority has become increasingly apparent in recent years. As Palestinian nationalism and Islamism has spread within the Arab community in Israel, and many Arabs (especially younger ones) have become more vocal and assertive in their demands for equality and more outspoken and demonstrative in their support for their Palestinian kin in the Occupied Territories, Israeli Jews have become increasingly alarmed by what many perceive as the growing radicalization of Arabs in Israel. This has had a significant impact on Israeli-Jewish attitudes and views toward the Arab minority. The perceived radicalization of the Arab minority has aroused deep fears among the Jewish majority and precipitated what has been aptly described as an "ethnocentric backlash."[45]

As Arabs have become more vociferous in calling for Israel to cease to be a Jewish state and instead become a "state for all its citizens," Israeli Jews have become more politically intolerant toward them; and as Arabs have become more strident in their opposition to Israeli policies and actions vis-à-vis Palestinians in the territories and Arabs elsewhere (such as in Lebanon), Israeli Jews have become more worried about the security risk that Arab citizens pose, especially in the event of another Palestinian intifada or Arab-Israeli war. Israeli Jews also increasingly fear that Arab demographic growth will eventually swamp Israel's Jewish population and nullify the Jewish state. Consequently, there has been a marked growth in support within the Jewish majority for a variety of measures aimed against Arab citizens, and even for the wholesale or partial removal of the Arab minority from Israel. Thus, heightened Jewish intolerance and fear has created fertile conditions in Israel for the passage of discriminatory and exclusionary government legislation.[46]

---

[44] Smooha, *Index of Arab-Jewish Relations in Israel 2004*, 38.

[45] Baruch Kimmerling and Joel S. Migdal, *The Palestinian People: A History* (Cambridge, MA: Harvard University Press, 2003), 212. In a similar vein, Oren Yiftachel writes that Arab demands for cultural and religious autonomy and for Israel to become a state of all its citizens have caused "an aggressive Jewish reaction bordering on panic [...]." Oren Yiftachel, *Ethnocracy: Land & Identity Politics in Israel/Palestine* (Philadelphia, PA: University of Pennsylvania Press, 2006), 173.

[46] An example of such legislation is the Nationality and Entry into Israel Law that passed on July 31, 2003, which denied citizenship and residency to Palestinians from the West Bank and Gaza who married Israeli citizens, thereby forcing these married couples to either live separately or leave Israel. The law effectively discriminates against Arab citizens of Israel because they are by far the most likely to marry Palestinians; hence their spouses are barred from entering Israel, unlike non-Jewish spouses from anywhere else.

The perception of a dangerously radicalized Arab minority really took hold within the Israeli-Jewish public as a result of the events of October 2000. More than anything else in recent history, the October 2000 events changed the way Israeli Jews perceived Arab citizens of Israel and focused popular Israeli-Jewish attention on the "problem" of the Arab minority.[47] Most Israeli Jews were outraged by what they regarded as the treasonous behavior of Arab citizens during the events of October 2000.[48] They saw the massive Arab protests that took place simply as demonstrations of solidarity with the second Palestinian intifada that had just begun in the West Bank and Gaza.[49] Many Israeli Jews were also shocked and appalled by the rioting, looting, and violence that occurred during the protests. It seemed that the violence and disorder that they had come to associate with the West Bank and Gaza was now occurring within Israel proper. It was suddenly apparent to large numbers of Jews in Israel that the people they had always regarded as "Israeli Arabs" were in fact Palestinians, or were at least becoming "Palestinized."[50] Having long denied or ignored the Palestinian national identity of Arab citizens of Israel, the realization among many Israeli Jews that Israel had a large number of Palestinians in its midst who identified and sympathized with Palestinians in the territories was deeply alarming. It had the immediate effect of exacerbating long-standing Jewish fears about the loyalty of Arabs in Israel, with almost three-quarters of Israeli Jews now believing that Arabs were disloyal to the state.[51] Hence, many Israeli Jews came to perceive Arab citizens as a danger to Israel's national security.

---

[47] In a poll carried out by the Dahaf Institute in March 2001, 55 percent of Israeli Jews reported that their view of Arab citizens had changed for the worse, and 50 percent said that they had a negative view of the Arab minority in Israel. Sever Plotzker, "Shift in Israel: Attitudes toward Peace," *Yediot Ahronot*, March 30, 2001.

[48] According to a survey conducted by the Israeli newspaper *Yediot Ahronot*, three out of four Israeli Jews defined the behavior of Arabs in Israel during the events of October 2000 as treason against the state. Cited in Ori Nir, "Not by hummus and za'atar alone," *Ha'aretz*, October 13, 2000.

[49] In a survey conducted in January 2000 about the reasons for the October 2000 demonstrations and riots in Israel, 44 percent of Jewish respondents identified the solidarity of the "Israeli Arabs" with the Palestinian struggle as the cause of the October events (only a quarter identified the Arabs' sense of discrimination as the cause). Michal Shamir, Tammy Sagiv-Schifter, "Conflict, Identity, and Tolerance: Israel in the Al-Aqsa Intifada," *Political Psychology* 27, no. 4 (2006), 571.

[50] Azmi Bishara, "Reflections on October 2000: A Landmark in Jewish-Arab Relations in Israel," *Journal of Palestine Studies* 30, no. 3. (2001), 54–67.

[51] Before the events of October 2000 in a poll taken in early 2000, 62 percent of Israeli Jews thought that Arabs in Israel were disloyal to the state. After the October events, that number rose to 73 percent in 2001. Asher Arian, *Israeli Public Opinion on National*

The October 2000 events, therefore, had a significant impact on Israeli-Jewish opinion vis-à-vis Arabs in Israel. Although many Israeli Jews always regarded Arab citizens with a degree of suspicion, this suspicion was considerably heightened by the events of October 2000. It was also regularly reinforced by the repeated references by Israeli-Jewish politicians and media pundits to Arabs in Israel as an actual or potential "fifth column." For instance, in an op-ed written during the October events, Dan Margalit, a popular commentator in the media wrote: "This total identification [with the Palestinians in the territories] and the absence of any voices in the Israeli Arab community publicly calling for an end to the violence gives rise to the suspicion that the members of this community constitute a fifth column."[52] Later, this view was put much more sharply by Effi Eitam, the leader of the right-wing National Religious Party (NRP) and then minister of housing in Prime Minister Sharon's government, in an interview on March 22, 2002: "I say that the Arabs in Israel overall are a bomb that is going to explode beneath the entire democratic system in Israel. [...] The Arabs in Israel are turning into a fifth column [...]. We need to consider whether Israel's democracy can continue to enable this public to go on taking part in it [...]. Arabs in Israel are a dangerous fifth column, like a cancer."[53] The image of the Arab minority in Israel as a ticking bomb was another recurring theme in Israeli-Jewish discourse after October 2000. As the prominent Israeli historian Benny Morris emphatically put it in a much-publicized interview: "The Israeli Arabs are a time bomb. Their slide into complete Palestinization has made them an emissary of the enemy that is among us. They are a potential fifth column. In both demographic and security terms they are liable to undermine the state."[54]

The belief among Israeli Jews that Arab citizens of Israel were a security threat also increased as a result of the second intifada – in a poll taken before the second intifada (in January 2000) about a quarter of Jewish respondents stated that Arab citizens were a security threat to the state; this figure increased to 39 percent in a January 2001 poll and to 50 percent in June 2002.[55] In another survey conducted at the height of the second

---

*Security 2003*, Memorandum no. 67 (Tel Aviv: Tel Aviv University, Jaffee Center for Strategic Studies, October 2003), 34.

[52] Dan Margalit, "A democracy on the defensive," *Ha'aretz*, October 5, 2000.

[53] Quoted in Ari Shavit, "A Leader is waiting for a signal," *Ha'aretz*, March 22, 2002.

[54] Ari Shavit, "Survival of the Fittest? An Interview with Benny Morris," *Ha'aretz*, January 9, 2004.

[55] Shamir and Sagiv-Schifter, "Conflict, Identity, and Tolerance," 577.

intifada in 2002, more than 70 percent of Israeli Jews described Arabs in Israel as a security threat.[56] The wave of Palestinian terrorist attacks carried out within Israel during the second intifada especially increased anti-Arab attitudes within Israeli-Jewish society.[57] The most blatant expressions of this were the calls of "Death to Arabs" in soccer stadiums and at the sites of terrorist attacks and in slogans like "No Arabs – No Terror Attacks" appearing in graffiti and on car bumper stickers.[58]

The rise in anti-Arab attitudes among Israeli Jews, however, was not just a passing phenomenon provoked by Palestinian terrorist attacks during the second intifada. Even after these attacks largely ceased, anti-Arab attitudes have continued to grow. Public opinion surveys carried out after the second intifada effectively ended in 2005 have revealed an increase in animosity toward Arabs within the Jewish public.[59] For example, a 2006 survey conducted by the Center against Racism showed a significant increase in negative feelings by Israeli Jews toward Arab citizens compared to the survey from the year before, including a doubling of the number of Israeli Jews expressing feelings of hatred toward Arabs.[60] In the survey, 75.3 percent of Israeli-Jewish respondents said that they would not live in the same building as Arabs (as opposed to 67.6 percent in 2005); 61.4 percent were not willing to have Arab friends visit their homes (a large increase compared to 45.5 percent in 2005); and more than half (55.6 percent) thought that Arabs and Jews should have separate entertainment and recreational facilities.

---

[56] Nadim Rouhana and Nimer Sultany, "Redrawing the Boundaries of Citizenship: Israel's New Hegemony," *Journal of Palestine Studies* 33, no. 1 (2003), 15.

[57] Daphna Canetti-Nisim, Gal Ariely, and Eran Halperin, "Life, Pocketbook, or Culture: The Role of Perceived Security Threats in Promoting Exclusionist Political Attitudes toward Minorities in Israel," *Political Research Quarterly* 61 (2008), 90–103. Israeli Jews became particularly alarmed when some Arab citizens were linked to suicide bombings in 2002. Consequently, in the summer of 2002, the Interior Ministry proposed taking steps to establish a new policy that revoked citizenship from Arabs charged with involvement in terrorism (this did not apply to non-Arab Israelis).

[58] Shimon Shamir, "The Arabs in Israel – Two Years after the Or Commission Report," Tel Aviv University, Konrad Adenauer Program for Jewish-Arab Cooperation (2006).

[59] The Association for Civil Rights in Israel (ACRI), "The State of Human Rights in Israel and the Occupied Territories 2007 Report," 14.

[60] In the survey, 49.9 percent of Jewish respondents said that they felt fear when hearing Arabic spoken in the street, 43.6 percent felt discomfort, 31.3 percent felt revulsion, and 30.7 felt hatred. In 2005, by comparison, 17.5 percent of Israeli Jews said they felt hatred toward Arabs. The survey also noted an alarming 26 percent rise in racist incidents against Arab citizens in 2006. Bachar Awawda and Alla Heider, "Index of Racism for 2006: Racism against Israeli Arabs – Citizens of the State of Israel," The Center against Racism, April 2007, http://www.no-racism.org/arabic/data/publications/index2006.doc.

Together with these anti-Arab social attitudes, political intolerance vis-à-vis Israel's Arab citizens has also increased within the Jewish public since the outbreak of the second intifada and the October 2000 events.[61] This is clearly apparent in the *Democracy Index* compiled by the Israel Democracy Institute (IDI), which has shown a gradual decline between 2000 and 2007 in support by the Jewish public for equal political rights for Arab citizens and the inclusion of Arab political parties in coalition governments. Whereas 46 percent of the Jewish public was in favor of Arab parties joining coalition governments in 2000, by 2007 this figure had dropped to only 22 percent (the lowest figure since the early 1990s according to the IDI's statistics).[62] The 2009 Democracy Index showed growing support among Israeli Jews for the stripping of political rights from Israel's Arab minority. For example, 73 percent of Israeli Jews agreed with the statement "a Jewish majority is necessary for fateful decisions for the country," compared with 62 percent who did so in 2003.[63] Further evidence of Israeli-Jewish political intolerance toward Arab citizens can be found in Smooha's *Index of Arab-Jewish Relations in Israel* – in the 2004 Index, just 65.5 percent of Israeli Jews thought that Arabs should be allowed to vote in Knesset elections, and only 48.8 percent thought Arabs should be allowed to become government ministers.[64] Young Israeli Jews are even more politically intolerant, with half of Jewish high school students between the ages of fifteen and eighteen stating in a survey carried out in February 2010 that they do not believe that Arab citizens are entitled to the same rights as Jews in Israel. Even more alarmingly, more than half of the students (56 percent in the survey) said they would deny Arabs the right to be elected to the Knesset.[65]

These opinion polls underscore what Elie Rekhess has accurately described as the "steep slide toward extremism" in Israeli-Jewish attitudes toward Arabs in Israel since October 2000.[66] The consequences of this for the political freedom of Palestinian citizens have been severe, as they have become less able to "mobilize within the confines of Jewish

---

[61] Shamir and Sagiv-Schifter, "Conflict, Identity, and Tolerance," 581.
[62] Israel Democracy Institute, "2007 Israeli Democracy Index."
[63] Israel Democracy Institute, "2009 Israeli Democracy Index"; Weiler-Polak, "Poll: Half of Israelis feel those born elsewhere can't be 'true Israelis,'" *Ha'aretz*, August 3, 2009.
[64] Smooha, *Index of Arab-Jewish Relations in Israel 2004*, 35.
[65] Or Kashti, "Poll: Half of Israeli high schoolers oppose equal rights for Arabs," *Ha'aretz*, March 12, 2010.
[66] Rekhess, "In the Shadow of National Conflict," 235.

tolerance and Israeli law."[67] Since 2000, a raft of legislation has been passed in the Knesset restricting the scope of permitted political activity, legislation clearly aimed at curtailing the freedom of expression of Arab political parties and individual Arab Knesset members. In May 2002, both the "Basic Law: the Knesset" and the "Law of Political Parties" were amended to ban parties and individuals that rejected Israel's identity as a "Jewish and democratic state" (not as a Jewish and/or democratic state, as the law was previously worded) or supported (in action or speech) "the armed struggle of enemy states or terror organizations" against the State of Israel.[68] In effect, this meant that, in the words of Nadim Rouhana and Nimer Sultany, "[Knesset] candidates and their parties must submit to the Zionist consensus in order to have the right to be represented in parliament [...]. And because the Zionist hegemony defines which organizations are terrorist and which states are 'enemy,' the law gives the [Central Elections] committee additional leeway to deprive those who deviate from this hegemony of the right to representation."[69] Indeed, as a result of this legislation the Knesset's Central Elections Committee (comprised of MKs from all the parties in the Knesset) banned Arab parties from participating in both the 2003 and 2009 parliamentary elections, although on both occasions Israel's High Court subsequently overturned the bans after they were appealed.

The activities of Arab political leaders in Israel have particularly come under critical scrutiny and have been subject to greater legal restrictions and penalties. A law passed in July 2002, for example, lifted the parliamentary immunity of Knesset members who rejected Israel's identity as a Jewish and democratic state or supported (in action or speech) "the armed struggle of enemy states or terror organizations" against Israel, thereby allowing them to be legally prosecuted. In June 2008, the Knesset passed a new amendment to the "Basic Law: The Knesset" that stated that any parliamentary candidate that visited an "enemy state" in the seven years before they became candidates would be considered to have supported armed struggle against the State of Israel unless they proved otherwise. The amendment, therefore, prevents politicians from running for a Knesset seat if they have visited an enemy state (such as Lebanon,

---

[67] Yiftachel, *Ethnocracy*, 182.
[68] Oren Yiftachel, "The Shrinking Space of Citizenship: Ethnocratic Politics in Israel," *Middle East Report*, no. 223, Vol. 32 (2002), 40–41.
[69] Rouhana and Sultany, "Redrawing the Boundaries of Citizenship," 11.

Syria, Saudi Arabia, or Iraq). Both pieces of legislation are clearly aimed at Arab politicians.

The most publicized and controversial instance of an Arab politician in Israel facing legal punishment was the case of Azmi Bishara. The "Bishara affair," as it became popularly known, broke out in 2007 following Israel's unsuccessful war against Hezbollah in Lebanon in the summer of 2006.[70] Bishara was accused of treason and espionage for helping Hezbollah during the war (he was alleged to have given Hezbollah information on strategic locations in Israel that it should attack with its rockets). Faced with these serious charges against him, Bishara fled the country rather than stand trial, which he claimed would not be a fair one. Whether or not Bishara is guilty or innocent of the crimes he is accused of committing (his supporters claim that he was being persecuted for his opposition to the 2006 Lebanon war and his vocal support for Hezbollah), his "exile" is seen by many Palestinians in Israel as an ominous indication of what might happen to all of them in the future.[71] Thus, the fate of Azmi Bishara has come to represent the potential fate of other Palestinian citizens of Israel who refuse to accept the status quo. As Bishara himself put it in an article written after his departure from Israel: "The Israeli authorities are trying to intimidate not just me but all Palestinian citizens of Israel. But we will not be intimidated. We will not bow to permanent servitude in the land of our ancestors or to being severed from our natural connections to the Arab world."[72]

Although Azmi Bishara is the most famous (or notorious, depending on your point of view) Arab politician to have faced legal prosecution by the Israeli state, he is by no means the only one. In recent years, a number of Arab political leaders have been indicted for various offenses, such as providing material support to terrorist groups (Ra'ed Salah, the head of the northern branch of the Islamic Movement[73]), visiting an enemy state (MK Said Naffaa), and assaulting police officers during demonstrations (MK Mohammed Barakeh, head of the Hadash party). This has given rise to a widespread belief within the Arab community that their political

---

[70] Bishara was earlier charged in 2001 with visiting an enemy state (Syria) and for incitement during a speech he gave, but both charges were later dismissed.

[71] Author's interview with Amal Jamal, professor of Political Science, Tel Aviv University, June 10, 2009, Ramat Aviv.

[72] Azmi Bishara, "Why Israel is after me," *Los Angeles Times*, May 3, 2007.

[73] Ra'ed Salah was arrested in May 2003 and accused of funneling money to Palestinian terrorist groups in the West Bank and Gaza. He was ultimately convicted on lesser charges and sentenced to forty-two-months imprisonment.

leaders are being systematically persecuted by the state.[74] While this may be something of an exaggeration, it is certainly true that there is less tolerance today within Israeli-Jewish society and among its political representatives toward the political activities of Arab citizens, especially if those activities are seen as challenging Israel's identity as a Jewish state. This intolerant political attitude is encapsulated in the words of Uri Borowski, then Prime Minister Sharon's advisor on Arab affairs who bluntly stated in an interview: "Anyone who is against the state as a Jewish state should sit in jail or leave."[75]

An even more disturbing trend than the rise of political intolerance among Israeli Jews for the future of Jewish-Arab relations in Israel is growing Israeli-Jewish support for proposals to rid Israel of some or all of its Arab population. The idea of forcibly expelling Arab citizens from Israel – euphemistically referred to as "transfer" in Israeli political discourse – had traditionally been advocated by right-wing extremists like Moledet party leader Rehavam Ze'evi[76] and earlier by Kach party leader Meir Kahane, but it never received much support from the Jewish public because it was generally deemed to be morally reprehensible. Since 2000, however, the idea of transfer has been raised more frequently[77] and has become more publicly acceptable. In a survey taken in 2003, one-third of the Israeli-Jewish public (33 percent) expressed support for the expulsion of Arab citizens from Israel – this was a 9 percent increase from 1991 when 24 percent of Israeli Jews supported the idea.[78] More popular than simply expelling Arabs from Israel – which is still widely considered to be morally wrong and politically unfeasible – is the idea of "voluntary

---

74  Mohammad Zeidan, the head of the Supreme Arab Follow-Up Committee, has denounced the state's "ongoing attack" against the leaders of the Arab public. Quoted in Sharon Roffe-Ofir, "Israeli Arab leader: Don't treat us like enemies," *Ynet*, January 14, 2010.

75  International Crisis Group, *Identity Crisis*, 25.

76  Moledet was a member of Sharon's National Unity Government and Ze'evi was the minister of tourism before his assassination by members of the Popular Front for the Liberation of Palestine in October 2001.

77  In an interview on Israeli television in December 2001, for instance, Avigdor Lieberman, head of the Yisrael Beiteinu party and then a minister in Sharon's National Unity government stated: "I do not reject the transfer option. We don't have to escape reality. If you ask me, Israel's number one problem [ … ] is first of all Arab citizens of the State of Israel. Those who identify as Palestinians will have to move to Palestine. Do I consider them citizens of the State of Israel? No! Do we have to settle scores with them? Yes!" Israeli television Channel Two's "Meet the Press" program, December 2001. International Crisis Group, *Identity Crisis*, 20. In January 2002, huge posters declaring "Only transfer will bring peace" appeared around the country. Sari Makover, "Danger: No Border Ahead," *Ma'ariv*, February 21, 2002.

78  Arian, *Israeli Public Opinion on National Security 2004*, 30.

transfer," which would involve government policies aimed at encouraging Arab emigration. This is increasingly supported by Israeli Jews, with 53 percent favoring this in a 2002 poll, increasing to 57 percent in 2003,[79] and rising to 62 percent in 2006.[80]

Another proposal that has gained popular support among Israeli Jews is that of "territorial exchange." The idea is to trade territory inside Israel that contains a large number of Arabs for territory in the West Bank that contains a large number of Jewish settlers. This would involve redrawing Israel's borders so that Arab-populated towns and villages situated to the west of the pre-1967 "Green Line" (in the Triangle and Wadi Ara regions) would be included in a future Palestinian state, whereas Israel would annex the large Jewish settlement blocs east of the Green Line. Although this idea was first raised in the early 1990s,[81] it has only gained public attention and serious political interest in the last decade.[82] The most outspoken proponent of a territorial exchange in recent years has been Avigdor Lieberman, head of the Yisrael Beiteinu ("Israel Our Home") party and a former member of the Likud (and one time Director-General of the Prime Minister's Office under Netanyahu), who started advocating for it in 2004 and has done the most to popularize the idea since then. He has found a receptive audience within the Israeli-Jewish public. Most Israeli Jews support transferring Arab communities currently in Israel to a future Palestinian state. In a survey carried out in 2007, 30 percent of Israeli Jews were in favor of the transfer of as many Arab communities as possible, another 17 percent were in favor of transferring a small number of communities, and 27 percent were in favor on condition that it would be undertaken with the consent of the Arab residents of those communities. Only a quarter of Israeli Jews were opposed to any kind of transfer.[83]

What lay behind Jewish public support for schemes to reduce the size of Israel's Arab population were demographic fears. Israeli-Jewish

---

[79] Arian, *Israeli Public Opinion on National Security* 2004, 30.

[80] Asher Arian, Nir Atmor, and Yael Hadar, eds., *Auditing Israeli Democracy 2006* (Jerusalem: The Israel Democracy Institute, 2006), 87.

[81] Joseph Alpher, "Settlements and Borders," Final Status Issues: Israel-Palestinians, Study No. 3, (Tel Aviv: Jaffee Center for Strategic Studies, Tel Aviv University, 1994).

[82] For instance, in an interview in April 2002, former Prime Minister Ehud Barak commented that a territorial exchange "makes demographic sense and is not inconceivable." Rouhana and Sultany, "Redrawing the Boundaries of Citizenship," 18.

[83] Yehuda Ben-Meir and Dafna Shaked, *The People Speak: Israeli Public Opinion on National Security 2005–2007*, The Institute for National Security Studies Memorandum No. 90 (May 2007), 81.

anxiety over the country's demographic future – specifically over whether and for how long Jews would remain a majority of the population[84] – has intensified over the last decade, stoked by the warnings of some demographers that Israel would soon lose its Jewish majority[85] and by the references of Israeli-Jewish politicians to the "demographic problem" represented by the Arab minority.[86] The so-called demographic threat to Israel's ability to remain a Jewish and democratic state has become a major political issue in Israel over the past decade (this threat pertains not only to the Arab minority within Israel but also to Palestinians in the Occupied Territories over whom Israel effectively rules). It was one of the primary justifications used in support of Israel's unilateral disengagement from the Gaza Strip in August 2005, as Prime Minister Sharon presented the Gaza disengagement as a means of preserving a Jewish majority in the state. It was also the major rationale behind the short-lived "convergence plan" proposed in early 2006 by Sharon's successor Prime Minister Ehud Olmert, which would have involved a unilateral Israeli withdrawal from much of the West Bank. Both of these plans were intended, at least in part, to substantially reduce the number of Palestinians living under Israeli control. As such, they reflected the importance that demographic concerns had come to play in Israel. In the words of Shlomo Brom, a former deputy national security advisor for strategic affairs and head of Strategic Planning in the IDF: "The most salient development in Israeli national security thinking in recent years has been the growing role of demography at the expense of geography."[87]

As long as there is no Palestinian state, the possibility that many Arab citizens of Israel may one day find themselves living in it – voluntarily

---

[84] In public opinion surveys conducted over many years, Israeli Jews have consistently ranked a Jewish majority as their most important value, more important than Greater Israel, democracy, and peace. In 2006, for instance, 54 percent of Israeli Jews felt this way. Ben-Meir and Shaked, *The People Speak*, 18.

[85] In particular, Israeli demographers Arnon Sofer and Sergio DelaPergola drew public and political attention to the "demographic threat" to Israel's future as a Jewish and democratic state. See Lily Galili, "A Jewish Demographic State," *Journal of Palestine Studies* 32, no. 1 (2002), 90–93.

[86] For example, in a widely publicized speech at the influential annual Conference on the Balance of Israel's National Security (dubbed the Herzliya Conference) in December 2003, Benjamin Netanyahu, then finance minister in Sharon's government, described Israel's Arab minority as a "demographic problem." Aluf Benn and Gideon Alon, "Netanyahu: Israel's Arabs are the real demographic threat," *Ha'aretz*, December 18, 2003.

[87] Shlomo Brom, "From Rejection to Acceptance: Israeli National Security Thinking and Palestinian Statehood," *United States Institute of Peace Special Report* no. 177, February 2007.

or not – remains a distant one. A much more immediate threat to the Arab minority is the campaign of incitement and delegitimization that has been waged in recent years by some right-wing Israeli-Jewish politicians, above all by Avigdor Lieberman. Lieberman has been compared to xenophobic far-right populist politicians in Europe like Austria's Jorg Haider and France's Jean-Marie Le Pen,[88] and to the late Meir Kahane, leader of Israel's neo-fascist (and now banned) Kach party.[89] While presenting himself as a pragmatist rather than an ideologue,[90] Lieberman has repeatedly emphasized the "problem" of Israel's Arab minority and argued that Jews and Arabs cannot live together and that Israel should find a way of ridding itself of its troublesome Arab minority. As he put it in one newspaper interview: "I want to provide an Israel that is a Jewish, Zionist country. It's about what kind of country we want to see in the future. Either it will be an [ethnically mixed] country like any other, or it will continue as a Jewish country."[91]

Lieberman has taken particular aim at Arab politicians, waging a vitriolic verbal war against them. In a speech in the Knesset on May 4, 2006, for instance, he called for the execution of three Arab Knesset members who visited Syria in 2006 (Balad MKs Azmi Bishara, Jamal Zahalka, and Wassel Taha), declaring: "The fate of the collaborators in the Knesset will be identical to that of those who collaborated with the Nazis. Collaborators, as well as criminals, were executed after the Nuremberg trials at the end of World War Two. I hope that will be the fate of collaborators in this house."[92] More recently, in August 2009, he publicly asserted that: "Our central problem is not the Palestinians, but Ahmed Tibi [head of the United Arab List] and his ilk – they are more dangerous than Hamas and [Islamic] Jihad combined."[93]

Lieberman's inflammatory anti-Arab rhetoric could easily be dismissed were it not for the fact that he has risen to a position of considerable power and influence in Israeli politics. Lieberman has enjoyed a great deal of political success since he founded Yisrael Beiteinu in 1999. After

[88] See, for instance, Akiva Eldar, "Let's hear it for the Haiders," *Ha'aretz*, November 12, 2006.

[89] Gideon Levy, "Kahane won," *Ha'aretz*, February 8, 2009.

[90] Joshua Hammer, "I'm a Realist," *The New York Review of Books*, March 25, 2010.

[91] Quoted in Harry de Quetteville, "Jews and Arabs can never live together, says Israel's vice PM," *The Sunday Telegraph*, November 5, 2006.

[92] "Israel's Lieberman and controversial comments," *Reuters*, April 1, 2009, http://www.reuters.com/article/worldNews/idUSTRE52U3FU20090401

[93] Herb Keinon, "FM: Tibi is more dangerous than Hamas," *Jerusalem Post*, August 5, 2009.

winning four seats in the Knesset election that year, the party went on
to win seven seats in the 2003 election (in an electoral alliance with the
NRP), and eleven seats in the 2006 election (this time by itself). Lieberman
subsequently became minister for strategic affairs and deputy prime minister in Ehud Olmert's government. In the most recent Knesset election
in February 2009, Lieberman's Yisrael Beiteinu party won 12 percent of
the vote and fifteen seats in the Knesset, making it the third largest party.
Lieberman has now become foreign minister in Benjamin Netanyahu's
Likud-led government, a position that puts him near the very top of the
political hierarchy in Israel.[94]

The key to Lieberman's rapid rise to power has been the electoral
support Yisrael Beiteinu has garnered from Jews from the former Soviet
Union (Lieberman is himself an immigrant from Moldova, and many of
the party's MKs and activists are from the former Soviet Union [FSU]).[95]
Over the last decade, Yisrael Beiteinu has become the "Russian" party
in Israeli politics, replacing Natan Sharansky's Yisrael Ba'Aliyah party,
which won just two seats in the 2003 elections and was subsequently
absorbed into the Likud party. Yisrael Beiteinu has successfully appealed
to the pervasive anti-Arab sentiment among Jewish immigrants from the
FSU.[96] In the run-up to the 2009 election, for instance, his party's election posters stated: "Only Lieberman speaks Arabic." Though oblique,
the message was unmistakable – "Lieberman knows how to deal with the
Arabs." It is not only "Russian" voters, however, who have been attracted
to Yisrael Beiteinu's anti-Arab message. The party has also drawn support

---

[94]  Yisrael Beiteinu also had four other ministerial positions in Netanyahu's government.
[95]  Two-thirds of its support (about 280,000 votes) in the 2009 elections came from immi-
      grants from the former Soviet Union. This accounted for ten of its fifteen Knesset seats.
      The Mossawa Center, "The Palestinian Arab Minority and the 2009 Israeli Elections,"
      The Mossawa Center, Haifa, Israel (March 2009), 29.
[96]  Opinion polls have shown that Jewish immigrants from the former Soviet Union (FSU)
      hold more anti-Arab views than native Israeli Jews. In a survey conducted by the Israel
      Democracy Institute in 2009, 77 percent of immigrants from the FSU supported pro-
      moting Arab emigration from Israel, as opposed to 47 percent of native Israeli Jews who
      supported such a policy. "Poll finds former Soviet olim less tolerant of Arabs than native
      Israelis," *Jerusalem Post*, August 3, 2009. Scholarly studies have also demonstrated that
      FSU immigrants exhibit higher levels of intolerance toward Arab citizens of Israel than
      native Israeli Jews. See Majid Al-Haj, "The political culture of the 1990s immigrants from
      the former Soviet Union in Israel and their views toward the indigenous Arab minority: A
      case of ethnocratic multiculturalism," *Journal of Ethnic and Migration Studies* 30, no. 4
      (2004), 681–696; and Eran Halperin, D. Canetti-Nisim, E. S. Hobfoll, and J. R. Johnson,
      "Heightened by failure to gain resources in a new society: Terror, resource gains and eth-
      nic intolerance," *Journal of Ethnic and Migration Studies* (2007).

from Jewish settlers in the West Bank,[97] despite the fact that Lieberman is not opposed to an Israeli withdrawal from much of the West Bank (though he actually lives in a settlement).

Yisrael Beiteinu's success in the 2009 election was part of a broader shift to the right within Israeli politics. The center-right Likud party was the biggest beneficiary of this, winning a total of twenty-seven Knesset seats (with 22 percent of the vote), fifteen more than it had in the previous Knesset. The center-left Labor party led by former Prime Minister Ehud Barak, by contrast, received only 10 percent of the vote and lost six seats. With only thirteen MKs, the once-dominant Labor party was now just the fourth largest party in the Knesset (behind Kadima, Likud, and Yisrael Beiteinu). The left-wing Meretz party also fared poorly, winning just three Knesset seats, two less than it previously had. The electoral decline of the parties representing the Zionist left (Labor and Meretz) – largely due to the cumulative impact on Israeli-Jewish public opinion of the failure of the Oslo peace process, the second intifada, and the wars against Hezbollah (in 2006) and Hamas (in 2008–2009) – resulted in a Knesset (the eighteenth) that was more right-wing, hawkish, nationalistic, and even chauvinistic than perhaps any that had come before it. This has had serious implications for the Arab minority.

Numerous pieces of legislation directly or indirectly targeting Arab citizens have been introduced in the present Knesset. The most threatening to the rights of Arab citizens were three parliamentary bills submitted in the summer of 2009 (mostly by MKs from Yisrael Beiteinu) that required pledges of loyalty to Israel as a Jewish and democratic state as a condition of citizenship, for getting a mandatory government-issued identity card, and for being sworn in as a member of the Knesset.[98] The oaths that these bills proposed essentially demanded that Arabs in Israel (as well as other Israelis) declare their allegiance to Zionist values.[99] Failure to do

---

97 Yisrael Beiteinu won a significant portion of votes in West Bank settlements in the 2009 election (for example, the party won 31 percent of the vote in the settlement of Ariel and 15 percent in Ma'aleh Adumim, the largest settlement bloc). The party also did well in the mixed Arab-Jewish cities of Beer Sheva (gaining 25 percent of the vote) and Haifa (16 percent of the vote). The Mossawa Center, "The Palestinian Arab Minority and the 2009 Israeli Elections," 29.

98 See Leslie Susser, "Fanning the Flames of Discontent," *The Jerusalem Report*, July 6, 2009.

99 The Citizenship bill sought to make Israeli citizenship conditional on a pledge of loyalty to Israel as a Jewish, Zionist, and democratic state and on a commitment to perform military or another form of national service. The ID bill required Israeli citizens in order to receive an ID card to declare: "I promise to be loyal to the state of Israel as a Jewish

so would mean losing their citizenship, being denied state benefits, and being barred from serving in the Knesset. The "Citizenship bill" and "ID bill" also required Arabs to serve in the IDF or perform some alternative kind of national service.

The idea that Israeli citizenship be made conditional on taking an oath of loyalty to Israel as a Jewish and democratic state and doing military or some other form of national service was championed by Lieberman and Yisrael Beiteinu in the run-up to the 2009 election with the slogan "No loyalty, no citizenship."[100] By making citizenship conditional, instead of an automatic right, Arabs who choose to live in Israel rather than a future Palestinian state could lose their citizenship and become permanent residents without the right to vote. The idea, therefore, complimented Lieberman's territorial exchange proposal, as both would have the effect of reducing the number of Israel's Arab citizens – whether by placing them under Palestinian rule or stripping them of their citizenship within Israel. Moreover, by linking citizenship to the performance of military service or some other kind of national service, the right of the vast majority of Arabs to Israeli citizenship is effectively called into question because (except for the small number of Druze Arabs and some Bedouin) they do not currently do the compulsory military service that other young Israelis do. In short, it delegitimizes the citizenship of most Arabs.

Although none of the proposed "loyalty bills" ultimately succeeded in becoming law, they still had a damaging affect in the message that they sent to both Jews and Arabs. According to Muhammad Zeidan, the director of the Arab Association for Human Rights, for Israeli Jews, "[t]he message is that the Palestinian community in Israel is not legitimate, that it is an enemy;" whereas for Arabs, "[i]t tells them that they are outsiders and raises the whole issue of their relationship to the state."[101] The bills certainly antagonized and infuriated Arab political leaders in Israel.

---

and Zionist state, the principles in the Declaration of Independence, the flag and the anthem. I promise to do compulsory military service in the IDF or some alternative form of national service, as stipulated by law." The bill concerning incoming Knesset members tried to change the oath of office from swearing allegiance to the "the state of Israel and its laws," to swearing loyalty to "the Jewish, Zionist and democratic state of Israel, its symbols and its values."

[100] The idea of a loyalty oath was first raised in 2003 when Prime Minister Sharon's adviser for Arab affairs recommended to a special ministerial committee charged with formulating proposals for government policy toward the Arab minority that in order to receive a necessary government-issued identity card, Israeli citizens first take an oath of loyalty to the state. Yair Ettinger, "PM's Arab adviser urges mandatory flag waving and loyalty oaths," *Ha'aretz*, November 5, 2003.

[101] Quoted in Susser, "Fanning the Flames of Discontent."

The chairman of the Supreme Arab Follow-Up Committee, Muhammad Zeidan, for instance, wrote a defiant letter to Prime Minister Netanyahu, President Shimon Peres, and Knesset Speaker Reuven Rivlin criticizing the proposed bills and calling on them "to stop the wave of racist incitement against the Arab citizens in Israel." He also asserted that: "A genuine sense of loyalty [among Arabs] will only come when people feel they are being treated fairly and with dignity. Israel's state institutions can't relate to the Arabs as a 'ticking time bomb' and in the same breath order them to be loyal."[102]

The loyalty bills are not the only pieces of legislation introduced in the current Knesset aimed at the Arab minority. In its 2010 annual report on racism, the Mossawa Center, an Arab advocacy group in Israel, described a total of twenty-one bills submitted to the Knesset in 2009 as "discriminatory and racist," a staggering 75 percent increase from the year before. Among these, the two most controversial bills targeting Arab citizens (in addition to the loyalty bills) were a bill that sought to criminalize public denial of Israel's right to exist as a Jewish state and a bill that banned public commemoration of the Nakba on Israel's Independence Day. The former bill banned the publication of writing that challenged Israel as a Jewish and democratic state and recommended a year in jail for anyone who violated this ban. Essentially, it was aimed at criminalizing the calls of Arab politicians and intellectuals for Israel to become a state for all its citizens.[103] As the bill's sponsor, MK Zvulun Orlev of the right-wing Jewish Home Party (the renamed National Religious Party), explained in an interview: "Influential elements in the Arab sector are making considerable public, political and financial efforts to undermine Israel's foundations as a Jewish and democratic state, and to turn it into a binational Jewish-Arab state. If these moves gain traction, the threat to the Jewish nation state will be enormous."[104] The bill passed its first reading in the Knesset, but it was subsequently defeated after an outcry in the media.

The "Nakba bill," as it became known, sought to ban public commemoration of the Nakba on Israel's Independence Day with a punishment of a three-year prison sentence (it was allegedly introduced in response to the mourning rallies held on Israeli Independence Day by many Palestinian citizens in recent years). The bill was initially approved

---

[102] Quoted in Susser, "Fanning the Flames of Discontent."
[103] Nadav Shragai, "Knesset okays initial bill to outlaw denial of 'Jewish state'," *Ha'aretz*, May 26, 2009.
[104] Quoted in Susser, "Fanning the Flames of Discontent."

by the Netanyahu government's Ministerial Committee for Legislation but was eventually watered down when it was put to a Knesset vote in March 2010. The revised version of the bill, which passed its first reading in the Knesset, made it illegal for state-funded organizations and groups (such as political parties or municipalities) to fund Nakba-related activities.[105] In a heated debate in the Knesset over the bill, MK David Rotem (a member of Yisrael Beiteinu, the party that introduced the legislation) declared: "[W]hen we are at war against a harsh enemy, we will legislate laws that will prevent him from hurting us."[106]

Taken together, these bills amount to an unprecedented assault against the rights of Arab citizens of Israel. Whether any of them are eventually enacted into law or not, they testify to the political atmosphere that has emerged in Israel over the past decade in which anti-Arab attitudes and policies have become increasingly mainstream and legitimate. As the security and demographic fears of the Jewish public have grown, so too has its suspicion and intolerance of the Arab minority; and these feelings have at times been manipulated and exploited by politicians like Lieberman. Consequently, the rift between Jews and Arabs in Israel – always wide – has now become dangerously deep and bitter.

## Conclusion

The increasing intolerance of the Jewish majority toward the political activities of the Arab minority has already led to the imposition of various legal restrictions on their political freedoms. The ability of the Arab minority to challenge the Zionist consensus in Israel and to demand changes to the character of the state has been steadily eroded over the past decade. Though Arab citizens of Israel still enjoy democratic rights, they cannot be taken for granted given the negative trends in Jewish public opinion that have been discussed in this chapter. Indeed, some observers have claimed that the rights of Arab citizens have already become more limited since 2000,[107] and that they are losing their substantive

---

[105] The bill also authorized the finance minister to decrease the budget for groups receiving government funding if they are involved in activities that deny the existence of Israel as a Jewish and democratic state, engage in racial incitement, violence or terrorism, or provide support for armed struggle or terrorism against the country.

[106] Quoted in Amnon Meranda, "'Softened' Nakba law passes 1st reading," *Ynetnews*, March 16, 2010.

[107] Yoav Peled, "Citizenship Betrayed: Israel's Emerging Immigration and Citizenship Regime," *Theoretical Inquiries in Law* 8, 2 (2007), 603–628.

meaning.[108] Some Israeli scholars have even argued that Israel is becoming an "ethnocracy" rather than a democracy,[109] while others have gone so far as to describe a process of "creeping apartheid" inside Israel.[110]

Although we believe that such descriptions are a little exaggerated and that Israel remains a democracy, albeit a seriously flawed one, the future of democracy in Israel – at least liberal democracy – is undoubtedly at risk.[111] The risk comes not only from what Amal Jamal terms the "majoritarian despotism of the Jewish majority" vis-à-vis the Arab minority,[112] but also from the general illiberal tendencies of large sectors of Israeli-Jewish society. That is, it is not only Arabs citizens toward whom many Israeli Jews have become increasingly intolerant, it also toward other Jews who publicly oppose and protest Israeli government policies and actions. So far, this intolerance of Jewish dissent has mainly been directed against Israeli human rights NGOs who have been accused of betraying the country and aiding the ongoing delegitimization of Israel.[113] Thus, a 2010 poll conducted by the Tami Steinmetz Center for Peace Research at Tel Aviv University found that 57.6 percent of Israeli Jews believed that "human rights organizations that expose immoral conduct by Israel should not be allowed to operate freely," and a majority also thought that there was too much freedom of expression in Israel.[114]

The most egregious manifestation of this intolerant attitude regarding the activities of human rights NGOs was a public campaign in 2010 against the New Israel Fund (NIF; a major funder of progressive, civil society groups in Israel) by *Im Tirtzu*, a right-wing Zionist student group, for allegedly providing support for the UN's Goldstone Report, which severely criticized Israel's conduct of the 2008–2009 Gaza War. During this campaign, the head of the NIF, Naomi Chazan, was vilified and crudely depicted on billboard posters across the country with a horn

---

[108] Jamal, "Nationalizing States and the Constitution of 'Hollow Citizenship': Israel and its Palestinian Citizens," *Ethnopolitics* 6, 4 (2007), 477.

[109] Peled, "Citizenship Betrayed."

[110] Oren Yiftachel, "'Creeping Apartheid' in Israel-Palestine," *Middle East Report*, no. 253 (Winter 2009); Oren Yiftachel, "Voting for Apartheid: The 2009 Israeli Elections," *Journal of Palestine Studies* 38, no. 3 (2009), 1–15.

[111] This view is shared by Knesset member Dov Khanin of the Hadash Party, who believes that democracy in Israel is fragile and under threat. Authors' interview with Dov Khanin, June 7, 2009, Tel Aviv.

[112] Jamal, "Nationalizing States and the Constitution of 'Hollow Citizenship,'" 477.

[113] Isabel Kershner, "Israeli Rights Groups View Themselves as Under Siege," *The New York Times*, April 5, 2010.

[114] Or Kashti, "Poll: Majority of Israel's Jews back gag on rights groups," *Ha'aretz*, May 7, 2010.

attached to her forehead.[115] A much more serious manifestation of this intolerance, however, was the introduction of a "transparency bill" in the Knesset in February 2010 that required any Israeli NGO that received funding from foreign governments (including the European Union) to register with the state's registrar of political parties, which would mean that they would lose their tax-exempt status and have a harder time raising money abroad. The bill would also make it a criminal offense for them not to declare that they are funded by "foreign state entities" in all of their publications, interviews, speeches, meetings, and so forth.[116] The bill overwhelmingly passed its preliminary parliamentary reading and will likely become law in the future.

It should by now be clear that Jewish-Arab relations in Israel are seriously deteriorating. Attitudes on both sides have hardened, mutual distrust has grown, fear has increased, and political opinion has become more radical and uncompromising. The Palestinian minority and the Jewish majority in Israel are caught up in a negative spiral in which the suspicion, fear, and animosity of one intensifies the suspicion, fear, and animosity of the other. Although the outcome of this negative spiral cannot be predicted, it clearly does not bode well for the future of Jewish-Palestinian coexistence in Israel. What, then, can be done to reverse this process and improve Jewish-Arab relations? How can a potential future internal conflict between Jews and Palestinians in Israel be avoided? The second part of this book will try to answer these crucial questions as we offer some suggestions for better managing, if not entirely solving, the Jewish-Palestinian conflict within Israel.

[115] Kershner, "Israeli Rights Groups View Themselves as Under Siege."
[116] Dan Izenberg, "Cabinet backs bill to register NGOs funded by foreign states," *The Jerusalem Post*, February 15, 2010.

PART II

MANAGING THE CONFLICT

# 5

# The Formation of the Jewish Republic

> I am certain that the world will judge the Jewish state by what it will do
> with its Arab population, just as the Jewish people will be judged by what
> it does or fails to do in this state.
>
> (Chaim Weizmann, Israel's first president)[1]

The first part of this book dealt in detail with the internal conflict between
Israel's Jewish majority and its Palestinian minority, and especially the
escalation of this conflict over the past decade. The second part of this
book now turns to the question of how to minimize or better manage this
conflict. Eliminating the conflict entirely is not something we believe to be
possible due to the depth of the cleavage between Jews and Palestinians in
Israel. How, then, can Jewish-Palestinian relations in Israel be improved
in any significant way? How can the State of Israel better meet the needs
of its Palestinian minority and how can the sense of loyalty and belonging
to the state on the part of the Palestinian citizens be enhanced? These are
the central questions that will be addressed in the rest of the book.

In order to seriously tackle the contemporary internal Jewish-Palestinian
conflict, it is essential to understand its underlying cause. It is our contention that the fundamental cause of the conflict lies in the character of
the Israeli state itself. The State of Israel can best be defined as a "Jewish
Republic," a state exclusively dedicated to what it views as Jewish interests, not to the interests of all its citizens (including its Palestinian citizens).
This kind of "ethnic state," and the policies which result from it, is at the

---

[1] Quoted in David J. Forman, "Israel Part II: The Reality – Israeli Arabs," *The Jerusalem Post*, February 12, 2010.

very core of the conflict between Israel's Jewish majority and its Palestinian minority. This is not to say that other factors have not also played a part in the conflict. In particular, the fact that Jews and Arabs have been locked in a long, bitter, and often violent struggle for control over the land has, of course, had a major impact upon Jewish-Palestinian relations in Israel, and indeed on the formation of Israel as a Jewish Republic in the first place. Were it not for the Arab-Jewish conflict that took place in British Mandatory Palestine and culminated in a "no-holds barred" war between the two ethno-national groups, Israel would no doubt have become a very different kind of state. But the fact that Israel became a Jewish Republic cannot simply be attributed to the Arab-Jewish conflict that preceded the state's founding, and continued after it. The establishment of Israel as a Jewish Republic was not an inevitable outcome of this conflict. Instead, it was a conscious choice made by the state's early leaders, especially by its first Prime Minister, David Ben-Gurion.

We argue in this chapter that a Jewish Republic emerged in the very early years of statehood largely as a result of some critical decisions made by Israel's leadership at the time. These decisions effectively determined the nature of the Israeli state for generations to come. Thus, the origins of Israel's internal Jewish-Palestinian conflict today lie in Israel's formative era. The decisions made during this period, particularly during the years 1948–1963 (when Ben-Gurion retired as Prime Minister), laid the basis for the Israeli state's approach towards its Arab minority, an approach that has for the most part prevailed to the present day.[2] Although through the years Israel has undergone a process of liberalization in many respects,[3] with some positive consequences for the Palestinian minority, the state itself has essentially remained a Jewish Republic, and its basic approach to the Palestinian minority has been generally consistent with this.

The argument presented in this chapter has enormous implications for the possibility of improving Jewish-Palestinian relations in Israel. If the internal Jewish-Palestinian conflict is deeply rooted in the nature of the

---

[2] Several scholars have written about the policy of the Israeli government toward the Arab minority in the early years of the state. See, for example Don Peretz, "Early State Policy toward the Arab-Population, 1948–1955," in Laurence J. Silberstein, ed., *New Perspectives on Israeli History: The Early Years of the State* (New York: New York University Press, 1991), 82–102, and Elie Rekhess, "Initial Israeli Policy Guidelines toward the Arab Minority, 1948–1949," in Silberstein. Ibid., 103–119.

[3] Thus, for example, the Israeli political system has become much more liberal in terms of recognizing gender differences, banning discrimination on the basis of sexual preferences, recognizing the standard "Western" liberties such as freedom of expression, and so forth.

Israeli regime that was established after 1948, as we strongly argue, then changes in that regime need to be implemented in order to significantly improve Jewish-Palestinian relations in Israel.

## A Jewish Republic or a Liberal Democracy?

Why did the State of Israel become a Jewish Republic? Such a question may at first seem strange or even naïve. After all, the establishment of the State of Israel in 1948 was the result of decades of nation-building by the Zionist movement and the culmination of its drive for Jewish national self-determination. Since a Jewish state was the overriding goal of the Zionist movement, unofficially at first and then officially after the Biltmore Conference in New York City in 1942,[4] it would seem that the State of Israel was destined to become a Jewish state, and that it couldn't become anything but a Jewish state.[5] But, the question is, what kind of Jewish state? Israel's founding fathers – Ben-Gurion, foremost among them – could have created in 1948 and during the formative years that followed a different kind of state than the one they actually created. In particular, Israel could have been established as a Western-style liberal democracy rather than an ethnic state, or in our terminology, a Jewish Republic.[6]

---

[4] A sovereign Jewish state was not the goal of all Zionists. Some, notably cultural Zionists and bi-nationalists, were opposed to Jewish statehood on either ideological or practical grounds. There was never a total consensus within the Zionist movement about its ultimate objective, but over time those advocating the establishment of a Jewish state came to dominate the Zionist movement and the political organs of the Jewish community in British Mandatory Palestine. On opposition to "statist Zionism" from leading Jewish thinkers see, Noam Pinko, *Zionism and the Roads Not Taken: Rawidowicz, Kaplan, Kohn* (Bloomington: Indiana University Press, 2010).

[5] The fact that the UN's partition resolution of November 1947 called for the establishment of an "Arab state" and a "Jewish state" in the area occupied by the British Mandate also gave a certain amount of international legitimacy to the idea of an ethnically defined Jewish state.

[6] Other options were theoretically possible, notably the establishment of a socialist republic, a bi-national state, or a theocracy (a state ruled according to Orthodox Jewish religious law), but none of these options were realistic in 1948. While many of Israel's founders were once committed socialists, Ben-Gurion and his colleagues in the ruling Mapai party had already decisively moved away from socialism in favor of nationalism long before 1948. See, Ze'ev Sternhell, *Nation-Building and Nationalism: Nationalism and Socialism in the Israeli Labor Movement, 1904–1940* (Tel Aviv:Tel Aviv University Press, 1995). A bi-national Jewish-Arab state was not a serious option in 1948 because it had no appeal to Israel's leadership or to the overwhelming majority of its Jewish community (only a small number of Jewish intellectuals, such as Martin Buber and Judah Magnes, and some members of the leftist Mapam party favored a bi-national state). Finally, a theocratic

As a full-fledged liberal democracy, the State of Israel would ensure full civil equality for all of its citizens as individuals, and the state would take a neutral (or at least as neutral as possible) position toward the different ethnic, national, and religious groups within it. In other words, the state would be concerned with the interests of all its citizens, rather than dedicate itself exclusively to the promotion of the interests of any particular group among them. The state's commitment to equality would most likely be enshrined in a constitution that would have included a comprehensive Bill of Rights, all protected by special majority for any significant change, an independent judiciary equipped with the prerogative of judicial review, and so forth. In the post-World War II era, with American liberalism and constitutionalism on the rise, the establishment of an Israeli liberal democracy would have been not only possible but even welcomed in many international quarters, especially in the West. It would have dramatically changed the entire complexion of the emerging Israeli polity.

But a liberal democracy of the type we imagine here (or a similar variety) was rejected in favor of an ethnic Jewish Republic. Unlike a liberal democracy, the Jewish Republic established in the late 1940s essentially emerged as an ethnic state, primarily committed to serving the interests of the dominant ethno-national group within it. Although the State formally accepted the equality of all its individual citizens, and declared its commitment to that equality in its foundational document (the 1948 Declaration of Independence), it subsequently violated its commitment in numerous ways, and became an ethnic state. It also became a "republic" in the sense that all individual citizens within it, Jews and Palestinians alike, have been judged by and rewarded according to their contribution to the ethnically defined common good, that is, by their contribution to the Jewish state and its Zionist agenda. By this criterion, however, "Israeli Arabs" (as they were defined by official Israel) could not become truly good Israeli citizens because they did not contribute to the state's Jewish-Zionist agenda.[7]

Jewish state was never likely since religious Jews were only a small minority of Israel's Jewish community in 1948 (although Ben-Gurion did make major concessions to the Orthodox and even the anti-Zionist ultra-Orthodox in order to unite all Jews in the struggle for a Jewish state).

[7] The fact that most Arab citizens of Israel, unlike Jewish citizens, do not serve in the IDF is the most obvious way in which they do not contribute to the Jewish Republic, and as such are regarded by the state and Israeli-Jewish society as lesser citizens. The state's decision not to require all Arabs to perform mandatory military service is, needless to say, understandable in the context of the ongoing Arab-Israeli and Israeli-Palestinian conflicts.

The tension between the Jewish Republic and liberal democracy has been in the air from the very beginning. Already the Declaration of Independence reflected two alternative value systems, espousing both liberal democratic values and, at the same time, ethno-national goals, declaring that the state would work on behalf of all of its citizens, on the one hand, and pursue Zionist ideals, on the other hand. Despite this dual promise, in practice the actual policies adopted by the state in the years after its establishment were consistent with the values of a Jewish Republic, rather than with the ideals of a liberal democracy.[8] Notwithstanding the establishment of many democratic institutions in the new state following its independence (such as a popularly elected parliament and a strong independent judiciary), the leadership of the state was exclusively committed to securing Jewish, and more specifically Zionist interests. Thus, the policies of the state, especially in the areas of immigration and citizenship, education, land policy, and economic development, were determined according to a Zionist agenda. In the Jewish Republic and consistent with its values, the Arab minority was not granted any collective political rights. Although individual Arabs received Israeli citizenship and most of the rights and privileges associated with it, they were not recognized, politically, as a national minority that the State ought to negotiate with. To the extent to which Israel became a democracy, therefore, it has emerged as an illiberal democracy, or as Sammy Smooha characterizes it, an "ethnic democracy."[9] We believe that the two sets of values included in Israel's Declaration of Independence could have been implemented in a much more balanced manner than they have been, and

[8] A major reason for this was the Arab-Jewish conflict that began in British Mandatory Palestine immediately following the United Nations' Partition Resolution of November 29, 1947 and then dramatically escalated. The civil war between Jews and Palestinian Arabs was then followed by an interstate war between the new Jewish state and the neighboring Arab states. More than any other single factor, the bitter and violent Arab-Jewish conflict made the emergence of an ethnic state in Israel much more likely than the emergence of a full-fledged liberal democracy. The literature on the Arab-Jewish conflict over Israel/Palestine is enormous. Useful reference books include Alan Dowty *Israel/Palestine* (Cambridge: Polity, Second Edition 2008); Ann M. Lesch and Dan Tachigi, *Origins and Development of the Arab-Israeli Conflict* (Greenwood: Connecticut, 1998); Avi Shlaim, *The Iron Wall: Israel and the Arab World* (New York: Norton, 2001); and Benny Morris, *Righteous Victims: A History of the Zionist-Arab Conflict 1881–2001*, (New York: Cambridge University Press, 2001).

[9] On the concept of "ethnic democracy" see Sammy Smooha, "Minority Status in Ethnic Democracy: The Status of the Arab Minority in Israel," *Ethnic and Racial Studies*, Vol. 13, 3 (1990): 389–413; and the critique by Oren Yiftachel, "The Ethnic Democracy Model and Its Applicability to the Case of Israel," *Ethnic and Racial Studies*, Vol. 15, 1. (1992): 125–137.

that a better balance must be achieved in the future, benefiting both the Jewish majority and the Palestinian minority (in Chapter 7, we propose ways of achieving this balance).

Perhaps the most important decision made by Israel's leadership in its formative era that determined the state's character as a Jewish Republic rather than a liberal democracy was the decision not to adopt a formal constitution for the new state.[10] Although upon declaring Israel's independence in 1948, the leadership of the state promised to elect a Constituent Assembly that would quickly adopt a formal constitution, shortly after the election for the Constituent Assembly the following year, Prime Minister Ben-Gurion announced that there was no need for a constitution after all. In the face of strong opposition both from within his own Mapai party, as well from parties on the left (the socialist Mapam party) and the right (the revisionist Herut party), Ben-Gurion opposed adopting a constitution on the grounds that it would limit the power of elected officials and put restraints on governmental actions, something that he saw as undemocratic.[11]

The non-adoption of a constitution in Israel's formative years was crucial in terms of enabling the establishment of a strong Jewish Republic. It effectively marginalized liberalism and civil liberties in Israeli political culture (ideas that are inherently linked to constitutionalism),[12] and it allowed the government to act without the normal restraints in implementing its agenda, particularly on issues concerning majority-minority relations (such as land expropriations, the imposition of the military government, etc.). This has had a very negative impact upon the relations between the Jewish majority and the Arab minority in Israel.

One of the main functions of a modern constitution, particularly in deeply divided societies, is to protect minorities against the whims of the

---

[10] Yonathan Shapiro, *Politicians as a Hegemonic Class: The Case of Israel* (Tel-Aviv: Sifriat Poalim, 1996); Philippa Strum, "The Road Not Taken: Constitutional Non-Decision Making in 1948–1950 and Its Impact on Civil Liberties in the Israeli Political Culture," in S. Ilan Troen and Noah Lucas, eds., *Israel: The First Decade of Independence* (Albany, NY: SUNY Press, 1995), 83–104.

[11] Chaim Zadok, one of Israel's top legal minds and a supporter of Ben-Gurion, said that Ben-Gurion had "a desire to govern without constitutional restrictions, taking whatever action he deemed best to put the state on a firm footing." Strum, "The Road Not Taken," 92. Ben-Gurion also opposed a constitution because he believed that the borders of the new state must be defined in the constitution, and he did not want to do so. Strum, "The Road Not Taken," 91.

[12] Yonathan Shapiro, "Where had Liberalism Disappeared in Israel," *Zmanim*, Winter 1996, 92–101 (in Hebrew); Rita J. Simon and Jean M. Landis, "Trends in Public Support for Civil Liberties and Due Process in Israeli Society," *Social Science Quarterly*, Vol. 71, No. 1 (1990): 93–104.

majority. In Israel's case, the Arab minority was particularly in need of constitutional protection because the ongoing Arab-Jewish conflict meant that many Israeli Jews, including government officials and members of the state's security forces, perceived "Israeli Arabs" as a security threat, making them likely targets of discrimination. Without having their rights enshrined in a constitution and a Bill of Rights, guaranteeing above all equality before the law, Arab citizens of Israel have largely been at the mercy of Israeli governments and the Jewish majority (Israel's Supreme Court has only rarely and belatedly intervened on their behalf, especially in the early, formative era). The Arab minority has been especially vulnerable to the Jewish majority's desire to control and marginalize it, a desire born out of the generally hostile relationship between Jews and Arabs inside and outside Israel. Thus, the fact that Israel became a Jewish Republic – an ethnic state and not a liberal democracy – has had huge implications for its treatment of its Arab minority.[13]

### Controlling the Minority

As a result of the war of 1947–1949, the Jewish community became a majority in the land in which they had been a minority for generations. The Jews suddenly had power not only over themselves but also over their longtime rivals, the Arabs. The new Jewish majority had a highly suspicious attitude toward the defeated minority, which was hardly surprising given the all-out civil war that Jews and Palestinians had just fought. Most Israeli Jews looked upon the 150,000 or so Arabs who remained in Israel after the war as a real or a potential "fifth column" in Israel's ongoing conflict with the Arab states surrounding it. Similarly, security-oriented Israeli leaders viewed "Israeli Arabs" as a threat, fearing that they might carry out espionage, sabotage, or even guerilla warfare against the state.[14] While there was little evidence that these suspicions were factually justified, they influenced the decision-making of the Israeli leadership concerning the Arab minority or were at least used as an excuse for harsh policies toward the minority.

Undoubtedly, the most important decision-maker during the formative years of Israel was David Ben-Gurion. As Prime Minister and Minister of Defense, Ben-Gurion had a decisive influence in all matters related to

---

[13] Lustick, *Arabs in the Jewish State.*
[14] See, for example, Yigal Allon, *A Curtain of Sand* (Tel Aviv: Ha'kibbutz Ha'meuchad, 1969), 322–323 (Hebrew).

the Arab minority. While he was naturally concerned about ensuring the security of the new and still very vulnerable state, he was also deeply committed to implementing a Zionist agenda and strengthening the country's Jewish character. Although Ben-Gurion often used universalistic language in talking about an egalitarian Israel, he was, above all, an ardent nationalist since his youth. He was single-mindedly committed to the Zionist project of establishing a Jewish state, not a Western-style liberal democracy. He saw himself as molding a new Jewish nation, not a civic Israeli nation in which people of different ethnic and religious backgrounds can equally belong. Ben-Gurion's approach to the governance of the state, therefore, was thoroughly ethno-national. Although he was obviously aware of the fact that Israel had a large number of Arab citizens living within it, as far as he was concerned, Jews and only Jews must govern the state. For Ben-Gurion, the Arab minority simply had to live under Jewish rule.[15]

Not all members of the Israeli leadership at the time, however, shared Ben-Gurion's ethno-national, exclusivist perspective. Some favored a much more accommodating, egalitarian, and inclusive approach to the Arab minority (the type of approach reflected in our own proposals in Chapter 7). Moshe Sharett (the Foreign Minister and later Prime Minister),[16] Yitzhak Greenboim (the first Interior Minister), Yitzhak Ben-Zvi (Israel's second President),[17] and Pinhas Lavon (later Defense Minister) were among those who advocated a more liberal position toward the Arabs (so too did members of the more left-wing Mapam party).[18] They believed that Jews had to set a positive example for majority-minority relations, particularly due to the Jewish people's history as victims of discrimination and persecution; and they were eager to prove that the Jewish state would treat its minority in a most humane and egalitarian manner possible.[19]

---

[15] In all of his numerous writings and speeches, there is no indication that Ben-Gurion ever deviated from this ethno-national outlook in regard to the Arab minority in Israel. Ben-Gurion's attitudes toward the Arabs was thoroughly and sympathetically explored by Shabtai Teveth, *Ben-Gurion and the Palestinian Arabs from Peace to War* (Oxford and New York: Oxford University Press, 1985), 191.

[16] See Gabriel Sheffer, "Sharett's 'Line', Struggles, and Legacy," in Troen and Lucas, eds., *Israel: The First Decade of Independence*, 143–169.

[17] Rekhess, "Initial Israeli Policy Guidelines toward the Arab Minority," 105–106.

[18] Segev, *The First Israelis*, especially 58.

[19] Shimon Shamir, "The Historical Perspective: Introductory Notes", *Skirot*, Tel-Aviv, Shiloach Center, 1976, 5, quoted in Rekhess, "Initial Israeli Policy Guidelines toward the Arab Minority," 104.

While it is important to acknowledge the presence of such liberal views as a way of identifying the options open to the state's leadership in those formative years, it is crucial to realize that an accommodating, inclusive approach to the Arab minority was not adopted by the state. The liberal perspective had little if any real influence on the state's actual policy toward the Arab minority during its early years, a policy that determined the trajectory of Arab-Jewish relations in Israel for decades to come. This policy was determined above all by Ben-Gurion. When it came to Arabs, Ben-Gurion was not a moderate. In fact he was a hardliner, both towards Arabs outside the state (that is, the neighboring Arab countries) as well as towards those inside the state (Israel's Arab citizens). Ben-Gurion's overall approach toward the Arab minority in post-1948 Israel can be summed up as one that emphasized separation and domination, rather than integration or cooperation.[20]

Of all the policies adopted by the Israeli state toward the Arab minority during its formative years, none was more symptomatic of and consequential for establishing negative majority-minority relations in Israel than the imposition of the Military Government (*Mimshal Tzvai* in Hebrew) on the Arabs, an institution that prevailed from 1948 to 1966. Areas heavily inhabited by Arabs were divided into five regions – Nazareth, Western Galilee, Ramle-Lod, Jaffa, and the Negev – and military officers, equipped with vast powers, were put in charge of each region, while the overall policy toward these areas and their inhabitants was set by the Ministry of Defense under Ben-Gurion.[21] The military government essentially gave the State total control over all aspects of Arab life. This level of control was designed to ensure the good behavior of the Arab population.

The establishment of the military government meant that, from the very start, the Arab minority was primarily looked upon and dealt with as a security problem, a challenge that had to be managed by military means and other instruments of control. Justified or not (and, on the basis of the available historical evidence, we regard the military government

[20] Ian S. Lustick, "Zionism and the State of Israel: Regime Objective and the Arab Minority in the First Years of Statehood," *Middle Eastern Studies*, Vol. 16, No. 1, January 1980, 127. On other fundamental divides within the Israeli society, Ben-Gurion was moderate and reasonable. With the Orthodox Jews, with whom he had deep philosophical disagreements, he reached already in 1947 the famous "Status Quo Agreement," recognizing their special interests in several crucial areas.

[21] By the time of its elimination, the military government covered 220,000 of a total of 260,000 Israeli Arabs.

as unjustified, at least in its depth and duration),[22] the military government had a profound long-term impact on Arab-Jewish relations. In many ways the military government amounted to the ghettoization of the Arabs, their physical separation from the Jewish majority. This had far-reaching psychological consequences. It clearly marked Arabs as a hostile population not to be trusted, and declared them to be politically and socially unintegratable, the "ultimate other."[23] The military government therefore exacerbated the already negative relationship between the Jewish majority and the Arab minority.

The nature of the state's general approach toward the Arab minority becomes even clearer when compared with its approach toward other cleavages within Israeli society. The state's leadership made a concerted attempt to overcome the many divides within the Jewish community, particularly the ones between religious and secular Jews, and between Ashkenazim (Jews originally from Europe) and Sephardim (Jews originally from the Middle East and North Africa).[24] These cleavages were energetically dealt with, through dialogue and compromise, and with a pronounced accommodationist spirit. The results were, on the whole, quite positive. By contrast, no equivalent effort was made by Israel's leaders to overcome the cleavage between Arabs and Jews, and there was no sustained attempt to integrate Arab citizens into Israeli society.

The only time that integration of the Arab minority was seriously considered by the state was during the brief existence of the Ministry of Minorities in Israel's first government in 1948. It was headed by Bechor Shalom Shitrit, a politician who grew up in Mandatory Palestine, spoke Palestinian Arabic, and had close ties to Israel's Arab community. Shitrit personally initiated the establishment of the Ministry prior to the declaration of the state. He had, in general, a liberal view about Jewish-Arab relations, and was a great believer in the possibility and desirability of Jewish-Arab reconciliation. He thought that the mission of his Ministry

---

[22] In assessing the military government, it is important to note that many people in Israel opposed it, an indication that it was not as absolutely necessary as the government at the time claimed. It was a subject of political disagreement, with some accusing Mapai of using the military government to bolster its political power. Civil libertarians in Israel were particularly uncomfortable with the military government and there was also unease within the judiciary.

[23] Peleg, "Otherness and Israel's Arab Dilemma," 258–280; and Ilan Peleg, "The Arab-Israel Conflict and the Victory of Otherness," in Russell A. Stone and Walter P. Zenner, eds., *Books on Israel, Vol. III* (Albany: SUNY Press, 1994), 227–243

[24] The "Status Quo Agreement" of 1947, for instance, was an attempt to tackle the deep division between secular and religious Jews. See, Asher Cohen and Bernard Susser, *Israel*

should be to try to integrate the Arabs into the Israeli society and convince them to accept living in a Jewish state.[25] After only a year, however, the Ministry of Minorities was abolished and Shitrit was dismissed from his post in June 1949 (although he remained Minister of Police). While some observers have argued that the Ministry was closed due to bureaucratic politics,[26] the fact remains that Ben-Gurion could have preserved the Ministry if he really wanted to, given his enormous power and authority at the time. After disbanding the Ministry, Ben-Gurion divided its functions among the different government departments, thereby eliminating a focal point for representing the concerns of the Arab minority. Shitrit, the most liberal member of the government (who suggested abolishing the Military Government as early as 1949), lost his ability to be a major player in determining the character of Jewish-Arab relations. To replace the Ministry of Minorities, a new position was created – Advisor to the Prime Minister on Arab Affairs. The first person appointed to the job was Joshua Palmon, a government bureaucrat and former intelligence officer who viewed the Arab minority through the lens of security and regarded it primarily as a security threat, as did most of his successors in that position.

## Conclusion

In the final analysis, in the clash between Jewish ethno-nationalism and the state's commitment to the ideals of democracy and equality, ethno-nationalism won decisively, especially in terms of the state's attitude toward the Arab minority. This was not inevitable, even if as an historical phenomenon it is not particularly surprising. The victory of ethno-nationalism was the result of a series of concrete decisions made by Israel's leading political actors, chiefly David Ben-Gurion. Our purpose in pointing this out is not to vilify Ben-Gurion, the person who deserves the most credit for the establishment of the State of Israel and for building a strong and successful state under very difficult conditions. Rather, our purpose is to emphasize that different choices could have been made and that a significantly more liberal democratic regime could have been established in Israel during its formative era. In particular, instead of pursuing a policy of separation and domination, the leadership of the state could have

*and the Politics of Jewish Identity: The Secular-Religious Impasse* (Baltimore: Johns Hopkins University Press, 2000).
[25] Rekhess, "Initial Israeli Policy Guidelines toward the Arab Minority, 1948–1949," 112
[26] Rekhess, ibid., 114–115

taken a more accommodating and inclusive approach to dealing with the Arab minority, as some moderates within Ben-Gurion's Mapai party and outside it suggested at the time.[27]

We have drawn attention in this chapter to Ben-Gurion's policy of separation and domination vis-à-vis the Arab minority not simply because it is of historical interest, but primarily because in our opinion this policy has been adopted, with slight variations, by successive Israeli governments (the only exception was Rabin's second government in 1992–1995). Ultimately, this policy has deepened the alienation of the Arab minority from the state and worsened relations between it and the Jewish majority. The alternative to a policy of separation and domination is one of integration and cooperation. What this policy might entail will be explored in the next chapter which looks at various options for how Israel can become a more democratic and inclusive state.

Before proceeding, however, it is important to point out a major implication of the argument that we have presented in this chapter. It is widely believed, especially among liberals and those on the left of the Israeli political spectrum, that Israel's problems began with its occupation of the West Bank, Gaza Strip, and East Jerusalem. According to this common view, until Israel conquered these territories in the war of 1967, the country was basically on the right path. Pre-1967 Israel is thus compared favorably to post-1967 Israel, with the former seen as more liberal and egalitarian, less nationalistic and chauvinistic.[28] In short, the period of 1948–1967 is often depicted and imagined as Israel's "golden age," which abruptly ended with the 1967 war and the occupation of Palestinian territories that ensued from it.

Our own view, as presented in this chapter, departs significantly from this conventional view. The Israeli regime that was established in 1948 and developed in the early years of the state was not at all liberal and egalitarian in its approach to its Arab citizens. On the contrary, for many years it governed them by harsh and draconian means, in a manner that resembled Israel's subsequent occupation of the West Bank and Gaza. Thus, while Israel's post-1967 Occupation undoubtedly undermines its democratic credentials, these credentials were shaky from the outset of statehood. The Jewish Republic that emerged in pre-1967 Israel was by no means a liberal democracy. Jewish ethno-nationalism was a dominant

---

[27] See Peretz, "Early State Policy toward the Arab-Population," 82–102; see also Rekhess, "Initial Israeli Policy Guidelines toward the Arab Minority," 103–119.

[28] See, for instance, Peter Medding, *The Founding of Israeli Democracy, 1949–1967* (Oxford & New York: Oxford University Press, 1990), 226.

force from 1948–1967, just as it has been since 1967. If anything, what we have witnessed since 1967 (e.g., the Occupation, the state-supported settlement project, and the political rise of the nationalist Right) has been the more overt expression of tendencies that were already evident in Israel during its formative era.

# 6

# Alternatives to Ethnic Hegemony

We can only hope to "manage," not to solve, conflicts arising from ethnocultural diversity. People who seek a "Solution" to ethnocultural conflicts are either hopelessly idealistic or murderously genocidal.

Will Kymlicka, Canadian political philosopher[1]

Bringing about a significant improvement in Jewish-Palestinian relations in Israel will not be easy. What can we learn from the experience of other countries where ethnic conflict is prevalent? This is the central question addressed by this chapter. In gaining insight into the Jewish-Palestinian conflict inside Israel and ways of better managing it, it is important to look at it comparatively, that is, to analyze this conflict as part and parcel of a large class of ethno-national conflicts in today's world. Although the Jewish-Palestinian conflict inside Israel might be different from other ethnic conflicts in certain respects (as every conflict is), it is surely not unique. Some analysts have an inclination to describe Israel, including majority-minority relations within it, as entirely unique. Contrary to this view, we believe that it is useful to view majority-minority relations in Israel, and ways of improving them, through a comparative lens.[2] We also believe that it is important to take a modest view with regard to the

---

[1] Will Kymlicka, *Finding Our Way: Rethinking Ethnocultural Relations in Canada*, (Oxford: Oxford University Press, 1998), 3.

[2] One of the best volumes dealing with the issue of Israel's uniqueness is Michael N. Barnett, ed., *Israel in a Comparative Perspective: Challenging the Conventional Wisdom* (Albany: State University of New York Press, 1996); especially useful is Barnett's introductory chapter titled "The Politics of Uniqueness: The Status of the Israeli Case," 3–28.

possibilities for improving inter-ethnic relations, realizing the limits of any possible "solution."[3]

This chapter, therefore, adopts a comparative approach, reviewing the different ways in which a variety of states deal with their majority-minority problems. Charged and even violent inter-ethnic conflicts are common in many polities. It is instructive to look at their experience and especially useful to identify cases and techniques in which ethnic conflicts have been dealt with effectively or in which ethnic tensions have been significantly reduced through political intervention. Thus, this chapter will identify several alternative models for dealing with conflict between majorities and minorities, including liberal democracy (based on equality among individuals), bi-nationalism (promoting equality among different ethno-national groups), and power-sharing governmental designs (including consociationalism or centralized power sharing, federalism, and territorial or functional autonomy). The pros and cons of each regime type will be analyzed in terms of several criteria, particularly their capacity to achieve normative goals such as equality, justice, and democracy; establish political stability; and gain international and domestic legitimacy. Looking at ethno-national conflict within a comparative framework will assist us in formulating recommendations for Israel and assessing the likelihood of Israel moving from hegemony to equality, both of which we will do in subsequent chapters.

## The Universality of Ethno-National Conflict

Like Israel, the vast majority of states in the contemporary world are ethnically mixed. These states may function within deeply divided societies in which different groups within the population view themselves, and are usually perceived by others within the society, as different in some fundamental way from other groups with whom they share the same political space. Put differently, in a large number of political systems one finds different "identity groups" competing with one another in the same political arena. This is an almost universal phenomenon in the contemporary world. The sources of the differences between identity groups are diverse – history and origins (imagined or real), language and religion,

---

[3] In general, democratic regimes have an inherent advantage in bringing about significant improvement in inter-ethnic relations, but their success cannot be guaranteed in a situation of sustained conflict in a deeply divided society.

race and culture, and narratives and mythology. Whatever the particular source of the difference, what is important politically is that both individuals and social groups have a deep sense of being unlike others with whom they share membership in the same society and citizenship in the same state. They often adopt toward those others an "us versus them" attitude.[4]

This reality is often a source of conflict within the political system, whatever its form. Thus, for example, both authoritarian and democratic regimes are likely to experience civil strife between identity groups if they function within the context of a deeply divided society. Ethnic conflict existed in Saddam Hussein's dictatorial Iraq and in today's authoritarian China, but it has also been in full force in newer democracies such as Slovakia following the Czechoslovak Velvet Divorce and the Baltic states, as well as within well-established democracies such as Canada or Belgium. Social divisions usually prevail despite democratic institutions. In fact, multi-national democracies, even more so than multi-national non-democracies, are often torn between the requirements of unity and homogeneity, on the one hand, and the reality of their own social diversity, on the other hand.[5] This is the reality faced by Israel today.

The key political factor in all deeply divided societies is the role of the state and its ability to successfully manage the forces of unity and diversity. Particularly important is the state's ability to prevent conflict between various ethnic groups from escalating to violent bloodshed. The more powerful nationalism is within a given multi-national state, the more difficult it is for the state to act as an effective, successful regulator of internal ethnic conflict. If individuals have supreme loyalty to their ethno-national group, and if this nation is but one component in a larger multi-national state, severe internal conflict between that nation and other nations within the state is almost inevitable. There is good reason, therefore, for deep pessimism with regard to the possibility of civic peace in an intensely nationalistic multi-ethnic environment.

Some scholars defend on normative grounds the model of nationalism in which nation and state coincide.[6] They argue that in a multi-ethnic

---

[4] Giovanni Sartori, "Understanding Pluralism," *Journal of Democracy*, Vol. 8, No. 4 (1997), 58–69, emphasizes this psychological aspect of the political process.

[5] Charles Taylor, "Foreword," in Alain-G. Gagnon and James Tully, eds., *Multinational Democracies* (Cambridge and New York: Cambridge University Press, 2001), xiii.

[6] Among those who support such a position are the Israeli scholar and politician Yael Tamir, *Liberal Nationalism* (Princeton, NJ: Princeton University Press, 1993); David Miller, *On Nationality* (Oxford: Clarendon Press, 1995).

society it is important to emphasize the unity of the state rather than emphasize its diversity lest diversity leads to conflict, that the majority has a right to define the character of the state, and that granting different groups collective rights negates the principle of equality before the law.[7] The reality of numerous contemporary societies (including Israel's), however, is that they are already deeply divided and their divisions are unlikely to disappear in the foreseeable future. Emphasizing unity and negating diversity under such circumstances is unlikely to promote ethnic accommodation; on the contrary, it is likely to be viewed by members of the minority as an attempt to assimilate them or ignore their demands.[8]

Whereas the majority in deeply divided societies should indeed enjoy the right to define the overall character of the state, the minority has a right to participate in the process through which this definition is made especially if it is a sizeable, distinct, and indigenous minority.[9] Moreover, the Canadian political theorist Will Kymlicka has made a strong argument that granting collective rights to minorities does not negate the democratic principle of equality before the law (that is, classical liberalism).[10] In fact, Kymlicka views "group-specific rights" as entirely consistent with liberalism. Like Kymlicka, we believe that liberal rights for individuals are necessary but insufficient for a just and stable order in deeply divided societies, and that collective rights for sizeable and distinct identity groups are also necessary.

Most contemporary conflicts in the world today are internal. By some counts, only about 10 percent of all contemporary conflicts in the world are international. Very few conflicts are classical interstate wars.[11] Hence, most analysts believe that "ethnic conflict has become today's most

---

[7] Among some of the most profound thinkers of that position, essentially liberal democratic, are Brian Barry, *Culture and Equality: An Egalitarian Critique of Multiculturalism* (Cambridge, MA: Harvard University Press, 2001); and Claus Offe, "Political Liberalism, Group Rights, and the Politics of Fear and Trust," *Hagar*, Vol. 3, No. 1 (2002), 3–17.

[8] On the Israeli and Turkish cases, see Ilan Peleg and Dov Waxman, "Losing Control? A Comparison of Majority-Minority Relations in Israel and Turkey," *Nationalism and Ethnic Politics*, Vol. 13, No. 3, (2007), 431–463.

[9] See Amal Jamal, "Collective Rights for Indigenous Minorities: Theoretical and Normative Aspects," in Elie Rekhess and Sarah Osacky-Lazar, eds., *The Status of the Arab Minority in the Jewish Nation State* (Tel Aviv: Tel Aviv University, 2005), 27–44. We share the view that an indigenous minority has more rights than an immigrant minority.

[10] Will Kymlicka, *Multicultural Citizenship: A Liberal Theory of Minority Rights* (Oxford: Oxford University Press, 1995).

[11] Pauline H. Baker, "Conflict Resolution Versus Democratic Governance: Divergent Paths to Peace?" in Chester A. Crocker and Fen Osler Hampson, with Pamela Aall, eds., *Managing Global Chaos* (Washington, DC: USIP Press, 1996), 563–571.

pervasive and dangerous expression of organized strife."[12] Most of these
ethnic conflicts stem from the drive of the majority ethnic group to dominate an ethnic minority. The ethnic majority's hegemonic behavior – its
desire to dominate other group(s) – is often the primary cause of ethnic conflict. Byman and Van Evera have identified a long list of conflicts
resulting from what they call "communal hegemonism."[13] They found
that of thirty-seven conflicts between the fall of the Berlin Wall (1989)
and 1996, no less than twenty-five conflicts resulted from a clash between
a hegemonic ethnic groups and other groups.[14] The conflict between Jews
and Palestinians within Israel fits this general pattern.

### Managing Ethnic Difference: Accommodation or Exclusion?

It is useful to distinguish between two different strategies that a state
might take toward the different ethno-national groups residing within it.
An exclusivist strategy is aimed at promoting the interests of the dominant ethno-national group and ignores or even suppresses the interests of
other ethno-national groups. It privileges one ethno-national group over
all others, often by making its preferential status a permanent feature of
the polity and establishing multiple institutions in order to perpetuate its
dominance. The state strives by all the means at its disposal to maintain
and even enhance the dominance of one ethno-national group. The state
essentially becomes the tool of the dominant ethno-national group. The
assumption is that the state belongs exclusively to the dominant ethno-
national group and that other groups have an inherently lesser status
in it. The state is certainly not a neutral zone for political competition,
including inter-ethnic competition, that it is envisioned to be in liberal
democratic states.

Unlike an exclusivist strategy, an accommodationist strategy tries to
harmonize relations between the different ethno-national groups by seeking at least partial satisfaction of all their interests. Although an accommodationist strategy might strive for integration and unity as a way
of establishing a stable political order, it does so through institutional
arrangements that reflect the interests of various ethno-national groups.
The key is that for the state to be accommodationist it must recognize its

---

[12] Airat R. Aklaev, *Democratizing and Ethnic Peace: Patterns of Ethnopolitical Crisis Management in Post-Soviet Settings* (Aldershot, UK: Ashgate, 1999).
[13] Ibid., esp. Table 4, p. 23.
[14] Daniel Byman and Stephen Van Evera, "Why They Fight: Hypotheses on the Causes of Contemporary Deadly Conflict," *Security Studies*, Vol. 7, No. 3 (1998), 1–50.

various ethno-national groups as legitimate and be genuinely sympathetic to ethnic diversity within it.[15] Ethnic diversity is typically accommodated in one of two ways. Either the state explicitly recognizes ethnic differences and caters to them, or it deliberately ignores ethnic differences.[16] The latter approach has been adopted in "Jacobin democracies" (such as France) where even the mere existence of ethnic groups is denied,[17] and in "libertarian democracies" (such as the United States) where ethnicity is socially recognized and legally tolerated[18] but politically not emphasized or even marginalized.

An accommodationist strategy is inherently more democratic than an exclusivist one, although exclusivism could always be defended (and often has been defended) as democratic by insisting that it implements the principle of majority rule and denies special rights for minorities. In deeply divided societies, accommodationism can be successful if it can demonstrate that it is ethically more just and politically more stable than exclusionism and if it can establish effective mechanisms for resolving ethnic conflict through democratic and peaceful means. An exclusivist strategy is not only democratically flawed but also unjust and unstable, particularly in the contemporary world. The denial of the legitimacy and possibly the very existence of an ethnic minority[19] is hardly a recipe for democracy, justice, or stability. An exclusivist strategy can lead states down the path of coercion, forced assimilation, and even population transfer and other forms of ethnic cleansing.

Despite the sharp distinction drawn here between exclusivist and accommodationist strategies, many states may well pursue both strategies at different times and to varying degrees.[20] States often pursue a mixture of exclusivist and accommodationist policies simultaneously. In the United States, for instance, liberalism (an accommodationist strategy)

---

[15] William Safran, "Non-Separatist Policies Regarding Ethnic Minorities: Positive Approaches & Ambiguous Consequences," *International Political Science Review*, Vol. 15, No. 1 (1994), 61–80.

[16] A. C. Van der Berghe, "Protection of Ethnic Minorities: A Critical Appraisal," in R. G. Wirsing, ed., *Protection of Ethnic Minorities: Comparative Analysis* (Oxford: Pergamon Press, 1981), 343–355.

[17] Note in this context the unsympathetic position of France toward the issue of recognizing minorities within the European Union.

[18] As, for example, in deducting financial contributions to ethnic or religious institutions.

[19] Examples include the dismissal of Breton identity as "folkloric" in France, the suppression of Kurdish identity in Turkey, denying the Hungarianess of most Transylvanians in Romania, and so forth.

[20] John Coakley, "The Resolution of Ethnic Conflict: Toward a Typology," *International Political Science Review*, Vol. 13, No. 4 (1992), 343–368 (esp. 345).

has coexisted with the more exclusivist "republicanism" and the thoroughly hegemonic ethno-centrism for generations.[21] Similar forces have been in competition within other polities, including Israel.[22] Nevertheless, the distinction is an important one because it helps us to think about how a state can change its policies toward the ethno-national groups within it. We can identify cases in which states have become more accommodationist (the United States, for example, over the last five decades or so) and cases in which states have moved in the opposite direction and become more exclusivist (e.g., Sri Lanka).[23]

In comparing accommodationist strategies to exclusivist ones, it is important to realize that regardless of its specific institutional arrangements, accommodationism is based on two fundamental ideas. First, accommodationism is based on the belief that social problems (including ethnic conflicts) can significantly benefit from "political engineering,"[24] the belief that a regime in a multi-ethnic society has to actively encourage moderation and try to control the destructive ethnic forces in the polity. Second, accommodationism is based on the belief in human equality as the foundation for the political order; it is deeply democratic. Whereas exclusivism upholds the superiority of one ethnic group over all other ethnic groups – due to its numerical advantage, historical rights, or even greater intrinsic worth – accommodationism upholds equality as a supreme value and a desired goal.

## Individual-Based and Group-Based Approaches to Ethnic Accommodation

There are many means of accommodating ethnic differences (see Figure 6.1). For analytical reasons, and for the purpose of identifying concrete

[21] Rogers M. Smith, "The 'American Creed' and the American Identity: The Limits of Liberal Citizenship in the United States," *Western Political Quarterly*, Vol. 41, No. 2 (June 1988), 225–251.

[22] Gershon Shafir and Yoav Peled, *Being Israeli: The Dynamics of Multiple Citizenship* (Cambridge: Cambridge University Press, 2002).

[23] R. N. Kearney, "Ethnic Conflict and the Tamil Separatist Movement in Sri Lanka," *Asian Survey*, Vol. 25, No. 9, 898–917; Neil DeVotta, "From Ethnic Outbidding to Ethnic Conflict: The Institutional Bases for Sri Lanka's Separatist War," *Nations and Nationalism*, Vol. 11, No. 1 (2005), 141–159.

[24] Giovanni Sartori, "Political Development and Political Engineering," *Public Policy*, Vol. 17 (1968), 261–298; and Peter H. Russell, "The Politics of Mega-Constitutional Change: Lessons for Canada," in Bertus de Villers, ed., *Evaluating Federal Systems* (Dordrecht: Juta & Co., 1994), 30–40.

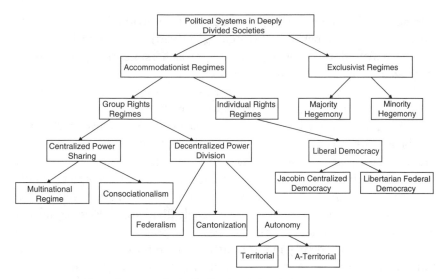

FIGURE 6.1. Classification of ethnically divided polities.

policies, it is useful to make a fundamental distinction between individual-based and group-based approaches to ethnic accommodation. An
individual-based approach is often referred to as "liberal democracy," or
simply as a "liberal" approach. It focuses on the rights of individuals and
treats social divisions – ethnic, religious, and so forth – as private matters
that ought not to be politicized, and hence they are not recognized by
the state. Liberal democrats prefer to de-emphasize ethnicity and instead
promote civic identities. In contrast to this, the group-based approach to
ethnic accommodation starts with the assumption that in deeply divided
societies, publicly recognizing different identities and granting representation to them is essential for achieving justice, equality, and stability.

In general, it is significantly easier for a dominant ethno-national group
to support an individual-based approach than a group-based one, although
some combination of the two is necessary for a long-term solution to
most ethno-national conflicts. There is likely to be much more opposition
to a group-based approach than to an individual-based approach from
members of the dominant ethno-national group because a group-based
approach, by definition, limits the power of the majority, whereas if the
majority group is truly dominant demographically, socially, economically,
and politically, it can sustain (or believe it can sustain) its power even if
a full-fledged, liberal democracy is established. Whereas substantial collective rights for a minority might well be viewed as endangering the very

essence of a hegemonic, ethno-national polity, individual rights are likely to be viewed as much less threatening. Nevertheless, some hegemonic polities have adopted a group-based approach as a strategy for conflict management and conflict reduction.

In the ongoing debate between liberals and group-rights advocates, the former argue that giving rights to groups "might lock in divisive national identities, unnecessarily heightening distrust between groups."[25] The problem with this is that ethno-national identities might already dominate a society and, if they do, then they need to be taken into account politically. Efforts to depoliticize ethnic identities are unlikely to be totally effective.[26] The more divided a society is, the less satisfactory individual-based, liberal democracy might be. In deeply divided societies, significant group rights are necessary for social peace and political stability. Although "pure" liberal democracy might be attractive on normative grounds, it is often problematic in practice because it might camouflage what is in reality the domination of the majority over the minority and particularly the privileged status of the majority in determining the polity's public life. Thus, the language, culture, and religion of the majority often dominate the public sphere. Hence, although an individual-based regime might be attractive to the dominant ethnic group within a society, it often does not meet the needs and interests of minorities.

Whereas group rights seem to be essential in managing inter-ethnic relations in deeply divided societies (such as Israel's), it is still useful to briefly examine individual rights regimes. Within such regimes, an important theoretical distinction ought to be introduced. The distinction is between liberal (or libertarian) democracy and Jacobin democracy. Among the fundamental ideas of liberal democracy are majority rule via periodic elections, the equality of individual citizens before the law, and the protection of fundamental freedoms via well-defined legal means. The state is presumed to be neutral in dealing with all distinct groups. Although collective rights are not granted to distinct groups in a liberal democracy, symbolic rights are often given to the dominant group even in liberal democracies: Official status is granted to the national church and the majority's language, flags might display religious symbols (most

---

[25] Jack Snyder, *From Voting to Violence: Democratization and National Conflict* (New York: W. W. Norton, 2000), 33.

[26] For such institutional arrangements, see Donald L. Horowitz, "Making Moderation Pay," in Joseph Monteville, ed., *Conflict and Peacemaking in Multiethnic Societies* (Lanham, MD: Lexington Books, 1991), 451–476.

often the Christian cross), anthems celebrate the history of the dominant group, and so forth.

Deviations from this "ideal type" of liberal democracy occur in a variety of cases. It includes special rights for minorities in the United States, where past discrimination is addressed through so-called affirmative action programs and where relations with Native Americans are regulated through agreements between the federal government and the Indian tribes. Other cases of special group rights in liberal democracies are found in New Zealand where the Maoris are recognized and even get parliamentary representation as a group, in the case of the status of Aborigines in Australia, in the policies toward the Swedish minority in Finland, or even in the status of Jews in post-War Germany.[27] These examples demonstrate that even in a liberal democracy there is a way to recognize some group rights. Whereas the "spirit" of a liberal democracy is to maximize individual rights, the reality of a deeply divided society (New Zealand), past discrimination (United States), cultural diversity (Canada), and other factors brings about compromises in which groups of people are recognized and granted special rights as groups while the overall character of the state, as protector of individual rights, is still maintained intact. This is highly relevant for the Israeli case.

The second individual-based model can be called the Jacobin model. As the name indicates, this model has its historical origins in the French Revolution,[28] in the notion of citizenship it developed, and in its impact on other countries.[29] Like liberal democracy, the Jacobin model is based on granting extensive rights to all citizens, but it differs from liberal democracy in taking a militant approach against ethnic groups and through its strong promotion of cultural uniformity and social homogeneity. The Jacobin model, therefore, emphasizes the enhancement of a unified national culture and language. In an already deeply divided society, in which divergent identities and conflicting interests are well established, Jacobinism might amount to the tyranny of the majority while completely

---

[27] A great source for the enumeration of special group rights in a variety of countries is Alexander Yakobson and Amnon Rubinstein, *Israel and the Family of Nations: The Jewish Nation-States and Human Rights* (New York: Routledge, 2009); an earlier version of this book appeared in Hebrew.

[28] Sudir Hazareesingh, ed., *The Jacobin Legacy in Modern France: Essays in Honor of Vincent Wright* (Oxford and New York: Oxford University Press, 2002).

[29] The French model was adopted, for example, by Italy after its unification, by Spain in the nineteenth century (despite the diversity of its peoples), by Ataturk's Turkey, and by many other countries.

ignoring or consciously marginalizing the existence of a distinct minority. Liberal democracy, on the other hand, may make serious inroads toward improving majority-minority relations by insisting on complete and constitutionally protected equality among individuals while augmenting it with significant group rights.

We believe that the best solution for long-term ethnic conflict lies in combining individual rights and group rights, especially for distinct, indigenous groups. In resolving ethnic conflict by combining individual and collective rights, it may be advisable to emphasize the primacy of liberal democracy and its fundamental principles but at the same time provide substantial group rights. The two approaches do not contradict one another; in fact they complement one another rather well, particularly in a deeply divided society. The deeper the divide in a society, the more individual rights are inadequate and the more group rights are needed to guarantee justice and peace.

Whereas ensuring individual rights is relatively straightforward – every citizen has an equal status to that of every other citizen – providing group rights is much more complex because one has to decide which groups within an existing polity deserve special recognition, let alone representation and even self-government. Which groups are to be privileged and on what grounds? To answer this crucial question, Will Kymlicka distinguishes between two kinds of minorities – a "polyethnic" or immigrant minority and a national minority, which he also calls "national groups" or "minority nations" (in using the word "nation" to describe non-immigrant minorities, Kymlicka emphasizes the indigenous nature of such minorities and clearly differentiates them from immigrant groups).[30] Kymlicka argues that national minorities deserve more rights than immigrant groups; in other words, that they deserve to be more accommodated by the majority.[31] We share this view both as a general proposition and in relation to Israel specifically.[32] But what specific collective rights should such groups enjoy? This, too, is unclear. The specific rights that indigenous peoples and national minorities should enjoy are, for the most part, ill-defined or even completely undefined. There is certainly no universal agreement on the precise rights these groups are entitled to.

[30]  Kymlicka, *Multicultural Citizenship*, 9.
[31]  Kymlicka provides five conditions for recognizing a group as a national minority: It must be present at the founding of the state; it must have a prior history of self-government; it must have a common culture; it must have a common language; and it must govern itself through institutions. See Kymlicka, *Multicultural Citizenship*.
[32]  For a similar view, see Jamal, "Collective Rights for Indigenous Minorities."

### Power Sharing versus Power Division

All group-rights regimes can be thought of as polities that establish mechanisms in order to restrain the power of the dominant group within society. The purpose is to create a more just and stable socio-political order. In deeply divided societies, group-based solutions might become highly attractive if in their absence ethnic conflict is present or highly probable. The relevance to Israel of a group-based approach to ethnic accommodation requires an extended analysis of such an approach.

When focusing on group-based rights, it is useful to distinguish between two alternative methods, power sharing and power division (see Figure 6.1). Power sharing is a solution in which distinct ethnic groups (often a majority and a minority) cooperate in running the central government via the membership of major ethnic parties in the central government or by other means. Power division is a design for the distribution of power emphasizing the avoidance of centralized and intense cooperation on a day-to-day basis between rival groups and their leaders. Whereas power sharing requires a higher level of trust among leaders of different ethno-national groups or at least their ability to work together through political coalitions, power division demands less trust and cooperative ability beyond the stage of agreeing on such division and, possibly, reviewing it from time to time. At the same time, both governmental modes are designed to solve ethnic problems in an accommodationist manner.

Power sharing often reflects a relatively even distribution of power among rival groups or, at least, a situation in which all groups participating in the governmental arrangement have substantial resources at their disposal. Examples for significant power sharing include Belgium and Northern Ireland. Power division typifies a situation in which there is a single dominant "nation" that grants considerably weaker but clearly distinct ethnic groups certain rights. Canada, Switzerland, and Spain are good examples for power division where weaker groups receive certain rights in their ancestral territories or even beyond them.

In reality, power sharing and power division may be and often are practiced simultaneously. A distinct minority, for example, might be guaranteed a measure of power in centralized institutions (e.g., positions in the governmental bureaucracy), which is a power-sharing technique, but also educational autonomy, a power-division method. Yet, for analytical reasons, it might be useful to keep this distinction in mind. Both techniques for accommodationism might be applicable in the case of Israel.

Power-sharing solutions include the establishment of a full-fledged multi-national regime (including bi-nationalism) and what has been called "consociationalism" (a concept developed by Arend Lijphart). Power sharing could be equal and extensive or less than equal and limited to certain areas. The level of power sharing in a multi-national state (such as a bi-national state) is complete and total between the ethno-national groups within the state. A consociational regime, however, might involve a more modest level of power sharing. In general, establishing true multi-nationality in today's world is extremely difficult. In a multi- or bi-national regime, the state belongs, on an equal basis, to two or more nations. This idea contradicts the self-perception of most countries in the contemporary world (including Israel).

Consociationalism typically involves such provisions as the creation of grand coalitions that guarantee joint control by different groups of the executive branch of government (including the policy-making cabinet), proportional representation to the different groups throughout the public sector (including the elected parliament, the civil service, and the budgetary allocations), substantial autonomy and self-government for ethnic communities, and constitutional veto power for the minority.[33] Whatever the specific arrangements, the essence of consociationalism is for a country to cope with its internal divisions and conflicts through "the politics of accommodation and reconciliation between the different ethnic groups."[34] The political solutions contained in Northern Ireland's Good Friday agreement of 1998, for example, were directly inspired by consociationalism.[35]

Full-fledged consociationalism is extremely hard to achieve in practice, particularly in a polity dominated by one ethnic group that is engaged in an active conflict with another ethnic group. Consociationalism is also normatively problematic because by giving the minority a veto power over public policy it negates majority rule, one of the most important of all democratic principles. Many liberal democrats view it as simply

---

[33] Among Arend Lijphart's numerous publications on consociationalism are *Democracies: Patterns of Majoritarian and Consensus Government in Twenty-One Countries* (New Haven, CT: Yale University Press, 1984), and *Democracy in Plural Societies: A Comparative Exploration* (New Haven, CT: Yale University Press, 1997).

[34] Sammy Smooha and Theodor Hanf, "The Diverse Mode of Conflict-Regulation in Deeply Divided Societies," *International Journal of Comparative Sociology*, Vol. 33, No. 1–2 (1992), 26–47 (quote is from p. 33).

[35] Brendan O'Leary, "The Nature of the British-Irish Agreement," *New Left Review* 233 (1999), 66–96; Brendan O'Leary, "The Protection of Human Rights under the Belfast Agreement," *Political Quarterly*, Vol. 72, No. 3 (July–September, 2001), 353–365.

"reinforcing and entrenching ethnicity in the political system"[36] and as an undemocratic model for conflict management.[37] Thus, although consociationalism might be useful and attractive on utilitarian grounds, it is democratically flawed. Despite these problems with consociationalism, there are some elements that could be positive and are easier to justify on normative grounds. Those elements amount to what can be regarded as "soft consociationalism." This might involve including members of the minority and their political parties in the government, and members of the minority could be actively recruited for positions within the public sector in an effort to enhance their presence and representation on the national scene. Autonomy and self-government could also be enhanced in certain areas such as education, language, and culture. Although these initiatives do not amount to full-fledged consociationalism, they may still blunt the sharper edges of an ethno-national conflict.

Although consociationalism might be problematic, especially in its full-fledged version, in some polities where conflict is prevalent, there might be "a simple choice between creating consociational democratic institutions or having no democracy at all."[38] Consociationalism is clearly preferable to the continuation of massive violence or to the perpetuation of hegemonic control.

In general, although consociationalism might work in a demographically balanced ethno-national situation, such as Belgium or Northern Ireland, it is unlikely to work in countries where one group enjoys a clear demographic and political advantage. Canada, Estonia, Israel, Slovakia, Spain, and Sri Lanka are some examples. In all of these situations, the dominant group is unlikely to share power in an equal manner (that is, agree to a hard form of consociationalism); although in the interest of stability, it might agree to some form of limited power sharing. Thus, hard consociationalism is possible only under certain conditions: a relatively mild conflict, a situation in which the main ethno-national struggle has already been settled in favor of the dominant group, rough equality between the parties, truly extraordinary leaders on both sides of the ethnic divide, and so forth. This combination, facilitating full-fledged consociationalism, is hard to achieve. In most hegemonic orders, built on

---

[36] Timothy Sisk, *Power Sharing and International Mediation in Ethnic Conflict* (Washington, DC, USIP Press, 1996), 39.

[37] Brian Barry, "Review Article: Political Accommodation and Consociational Democracy," *British Journal of Political Science*, Vol. 5, 4 (October 1975), 477–505.

[38] John McGarry and Brendan O'Leary eds., *The Politics of Ethnic Conflict Regulation* (London and New York: Routledge, 1993), 36.

huge differentials of power between majorities and minorities and serious inter-ethnic hostility, the likelihood of hard consociationalism is low.[39]

A quick look at some actual cases demonstrates the limits of consociationalism. Over the last several decades, a few consociational arrangements (Czechoslovakia, Cyprus, and Lebanon) have collapsed,[40] and others (Belgium[41]) have moved from consociationalism to federalism, or from "power sharing" to "power division" in our language. Only Northern Ireland has moved in a consociational direction, and the Northern Irish situation is quite unique – it is not an independent state but part of the United Kingdom; the "mother countries" of the battling minorities (the United Kingdom and the Republic of Ireland) pushed hard for a political settlement, and the demographic situation became more balanced. No independent, sovereign state that could be described as hegemonic has moved in a genuinely consociational direction over the last several decades. In an era of greater public involvement in politics, "hard consociationalism," requiring agreements between leading elites, is even less likely than before. Grassroots pressures often push leaders toward uncompromising positions rather than toward quiet, behind-the-scenes, pragmatic deals with ethno-national rivals that is the essence of hard consociationalism. Thus, the chances of successfully maintaining an effective genuine power-sharing arrangement (that is, one in which two parties or more have veto power over changes) are low today.

Another group-rights regime is multi-nationalism, and specifically bi-nationalism. Multi-nationalism could be looked on as a form of radical consociationalism, an entirely egalitarian power sharing from a nationalist perspective. In this regime type, one or two nations share power on a completely equal basis, at least theoretically. Examples include the old Austro-Hungarian Empire after 1867, Czechoslovakia following World

---

[39] Genuine consociationalism in Israel is limited to the relationships between Jewish groups, particularly Orthodox and secular ones: See Asher Cohen and Bernard Susser, "From Accommodation to Decision: The Transformation of Israel's Religio-Political Life," *Journal of State and Church*, Vol. 38, No. 4 (1996), 817–839; and Eliezer Don-Yehiya, *Religion and Political Accommodation in Israel* (Jerusalem: The Floersheimer Institute for Policy Studies, 1999).

[40] On the case of Czechoslovakia, see Ilan Peleg, *Democratizing the Hegemonic State: Political Transformation in the Age of Identity* (Cambridge: Cambridge University Press, 2007), especially 139–145; on the case of Cyprus, see Peleg, *Democratizing the Hegemonic State*, especially 145–153.

[41] On changes in the Belgian case, see Liesbet Hooghe, "Belgium: From Regionalism to Federalism," in John Coakley, ed., *The Territorial Management of Ethnic Conflict* (London: Frank Cass, 1993), 44–68.

War I and then World War II, and modern Belgium.[42] Bi-nationalism rarely works in reality. It contradicts the very nature of the modern nation state; it is the precise opposite of the nation state. In a country with a clear ethno-national majority and an already existing majority-minority conflict, bi-nationalism is unlikely to be accepted by the majority group; and if it is somehow adopted or enforced, it is likely to result in great instability. Therefore, there are practically no good examples of successful bi-national regimes in the world today.

In addition to the power-sharing mechanisms that are available for easing inter-ethnic conflicts, there are several power-division mechanisms. Power division includes solutions such as federalism and autonomy. In general, power-division regimes in multi-ethnic societies seem to have a better chance of success than power-sharing regimes. In fact, the poor track record of power sharing might serve as an indirect endorsement for power division in situations where group rights, in addition to individual rights, are necessary.

One power-division regime that has gained popularity in recent decades is federalism. The fundamental idea behind federalism is the division of power between the central government (where presumably the dominant ethno-national group leads) and the territorial units of the state (units that often represent distinct history, religion, and ethnicity). The territorial units allow diversity to come to fuller expression, balancing the centralized dominance of the state as a whole. The most important question is whether a federal solution is likely to resolve an internal ethnic conflict in a way that will achieve justice, stability, and democracy or at least enhance those values in a significant manner.

In theory, federalism might be perceived positively as a way of recognizing diversity,[43] combining unity and diversity in multi-ethnic polities, and trying to maintain the integrity of the state while recognizing its ethnic components. Federalism might give ethnic minorities a measure of protection against majoritarian arbitrariness through the use of constitutional means (such as constitutional provisions that cannot be changed by simple majorities). Federalism can be especially useful if a minority ethnic group resides in a particular and well-defined region (presumably the minority's ancestral homeland) rather than being spread around the entire territory of the state, if granting federal rights is judged by the

---

[42] Hooghe, *Belgium.*
[43] Enric Fossas, "National Plurality and Equality," in Ferran Requejo, ed., *Democracy and National Pluralism* (New York: Routledge, 2001), 64–83.

minority to satisfy its demands, and if the majority does not view the federal arrangement as a prelude to secession or an invitation to separatism. However, a federal solution requires, as a pre-condition, the absence of a total breakdown in majority-minority relations or highly tense and hostile relations between the majority and minority; otherwise the dominant majority is unlikely to allow it.

In situations where full-fledged, ethnically based federalism is not possible (that is, in most of the cases in today's world, including Israel) semi-federalist arrangements are more likely and more promising.[44] So is devolution, or "devolutionary federalism,"[45] a process in which powers are systematically transferred from the center to the constituent governmental units, as has happened in such countries as Spain and the United Kingdom. Semi-federalism and devolution have the advantage of recognizing the national or ethnic uniqueness of certain areas, such as the Basques Country and Catalonia in Spain or Scotland and Wales in the UK, while leaving ultimate power in the hands of the central government, thus assuring the majority that separatist moves by the minority can be halted or reversed (although this will probably not be enough to win the support of nationalists within the majority for whom any recognition of minority rights, particularly with a territorial component, is an ideological anathema).

Most countries with a dominant ethno-national group and an active conflict with a restive minority are unlikely to look kindly on robust federalism. Federalism is especially unattractive in bi-national societies, where there are long-term inter-ethnic disputes. If Belgium disintegrates, it could be the final nail in the coffin for the ethnically based federal design in its bi-national application. Although ethno-federalism might be easier when there are more than two groups, there are few if any of these cases.

In theory, in order for ethno-territorial federalism to be effective as a mechanism for solving ethnic conflict it must be based on the principle that the federal agreement cannot be changed without the mutual consent of both the center (representing the state and, in fact, the dominant ethno-national group) and the federal units (representing the minority groups). However, such an agreement is unlikely to be reached because

---

[44] On the case of Spain in the post-Franco era, see Luis Moreno, *The Federalization of Spain* (London: Frank Cass, 2001).

[45] Koen Lenaerts, "Constitutionalism and the Many Faces of Federalism," *American Journal of Comparative Law*, Vol. 38, 1 (1996), 205–263.

the dominant ethno-national group is likely to view it as extremely dangerous and threatening.

The major problem with federalism in a multi-ethnic state is that such federalism can easily lead to the evolvement of a separatist movement and eventually to secession. Once an ethnic unit is created within a polity it could become, even if it is not intended to become, a focal point of conflict and finally withdrawal from the union. Such withdrawal might result in war. The history of post–Cold War Czechoslovakia, the Soviet Union, and Yugoslavia point out the difficulties of sustaining any kind of ethno-territorial federalism, particularly in the absence of a centralized, authoritarian government. In an era of nationalism, the political dynamics in any ethnically based federal system may push the polity toward dismemberment. This could be the situation especially if an ethnic minority feels underrepresented at the federal level, economically exploited by the center, and underappreciated as a distinct ethno-national group within the federation.

A more successful design than federalism and potentially more promising for the Israeli case might be that of autonomy. Autonomy is a group-based design that gives a particular ethnic group or a region with an ethno-national character a measure of control over some aspects of their life.[46] Autonomy might be granted to a group on a territorial or non-territorial basis but under the full control of the state. Non-territorial autonomy is particularly attractive when members of an ethnic minority are spread out throughout the state.[47] In such a case, all individuals belonging to the ethnic minority might be given "personal autonomy," granting them specific and well-defined rights.

Autonomy is clearly distinct from other forms of group rights. Whereas consociationalism amounts to centralized power sharing among different groups, autonomy is about decentralized power division. Whereas federalism is invariably territorial, autonomy may or may not be. Whereas federalism limits the power of the central state, usually through inflexible constitutional arrangements, autonomy does not limit the power of the state to change the constitutional arrangements through legislation. So although autonomy shares with other group-rights regimes some characteristics, it also has some features that make it unique. Its attractiveness

---

[46] On autonomy, see Ruth Lapidoth, *Autonomy: Flexible Solutions to Ethnic Conflicts* (Washington, DC: United States Institute for Peace, 1996).

[47] John Coakley, "Approaches to the Resolution of Ethnic Conflict: The Strategy of Non-Territorial Autonomy," *International Political Science Review*, Vol. 15, No. 3 (1994), 217–314.

is in being a compromise between the demands of the state and its ethno-national majority (demands to be the final arbiter in issues related to the overall constitutional order) and the demands of the minority (demands to have its uniqueness recognized and institutionalized). While allowing groups to hold on to and promote their distinct identity and even exercise control (although not necessarily exclusive control) over issues of special concern to them, autonomy allows the larger entity – in effect the state and the majority – to promote their interests.[48]

Autonomy is, thus, a mechanism for dealing with competing claims. Although some analysts view autonomy as a type of consociationalism, for analytical reasons it is important to emphasize that most autonomies are focused on a division of power rather than on power sharing. Whereas consociationalism necessitates close cooperation between majorities and minorities in central government (including at the cabinet level), auton-omy facilitates avoidance (rather than cooperation) because it separates powers. At the same time, both consociationalism and autonomy imply recognition of and representation for the minority group and attention to its collective interests. Furthermore, in reality, consociationalism and autonomy can be combined.

Although autonomy might mean different things to different people, the word itself implies a step toward the recognition of the collective rights of a minority group and its members. Once autonomy is estab-lished, it could change in a variety of ways. In today's world it is likely to expand and become more robust rather than weaker. Although auton-omy cannot eliminate ethnic differences, by recognizing them formally and openly it tries to better manage them.[49] The management potential of autonomy is promising precisely because the application of the concept to different situations is elastic and flexible. Part of autonomy's flexibil-ity is in neither demanding a territorial component (a feature that could lead to secessionism) nor insisting on a permanent transfer of power from the center to the periphery. Thus, countries such as India and Spain have been using autonomy quite creatively and flexibly over the last several decades.

Proponents of the centralism that has traditionally been a feature of unitary European states are often uneasy about autonomy, but it is

---

[48] Jash Ghai, ed., *Autonomy and Ethnicity: Negotiating Competing Claims in Multiethnic States* (Cambridge & New York: Cambridge University Press, 2000), 8.

[49] For the distinction between eliminating versus managing ethnic differences, see McGarry and O'Leary, *The Politics of Ethnic Conflict Regulation*, esp. Ch. 1.

interesting to note that even some of the highly centralized counties in Europe have moved toward greater autonomy for their ethno-national regions. Since 1997, for instance, the United Kingdom, a unitary state par excellence, has undergone a process of devolution, giving recognition and powers to regions with a distinct ethno-national character (Scotland, Wales, and Northern Ireland). Spain in the post-Franco era has established a complicated system of autonomies, in the process dismantling one of the most authoritarian and centralized governmental structures in Europe. Even France, the country that gave the world the highly centralized Jacobin model, has moved toward giving Corsica more autonomy.

Despite the potential attraction of autonomy for improving majority-minority relations, like federalism it is not free of problems. There are at least four specific issues that need to be considered in establishing autonomy in any multi-ethnic society (including Israel). First, autonomy could be seen by the state and its ethnic majority as a first step toward separatism and independence on the part of the minority, particularly if autonomy is territorially based. Second, autonomy could be perceived as creating inequality among individuals and groups, because those who enjoy autonomy might have more rights than others. Third, in a situation of ethnic conflict, leaders of the majority might find it politically difficult to offer autonomy to a minority, and the existence of a militant minority may make concessions to that minority even more politically difficult. Finally, there might be legitimate concern that autonomy for one group could lead to similar claims by other groups, leading to the eventual dismemberment or significant weakening of the state.

Most of these problems, though real, can be dealt with, especially if the proposed autonomy for a particular ethnic minority is limited in scope (covering certain areas such as culture and education but not other areas such as foreign affairs and monetary matters), is non-territorial (given to persons and not to regions), and is constitutionally revocable by a legitimate process determined in advance and agreed to by the majority and the minority. Although non-territorial autonomy might not be completely satisfying for ethnic minorities, it is clearly preferable to no solution at all, a situation that leaves the ethno-national majority in complete control. Thus, we agree with John Coakley that "there is something of value in non-territorial approaches to the resolution of ethnic conflict."[50] The alternative to autonomy is often either the indefinite continuation of the hegemony of the majority or the evolvement of a separatist movement

---

[50] Coakley, "Approaches to the Resolution of Ethnic Conflict," 312.

and increased violence. Most states can learn to live with limited non-territorial autonomy, especially if the alternative is civil strife, occasional violence, and political instability.

In the final analysis, the adoption and implementation of autonomy is a function of its attractiveness in comparison to other minority-recognition schemes. In the case of autonomy, it is useful to compare it to two alternative governmental designs, consociationalism and federalism. From the perspective of the state and the dominant ethno-national majority, autonomy is clearly preferable to the other two designs, especially in their robust versions.

## Conclusion

In examining different regimes comparatively, as we have done in this chapter, we can gain useful insights into the Israeli case. Having briefly reviewed a variety of models for managing ethnic differences, it seems to us that a group-based, power-dividing approach is the most promising one for Israel to take in managing its majority-minority relations. This is the approach that we will apply to Israel in the next chapter (Chapter 7). Whether the Israeli regime is actually capable of making a fundamental change in its approach to the Palestinian minority is a question that we will address in Chapter 8.

# 7

# Neither Ethnocracy nor Bi-nationalism

## Seeking the Middle Ground

> It is inconceivable that we will continue the way we are going, because we are not only a Jewish state, we are also a democratic state. We can't run away from it. If we really mean to be democratic, then we have to be democratic. And that may create certain challenges to the Jewish nature of the State of Israel.
>
> (Ehud Olmert, prime minister of Israel, 2006–2009)[1]

The history of Arab-Jewish relations in Israel and majority-minority relations around the world leads us to conclude that Israel's future depends on how it treats its Palestinian minority and more generally on the type of majority-minority relations it develops. Whereas many analysts tend to concentrate on Israel's "external Palestinian problem" – its relationship with the Palestinian population in the territories taken in the 1967 war – we believe that its "internal Palestinian problem" is equally serious. The goal of this chapter is to offer a comprehensive agenda for improving the way in which the internal Palestinian problem is managed.

This chapter provides a systematic program for transforming the relationship between the Jewish majority and the Palestinian minority in Israel, and through this transformation enhancing the quality of Israel's democracy and its long-term political stability. It argues that in order to significantly repair the deteriorating majority-minority relations within it, Israel needs to create a political structure and establish patterns of political behavior that are significantly more congruent with the actual nature of its society. There is a glaring incompatibility today between the

---

[1] Quoted in Bernard Avishai, *The Hebrew Republic: How Secular Democracy and Global Enterprise will Bring Israel Peace at Last* (Orlando, FL: Harcourt, 2008), 236.

bi-national nature of Israeli society and its uni-national political structure. Although Israeli society is bi-national and increasingly diverse, the
political structure of the country has remained completely uni-national,
dominated by a single national group and shaped by its internal politics. The development of a more congruent political structure is, in the
long run, in the interests of both the Jewish majority and the Palestinian
minority in Israel.

Israel's increasingly bi-national nature is clearly apparent in its demographic trends. Despite the state's persistent efforts to maintain and
enhance the Jewish majority in the country, non-Jews are already at least
a quarter of the population. There are now numerous mid-size Israeli
towns (where the population is between 5,000 and 10,000 residents) that
are mostly Arab, and the numbers of towns with larger Arab populations (more than 10,000) are growing. Arabs live side-by-side with Jews
in at least six mixed cities (Acre, Haifa, Jaffa, Lod, Ramle, and Upper
Nazareth), and many Arabs are moving into traditionally Jewish towns
such as Carmiel, Rehovot, Hadera, Nahariya, Eilat, and Beersheva. This
changing demographic reality has not been reflected in power sharing,
particularly on the national level.[2]

Given these demographic trends and the worsening state of Arab-Jewish
relations in the country, those of us concerned with ensuring a stable
future for Israel and interested in improving the quality of its democracy
ought to examine ways of transforming the Israeli political reality. This is
what we will do in this chapter. Five alternative options are available for
the State of Israel in terms of its overall approach to majority-minority
relations.[3] First, the state can try to maintain the status quo in majority-
minority relations, despite the frictions and occasional outbursts between
its two ethno-national groups. Second, the state may try to promote moderate changes toward increased democratization and equality between its
ethno-national groups, gradually dismantling the most flagrant violations
of its democratic credo but without significantly changing its character
as an essentially ethnic state. Third, the state might decide to radically
transform itself in the direction of full inclusion of the minority by moving decisively toward a liberal-democratic order or even a consociational

---

[2] For more details, see Chapter 1.

[3] Nadim Rouhana, "Israel & Its Arab Citizens: Predicaments in the Relationship between
Ethnic States and Ethnonational Minorities," *Third World Quarterly* 19, 2 (1998), 277–
296, identifies only three options: (1) maintain the status quo; (2) full integration; and (3)
full separation. We find Rouhana's conceptualization too crude; it does not capture the
full gamut of options, some of which are politically practical.

order (power sharing between its two ethno-national groups). Fourth, Israel might decide to further ethnicize itself by strengthening the hegemonic control of its Jewish majority, as has already been done over the last few years.[4] Fifth, the state may move toward a radical ethno-national structure by completely marginalizing the minority, significantly limiting its rights, or even ridding itself of its Arab citizens entirely.[5]

In one way or another, all of these options have been on the table in Israel, although not all of them have been promoted with equal ardor at all times. The perpetuation of the status quo, reflected in the definition of Israel as a "Jewish and democratic state," has been favored by the majority of Israeli Jews and by most of the country's public, political organizations, including official state organs.[6] This status quo option has enjoyed the force of inertia on its side. The second option, increased democratization and equality, has been promoted through demands for more equal distribution of budgets, increased representation in governmental positions for members of the minority, and so forth; yet, those actions have been fairly minor and cosmetic.[7] The third option, a decisive movement toward either full-fledged liberal democracy and/or group-based power sharing has not yet been tried. It is the one that we strongly endorse in this book. The fourth option, the further ethnicization of the country, has been promoted, according to our own analysis and that of others, by the state over the last few years via increased majoritarianism.[8] The last option, the radical ethnicization of Israel, has been promoted by a

---

[4] Yoav Peled, "Citizenship Betrayed: Israel's Emerging Immigration and Citizenship Regime," *Theoretical Inquiries in Law* 8, 2 (2007), 603–638; Yoav Peled & Doron Navot, "Ethnic Democracy Revisited: On the State of Democracy in the Jewish State," *Israel Studies Forum*, Vol. 20, No. 1 (2005), 3–27; Yoav Peled, "The Evolution of Israeli Citizenship: An Overview," *Citizenship Studies*, Vol. 12, No. 3 (June 2008), 335–345; Leora Bilsky, "'Speaking through the Mask': Israeli Arabs and the Changing Faces of Israeli Citizenship," *Middle East Law and Governance*, Vol. 1, No. 2 (2009), 166–209.

[5] Israeli Jewish politicians such as Meir Kahane, Effi Eitam, Avigdor Lieberman, and many others have recommended such options through the years.

[6] Ilan Peleg, "Israel between Democratic Universalism and Particularistic Judaism: Challenging a Sacred Formula," *Report to the Oxford Centre for Hebrew and Jewish Studies* (2002–2003), 5–20; Alan Dowty, "Is Israel Democratic? Substance and Semantics in the 'Ethnic Democracy' Debate," *Israel Studies*, Vol. 4, No. 2 (Fall 1999), 1–14; Ruth Gavison, "Jewish and Democratic? A Rejoinder to the 'Ethnic Democracy' Debate," *Israel Studies*, Vol. 4, No. 1 (Spring 1999), 44–72; Dafna Barak-Erez, ed., *Jewish and Democratic State* (Tel-Aviv: Tel-Aviv University Press, 1996), (Hebrew).

[7] The 2010 decision to allocate more than 800 million shekels to the "Arab sector" might signal a change in this policy.

[8] See Chapter 4 in this volume as well as Peled and Navot, "Ethnic Democracy Revisited," 3–27; and Peled, "Citizenship Betrayed," 603–638.

growing number of political figures on the right and has recently become more popular, as shown in the results of the 2009 election.[9]

Given these options, this chapter focuses on the possibility of introducing changes in Israel's political system that would transform the country from an ethnically hegemonic and therefore democratically flawed polity to a more egalitarian and inclusive democracy. We believe that such a transformation can be achieved without endangering the vital interests of Israel's Jewish majority and that, in fact, it will protect those vital interests by better integrating the minority and strengthening within it a sense of belonging to the state. In the absence of a transformation, a further deterioration of majority-minority relations in Israel seems inevitable. This is as dangerous to the interests of the majority as it is to the interests of the minority. Hence, this chapter identifies the changes that the State of Israel has to adopt in order to transform it from being an ethnic democracy (a regime form that is by definition democratically flawed[10]) to becoming an inclusive, egalitarian democracy. These changes involve a package of individual rights to all Israeli citizens (carried out in the tradition of liberal democracy) and group-based rights in various forms.

In examining the relationships between Jews and Arabs in Israel and in the Middle East in general, it is important to emphasize the somewhat paradoxical nature of these relationships. On the one hand, Arab-Jewish relationships have been negative almost from the very beginning of the Zionist project in Eretz Israel; on the other hand, these relationships have never been static – on the contrary, Arab-Jewish relations have always been characterized by change, both in a negative and in a positive direction. The historical record clearly shows that Arab-Jewish relations in general have seen substantial changes through the years,[11] and most importantly in terms of this book, that a great deal of change has also occurred in Arab-Jewish relations within Israel.[12] These relationships are

---

[9] In fact, the increasing pressure to further ethnicize Israel and, thus, strengthen its hegemonic character has motivated to a large extent the writing of the current volume.

[10] Ilan Peleg, "Israel as a Liberal Democracy: Civil Rights in the Jewish State," in Laurie Eisenberg and Neil Caplan, eds., *Review Essays in Israel Studies: Books on Israel*, Vol. 5 (Albany: State University of New York Press, 2000), 63–80.

[11] For example, following the Suez or Sinai campaign in 1956, Arab-Israeli relations experienced a period of relative calm; and following the Oslo Accords in 1993, there was a period of hope for eventual peace in the region.

[12] According to Yoav Peled and Gershon Shafir, citizenship discourses between Jews and Arabs have changed through the years. They distinguish between different citizenship discourses in the relationships between Jews and Arabs in Israel, identifying them as the liberal, republican, and ethno-national discourses. Shafir and Peled, *Being Israeli: The Dynamics of Multiple Citizenship* (Cambridge: Cambridge University Press, 2002);

not characterized by a constant level of hostility at all times; they are fundamentally fluid, not fixed.[13]

The perspective that emphasizes the possibility of change in Arab-Jewish relations, and particularly the possibility of introducing initiatives to promote a better relationship between Arabs and Jews within Israel, is important for understanding the rationale behind this chapter. We believe that such initiatives are necessary for improving the quality of Israel's democracy and ensuring its overall stability. We also believe that large-scale political initiatives can succeed. Political engineering has led to positive results in numerous other overly ethnicized situations.[14] Creative political action can foster better relationships between ethno-national groups and avert violence and other forms of instability. Nevertheless, although we firmly believe that peaceful political transformation is possible, we recognize that it is not easy to initiate and implement, especially when there is a serious, ongoing, and deeply rooted ethno-national conflict, as is the case in Israel.[15]

Yoav Peled, "Strangers in Utopia: The Civic Status of the Palestinians in Israel," *Teoria U'Vikoret*, Vol. 3 (1993), 21–35; and Yoav Peled, "Citizenship," in Uri Ram and Nitza Berkovitch, eds., *In/Equality* (Beer-Sheva: Ben-Gurion University of the Negev Press, 2006), 31–37.

[13] Other scholars have taken a similarly dynamic perspective in viewing the Arab-Jewish relationship. Ian Lustick, for example, has argued that Arab-Jewish relations have evolved historically from increasing but uncalculated hostility in the earliest period (1882–1925) to unilateral "pedagogy of force" between 1925 and 1968 (the use of the Iron Wall policy by the Jews to convince the Arabs that Zionism cannot be defeated by the use of force), then to a period (1969–1993) in which the Israelis demanded that the Arabs merely recognize their existence, and finally to the period since the mid-1990s marked by Israeli abandonment of efforts to "teach" the Arabs anything and by Arab/Muslim rejection of the existence of a Jewish state in the Middle East. Ian S. Lustick, "Abandoning the Iron Wall: Israel and 'The Middle Eastern Muck,'" *Middle East Policy*, Vol. 15, No. 3 (Fall 2008), 30–56.

[14] On the notion of political engineering in general, see Ilan Peleg, *Democratizing the Hegemonic State: Political Transformation in the Age of Identity* (Cambridge University Press, 2007), especially 4, 6–7, 109, and 206–208. Relatively recent cases of successful political engineering include Spain, Canada, and Northern Ireland. On the Canadian case, see for example, Peter H. Russell, "The Politics of Mega-Constitutional Change: Lessons for Canada," in Bertus de Villers, ed. *Evaluating Federal Systems* (Dordrecht: Juta & Co., 1994), 291–311. On the Spanish case, see Andrea Bonime-Blanc, *Spain's Transition to Democracy: The Politics of Constitution Making* (Boulder, CO: Westview Press, 1987). On Northern Ireland, see John McGarry, "'Democracy' in Northern Ireland: Experiments in Self-Rule from the Protestant Ascendancy to the Good Friday Agreement," *Nation & Nationalism*, Vol. 8, No. 4 (2002), 451–474.

[15] See As'ad Ghanem, *The Palestinian-Arab Minority in Israel, 1948–2000* (Albany, NY: State University of New York Press, 2001); Nadim Rouhana, *Palestinian Citizens in an Ethnic Jewish State: Identities in Conflict* (New Haven, CT: Yale University Press, 1997); Peleg, *Democratizing the Hegemonic State*, especially 173–179; Oren Yiftachel,

Reversing the negative trajectory of Jewish-Palestinian relations in Israel, a trajectory that was set in the early years of the state,[16] first requires the formulation of a "grand strategy" for change and then the implementation of detailed and practical ideas that correspond to that strategy. Our grand strategy has several elements that form a coherent whole, a set of changes that we have conceived of as positive initiatives toward a more inclusive and more stable Israeli political system. The strategy has three main elements. First, a new state definition, involving a change in the definition of the State of Israel that creates a new ideological framework for majority-minority relations. Second, a new rights regime based on a balanced combination of individual and collective rights for all Israelis, in material and symbolic areas alike, as a way of improving majority-minority relations. Third, a new socio-political contract between the majority and the minority, based on genuine equality in rights and on encouraging voluntary civilian service to the state by Palestinian citizens in an effort to ease the concerns of many Israeli Jews over the loyalty of Arabs to the state.

Although this grand strategy is very ambitious, all of its elements are necessary to bring about a real transformation, and they are all intimately connected. There should be a comprehensive effort to implement all of them. At the same time, changes in one area should not be regarded as pre-conditions to changes in another area. Although a real transformation of the Israeli polity requires attention to all those areas, not all of them need to be addressed or implemented simultaneously.

### Redefining the Israeli State

Complex issues of identity and self-definition have challenged the State of Israel from the very beginning of its sovereign existence.[17] Although

---

*Ethnocracy: Land & Identity Politics in Israel/Palestine* (Philadelphia, PA: University of Pennsylvania Press, 2006); Lustick, *Arabs in the Jewish State*; and Smooha, "Minority Status in an Ethnic Democracy: The Status of the Arab Minority in Israel," *Ethnic & Racial Studies* 13, 3 (1990), 389–413. Sammy Smooha, "Ethnic Democracy: Israel as an Archetype," *Israel Studies* 2, 2 (1997), 198–241; and Sammy Smooha, "Types of Democracy & Modes of Conflict Management in Ethnically Divided Societies," *Nations & Nationalism* 8, 4 (2002), 423–431.

[16] As we argued in Chapter 5.

[17] Many of the challenges are rooted in questions related to the nature of Jews as a community of people – are Jews primarily a "nation," a "religious group," an "ethnicity" or all of these wrapped into one; who belongs to the group and by what criteria; is "Jewishness" an objective reality or a "subjective" perception by non-Jews?

not all of Israel's identity issues relate directly to the relationship between the Jewish majority and the Palestinian minority within the state, many of those issues have direct implications for that relationship. The definitional issues of Israel are important for improving majority-minority relations in the country because they determine the very essence of Israeli citizenship – the definition of who belongs to the Israeli political community and who does not belong (regardless of their formal status as an Israeli citizen), the nature of their individual and collective status within the political community, and what rights and duties they have within that community.

The State of Israel has defined itself in its 1948 Declaration of Independence as "the state of the Jewish people," a particularistic definition emerging from the Zionist movement. It has also defined itself as a democratic state with commitments to full equality, a definition that has universalistic connotations. For a long time, Israel has now declared itself to be both "Jewish and democratic," a definition included in two important Basic Laws introduced in 1992 and in numerous other documents. Although this precise definition was not included in the Declaration of Independence, this foundational document includes commitments to both "halves" of Israel's identity.

Despite this dual commitment, the development of the State of Israel in general and the relationship between its Jewish majority and its Palestinian minority in particular indicate that the Jewishness of the state has been maintained more forcefully than its democratic character. We believe that a key for Israel's future lies in the re-calibration of the balance between the Jewish and the democratic commitments of Israel. Such a re-calibration will enhance the quality of Israel's democracy and establish a more stable socio-political order.

In terms of a definitional change, what is required is a change from the well-established exclusively Jewish definition of the State of Israel to one that recognizes and legitimizes the ethno-national diversity of Israeli society and gives that diversity fuller institutional expression.[18] A new definition should reflect a balanced and inclusive approach that combines what is politically feasible with what is just. In developing alternative definitions for the State of Israel it is important to emphasize that it is unrealistic to believe that the Jewish majority in Israel will give up its insistence on defining the state in a way that resonates with its identity as

[18] See Safran, "Non-Separatist Policies Regarding Ethnic Minorities: Positive Approaches & Ambiguous Consequences," *International Political Science Review* 15, 1 (1994), 72.

a community of Jews, reflective of Jewish history in general and Jewish connection to the land in particular. This connection ought to be reaffirmed, thus responding to the fundamental identity of most Israeli Jews. However, such reaffirmation must be balanced against the basic needs and rights of Israeli citizens who are not Jewish, particularly Palestinian Arabs.

Starting with this set of requirements, at least four alternative definitions for the Jewishness of the State of Israel are possible, including the oft-repeated and widely accepted definition of Israel as "a Jewish State." Other definitions, belonging to the same general family, include the "State of the Jews" (which is a direct translation of Herzl's famous treatise, *Der Judenstaat*), a "Jewish Homeland," and the "State of the Jewish People" (a formula used in the Declaration of Independence). All these definitions of the State of Israel reflect the notion that Jews deserve a state of their own in their ancestral homeland. This notion has not only been supported by almost all Israeli Jews (and most non-Israeli Jews) but has also been widely endorsed internationally, including by the UN General Assembly in its 1947 Partition Resolution and by many others. It can also be persuasively argued on normative grounds that the ethno-national majority residing in a state has a right to define the overall character of the state, as is the situation in numerous countries around the world.[19]

The problem, however, with all definitions of the state that are exclusively Jewish is that they lead to a citizenship discourse that is ethno-national. In such a discourse, the status of both individuals and groups within the society is determined by their ethnicity rather than by their citizenship. Thus, an ethno-national discourse produces a situation that is incompatible with the equality of all citizens and is, therefore, flawed from a democratic perspective. Therefore, a broader definition of the state is needed.

In the case of Israel, the ethno-national discourse, dominant since the state's formative era,[20] has generally trumped the liberal discourse granting equal rights to all citizens, regardless of ethnicity, nationality, or religion. This ethno-national discourse has been based on a distinction between Jews and non-Jews, giving the latter secondary status. In addition to the ethno-national discourse, Israeli political culture has also been

---

[19]  This general argument is made by Alexander Yakobson and Amnon Rubinstein, as well as by Ruth Gavison in many of her writings including her *Israel as Jewish and Democratic State: Tensions and Opportunities* (Jerusalem: Van Leer Institute, 1999).

[20]  See Chapter 5.

dominated by a "republican discourse," granting rights to individuals and groups in accordance with their contribution to society.[21] The republican discourse has been almost as discriminatory as the ethno-national one. The combination of ethno-nationalism and republicanism has dominated Israel's political scene, negating the universalistic and egalitarian demands of liberalism, despite the fact that the Israeli polity has maintained many specific liberal rights: free election, rights of expression and association, judicial review, and so forth.[22]

There has been an inherent tension in Israel between the different citizenship discourses specifically in regard to the Palestinian minority. On the one hand, Israel's democratic commitment means that Palestinian citizens are, in principle, equal to Jewish citizens. On the other hand, the ethno-nationalist discourse assumes that Jews ought to be privileged in Israel because as a Jewish state, Israel is, by definition, "their" state. This tension is intensified by the republican discourse within Israeli political culture that maintains, in effect, that because Jews contribute more to the goals of the society (by serving in the army, for example), they are entitled to more rights. Moreover, the state itself is committed, as a collective body, to the implementation of Jewish and Zionist goals that are superior even to the will of the majority.[23]

The dominance of the ethno-national and republican citizenship discourses within Israel has resulted in the disempowerment of the Palestinian minority. Although Palestinian citizens enjoy many of the rights that flow from the liberal discourse in Israel (such as freedom of religion, expression, and assembly, and the right to participate in the country's political life), the relative marginality of that discourse itself and the significant impact of the other two discourses (the ethno-national and the republican) means that they are, as non-Jews, unequal with Jewish citizens. Our proposal for a redefinition of the state along with the specific changes we propose in the next section is designed to create a more equal situation between Jews and non-Jews in Israel.

---

[21] For this argument, see Shafir and Peled, *Being Israeli.*

[22] It is not unusual for a variety of contradictory discourses to exist side-by-side as shown, for example, in the American case by Rogers M. Smith, "The 'American Creed' and the American Identity: The Limits of Liberal Citizenship in the United States," *Western Political Quarterly* 41, 2 (1988), 225–251.

[23] Ben-Gurion's argument in regard to the Law of Return is very instructive in this regard. He saw the law as preceding to and superior to all other powers of the State, including that of the Knesset. His position was clearly "republican" and not democratic.

In redefining the state in a balanced manner, it ought to be remembered that the right of the majority to define the character of the polity, as part and parcel of the democratic principle of "majority rule," must be complemented by granting significant minorities the right to actively participate in the process through which the definition of the state in which they reside is made and in determining the character of the political institutions that emerge as a result of that definition. Democracy means, among other things, protection of minorities from the tyranny of the majority and their meaningful political participation. This protection from the majority and meaningful political participation must be applied to the Palestinian minority particularly because it is an indigenous group living in its ancestral land.[24] In regard to the definition of the state, it could be argued that it should reflect not only the perspectives and interests of the majority but the minority's perspectives and interests as well, even if the minority should not be given a veto power over the definition of the state. The key for a just and stable solution is to devise a balanced solution in which the interests of both groups are reflected in a revised definition of the state.

There are several arguments for bringing the minority into the process of determining the definition and the nature of the Israeli polity. First, the rights of the minority were recognized, and commitments to protect them were made, in historical documents endorsing the creation of a Jewish community and then a Jewish polity in Palestine, including the 1917 Balfour Declaration and the 1947 Partition Resolution.[25] The Balfour Declaration, for instance, while endorsing the establishment in Palestine of a "national home for the Jewish people," declared that "nothing shall be done which may prejudice the civil and religious rights of existing non-Jewish communities in Palestine."[26] Second, the rights of minorities – and particularly sizeable, distinct, and indigenous minorities – are increasingly recognized in the world today, although the level of

[24] Amal Jamal, "Collective Rights for Indigenous Minorities: Theoretical and Normative Aspects," in Elie Rekhess and Sarah Osacky-Lazar, eds., *The Status of the Arab Minority in the Jewish Nation State* (Tel Aviv: Tel Aviv University Press, 2005), 27–44, (see also note 32).

[25] Both documents reflect the sensitivity of the international community to the issue of the relationship between the Jewish and the Arab communities from the early days of the Zionist movement.

[26] Walter Z. Laqueur & Barry Rubin, eds., *The Israel-Arab Reader: A Documentary History of the Middle East Conflict*, 4th ed., (New York: Penguin Books, 1984), 18.

specificity of that recognition leaves a lot to be desired.[27] Third, only by bringing the Palestinian minority into a genuine dialogue with the Jewish majority on the very nature of the state can we hope to create the level of satisfaction that is necessary for long-term socio-political stability.

Given the insistence of the Jewish majority on defining the state as "Jewish" in any of the four ways previously mentioned (that is, to define the State of Israel in ethno-national-religious terms rather than in civic terms) and the right of members of the Palestinian minority to be included in the determination of the polity's character and the nature of its institutions, can there be a compromise position that responds to both concerns? Despite the self-evident difficulties in finding a compromise, we believe that this question can be answered in the affirmative. We are convinced that finding this middle ground is essential to Israel's future.

A variety of alternative definitions could be adopted in order to signal a shift from almost complete Jewish exclusivity to at least partial majority-minority accommodation. Such accommodation would require that in addition to the definition of the state as "Jewish," recognition and protection of the status of the minority within the state will be enacted. So far, to the extent to which Israel has committed itself to universalistic ideals, it has defined itself as "democratic" in addition to being "Jewish." We believe that this definition has been too vague, too narrow, and insufficiently prescriptive. It has failed to create a strong democratic system in which minority rights are actively protected. There is a consensus today that despite the state's commitment to democracy, the minority has always been marginalized and discriminated against.

In recognition of this, suggestions have been made to define the state not merely as "democratic" but also as a "state of all its citizens," and even as a "state of all its nations" (*medinat kol leumiah* in Hebrew). Given the great implications of the definitional question, it is not surprising that these formulae have strong supporters and equally passionate detractors. It seems, however, that although a "state of all its citizens" is compatible with the "Jewishness" of the state, the redefinition of Israel as "a state of all its nations" is incompatible with the state's Jewishness in any of its versions. Moreover, because the majority insists on defining the state as "Jewish," it needs to accommodate the demand to define Israel, in addition, as the "state of all of its citizens." Otherwise, an Arab (or any

---

[27] See, for example, the European Human Rights Convention. For general analysis of the rights of indigenous minorities, see Jamal, "Collective Rights for Indigenous Minorities."

other non-Jew) in Israel might and should feel excluded. The "state of all its citizens" is, thus, the countervailing force, the balancing act, to an Israel that insists on a collective definition as Jewish.

The formulae of a "Jewish State," a "State of the Jews," or the "State of the Jewish People" have been adopted in several official documents, including Israel's Declaration of Independence, several Basic Laws (and regular laws), Supreme Court rulings, and so forth. These formulae are problematic if they stand alone rather than being complemented by recognizing Israel as a diverse society in which a large number of non-Jews reside and where they should enjoy full citizenship. By themselves, these traditional definitions project an exclusive perspective in a polity that is, and has always been, bi-national and that has a large, distinct, and indigenous national minority within it. This incongruence between the state's definition and the socio-political reality is highly problematic, both theoretically and in terms of its practical implications. The various exclusive formulae have been translated, in reality, to a set of problematic practices in a variety of political areas (such as excluding Arab parties from participation in government coalitions), legal limitations (such as limiting the sale of lands in large areas of Israel to Jews), and significant economic inequalities between Arabs and Jews.

Yet, the two alternative definitions that have been proposed as replacing Israel as "democratic" are equally problematic if they are to stand on their own (that is, without a Jewish component as part of the state definition). "A state of all its citizens," with its emphasis on the individual, is a liberal democratic ideal that ignores the unique circumstances under which Israel came into being and its very raison d'être; it ignores the ideals of Zionism to which almost all Israeli Jews, and by now most Jews in the world, continue to subscribe. Deserting completely the collective perspective of the majority is unjust and unpractical. The formula of a "state of all its nations" is even more problematic; rather than claiming a liberal state, it endorses, at least implicitly, a bi-national polity, negating Zionism in an even more fundamental manner than a "state of all its citizens." The demand for multi-nationalism or bi-nationalism in the Israeli context is unjust, particularly once a Palestinian state is established side-by-side with Israel; it is also impractical and potentially destabilizing a political situation that is already volatile.[28]

---

[28] Genuine multi-nationality contradicts the self-perception and the very essence (the raison d'être) of most modern countries. For all intents and purposes, it simply does not work in the contemporary world. Protected status for national minorities, on the other hand, does work.

Given the complexity of the issue – the definition of the State of Israel in a way that could satisfy both the majority and the minority – it seems to us that there are two compromise solutions that might respond to the concerns of both Jews and Palestinians as part of an overall strategy for improving their relationship. First, Israel might drop all definitional references to its ethno-national character (that is, its "Jewish state" definition) yet continue to maintain some of its particularistic institutions. After all, few states explicitly define themselves by their religion, ethnicity, or nationality, although practically all of them have an official language and a particularistic culture. Most states also recognize special holidays that are linked to the religion of most of their citizens and to their historical legacies and traditions. This solution, although theoretically possible, is unlikely to be possible in reality because the vast majority of Israeli Jews insist on Israel's definition as a "Jewish" entity.

A second possible solution for the definition of the state would be to identify Israel as both "the Jewish homeland and a state of all its citizens." This formula combines the majority's perspective by adopting the main component of its ethno-national-religious identity and the minority's position by reaffirming the country's civic-democratic identity. Moreover, by changing the existing formula from a "Jewish state" to "Jewish homeland," the collective definition is softened. The definition of Israel as a "Jewish state" imposes on it prescriptive and legal demands. The polity is expected to behave "Jewishly" in all areas – immigration, education, land ownership, religious institutions, and so forth. Moreover, if it is a "Jewish state," all its state symbols ought to be Jewish. On the other hand, "homeland" is significantly less prescriptive, more amorphous, and less demanding than "state." "Homeland" is an historical designation of a land that often lacks even clear borders (as is the case with Eretz Israel), whereas "state" is an institutional term referring to a well-defined political structure.

By designating Israel as a "state of all its citizens," in addition to the "Jewish homeland," the definition of the state shifts in an individualistic, liberal, and truly democratic direction, insisting on the legal equality of all citizens as "owners" of the state, thus giving members of Israel's Palestinian minority a measure of recognition and protection. It seems to us that such a combined definition, although somewhat cumbersome and wordy, could move Israel toward a more inclusive and more stable future without threatening the majority's sense of influencing the public sphere.

Whereas traditionalists might oppose the dual nature of our proposed definition, the fact is that the Jewish majority in Israel has already accepted the duality of the state by enshrining the formula of Israel as Jewish and democratic. Through our proposal, the dual commitment of the state will not only be reaffirmed but also strengthened, particularly if it is accompanied, as it must be, by more practical steps toward the establishment of a significantly more inclusive polity. Our proposal would signal a decisive, purposeful move toward the recognition of the rights of the minority or, at least, its members as individuals. The proposed change will improve Israel's democracy, pushing it forward from being inherently flawed toward a better democratic condition. As long as Israel's definition is mostly (even if not entirely) particularistic, that is "a Jewish state," while facing a bi-national society, it will continue to experience great tension with democracy. Particularistic self-definitions tend to be in great tension with the requirements of democracy, especially in a situation of serious, historical, and active ethno-national conflict. In Israel's case, the country's self-definition as a "Jewish state" has been construed very broadly. It has had not merely symbolic expressions – reflected in the anthem, flag, language, national holidays, historical heroes, and so forth – but many material expressions as well – land allocations, budgetary priorities, appointments to governmental positions, immigration policy, and so forth. The proposed dual definition as both the "Jewish homeland" and "a state of all its citizens" is intended to introduce a better balance, and thus be more democratic.

The examples of the Scandinavian countries, the United Kingdom, the Netherlands, and many other countries indicate that particularism can be balanced with democracy and equality, especially if it is limited to symbolic, non-material issues. The formula of "state of all its citizens" might give members of the minority a sense of belonging to a polity that also defines itself as the Jewish homeland. Without such a complementary definition, Israel is destined to live with its inequalities, a condition that might deteriorate in times of crisis and conflict, as indeed it has recently. The point of our proposal for a dual definition is that Israel can become a significantly stronger democracy only if it declares itself to also be a "state of all its citizens." Such a declaration would constitute an act of inclusion toward a minority that has justifiably felt itself excluded for a very long time. The proposed definition could be thought of as a countervailing force to exclusivist, nationalist, and even non-democratic forces within Israel's political system.

Whatever might have been the intentions of Israel's founding fathers, they have not been able to produce in Israel a model democracy. Although

conditions for the establishment of a model democracy were never promising, given the intensity of the Arab-Jewish conflict and other divisions
within the Israeli society, after six decades a significant improvement is
possible and desirable. In the absence of a dramatic change, further escalation in the majority-minority conflict, and with it further deterioration
in the quality of Israel's democracy, is likely. The necessity for a more specific definition of the State of Israel – not merely as a "democratic" state
but also as a "state of all its citizens" – is particularly clear in view of the
evidence that, to date, the definition of the state as "democratic" has not
produced equality between Jewish and Arab citizens. The empirical data,
indicating that a pattern of continuous discrimination persists, is comprehensive and incontrovertible.[29]

## A New Rights Regime

In dealing with majority-minority relations in Israel, we need to progress
beyond issues of state definition and develop pragmatic proposals for
reversing the negative trends within Israeli society and politics. We believe
that the way to improve Arab-Jewish relations in Israel is through the
significant expansion of both individual and collective rights. Individual
members of the Palestinian minority must be dealt with and recognized
as completely equal citizens in all areas; and the collective rights of the
Palestinian minority should be significantly increased in several areas.
A solution cannot be found exclusively in either individual or collective
rights, only in their close combination (while at the same time taking into
account possible tensions between the two sets of rights). Classical liberalism, with its exclusive focus on individual rights, is simply insufficient
in responding to the needs of bi-national (and not merely multi-cultural)
societies, such as Israel's.[30]

---

[29] Practically all analysts agree that patterns of discrimination between Jews and Arabs characterize Israel. See, for example, Ghanem, *The Palestinian-Arab Minority in Israel*; Lustick,
*Arabs in the Jewish State*; David Kretzmer, *The Legal Status of the Arabs in Israel* (Boulder,
CO: Westview Press, 1990); Yoav Peled, "Ethnic Democracy and the Legal Construction
of Citizenship: Arab Citizens of the Jewish State," *The American Political Science Review*
86, 1 (1992), 432–443; Ilan Peleg, "Jewish-Palestinian Relations in Israel: From Hegemony
to Equality," *International Journal of Politics, Culture and Society* 17, 3 (2004), 415–437;
Rouhana, "*Palestinian Citizens in an Ethnic Jewish State*;" Shafir & Peled, *Being Israeli*;
Yiftachel, *Ethnocracy*. Even official documents of the State of Israel do not question this
conclusion.

[30] We are closer in our approach to the issue of individual rights versus collective rights to
"group rights analysts" such as Will Kymlicka and Ferran Requejo.

The Israeli state already recognizes Arabs as a group in a variety of ways.[31] Arab children are entitled to education in Arabic, Muslims have their own religious institutions, there are broadcasts in Arabic on state radio and television stations, and so forth. Yet these rights have never amounted to explicit political recognition. Israel not only needs to formally recognize Arabs as a "national minority" but also grant them more collective rights that give concrete expression to this enhanced status. The granting of extensive collective rights to the Palestinian minority in Israel is morally justified and politically necessary for several reasons: the significant size of the minority both in absolute terms and relative to the size of the population in the country; the deep historical roots of the minority in the land (as an indigenous and not an immigrant minority);[32] the fact that members of the minority share all the elements of a distinct culture (including language, music, folklore, food, etc.); the fact that as a minority, Palestinians are not only a distinct group in and of themselves but also very different from the majority in terms of ethnicity, religion, culture, language, and history; finally, the historical conflict between the majority and the minority that requires the protection of the minority.

Officially recognizing that Arab citizens of Israel constitute a national minority and have a Palestinian national identity does not mean that they should not also be regarded as full-fledged Israeli citizens and members of the Israeli public. It is essential for the state and for Israeli-Jewish society to accept the possibility that Palestinians in Israel can be loyal to both their nation, the Palestinian nation, and to their state, the State of Israel. The dual identity of Palestinians in Israel – as Palestinians and Israeli citizens – should be publicly and formally accepted. To expect or demand that they completely abandon one of these identities is unnecessary and unrealistic. In many contemporary democracies it is possible for people to have different national and civic identities; for example, being Catalan and Spanish in Spain or Scottish and British in the UK. Palestinians in Israel should also be allowed to be both Palestinian and Israeli and not be forced to choose between these two identities. The new definition of the State of Israel that we have offered – as the Jewish homeland and a state

---

[31] Moreover, Arabs and Muslims were also recognized as a community by previous regimes in Palestine, including the Ottoman Empire and the British Mandate.

[32] Jamal, "Collective Rights for Indigenous Minorities," 27–44, calls the Palestinians in Israel "an original nation," equivalent to "an indigenous nation" and distinct from a "national minority" or "an immigrant minority." From our perspective, Palestinian Arabs are surely not immigrants and should be considered indigenous or original groups as well as a national minority.

of all its citizens – allows Palestinians in Israel to fulfill this dual role as both Palestinians and Israeli citizens.

The approach taken in the previous section in regard to the definition of the state should be translated into practical proposals designed to create more equality between the Jewish majority and the Palestinian minority in Israel. Although absolute equality might not be possible in a country where the majority identifies the state with one nation, equality can be increased in as many areas as possible. Several specific policies can be implemented in an effort to maintain Israel as both a Jewish homeland and strengthen the sense that it is also a state of all its citizens. Whereas Israel is already a "Jewish state" in numerous ways related to both its domestic and foreign policy – its immigration policy, development and settlement programs, educational and cultural curricula, symbolic order, and so forth – it can and should transform itself into a state of all its citizens without losing its overall character as the homeland of the Jewish people.

It is impossible to review here every aspect of Arab-Jewish relations that requires attention. Here are, however, a series of ten policies (some easier than others to implement) that we believe to be important in enhancing the rights of Palestinians in Israel both as individual citizens and as a distinct national minority:

1. Establishing functional autonomy for Palestinians in some areas of public life as a fully recognized national minority. By "functional autonomy" we mean the right of members of the minority to manage their lives in certain areas such as education, religion, and culture. Whereas we do not support territorial autonomy of any kind because such autonomy might be considered or perceived as a prelude to secessionism, functional and non-territorial autonomy could be helpful in reshaping majority-minority relations in Israel. Especially important in this regard is the field of public education in Arabic.[33] It should involve Palestinian management of the Arab educational system, significant influence over the curricular content of education in that sector, and the establishment of an Arab university. Such steps could empower the minority without endangering the political sovereignty or territorial integrity of the state. Autonomy is an attractive compromise between the majority's

---

[33] It is important to note that Israel has had a separate Arabic language educational system from its very beginning, although it has never been truly autonomous.

desire to control the public sphere and the minority's desire to have its unique position and identity recognized.[34]

2.  Nominating Palestinian citizens to positions of responsibility within the Israeli polity particularly in all parts of the government bureaucracy and especially in higher-up policy-making capacities in areas directly connected to the lives of the Palestinian community.[35] Although such a process has already begun with official governmental support, it has progressed slowly (a recent report identified only slightly more than 6 percent of Israel's government employees as Arabs). The right of Palestinians to occupy important positions is fundamental to their equality as individuals, but their representation in various governmental organizations could also be regarded as a group right. The fulfillment of this right could enhance the commitment of the minority to the state. The country has to move beyond token appointments of Arabs as officials and judges.

3.  Improving the overall economic conditions of the Palestinian minority through long-term development plans and equal financial allocations to Arab municipalities. The economic sphere is of particular importance in view of the fact that a large number of Palestinians in Israel (about 50 percent) live under the poverty line.[36] Statistics published by the government indicate that resources invested by the state in crucial areas related to the "Arab sector" (e.g., education, housing, industrial development, employment, welfare, and infrastructure) are a fraction of the resources invested in the "Jewish sector." The State of Israel should also focus in coming years on fair-employment and fair-housing laws, guaranteeing equality in these two crucial areas. Another focal point should be larger budgetary allocations to the improvement of the infrastructure in Arab villages and towns. The recent decision by the Israeli government, initiated by Minister for Minority Affairs Avishay Braverman, to designate 800 million shekels (around $214 million)

---

[34] Many countries have used autonomy as a governmental vehicle for easing relations between their ethnic groups. An example is post-Franco Spain. For general analysis of autonomy, see Ruth Lapidoth, *Autonomy: Flexible Solutions to Ethnic Conflicts*, (Washington, DC: United States Institute for Peace, 1996).

[35] Thus, for example, Palestinians should be directly involved in the economic development of areas in which they reside, running institutions from which they receive services, etc.

[36] On the welfare gap, see Khawla Abu-Baker, "Social and Educational Welfare Policy in the Arab Sector in Israel," *Israel Affairs*, Volume 9, Issue 1–2 (2003), 68–96.

as an investment plan for Arab communities, the largest-ever plan of its type, is definitely a move in the right direction.[37]

4. Adopting an aggressive anti-discriminatory policy in order to protect Palestinian citizens against official or unofficial mistreatment by public or private entities, including individuals. This could be done by establishing a state agency to deal actively and proactively with all forms of discrimination against members of the Palestinian minority, as individuals or as a group, whether carried out by governmental organizations, private economic firms, or individual citizens.[38] Hate crimes against Palestinian citizens ought to be prosecuted with particular vigor. The anti-discriminatory policy should combine the forces of the government (including the public education system) and non-governmental organizations.

5. Introducing symbolic changes that can bolster a sense of shared citizenship and a feeling that the state belongs to all of Israel's citizens. For instance, adding an additional stanza to the national anthem, *Hatikvah*, which might emphasize the symbolic value of Jerusalem/al Quds as a place where all great monotheistic religions meet, could be a step toward inclusiveness. The initiation of a public holiday called Citizenship Day,[39] or a day celebrating peace (if and when peace is established), are additional ideas for the promotion of shared symbols in a society in which such symbols do not currently exist.

6. Resolving the problems of land and housing that are a constant source of friction between Palestinians in Israel and the state authorities. This includes legalizing existing Arab homes in Arab towns and villages in Israel that have been built without official permits (because such permits are almost impossible to obtain due to various legal and bureaucratic obstacles[40]), increasing the amount of land available to Arab municipalities for their expansion, and formally recognizing all the "unrecognized villages" (many of which are desperately poor and lack basic services like water or electricity, particularly the thirty-six unrecognized villages

---

[37] Similar plans in the past, however, have remained a dead letter. The test of the 2010 plan will be in its implementation.

[38] Similar agencies have been established in other countries, including the United States.

[39] The United States enacted a Constitution Day (previously known as Citizenship Day) in 2004. It is marked usually on September 17.

[40] Fadi Eyadat, "Israeli Arabs have no choice but to build illegally," *Ha'aretz*, July 29, 2010.

in the Negev that are inhabited by approximately 90,000 Bedouin Arabs).[41] Improving the living conditions of the Palestinian minority and especially ensuring its equal access to housing and land will remove one of the biggest problems in the current relationship between the state and the Palestinian minority. At a minimum, the state should stop demolishing Arab homes and villages, something it continues to do on a regular basis.[42]

7. Initiating affirmative action programs as a way of better integrating Palestinian citizens into Israeli society. Affirmative action programs – particularly in government bureaucracies, institutions of higher education, and the business community – could help in narrowing the economic gaps between Jews and Arabs. Although affirmative action is, by definition, a violation of the equality principle, in some situations it is necessary to solve historical problems in multi-ethnic societies. In the Israeli context, affirmative action can serve a valuable role both materially and symbolically.

8. Enhancing the political representation of the Palestinian minority by formally recognizing its representative institutions (such as the High Follow-up Committee for Arab Citizens), negotiating with them, and including Arab parties in government coalitions. This could also encourage moderation on the part of Arab leaders, organizations, and political parties. Power sharing in the central organs of the state, particularly in the executive branch and in the legislature, is a useful mechanism for the enhancement of cooperation between diverse groups in deeply divided societies (as demonstrated in the examples of Northern Ireland, Canada, Spain, and Belgium). Since 1948, none of Israel's thirty-two coalition governments have included Arab parties. Only two Arabs have ever served as government ministers (out of close to 680 such appointments), and only one Arab has been appointed a Supreme Court judge out of almost 60 such appointments.[43]

[41] See Human Rights Watch, "Land and Housing Rights Violations in Israel's Unrecognized Bedouin Villages," March 30, 2008; and The Negev Coexistence Forum for Civil Equality, *The Bedouin-Arabs in the Negev-Naqab Desert in Israel*, August 2009, 3–4. For a description of a typical "unrecognized" village, see Rachel Leah Jones, "Ayn Hawd and the Unrecognized Villages," *Journal of Palestinian Studies*, Vol. 31, No. 1 (Autumn 2001), 39–49.

[42] See, for example, Jack Khoury and Yair Yagna, "Police destroy dozens of buildings in unrecognized Bedouin village in Negev," *Ha'aretz*, July 28, 2010.

[43] See Oren Yiftachel, "Ghetto Citizenship: Palestinian Arabs in Israel," in Nadim Rouhana and A. Sasagh, eds., *Israel and the Palestinians: Key Terms* (Haifa: Mada Center for Applied Research, 2009), 56–661.

9. Protecting and strengthening the equal citizenship of Palestinians in Israel through the introduction of a Basic Law that guarantees the citizenship of all Israelis as inalienable and inviolable. Several developments over the last few years have threatened the status of Palestinians as equal citizens or eroded their sense of equal citizenship. The heavy-handed reaction of the Israeli police toward demonstrations by Palestinian citizens (in comparison, for example, to their significantly softer reactions toward demonstrations by ultra-Orthodox Jews or Jewish settlers), and particularly the killing of thirteen demonstrators during the October 2000 events, is one example. Another is the denial of the right of Palestinian citizens in Israel to family unification via marriage with non-citizens (mostly from the Occupied Territories).[44] The citizenship of Palestinians in Israel has also been threatened by the proposal to move the border between Israel and the West Bank eastward so as to deprive a large number of Palestinians (close to 20 percent) of their citizenship.[45]

10. Strengthening the status of Arabic as an official language of the country. Arabic has been an official language since Israel's establishment. In reality, however, it is today not only dominated by Hebrew but also by English. In the mid-1980s, then Education Minister and later President of Israel Yitzhak Navon made the study of Arabic mandatory in all Israeli schools, but the new policy was widely ignored. The strengthening of the knowledge of Arabic could be positively perceived by the Palestinian minority and strengthen integrative processes in the country.

All of the practical changes that we recommend can significantly improve Arab-Jewish relations inside Israel. Collectively, the changes amount to a new social contract or grand bargain between the majority and the minority in Israel. Of particular importance are our proposals to recognize Israel's Palestinians as a national minority and to significantly enhance their collective rights, including granting them broader autonomy. Although we do not believe that our proposals will completely

---

[44] This ban was enacted by the Knesset in July 2003; the law was amended in July 2005. On May 14, 2006, Israel's High Court of Justice turned down the appeal to declare the law unconstitutional by a slim (6:5) majority, with Chief Justice Barak voting with the minority. See Na'ama Carmi, "The Nationality and Entry into Israel Case before the Supreme Court of Israel," *Israel Studies Forum*, Vol. 22, No. 1 (Summer 2007), 26–53.

[45] Peled, "Citizenship Betrayed," 603–638, assesses the number of Palestinians that might lose their citizenship if the border is moved at 150,000–200,000.

resolve the conflict between the Jewish majority and the Palestinian minority or between the state and the minority, we do think that they could substantially improve Israel's ability to manage the conflict in a way that will improve majority-minority relations and, thus, make further escalation, including large-scale bloodshed, less likely.[46]

Our proposals for improving the relationship between the Jewish majority and the Palestinian minority are based on a dynamic view of that relationship. Although the overall trajectory of this relationship was determined when the State of Israel was established in 1948, different levels of inter-ethnic conflict have evolved over time. This is also likely to be the pattern in the future. Thus, continued exclusion of the minority by the majority and the state will probably lead to heightened hostility and even violence. An energetic action in the direction of inclusion will lower such hostility and make violent outbursts less likely.

None of our proposals, or even all of them together, will turn Israel into a bi-national state or undermine the country's "Jewishness." We believe that Israel should maintain its Jewish identity, but that identity should not be taken as a license for discrimination against non-Jews. Hence, the status of non-Jews in Israel, particularly Palestinian citizens, ought to be enhanced and actively protected by the State of Israel. Nevertheless, several practices can and should be maintained in Israel as a "Jewish homeland." Among the institutionalized practices that ought to be maintained are Israel's Law of Return, the existence of special relations between the State of Israel and organizations such as the Jewish Agency, and the central place of the Hebrew language and culture in Israel.

Although the ten proposals we put forward might be perceived as concessions by the Jewish majority to the Palestinian minority, they are, in fact, mutually beneficial to both majority and minority. They are designed to improve the quality of Israel's democracy by increasing the rights of the minority without reducing the Jewishness of the state. It is our belief that Israel will be politically strengthened if it treats its Palestinian citizens as individuals with complete equality and recognizes their status as a national minority. This will fortify the internal cohesion of the country. In the absence of the type of reforms we propose, the quality of Israel's democracy will remain relatively low and its political stability might well

---

[46] In general, we do not believe that there is a perfect solution to this long conflict and possibly all conflicts in deeply divided societies. But it is important not to make perfection the enemy of the good and to try to improve relations as much as possible.

deteriorate, despite or even because of a resolution of Israel's conflict with the Palestinians in the West Bank and Gaza.[47]

Most of the proposals we make in this chapter do not harm the rights of members of the Jewish majority in any way. Those that do impact such rights are just and necessary responses to long-term discrimination against the Palestinian minority. Thus, special actions on behalf of the nomination of more Palestinian citizens for public offices and an aggressive affirmative action program might divert some resources toward the minority, but they are compatible with Israel's basic commitment to democracy and equality. The establishment of an anti-discriminatory policy and the introduction of symbolic changes are even less costly to members of the majority but highly beneficial to members of the minority and to the Israeli polity as a whole.

Nevertheless, convincing the Jewish majority to end all forms of discrimination against Palestinians as individuals and to grant the Palestinian minority substantial collective rights including autonomy in certain areas will not be an easy task given the hostility and suspicion that many Israeli Jews currently feel toward the Palestinian minority. We believe that the Palestinian minority itself, through its rhetoric and behavior, can help to reduce some of this hostility and suspicion. In particular, the leadership of the Palestinian minority, although fully entitled to fight for the demands of their constituents by all peaceful and democratic means at their disposal, should avoid using provocative language or taking provocative actions. For instance, it is politically imprudent and un-helpful for leaders of the Palestinian community in Israel to denounce the state as "colonial" and "imperialistic," to participate in activities aimed at delegitimizing the State of Israel, or to make highly publicized visits to Arab states that are still officially in a state of war with Israel. Even legitimate language and activity can be counterproductive in terms of bringing about national reconciliation.

Some Israeli Jews have recently argued that Jewish concerns about the loyalty of Palestinian citizens of Israel could be eased if they performed mandatory military service, as Israeli Jews do (except for ultra-Orthodox Jews).[48] In theory, such a proposal seems reasonable because it would clearly demonstrate their allegiance to the state and allow young Palestinian citizens of Israel to receive the material benefits conferred on those who perform military service in Israel. In practice, however,

---

[47] For more on this point, see the Conclusion.
[48] Moshe Arens, "Allegiance by choice," *Ha'aretz*, August 3, 2010.

imposing mandatory military service on the Palestinian minority would be very problematic as it could force Palestinian citizens of Israel to fight against other Palestinians (mostly in Gaza and the West Bank). This would put them in a position in which they would have to betray either their state or their nation. Conscripting Palestinian youth into the IDF, therefore, is bound to be a recipe for conflict.

A more feasible option that might be attractive to many Palestinian youth in Israel is voluntary civilian service, involving helping individuals (e.g., the elderly and the disabled) and communities in need (including Palestinian communities in Israel), providing emergency services, improving infrastructure (a major need in Arab villages and towns), beautifying the environment, and so forth. Israel already has a voluntary national service program that was originally set up to provide an alternative to military service for Orthodox women. In recent years a small but growing number of Palestinian high-school graduates have taken part in this program,[49] and there is good reason to believe that many more would be willing to participate.[50] The state should, therefore, significantly expand this civilian service program, while maintaining its voluntary nature and ensuring that it is completely separate from the IDF. Rather than being conceived as a test of the loyalty of Palestinian citizens, an expanded voluntary civilian service program should be seen as a means of facilitating cooperation between young Jews and Arabs, working on behalf of Israeli society as a whole, and offering a shared experience in an increasingly divided society. Moreover, for young Arab volunteers, it will provide them with immediate economic benefits (in the form of a monthly stipend) and help them acquire skills that could boost their prospects for future employment.[51] Just as military service has helped young Israeli Jews enter and advance in the workforce, so too can civilian service help Palestinian citizens of Israel.

[49] The number more than doubled from 280 in 2007 to almost 600 in 2008. Yoav Stern, "Opposition to national service in Israel's Arab sector is bitter," *Ha'aretz*, August 4, 2008.

[50] On the growing popularity of civilian service among Palestinian youth in Israel, see Yuval Azoulay, "Number of Israeli Arab National Service Volunteers Doubles," *Ha'aretz*, December 20, 2007. A survey indicated that more than 75 percent of Palestinian youth would be willing to participate in a volunteer program if it offered benefits similar to those granted for military service. Ken Ellingwood, "Israeli Arabs Split over National Service Plan," *Los Angeles Times*, January 2, 2008, http://www.latimes.com/news/nation-world/world/la-fg-service2jan02,1,4215318.story?ctrack=1&cset=true.

[51] On the benefits of a voluntary civilian service program for Arab youth, see Amnon Beeri-Sulitzeanu, "A Different Kind of Service," *Ha'aretz*, August 13, 2010.

## Conclusion

In order to better manage Jewish-Palestinian relations within Israel, the state needs to move, gradually but decisively, from being an exclusively Jewish polity to become a more inclusive, pluralistic egalitarian democracy that balances the rights of the majority and the minority in a better way than it does now. We believe that this can be done only by enhancing the rights of Palestinian citizens in a variety of areas. Doing this is essential for reversing the currently deteriorating relationship between Jews and Palestinians in Israel. The dangerous nature of this deterioration cannot be exaggerated. Increasing anti-Arab discrimination, the decline of democratic norms, and even large-scale violence within Israel is likely in the absence of creative solutions. Ethnic overbidding on both sides of the ethno-national divide is particularly dangerous, as has been proven in numerous other ethnic conflicts as well as in the Israeli-Palestinian conflict at large.

In trying to improve Arab-Jewish relations in Israel in a comprehensive and balanced manner, it is important to take a combination of perspectives. First is a normative perspective, reflected in an effort to produce a solution that is just and equitable.[52] Second is a political perspective, with the aim of producing a much more stable solution that can minimize violence and enhance inter-ethnic dialogue within the Israeli polity. And third is a pragmatic perspective, seeking a solution that can actually be "sold" to both sides by their leaders and that might be sustainable in years to come.

In terms of these perspectives, the current situation in Israel is quite weak in a normative sense – most analysts consider the country's democracy to be deeply flawed. The current situation is also quite weak from a political perspective – it has resulted in growing ethno-national conflict marked by occasional violent outbursts. The challenge lies in three crucial questions that are central to the pragmatic perspective: Can the Israeli polity actually carry out the transformation offered in this chapter, can it be "sold" to the Israeli public (particularly the Jewish majority) by its leaders, and can it be implemented and then sustained? Our answer to these three questions is "yes," although implementing the transformation will certainly not be easy.

---

[52] This is often subsumed under the value of "democracy," but it is important to note that as a concept democracy is "essentially contested" and not always useful for political communication. W. B. Gallie, "Essentially Contested Concepts," in Max Black, ed., *The Importance of Language* (Englewood Cliffs, NJ: Prentice-Hall, 1962), 121–146.

If Israel chooses to ignore the deterioration in Arab-Jewish relations that we discussed in earlier chapters, the future of the country is bleak indeed. We believe that a more stable future lies with the political middle ground as we have outlined it in this chapter. This middle ground rejects the continuation of the current Israeli ethno-national regime, although it does not accept bi-nationalism as either just or viable. Between what might be called "hard consociationalism," which gives the minority veto power over the will of the majority, and "soft consociationalism," which involves autonomy and other limited forms of power sharing, the middle-ground solution endorses the latter.

Fundamentally, our approach seeks to accommodate the desires of most Israeli citizens, the majority that insist on Israel as a Jewish entity, while also catering to the legitimate demands of those who do not share the ethnicity, nationality, or religion of the majority. Certain collective rights can and should be given to the Palestinian minority without endangering the essential character of the state. Although the transformation of Israel into a bi-national state, or efforts to bring it about, must be rejected as unjust, unnecessary, and destabilizing, significant changes in the existing Israeli regime ought to be implemented by following the transformation program outlined in this chapter or a similar program.

A balanced approach on behalf of transformation is the key to success in the very challenging political environment of Israel. Determining the precise rights of the minority in the state ought to be guided by both the art of the possible and by what is just. Thus, some of the Vision documents demand a veto power for the minority. This demand is incompatible with Israel's majoritarian democracy and has no chance whatsoever of being accepted by the majority. Many in the majority would see the acceptance of such a demand as "the end of the Jewish State."[53] Yet, the participation of the minority in any decision regarding it could be promoted by another, more modest, proposal in the Vision documents: the creation of a parliamentary committee to deal with all bilingual and multi-cultural issues in Israel. This is just one of many examples of looking for the middle ground in Israel. It is an approach we endorse wholeheartedly.

---

[53] This is, for example, the opinion of the Israeli sociologist Sammy Smooha in an interview about the Vision documents with Uriel Abulof, *Eretz Acheret*, Issue 39, April–May 2007, 34.

# 8

# Israel's Challenge

## *Moving from Hegemony to Equality*

> Israel is going through a very complex period and its long term future depends not only on reaching peace and security with the Arab world on the basis of two states for two peoples, but also on being able to create a new domestic balance in which the Arab citizens of Israel feel part of the state, with the equality and partnership they have been seeking for years, but which has been denied them by successive Israeli governments.
>
> Avishay Braverman, Labor Knesset member and minister for minority affairs in the Netanyahu government, July 2009[1]

Perhaps the greatest challenge facing the State of Israel today is that of developing a significantly stronger, more inclusive democracy that can better balance the interests of the Jewish majority and the rights of the Palestinian minority. In the previous chapter, we outlined how Israel can successfully meet this challenge. The changes that we proposed entail a fundamental transformation of Israel's ethno-national regime. Many Israeli Jews will no doubt be strongly opposed to such a transformation and will therefore resist it. This is to be expected. Ethnic majorities in multi-ethnic states are bound to oppose changes that enhance the position of the minority, especially if those changes involve giving the minority not just equal individual rights but also collective rights.[2] Dominance within the state is often perceived by the majority to be its right, part of the "natural order"

---

[1] Quoted in Susser, "Fanning the Flames of Discontent," *The Jerusalem Report*, July 6, 2009, 11.

[2] The changes in Northern Ireland over the last dozen years or so demonstrate this reality. They came about only after many years of violence as well as demographic changes in favor of the minority.

of things.[3] Indeed, the majority often regards its rights and privileges as guaranteeing its very survival as a group. Thus, any perceived challenge to these rights and privileges may be seen by members of the majority as a serious threat to their future. This is likely to provoke stiff resistance.

In Israel's case, the Jewish majority can be expected to resist significantly improving the status of the Palestinian minority in the country for two additional reasons. First, because of their continued adherence to Zionist ideology, the vast majority of Israeli Jews view the State of Israel as the exclusive possession of the Jewish nation, a community that includes both Jews who reside in Israel and those who reside in the worldwide Jewish Diaspora. Second, the long and bloody struggle between Jews and Arabs over Israel/Palestine makes Israeli Jews even less willing to offer any concessions to the Palestinian minority.

Just as the opposition of the Jewish majority to a transformation of Israel's ethno-national regime is to be expected, so too is support for this from the Palestinian minority. Any sizeable ethnic minority, and especially an indigenous minority with a national consciousness, deserves significant recognition and rights. Such a minority, in all likelihood, will try to establish equal status with the majority and transform the state from an ethnic state to a civic or even a multi-national state. In this respect, the Israeli case is typical and quite similar to that of other multi-ethnic states, although the unique factors in the Israeli case ought not be ignored.

This chapter examines the process through which Israel may change from being an ethnic state (albeit with many democratic characteristics) to becoming an egalitarian, inclusive democracy. How can this change happen? In general, there are two ways this can take place. A transformation can occur through large-scale, political engineering initiated and directed by Israel's state institutions, or it can occur through the active resistance of the minority population (assisted by liberal elements within the majority), possibly involving violent clashes between the minority and state authorities (as well as with nationalist elements in the majority), and growing international pressure. We believe that unless the State of Israel becomes energetically involved in promoting the first transformation and begins a peaceful process of reconciliation through inter-ethnic dialogue, active resistance to the status quo by the minority will increase and violent outbursts will occur with higher frequency and intensity.

---

[3] Describing this natural order as "hegemonic," in the sense that it is considered unchangeable, corresponds to the use of the word by Antonio Gramsci. See Robert Bocock, *Hegemony* (Chichester, West Sussex: Tavistock Publications, 1986).

## Transforming Hegemony

Israel is a majority-based regime with many democratic institutions and norms, including free elections for a representative parliament to which Arabs as individuals and as parties are chosen.[4] As a democracy, albeit a flawed one, we believe that Israel is capable of becoming significantly more inclusive and egalitarian. Whereas in minority-based hegemonic regimes a transformation is impossible without demolishing these regimes completely (as was done, for example, in South Africa in the 1990s), in majority-based hegemonic regimes a transformation is possible, although it is still extremely difficult to bring about. In principle, majority-based hegemonic regimes can become more pluralistic through the provision of extensive individual rights and even significant group rights. The key to such a development is to find a way in which a transformation can occur without undermining the majority's feeling that it can control its destiny and take the leading role in the state.

In looking at the type of majority-based hegemony that Israel represents, it is important to realize that many segments of the society have a genuine commitment to democratic ideals such as freedom of expression and other fundamental freedoms. At the same time, the emphasis in that kind of regime, emerging against the background of severe inter-ethnic conflict, is more on the rule of the majority than on the protection of the minority. However, a commitment to even some democratic principles might open the door for the adoption of other democratic principles. Moreover, in majority-based hegemonies such as Israel, if the majority is truly in control of the polity (politically, economically, militarily, and culturally) and has confidence in the durability of its control, the use of violence against the minority might be minimal. Parliamentary majorities, watchful executive office holders, and independent courts often replace brute force as mechanisms for maintaining the control of the majority in a hegemonic position. The more confident the majority is, the more it tends to offer the minority deals that improve its overall condition, even if those deals fall short of complete equality. The role of the leadership here is of the utmost importance. If the leaders of the majority understand that total dominance and control by the majority is ultimately not in its interests, hegemonic rule might be gradually blunted and its sharper edges abolished.

---

[4] Efforts to interfere with the open election process have failed in the last few elections, although the existing law threatens parties who oppose Israel as "Jewish and democratic" with disqualification, as indeed was done to al-Ard.

A transformation from exclusivism to accommodationism in a majority-based hegemony is entirely possible, therefore, although it is by no means easy, particularly not in circumstances of persistent inter-ethnic conflict. A difficulty in bringing about such a transformation is the problem of "ethnic outbidding."[5] This is when politicians try to enhance their nationalistic credentials and increase their popular appeal by catering to their ethnic constituencies and presenting anti-minority positions rather than inclusive, accommodating ones. This can be seen in Israel over the last few years in the anti-Arab campaign of Avigdor Lieberman and his party, Yisrael Beiteinu. Lieberman's political success demonstrates the effectiveness (as well as the potential danger) of "playing the ethno-nationalist card."

The phenomenon of ethnic outbidding means that it can actually be more difficult in a democracy than in a non-democracy to deviate from an ethno-nationalist line. Nevertheless, the more democratic a state is, the more difficult it becomes to maintain and justify ethnic exclusivity because it goes against the grain of the very essence of democracy. The engine that creates transformation (or at least significant pressure for transformation) in a hegemonic regime that maintains a democracy is the collision between the ideological and political tenets of such a regime and the demands of democracy. Thus, democratization might bring about opposition to ethnic exclusivity, as demonstrated in several post-Communist East European countries (such as Estonia, Latvia, and Slovakia).

In the long run, hegemonic exclusivism of the ethnic type is likely to decline. It completely contradicts the values of democracy, equality, and self-determination prevalent in the world today, and it breeds opposition and even radicalism. Through subjugation, isolation, avoidance, and displacement of ethnic groups,[6] hegemonic majorities and their states might be able to postpone their own transformation but not totally avert it.

The struggle for the transformation of a hegemonic system is often focused on control over, access to, and participation in the public sphere. In an ethnically hegemonic state, the public sphere is structured in a way

[5] See Neil DeVotta, "From Ethnic Outbidding to Ethnic Conflict: The Institutional Bases for Sri Lanka's Separatist War," *Nations and Nationalism* 11, 1 (2005), 141–159, on a case that has deteriorated quite tragically; see also Timothy Sisk, *Power Sharing and International Mediation in Ethnic Conflict* (Washington, DC: U.S. Institute of Peace, 1996),17.

[6] Donald Rothchild and Victor Olurunsola, eds., *State vs. Ethnic Claims: African Policy Dilemmas* (Boulder, CO: Westview Press, 1986), 240–241.

that gives the majority a decisive advantage over the minority.[7] Thus, important resources such as land (often defined as the "national patrimony"), the military (and especially the domestic intelligence operation), or the mass media are likely to be under the control of the hegemonic majority. A hegemonic system cannot be transformed unless the minority can get access to the power resources controlled by the majority and by the state – land, governmental positions on all levels and of all types (but particularly on the policy-making level), the educational system, the media, and so forth. Thus, the key for a transformation in an ethnically hegemonic polity is the willingness of the dominant majority, and specifically its political leadership, to accept the minority as a significant participant (even if not a completely equal participant) in governing the country.

The majority might react to the challenge from the minority in five distinct manners (the following list develops some of the ideas raised in Chapter 7):

1. Reaffirm the status quo. Despite the tension between the ethnic nature of the state and the democratic forces within it, the hegemonic state may decide to maintain the status quo, despite its unequal nature.[8] Given that changes are invariably risky by generating unpredictable processes, the political leadership might find the maintenance of the status quo attractive, particularly if the dominant ethnic group is (or feels that it is) in firm control and the costs associated with hegemony are tolerable or perceived as such.

2. Accept cosmetic changes toward increased democratization and equality. In view of the pressure to liberalize, the ethnic state may agree to gradually dismantle the most flagrant forms of civil inequality and discrimination but without genuinely changing the character of the hegemonic regime. Moderate transformation might be carried out on an experimental basis, testing the water toward the possibility of more fundamental changes.[9] It is an attractive option to the majority, especially if the transformation is reversible.

---

[7] Will Kymlicka, *Multicultural Citizenship: A Liberal Theory of Minority Rights* (Oxford: Oxford University Press, 1995); Jeff Spinner, *The Boundaries of Citizenship: Race, Ethnicity and Nationality in the Liberal State* (Baltimore, MD: Johns Hopkins University, 1994).

[8] Among the many examples for the reaffirmation of the status quo are countries such as China and Malaysia.

[9] Spain in the post-Franco era has, in effect, adopted such a policy. The transfer of power to the "autonomies" has been gradual. See Luis Moreno, *The Federalization of Spain* (London: Frank Cass, 2001).

3. Adopt radical revision toward genuine democracy and equality. A hegemonic state may decide to dramatically change its character and become significantly more pluralistic.[10] Such a change is, by definition, mega-constitutional in the sense that it does not merely adjust an existing constitution but transforms it by creating a genuinely "new order." Radical revisions often occur under special circumstances such as war, the collapse of a regime, or large-scale violence, but they could occur through peaceful, political initiative.

4. Introduce mild changes toward the further ethnicization of the polity. The hegemonic state might decide to strengthen its ethnic character but do so in a relatively mild manner, without completely changing its fundamental character. Internal pressures, such as competition among leaders of the majority, would normally be responsible for such a move.[11] Mild changes might include the strengthening of the religious institutions of the majority,[12] symbolic changes (in flags, anthem, etc.) that emphasize the preferable position of the majority, as well as the cultural and linguistic domination of the majority within the polity.

5. Push toward full-fledged ethnicization of the hegemonic polity. The ethnic majority and its elite might adopt radical initiatives to transform the multi-ethnic state to a purely mono-ethnic polity. In doing so, it might use harsh means, including ethnic cleansing, forced assimilation, apartheid, and even full-fledged genocide.[13]

Within Israeli politics today, there is an effort to sustain the status quo (option 1), pressure for the introduction of some relatively modest changes toward greater inclusion (option 2), and equally powerful pressure for the further ethnicization of the polity (option 4). Hence, Israel is very much at a crossroads in regard to its majority-minority relations. Only time will tell whether it has decided to liberalize itself or go in the opposite direction.

---

[10] Examples include post-Franco Spain, Northern Ireland today, or post-apartheid South Africa. See Ilan Peleg, *Democratizing the Hegemonic State: Political Transformation in the Age of Identity* (Cambridge: Cambridge University Press, 2007), ch. 5.

[11] Examples include Russia in the post-Yeltsin era (under the leadership of Vladimir Putin), India under the BJP, etc.

[12] In Sri Lanka, for example, Buddhism became the state religion, thus strengthening the position of the Sinhalese vis-à-vis the Tamils.

[13] Examples include South Africa under apartheid after 1948, Turkey in 1915, Serbia under Milosevic, Rwanda in 1994, Pakistani action in Bangladesh in the 1970s, and so forth. See Peleg, *Democratizing the Hegemonic State*, especially ch. 6, 183–191.

It is useful to look at three distinct dimensions of a possible transformation in Israel. First is the direction of the change that Israel might adopt toward greater inclusion or exclusion – will Israel's political elite decide to push toward enhanced democratization and equality (that is, work toward ethno-national accommodation) or toward increased ethnicization of the polity (that is, increase the hegemony of the Jewish majority)? At the moment, Israel is not moving toward more equality; on the contrary, it has been moving toward increased hegemony.[14]

Second are the dimensions of the change – will the changes introduced be mild or radical? In general, it is difficult to be optimistic about the likelihood of a major change in Israel. The Israeli political system has been slow and hesitant in responding to Palestinian issues in general – inside and outside Israel – and there are no signs that this non-reactive inclination is about to change. At the same time, Arab-Jewish relations in Israel have deteriorated so significantly over the last decade that minor changes are now clearly insufficient.

Third, there is the mechanism of change that is the way in which a transformation in Israel might be brought about – will it be the result of violent or peaceful events? Will it be elite-initiated or public-induced? Will it come as a response to internal or international pressures? To date, the Jewish majority in Israel has supported the country's political elite in its relations toward the minority, both in terms of exclusionary and non-democratic actions (e.g., the imposition of the military government between 1948 and 1966) and in terms of inclusionary and liberal action toward the minority (e.g., allowing Arab parties to run in the parliamentary election). Whereas violent actions have not brought about immediate results, they have put the issues of the Arab minority on the public agenda on more than one occasion. Thus, following the events of October 2000 there was significant domestic pressure to seriously tackle the fundamental causes of those events. As to the source of pressure to transform the system, it has to come from the inside the country, not from the outside. It will ultimately be up to the Israeli system itself to change.[15] Although Jews in the Diaspora, especially American Jewry, are actively engaged in the issue of Arab-Jewish relations in Israel and have supported numerous initiatives to promote Arab-Jewish equality and coexistence,[16]

---

[14] See, in particular, Chapter 4 in this volume for empirical substantiation of this claim.
[15] International pressure on Israel has been limited, almost exclusively, to the issue of the future of the Occupied Territories.
[16] American Jewry, for example, has established the Inter-Agency Task Force on Israeli Arabs, a coalition of Jewish organizations, foundations, and philanthropists to promote

such efforts, though important, cannot substitute for social and political action within Israel. Individuals and groups in the Jewish Diaspora can support and encourage the reform efforts of Israelis, but they cannot themselves change the country from the outside.

Although, in general, domestic developments in Israel might prove more important than international ones in transforming the Israeli political system, the worldwide Zeitgeist is not unimportant in terms of the future of Arab-Jewish relations. Many states around the world are becoming more pluralistic and moving in the direction of recognizing minorities and granting them significant collective rights. If the status quo in Israel is sustained or if Israel becomes more exclusionary, it will find itself increasingly at odds with contemporary democratic political culture. Conversely, if Israel becomes more inclusive and pluralistic, it will reach the level of inclusive democracy that currently exists in other Western polities with ethnically diverse societies. Thus, although the typical West European nation-state was initially built on a centralized, unified, Jacobin concept of national integration, today there is a trend toward the recognition of cultural diversity, regional variance, ethno-national representation, and even significant autonomy. The politics of recognition and difference is king,[17] despite significant pressures in the opposite direction.[18]

The key for bringing about a transformation in Israel lies in understanding that like all polities, the hegemonic ethnic state is an invention, a political creature "imagined" to represent a group of people who reside in the state as well as possibly outside of it.[19] This imagined community, in the language of Benedict Anderson, views itself as a nation, rooted in common ethnic descent, shared history and destiny, common language and possibly religion, and so forth. The national construct is often linked to a territory. Whereas hegemonic states might present themselves historically and culturally as uniform entities, their minorities, those who do

---

the issue of Arab-Jewish equality in Israel. The Task Force's goal is to increase awareness of the economic gaps in Israel and to help fund Arab economic development. British Jewry has recently set up a similar task force in the United Kingdom.

[17] Iris Marion Young, *Justice and the Politics of Difference* (Princeton, NJ: Princeton University Press, 1990); Chantal Mouffe, "Which Public Sphere for a Democratic Society?" *Theoria* 99, (June 2002), 55–65.

[18] Thus, what might be called the "anti-Burqa" legislative initiatives ought to be recognized as steps away from the recognition of the other and toward more exclusionary politics.

[19] Many states view themselves as representing nations who are not all "in residence" in the national state – Ireland, Poland, Israel, and Greece are some examples. See Alexander Yakobson and Amnon Rubinstein, *Israel and the Family of Nations: The Jewish Nation-State and Human Rights* (New York: Routledge, 2009), for a large number of examples.

not "fit" their particular national construct, are constant reminders of the inherent artificiality, as well of the volatility, of the national polity within which those minorities reside.

In the case of Israel, the definition of the political community might be more complex than in most other cases of modern nationalisms, particularly because of the relative newness of the Zionist idea that brought Israel into being and the very fact that Jews have been spread all over the world, in so many different communities, and for such a long period of time. Israeli nationalism, based on the country's "Jewishness" and "Judaism"[20] to the exclusion of those who are non-Jews, is as invented and imagined as any.

The key for possibly transforming Israel is to be found in the settling or at least moderating the tension between Israeli citizenship (shared today by those defined as Jews and many who are not) and Jewish nationalism as defined by the state or by its majority. This nationalism is limited to those defined as Jews.[21] Being a member of the Jewish nation gives an individual citizen of Israel great advantage today, but it is a tension-inducing condition in terms of the relationship between the state and the minority. The resolution or moderation of that tension, created by the incongruence between citizenship and nationhood, is a key to the possible transformation of the hegemonic ethnic state into a more inclusive and more democratic state.

Political transformation is particularly likely or at least possible in cases where the imagined national community has created a polity that is democratically flawed (e.g., by negating equality to minorities), politically unstable (e.g., generating violence), or lacking legitimacy (e.g., heavily criticized externally and even internally). Those conditions (some of which clearly exist in contemporary Israel) might cause the hegemonic state to "re-imagine" itself in a more realistic, just, and democratic manner by restructuring its institutions in a more pluralistic fashion. If Israel is to change, it must be capable of re-imagining itself in a way that is at least somewhat different than its traditional definition has been.

If a multi-national state decides to reconstruct itself and become a more inclusive, pluralistic, and democratic entity, the repertoire of options available to it is quite varied. First, if the dominant ethno-national group

---

[20] There are bitter disagreements among Jews as to the meaning of those terms themselves and, consequently, as to who really belongs to the nation.

[21] This definition of "Jewish" is, in and of itself, problematic and intensely debated in Israel and beyond.

views itself as the sole sovereign, the possessor of the national territory, and the "owner" of the polity, it might nevertheless decide to grant certain collective rights to other distinct groups within the polity.[22] Secondly, the multi-national ethnic state could chose to reconstitute itself as a confederation of several nations. Such a reconstitution is a dramatic act, a far cry from merely granting some collective rights to distinct ethnonational groups. Thirdly, a multi-national hegemonic state could become a liberal democracy; that is, it could transform itself into a state of all its citizens, emphasizing individual equality and completely de-ethnicizing its public life.

The first option is readily available to Israel because the state has already given Palestinian citizens some cultural and religious rights. Thus, it could give them more collective rights, particularly political rights, including autonomy in certain areas and official political recognition. The second option is close to impossible in Israel because it negates the essence of the Jewish, Zionist state, and is very unlikely to be accepted by the Jewish public, the main constituency in Israel's political system. A combination of the third option (complete individual equality) and the first option (recognition and enhancement of group rights) is not incompatible with the continuing existence of an Israeli ethno-national system. In fact, the State of Israel could and indeed ought to guarantee both equal individual rights and extensive group rights for its Palestinian citizens, and it can do this without endangering its own identity as a Jewish and Zionist state.

A political system that is based on pure individualistic justice,[23] or on pure communitarian justice,[24] is likely to be insufficient to solve the very difficult dilemmas faced by Israel today. What could be called "national communitarianism," built around the dominant ethnic group,[25] is particularly unjust and is an invitation for instability and even violence in a deeply divided society. A genuine liberal democracy, complemented by what might be called "soft consociationalism" (or "robust multi-culturalism") fits such a society a lot better. This has to be the goal of the transformation process in contemporary Israel.

---

[22] Such a constitutional change does not necessarily mean a redefinition of the state. If the majority insists on identifying the state with its traditions, exclusively or primarily, it may still award the minority a status of a "national minority."

[23] John Rawls, *A Theory of Justice* (Cambridge, MA: Belknap Press of Harvard University Press, 1971). Rawls represents an ideal model of liberal democracy.

[24] Michael Sandel, *Liberalism and the Limits of Justice* (Cambridge and New York: Cambridge University Press, 1982).

[25] Tamir, *Liberal Nationalism*.

For most hegemonic polities, the granting of equal rights to individuals – a liberal democratic transformation – might be relatively easy, especially in a formal, legalistic manner. Israel is already there, although more in theory than in practice. The creation of shared citizenship via recognition of and representation for non-dominant groups, however, is a much tougher process. In many cases, including Israel's, it might contradict the very essence of how the majority views "its" state. The success of that project depends on the ability of the political elite to educate the populace, especially the majority, and to persuade it that the transformation of the hegemonic state into a multi-ethnic state means the creation of a more just and more stable democratic order that could work for the benefit of all citizens. Although Israel does not appear to be ready at the present time for this kind of transformation, the examples of other states demonstrate that transformation is possible.

The transformation from hegemony to multi-ethnic democracy amounts to dual challenge. First, it is a challenge to nationalism, and particularly the idea that nationalism should lead to a state that expresses exclusively the interests of a single ethno-national group. This challenge is particularly pointed when a uni-ethnic polity exists in a deeply divided society, as is indeed the situation in Israel. Second, multi-ethnicity is a challenge to liberalism, particularly the idea that ensuring equal citizenship for all individuals can solve all problems within a hegemonic state. Although the idea of individual equality is laudable and necessary for both democracy and stability, it is an insufficient remedy for the problems of societies that are already deeply divided along ethnic lines. In this regard, Israel is a classic case. Liberalism in its unadulterated, pure form might be a just and stable solution only in relatively homogenous societies, those very societies that ironically have often established their homogeneity through ethnic cleansing and the marginalization of other ethno-national or cultural groups. Liberalism has inherent difficulties in responding to the challenges of nation building in multi-national societies,[26] particularly during the early history of such societies.[27] In the case of Israel, whereas liberalism must be part of the solution, it cannot be the entire solution.

---

[26] Alan Patten, "Liberal Citizenship in Multiethnic Societies," in Alain-G. Gagnon and James Tully, eds., *Multinational Democracies* (Cambridge and New York: Cambridge University Press, 2001), 279–298.

[27] Jeff Spinner, "Unoriginal Sin: Zionism and Democratic Exclusion in Comparative Perspective," *Israel Studies Forum*, Vol. 18, No. 1 (Fall 2002): 26–56.

These limitations in regard to both nationalism and liberalism ought to be recognized in the process of contemplating the transformation of Israel's hegemonic system. In regard to nationalism, it is important to note that large forces in the contemporary world such as globalization are unlikely to overwhelm nationalism. Globalization is hardly an alternative to nationalism. On the contrary, in numerous situations it encourages nationalism as an antidote to itself. If excessive nationalism is to be fought successfully, it is on the state level that it ought to be challenged. Nationalism is a natural human force, and as such it cannot be eliminated.[28] On the other hand, it should be steered, directed, and channeled in acceptable, positive directions.

Liberalism also has to be approached as a "given," a fixture within any democratic society. In a hegemonic state that might be considering transformation, it means that special group rights for the minority will be resisted by the majority, often in the name of opposition to "reverse discrimination." The way to implement what is technically an "illiberal solution," a solution based on group rights, is by exposing societal inequalities resulting from both historical processes and discriminatory policies and pointing out in some detail how group rights might help in erasing those inequalities.

## Examples of Transformation

Most hegemonic regimes have a strong and natural tendency to resist their own transformation. The Israeli political system can be expected to behave similarly. Like other hegemonic systems, the Israeli polity has a certain built-in inertia. Analytical insight and normative conviction as to why Israel needs to change cannot easily reverse a long-term historical trajectory. Nevertheless, an examination of other cases indicates that a wide variety of conditions might either force regimes to change or make a change highly desirable. A transformation is often the result of a major crisis – a war, a revolution, and so forth – or the result of recognition that the polity has to change in order to survive.

Several cases of transformations are interesting to look at in terms of their potential relevance for the Israeli case. They could assist us in identifying factors that explain how a hegemonic state might overcome its own resistance to transformation. One such case is post-Franco Spain. Spain did not change primarily as a result of external forces (such as

---

[28] Yael Tamir, *Liberal Nationalism* (Princeton, NJ: Princeton University Press, 1993).

pressure from other European countries) but as a result of a regime-initiated transformation.[29] The conservatives who were in power following Franco's death knew that they could not stay in power without excessive repression, whereas those who were in opposition (many of them Catalans and Basques) did not have sufficient power to overthrow the regime.[30] Hence, the transformation did not come about as a result of violent action but through multi-party negotiation. The result was a process of deliberate transformation in which the country was democratized, decentralized, and, most importantly for the Israeli case, multi-ethnicized. The essence of this transformation was the replacement of the artificially imposed unitary structure (a problem in most hegemonic states) with a pluralistic regime that accepted the diversity of Spanish society but without the dismemberment of the state. The quasi-federalism[31] or semi-federalism that emerged[32] from the process is impressive; it has facilitated the recognition of both the regional and the ethno-national diversity of the country.

The transformation of Spain, though not without its problems, has undoubtedly been good in terms of democracy, equality, and stability within the country. Spain in the post-Franco era has emerged as a vibrant democracy with increasing equality of individuals and most distinct groups. Violence has been limited to radical elements among the Basques. Although the differences between Spain and Israel are huge (as is the case between any two situations), the Spanish process is highly relevant for what Israel could do. There are several lessons to be learned from Spain's example. First, despite the impact of the past, often understood as preventing change or significantly limiting change, it is never a total impediment to changes in the future. Second, sometimes a tragic past actually helps to bring about a better future. In Spain, the tragic history of the country, particularly the Civil War, moderated the position of all parties following Franco's death, thus facilitating an agreement. Third, Spain provides an example of the power of political engineering through

---

[29] The truth of the matter is that whereas internal factors were more responsible for the transformation than international factors, the latter were also important, particularly the desire of the Spanish business community to integrate economically into Europe. Andrea Bonime-Blanc, *Spain's Transition to Democracy: The Politics of Constitution Making* (Boulder, CO: Westview Press, 1987).

[30] Juan Linz & Alfred Stepan, *Problems of Democratic Transition and Consolidation* (Baltimore, MD: Johns Hopkins University, 1996).

[31] Bonime-Blanc, *Spain's Transition to Democracy*, 84.

[32] Luis Moreno calls Spain "an example of devolutionary federalism" in his *The Federalization of Spain*, 25.

multi-party agreement. Fourth, the Spanish case demonstrates the crucial role of practical and moderate leadership in the process of producing an acceptable solution to highly complex conflicts, as well as the important role of popular support. Finally, the case of Spain also demonstrates the importance of maintaining flexibility even after a constitutional compromise has been hammered out. Since the constitution of 1978, several components of the constitution have been changed, further enhancing the system's effectiveness and stability.

Canada is another example of a state that has successfully gone through a transformation, overcoming the resistance to it. The Canadian case is even more relevant for Israel. Like Israel, Canada has been a pluralistic mosaic from its very beginning.[33] Although English hegemony was established, the "French factor" was always present. Complex mechanisms were therefore devised in order to facilitate that hegemony while recognizing the status of the minority (as was the case in Israel). For example, whereas the Anglican Church had an official status in Canada as a British colony, the Catholic Church was granted official status in Quebec in the late eighteenth century.[34] Once Canada became independent in 1867, the English majority quickly established control over most aspects of public life, particularly a dominant position in the central government and in leading the national economy. The flag adopted was a modified Union Jack, and immigrants were expected to go along with "Anglo conformity."[35]

Only after World War II has this hegemonic model begun to change, transforming the "essence" of Canada in a pluralistic direction. This change reflected the decline of Britain as a world power and the significant weakening of Canada's links to Britain, but also the rising assertiveness on the part of the Quebecois. New policies in the 1970s encouraged immigrants to "maintain various aspects of their ethnic heritage."[36] A new symbolic order was introduced,[37] with a neutral flag (a red maple leaf), a new national anthem, and most importantly a new status for the

---

[33] Peter Kivisto, *Multiculturalism in a Global Society* (Oxford and Malden, MA: Blackwell Publishing, 2002), 85.

[34] Leslie L. Laczko, "Canada's Pluralism in Comparative Perspective," *Ethnic and Racial Studies*, Vol. 17, No, 1 (January 1994), 20–41 (esp. 31).

[35] Will Kymlicka, *Finding Our Way: Rethinking Ethnocultural Relations in Canada.* (Oxford: Oxford University Press, 1998), 44.

[36] Ibid.

[37] Raymond Breton, "The Production and Allocation of Symbolic Resources: An Analysis of the Linguistic and Ethnocultural Fields in Canada," *Canadian Review of Sociology and Anthropology*, Vol. 21 (1984), 123–140.

French language. The country declared itself bilingual.[38] It is important to note, however, that despite the growing recognition of the French culture and language, and the power given to Quebec as a province, total equality was not established. At the same time, Canada has become significantly less hegemonic, and more liberal, inclusionary, and pluralistic.[39] The relevance of this for Israel is self-evident.

Although Canada has shifted toward a more open and inclusive political order, this transformation has not been easy or universally accepted – numerous Canadians have seen the change as problematic. The 1988 Multiculturalism Act, for instance, was criticized as divisive. Many Quebecois felt that multi-culturalism diluted their special rights as one of Canada's two Founding Nations. In English Canada, many have viewed multi-culturalism as harming national unity; whereas others saw it as anti-liberal. However, transformation occurred despite the resistance of many within the hegemonic majority.

The cases of Spain and Canada demonstrate the capacity of countries to transform themselves despite strong resistance to transformation. Other countries also demonstrate the possibility of overcoming opposition and making major changes, notably the United Kingdom,[40] Northern Ireland,[41] and South Africa.[42] In the case of the United Kingdom, a unitary centralized polity initiated (in 1997) a process of "devolution," transferring power from the parliament in Westminster to Scotland and Wales

---

[38] In regard to language rights, the personality principle was adopted in Canada – language rights are given to individuals and may be exercised anywhere in the land (unlike the more limited territorial principle in regard to language education that applies in Belgium, Spain, or Switzerland). Jean Laponce, *Languages and Their Territories* (Toronto: University of Toronto Press, 1987); Carol L. Schmid, *The Politics of Language: Conflict, Identity, and Cultural Pluralism in Comparative Perspective* (Oxford: Oxford University Press, 2001); Ayelet Harel-Shalev, "The Status of Minority Languages in Deeply Divided Societies: Urdu in India and Arabic in Israel – A Comparative Perspective," *Israel Studies Forum*, Vol. 21, No. 2 (2006), 28–57.

[39] Eva Mackey, *The House of Difference: Cultural Politics and National Identity in Canada* (London and New York: Routledge, 1999), 5; Gordon E. Cannon, "Consociationalism vs. Control: Canada as a Case Study," *Western Political Quarterly*, Vol. 35, No. 1 (1982), 50–64.

[40] Vernon Bogdanor, "Devolution: Decentralization or Disintegration?" *The Political Quarterly*, Vol. 70, No. 2 (1999), 185–194; Peleg, *Democratizing the Hegemonic State*, 122–127.

[41] John D. Cash, "The Dilemmas of Political Transformation in Northern Ireland," *Pacifica Review*, Vol. 10, No. 3 (1998), 227–234; Peleg, *Democratizing the Hegemonic State*, 153–157.

[42] Adrian Guelke, "Ethnic Rights and Majority Rule: The Case of South Africa," *International Political Science Review*, Vol. 13, No. 4 (1992), 415–432; Peleg, *Democratizing the Hegemonic State*, 158–167.

and thus giving birth to a quasi-federal system.[43] In Northern Ireland, a consociational political system was adopted through a large-scale constitutional reform; and in the case of South Africa, a dramatic change toward majoritarian rule was made.[44] Whereas all these examples indicate the capacity of political systems to significantly change, there are plenty of counter-examples indicating that political systems might equally move toward sustaining and strengthening their hegemonic regimes.[45] In some cases, such as Sri Lanka,[46] Rwanda,[47] and Milosevic's Serbia, a radical change toward hegemony has occurred, leading to large-scale violence; whereas in other cases, such as Russia and India,[48] ethnicization may be more moderate.

## The Prospects for Change

It is impossible to safely predict whether Israel will follow the examples of countries that have moved toward recognition of their own diversity. Israel's present political climate is not promising in this regard. The current Israeli government coalition led by Prime Minister Netanyahu that came into power in 2009 includes parties that are very nationalistic, anti-universalistic, and anti-Arab (e.g., Yisrael Beiteinu). The leading party in the coalition, Likud, has always been a fundamentally nationalist party, despite the presence of some liberals within it.[49] Other parties in

---

[43] Jonathan Bradbury and James Mitchell, "Devolution: Stability, Uncertainty and Crisis," *Parliamentary Affairs*, Vol. 55, No. 2 (2002), 299–316.

[44] Adrian Guelke, *Rethinking the Rise and Fall of Apartheid* (New York: Palgrave Macmillan, 2005); Kristin Henrard, "Post Apartheid South Africa: Transformation and Reconciliation," *World Affairs* 166, 1 (summer 2003), 37–55.

[45] Peleg, *Democratizing the Hegemonic State*, ch. 6.

[46] Maya Chadda, "Between Consociationalism and Control: Sri Lanka," in Ulrich Schneckener and Stefan Wolff, eds., *Managing and Settling Ethnic Conflicts* (New York: Palgrave, 2004), 94–114; DeVotta, "From Ethnic Outbidding to Ethnic Conflict," 141–159.

[47] Helen M. Hintjens, "Explaining the 1994 Genocide in Rwanda," *The Journal of Modern African Studies*, Vol. 37, No. 2 (1999), 241–286.

[48] Amatendu Misra, "Politics of the Hindu Right: Emergence and Growth of the Bharatiya Janata Party," *Politics, Administration and Change*, Vol. 32, No. 2 (July–December 1999), 36–55.

[49] It is important to note that in July 2010 Dan Meridor, a Likud minister, expressed his strong opposition to an amendment in the Citizenship Law that required prospective Israeli citizens to declare allegiance to Israel as a "Jewish, democratic state," thereby delaying a cabinet vote on the matter. In raising the issue, Meridor (who was supported by Benny Begin, another Likud minister and son of Menachem Begin) quoted Ze'ev Jabotinsky. See Barak Ravid, "Meridor: Loyalty oath will only make Israeli Arabs more extreme," *Ha'aretz*, July 19, 2010.

the current government are religious nationalists (e.g., Shas) who regard all non-Jews in Israel, not only Arabs, as aliens;[50] whereas others are closely linked to the settler movement, the most radical element of the Israeli public.[51] The present government, therefore, is extremely unlikely to launch or even accept a liberalization program of any kind, although it might approve some limited initiatives for Israel's Arab citizens, mainly by focusing on reducing the economic gaps between Jews and Arabs, but even this is questionable given the strong ethnocratic orientation of many of its members.

The composition of the current Israeli government is indicative of a broader fact about contemporary Israeli politics, namely the unprecedented weakness of the Left (represented by parties such as Meretz, which now has been reduced in the 2009 elections to just three Knesset members) and Center-left (represented by the decimated Labor party, with only eleven Knesset members). Because the Left and at least some in the Center-left are traditionally the bearers of the universalist, liberal vision in Israel, the political decline of the Israeli Left and Center-left indicates the general decline of the universal-liberal vision in Israel's political landscape.

Whereas the power of the Left and Center-left in Israel has declined in recent years, the power of the Right has increased. The Israeli Right's nationalist agenda essentially amounts to sustaining and even enhancing Israel's exclusivist Jewish character. Not only has the traditional Right (in the form of the Likud party) returned to power, but a New Right (represented by Avigdor Lieberman's Yisrael Beiteinu party) has also gained influence, largely by emphasizing the threat posed by Israel's Arab minority. The appointment of Lieberman as Israel's foreign minister in the current government is important in this regard because it has given his ideology and confrontational style of politics much greater visibility and even legitimacy. Thus, the discriminatory, anti-Arab legislation that have recently been proposed by right-wing politicians in Israel are surely a sign of things to come.

If one looks at the Israeli political scene from the perspective of the attitude of the Jewish majority toward the Palestinian minority, and

---

[50] Thus, for example, the interior ministry under Shas leader Eli Yishai has pursued a very tough policy toward foreign workers, including their Israel-born, Hebrew-speaking children.

[51] Since 1967, several political parties have been linked to the settlement movement. This includes the Mafdal (National Religious Party), the Tehiyah, and today the National Union (Ichud Leumi).

particularly from the perspective of the various types of nationalism represented, four different camps can be identified. The largest camp might be called the "moderate nationalists." They are people, numbering around 60 percent of the Jewish population in Israel, who support the status quo and would like to maintain the Jewish and Zionist character of the State of Israel. They accept the formula of "Jewish and democratic" as an ideal to be maintained and believe that this ideal has, in fact, been achieved. Although members of this dominant camp among the Jewish majority believe that Arab citizens as individuals ought to be treated as equals, they tend to oppose extensive collective rights for the Arab minority, especially beyond the rights already given to the minority. In this sense, people belonging to this camp are genuinely "nationalists," supporters of the superior status of the Jewish majority. As pragmatists and moderates, however, members of this camp support efforts to close the economic gap between Arabs and Jews, as well as other changes, but only within the existing Israeli polity. Moderate nationalists accept the inevitability of the two-state solution but mostly in order to guarantee the "Jewishness" of the State of Israel. In terms of their political affiliation, most members of this camp tend to vote for the centrist parties (Kadima and Labor), whereas some might vote for the Likud.[52] These parties currently control sixty-eight seats in the Knesset, a clear majority.[53]

A second camp within the Israeli-Jewish majority can be called the "extreme nationalists." We estimate this camp as between 20 percent and 30 percent of the Jewish public. People who belong to this camp believe that between democracy and "Jewishness," however these might be defined, the latter should prevail. Hence, they prefer the Jewish-Zionist character of the state over democracy, and they want exclusive Jewish control over the state. Extreme nationalists tend to perceive the outside world, particularly all Arabs, with suspicion, hostility, and disdain. They regard Arab citizens as a potential security threat and favor tight control over them. Many believe that Israel will eventually have to expel the Arabs, either through war or through an agreement with the PA that will swap Israeli settlement blocs in the Occupied Territories for Arab-inhabited

---

[52] Some Likud politicians, such as Reuven Rivlin and Dan Meridor, are moderate nationalists, whereas others are closer to being extreme nationalists.

[53] Among the intellectuals that argue for a liberal-nationalist position, one can find people such as Ruth Gavison, Amnon Rubinstein, Yael Tamir, Alexander Yakobson, and many other members of the Israeli academia. The Israeli legal community, headed by the Supreme Court, has also been supportive of the status quo, although on some issues they have been "pushing the envelope" toward a liberal interpretation of the law.

areas of Israel (particularly in Wadi Ara and the Triangle). Members of this camp support far-right parties such as the National Union (currently composed of Moledet, Hatikva, Eretz Yisrael Shelanu, and Tkuma), the Jewish Home party, and Yisrael Beiteinu – together these parties have twenty-two seats in the current Knesset.

The third camp among Israeli Jews might be called the "liberal nationalists." The liberal belief system of these Israeli Jews, only about 7 percent to 8 percent of the Israeli-Jewish public, emphasizes democracy and equality as core values. More specifically, members of this camp promote full equality for Arabs and Jews as individuals, the enhancement of the collective rights of the Palestinian minority though cultural autonomy (but not bi-nationalism), and the genuine integration of Palestinian citizens into all aspects of Israeli society, culture, economy, and politics. This camp, however small, espouses some of the fundamental ideals of Western democracy with its emphasis on civic equality. It is important to emphasize, however, that members of this camp do support maintaining the Jewish character of Israel. Most people in this camp endorse the central elements of Zionism, including the Law of Return that grants preferential treatment to Jewish immigrants to Israel and the special relationship between Israel and Jewish communities around the world. Yet, liberal nationalists are strongly opposed to any form of discrimination against Israeli citizens. Supporters and members of the Meretz party as well as some supporters and members of the Labor party represent this liberal nationalist attitude, as do many Israeli NGOs working on behalf of Arab-Jewish equality and coexistence (such as the New Israel Fund, Sikkuy, the Abraham Fund, and Merchavim). The proposals we made in Chapter 7 are generally in accordance with the views of this camp.

The fourth, and by far the smallest camp among Israeli Jews are the "anti-nationalists." Individuals who belong to this camp are opposed, as a matter of principle, to the existence of a Jewish state, either because they are philosophically anti-nationalist or, more often, because they view the Zionist project as imperial and colonial. Some anti-nationalists support the transformation of Israel into a bi-national state (in the territory of Israel proper in its June 4, 1967, borders), whereas others prefer one democratic state covering all the territory of Israel/Palestine (i.e., over all the territory of the former British Mandate of Palestine). We estimate the size of this camp to be only 1 percent to 2 percent of Israeli Jews. They tend to vote for the non-Zionist, Arab-Jewish Hadash party.

The struggle between these four camps will continue in the years to come. The major struggle is likely to be between the dominant Zionist

camps that we have called the "moderate nationalists" and the "extremist nationalists" to their right. A decisive movement toward a two-state
solution, supported by the majority of the moderate nationalists, will
generate intense debate about majority-minority relations in Israel. The
extremists are likely to argue, as they already have, that "Israeli Arabs"
have to be "dealt with" in the context of adopting a two-state solution,
whereas many moderate nationalists will probably oppose the extremists' radical "solutions." The debate between these two now-dominant
camps over this issue will be part of a larger debate over the nature of the
Jewish Republic.

However, the struggle between the moderates and the extremists will
not be the only one waged. Liberal nationalists will also be part of the
debate over majority-minority relations in Israel and over the character
of the state in general. The liberal nationalists will argue for the need for
more extensive changes to the existing Israeli regime – the transformation
from the current hegemony to a significantly more inclusive, egalitarian
democracy. In arguing for the necessity of introducing more significant
changes, the liberals will have to convince moderate nationalists that
these changes are not merely in the interest of the Palestinian minority
but also that of the Jewish majority and the state itself.

The proposals offered in this book can be looked on as an agenda for
change in Israel, particularly as it applies to the relationship between the
Jewish majority and the Palestinian minority. The effective promotion
of this agenda requires the establishment of a broad coalition of political forces that have traditionally belonged to different "camps" in Israel.
This coalition must include, not only Israeli Jews who are liberal nationalists, but also those who are moderate nationalists. By itself, the Israeli
Left lacks the political power to carry out the kind of agenda we have
proposed (and there is little reason to expect that the Left will experience
a major improvement in its political fortunes any time soon). The Left
needs to find allies in the center and even on the right of Israel's political
map. Although this may seem highly improbable, it is worth bearing in
mind that a similarly broad coalition now exists in Israel in support of the
two-state solution. Such a coalition in favor of a Palestinian state (which
includes some members of the Likud party and Yisrael Beiteinu, as well
as members of Kadima, Labor, Meretz, and Hadash) would have been
unthinkable in the past. Once, support for a Palestinian state was con-
fined to the far-left margins of Israeli politics, whereas today there is an
overwhelming consensus among Israeli Jews in support of it (even though
many Israeli Jews remain deeply skeptical of Palestinian intentions). Thus,

just as most Israeli Jews have come to accept the necessity of a Palestinian state – for the sake of Israeli, not Palestinian, interests – so too, it is quite possible that in the future they will also come to recognize the need for major changes in majority-minority relations in Israel.

Of course, it is not just Israeli Jews who will need to support the kinds of changes we have advocated in this book. Palestinian citizens of Israel must also actively support them (and not just passively). Such support is not guaranteed. There are now vocal and influential segments of the Palestinian minority who reject any kind of integration in Israel and shun cooperation with Israeli Jews altogether. They will not be satisfied with anything less than a bi-national state in Israel. For the time being at least, these radical elements are a minority among Palestinians in Israel. Most Palestinians in Israel are more moderate and thus much more likely to support the changes we propose. They will need to join together with Israeli Jews to create a strong majority in support of Arab-Jewish accommodation and reconciliation in Israel. This Arab-Jewish alliance is necessary to push for change and to counter the extremists on both sides. Unless such an alliance emerges, the future of majority-minority relations in Israel looks very bleak.

### Conclusion: Future Scenarios

If no major change occurs and majority-minority relations continue to deteriorate in Israel, a number of negative scenarios might occur in the future. These scenarios are very worrying in terms of the stability of the state and the quality of its democracy. In this section, we identify these scenarios and try to assess their likelihood. It is important to note that several of these negative scenarios might reinforce one another.

Scenario #1 is increasing Arab political separatism. The Arab public will withdraw from Israeli politics (a majority of Arab voters will boycott Israeli elections), and there will be growing Arab demands for political autonomy, not just cultural autonomy. This type of separatism has already occurred since the 2001 elections with reduced participation of Palestinian citizens in national elections. There is a significant danger, with high level of probability that Arab political separatism will increase. Although this separatism will not amount to territorial secession, it could be politically highly negative. Whereas cultural separatism (in the form of strengthening the Arab educational system, for example) is tolerable, political separatism is a lot more dangerous from the perspective of the long-term stability of the Israeli polity.

Scenario #2 is the intensification of Jewish exclusionism toward the Arabs in Israel, entailing the increasing erosion of the rights of Arab citizens and their gradual exclusion from the Israeli political system. This is also already happening as the growing intolerance of the Jewish majority toward the political activities of the Arab minority has led to the imposition of various legal restrictions on their political freedoms. Consequently, the ability of the Arab minority to challenge the Zionist consensus in Israel and to demand changes to the character of the state has been steadily eroded over the past decade.[54] Indeed, some observers have argued that an ongoing process of "creeping apartheid" has been occurring inside Israel.[55] The further marginalization of Palestinian citizens of Israel could turn the country from being an "ethnic democracy," a flawed and illiberal democracy, to a full-fledged ethnocracy.[56]

Scenario #3 is the significant increase in inter-communal violence between Palestinians and Jews in Israel, an increase that could easily lead to a serious escalation with unpredictable results. This will include more frequent and bloodier clashes between Jews and Arabs in mixed towns (which are growing in number) and in mixed regions of the country (such as the Negev and the Galilee). It is important to note in this context that even towns with a long history of inter-communal relations, such as Jaffa and Acre, have experienced episodes of inter-communal violence in recent years. In Acre, for example, in October 2008, thirty homes, one hundred cars, and eighty shops, both Jewish and Arab, were attacked in the course of two weeks of clashes between local Arabs and Jews.[57] The policy of the government – preventing the expansion of Arab villages and towns – force many Arabs to move into Jewish towns, a demographic process that generates more tension, conflict, and occasional violence.

Scenario #4 is the outbreak of an Arab intifada inside Israel. Such a development would mean that a significant number of Arab citizens will become involved in a mass uprising against the state. This could include

---

[54] For this claim, see Amal Jamal, "Nationalizing States and the Constitution of 'Hollow Citizenship': Israel and its Palestinian Citizens," *Ethnopolitics* 6, 4 (2007), 477.

[55] Oren Yiftachel, "'Creeping Apartheid' in Israel-Palestine," *Middle East Report* 39, 253 (2009): 7–15.

[56] Oren Yiftachel, *Ethnocracy: Land & Identity Politics in Israel/Palestine* (Philadelphia: University of Pennsylvania Press, 2006). See also Yoav Peled, "Citizenship Betrayed: Israel's Emerging Immigration and Citizenship Regime," *Theoretical Inquiries in Law* 8, 2 (2007), 333–358.

[57] The Mossawa Center has warned that "[t]he situation in Acre is an early-warning signal of a potentially explosive country-wide conflict between Arabs and Jews." Mossawa Center, "Akko: City on the Front," December 2008, 8.

violent protests, demonstrations and marches, and large-scale civil disobedience (along the lines of the first Palestinian intifada). Although we do not view this scenario as very likely at the present time (mid-2010), the nature of popular uprisings is that they are unpredictable and have a life of their own. Whereas an internal uprising would be very costly to the minority, and the leadership of the Palestinian community might therefore be risk-averse, events could spiral out of control. Furthermore, the lack of a resolution of long-term ethnic problems can sometimes lead to large-scale violence.[58]

Scenario #5 is the possibility of the involvement of Palestinian citizens of Israel, as individuals or in groups, in terrorist activities inside Israel. Radical groups within the Arab population could form and engage in terrorist activities, or members of the Arab population could join outside radical groups (such as Hamas and Hezbollah) and engage in terrorist activities on their behalf. To date, only a small number of Palestinian citizens of Israel have been involved in terrorist activities against the state. During the second intifada, however, there was a significant increase in the number of Arab citizens involved in terrorism.[59]

Scenario #6, the internationalization of the issue of Arab equality within Israel, is a lot more likely than either internal Palestinian terrorism or an internal intifada. Such a process will amount to increasing pressure on Israel to significantly improve the status of its Palestinian citizens and meet accepted international standards in regard to minority groups. To date, the international community has focused almost exclusively on the status of the West Bank and Gaza. In the last few years, however, there has been a growing effort by Palestinian NGOs, as well as some Jewish-Arab organizations, to raise international awareness about the issues of the Palestinian minority in Israel. Thus, for example, the Arab civil rights organization Adalah has appealed to the EU to raise the issue of the proposed "loyalty oaths" in meetings with Israeli diplomats.[60]

Scenario #7 is the fusion of the internal and external Palestinian issues. This scenario will involve Palestinians in Israel and in the West Bank and Gaza uniting together in a common struggle, probably demanding

---

[58] The case of Northern Ireland, Sri Lanka, and Rwanda are some examples.

[59] In 1999, only two Arabs were found to be involved in terrorist activity; in 2001 the number had increased to thirty, and the next year to seventy-seven. Figures in International Crisis Group, "Identity Crisis: Israel and its Arab Citizens," *Middle East Report* 25, 1 (March 2004), 25.

[60] Authors' interview with Hassan Jabareen, general director of Adalah, Haifa, June 24, 2009.

a single bi-national state in Israel/Palestine.[61] If the effort to establish a Palestinian state fails and Israel's Palestinian minority remains marginalized, the campaigns on behalf of Palestinian rights in the Occupied Territories and in Israel proper might merge into a joint demand for political equality within the entire area of Israel/Palestine. Hence, this scenario will become more likely as the possibility of a two-state solution declines.[62] This scenario will be explored more fully in the Conclusion, which focuses on the connection between Israel's internal and external Palestinian "problems."

---

[61] Belgium is a model for such bi-nationalism. Although it is not a particularly successful state, it is much superior to the occupation and the marginalization that has characterized Jewish-Palestinians relations.

[62] The one-state solution has been suggested in the past by the Palestinian-American intellectual Edward Said but is now advocated by many others, including Yehuda Shenhav in *The Time of the Green Line* (Hakibbutz: Hameuchad, 2010); see also Dmitry Reider, "Who Is Afraid of the One-State Solution?" *Foreign Affairs*, March 31, 2010.

# Conclusion

## A Comprehensive Resolution of the Palestinian Problem

> Israel's Arabs are part of the same thing – together with the Palestinians – and there is no use solving the Palestinian problem without solving the Israeli Arab problem. Returning to the 1967 borders will bring neither peace nor security, but will transfer the conflict into Kfar Saba and Raanana [towns inside Israel]. So when you try to solve the problem, you must solve the whole thing.
>
> Avigdor Lieberman, foreign minister and deputy prime minister, 2009-present[1]

The main purpose of this book has been to draw attention to the escalating conflict within Israel between its Jewish majority and its Palestinian minority and to offer our ideas for how this conflict can be alleviated. This is not just an issue of domestic importance to Israel that threatens the country's internal stability and even its democratic regime. It is also an issue that is inextricably linked to the Israeli-Palestinian conflict, a conflict with massive regional and even global repercussions. We believe that the existence of a sizable Palestinian national minority within Israel has major implications for how the State of Israel should define itself and behave and for how the long-running conflict between Israel and the Palestinian nation should be resolved. Simply put, it means that it is highly problematic for the State of Israel to define itself as an exclusively Jewish state, and that it is wrong to believe that the conflict between Israel and the Palestinians can be solved by the two-state solution alone, that is a Jewish state and a Palestinian state. Thus, we have to rethink the future of Israel and the solution to the Israeli-Palestinian conflict.

[1] Attila Somfalvi, "Lieberman defends PR, slams opposition," *Ynet*, June 6, 2010.

At a time when the international community, led by the United States, is actively promoting the two-state solution and the establishment of a Palestine state, this rethinking is urgently needed.

The problems of the Palestinian minority in Israel, specifically their second-class status within the country and their troubled relations with the Jewish majority, have been ignored by Israeli Jews, by Israeli governments, by Arab governments, by American governments, and by the international community at large for far too long. This neglect has allowed these problems to fester and grow, and it has led to increasing frustration and discontent among Palestinian citizens of Israel. While the world's attention has been focused on the predicament of Palestinians in the West Bank, Gaza Strip, and East Jerusalem, the predicament of Palestinians in Israel – albeit better than that of Palestinians in these territories – has been largely overlooked. At best, it is regarded as a domestic Israeli matter, one that has little if anything to do with the conflict between Israel and the Palestinians. Without wishing to deny the importance of ending Israel's occupation of Palestinian territories and improving the lives of Palestinians in the territories, we believe that improving the status of the Palestinian minority in Israel and its relations with the Jewish majority is also critically important and needs to receive much more attention, both inside and outside Israel. Unless this happens, we fear that Arab-Jewish tension within Israel will continue to escalate, potentially leading to violent confrontations, loss of Palestinian civil rights, rising terrorism, and even an internal intifada. In short, what this book calls "the conflict within" could well explode. To go on ignoring and neglecting the issue of the Palestinian minority in Israel, therefore, is very dangerous because the future of Arab-Jewish coexistence in the country is now at risk.

Some might argue that we are being overly alarmist and that Arab-Jewish relations in Israel are not nearly as bad we suggest. To be sure, at first sight there is little evidence of conflict between Palestinians and Jews in Israel. Violence remains rare, and interpersonal relations are normally civil. However, beneath the surface of daily life tensions are increasing, and attitudes and perceptions on both sides are worsening (as we have shown in Chapters 3 and 4). Radical political views have gained ground among Palestinians and Jews in Israel. Extremists within both communities have fanned the flames of hatred and become more vocal and prominent. At present, both Jews and Palestinians are locked in a vicious circle in which the radicalism of one feeds the radicalism of the other. Although most Palestinians and most Jews in Israel are still politically moderate and favor coexistence, the political trends within both communities – with Palestinians in Israel becoming more assertive and more nationalistic, and Israeli Jews becoming less tolerant and more right-wing – point toward growing conflict between the two groups.

The first part of this book described in detail the deteriorating relationship between the Jewish majority and the Palestinian minority and discussed the reasons for this deterioration. In doing so, it basically made the case for why major action must be taken to improve the status of the Palestinian minority and better manage majority-minority relations in Israel. The second part of this book considered both theoretically and practically what changes Israel could and should make with regard to its treatment of the Palestinian minority. It argued that since its establishment in 1948, the State of Israel has never really been a liberal democracy, but a Jewish Republic that has consistently pursued an exclusionary rather than an inclusionary policy toward its Palestinian minority. Consequently, it has alienated, not integrated, its Palestinian citizens and entrenched the division between the Jewish majority and the Palestinian minority.

To overcome this legacy, the Israeli state needs to become much more accommodating of its Palestinian minority. It must recognize the Palestinians as a national minority, increase their collective rights (including granting them cultural autonomy), enhance their political representation, raise their socio-economic level, and safeguard their individual rights. The policy recommendations we made in Chapter 7 amount to a complete transformation of Israel's approach toward its Palestinian minority. Minor, cosmetic changes are not enough. The grievances of the Palestinian minority are deep and their current demands are far-reaching, as the Vision documents published in 2006–2007 attest. Whereas we do not think that all of these demands can or should be satisfied (in particular, we oppose the call contained in the Vision documents for Israel to become a completely bi-national state),[2] we do believe that Israel must seriously respond to these demands and that many of them can be met without Israel abandoning its Jewish character. We have tried to suggest how Israel can maintain its "Jewishness" and at the same time accommodate its Palestinian minority.

---

[2] In our opinion, it is unfair to demand a Palestinian nation-state in the West Bank and Gaza while insisting that Israel cease to be a Jewish nation-state and instead become a bi-national state (as the Vision documents do).

We hope that our proposals will be adopted by Israeli governments in the near future, or at least that they will help generate a real dialogue between representatives of the country's Jewish and Palestinian citizens. The growing awareness among Israelis, including Israeli politicians of all political stripes (left, right, and center), of the deteriorating relations between Jews and Arabs provide some reason to believe that such a long overdue dialogue may at last occur. The broad consensus that exists within Israel about the problematic nature of majority-minority relations in the country is a necessary starting point for any kind of serious reckoning with the issue. However, given the political trends we have discussed in the book (especially in Chapters 2–4) and the political forces within Israel that are opposed to change (discussed in Chapter 8), we are pessimistic about the prospects for a major improvement in the status of Palestinians in Israel and in Jewish-Arab relations. For this to happen, the Jewish majority essentially has to be willing to give up the hegemony it has always enjoyed in Israel, and thus far it has shown no inclination to do this.

## Arab-Jewish Relations and the Israeli-Palestinian Conflict

The single biggest factor inhibiting the willingness of Israeli Jews to relinquish their hegemony and support real equality between Jews and Arabs in Israel is the ongoing Israeli-Palestinian conflict. Unlike many other cases of ethno-national hegemony mentioned in this book, in Israel's case the dominant ethno-national majority is essentially at war with the kin of the ethno-national minority. This greatly complicates majority-minority relations in Israel. The behavior and beliefs of Israeli Jews vis-à-vis Arabs in Israel must be understood within the context of the long, bitter, and bloody conflict between Jews and Palestinians and their respective national movements. This conflict has profoundly shaped how the Jewish majority in Israel has treated the Palestinian minority from the very beginning of Israeli statehood, and it will continue to do so as long as the conflict continues. There is, therefore, little chance that a dramatic improvement in relations between Jews and Palestinians inside Israel will occur while the wider Israeli-Palestinian conflict remains unresolved.

Although the Israeli-Palestinian conflict is certainly not solely responsible for the deteriorating relations between Jews and Palestinians within Israel, the conflict undoubtedly contributes to this deterioration in a number of ways. First, it is because of the Israeli-Palestinian conflict that Israeli Jews perceive "Israeli Arabs" as a security threat and a potential fifth column.[3] The fear and suspicion that many Israeli Jews harbor toward Arabs as a result of the conflict makes them less willing to make "concessions" to the Arab minority, because they worry that doing so might be perceived as weakness and could embolden the Arabs. The lack of trust also means that Israeli Jews fear that any concessions will be exploited by the Arab minority. As long as this zero-sum mentality prevails among the Jewish majority, there will be little inclination to make major concessions to the Palestinian minority (such as granting them collective rights). The Jewish majority will not willingly give up its position of dominance over the Palestinian minority while simultaneously engaged in a conflict with the Palestinian nation at large.

Second, the Israeli-Palestinian conflict also affects the perceptions and attitudes of Palestinians in Israel. To the extent that Palestinians in Israel perceive the Israeli state as violently oppressing Palestinians in the territories, they are hardly likely to feel any sense of loyalty to this state or want to identify with it in any way. They are also likely to feel some degree of antagonism toward Israeli Jews who support "the Occupation" and Israel's military offensives against Palestinians and other Arabs (such as Hezbollah in Lebanon). This increases the acute sense of alienation felt by Palestinian citizens of Israel vis-à-vis the Israeli state and Israeli-Jewish society, which in turn feeds radical forces within the Palestinian community. Thus, the conflict weakens the desire of many Palestinian citizens to integrate into Israeli society and politics and strengthens their political separatism instead.

Third, extremist politicians in both communities exploit the Israeli-Palestinian conflict for their own political purposes. Examples abound of Jewish and Arab political figures taking advantage of the conflict to increase their political appeal and advance their agendas. Avigdor Lieberman, for instance, capitalized on the 2008–2009 Gaza war to promote his anti-Arab platform,[4] and this significantly helped his Yisrael Beiteinu party at the polls in the February 2009 election. Similarly, Sheik Raed Salah, the firebrand leader of the Northern Branch of the Islamic Movement, gained a great deal of attention for his participation in the much publicized Gaza flotilla incident in May 2010 (especially as a result

---

[3] It should be noted that this perception is not entirely baseless because a few Palestinian citizens of Israel have been involved in terrorist activities. See, for example, Amos Harel, "Two Israeli Arabs arrested on suspicion of planning attacks," *Ha'aretz*, December 6, 2007.

[4] Isabel Kershner, "Gaza War Gives Bigger Lift to Israel's Right Than to Those in Power," *The New York Times*, January 26, 2009.

of initial false rumors that he had been killed by Israeli commandos onboard the Turkish vessel *Mavi Marmara*).[5] By raising the visibility and boosting the appeal of political extremists on both sides, therefore, the conflict increases the political polarization between the Jewish and Arab communities in Israel.

Finally, because the Israeli-Palestinian conflict generally dominates the political agenda in Israel, other issues get less public and political attention. Despite now being widely acknowledged in Israel to be a crucial, even an existential, issue for the country's future, the issue of Arab-Jewish relations inside Israel and the status of the Arab minority still gets neglected because of the heavy focus on the conflict and on relations between Israel and the PA. It only receives occasional and passing attention, and even then often in the context of a flare-up of Israeli-Palestinian violence in the Occupied Territories.

The extremely negative impact that the Israeli-Palestinian conflict has on Arab-Jewish relations in Israel is even worse when Israeli-Palestinian violence or Israeli-Arab violence in general spikes. As the level of violence increases, so too does the tension and animosity between Jews and Palestinians in Israel, as they tend to immediately take opposite sides. When all-out wars break out, Jewish-Palestinian relations inside Israel severely deteriorate, as occurred with Israel's recent wars in Lebanon (in July-August 2006) and Gaza. Indeed, even though eighteen Arab citizens of Israel were actually killed by Hezbollah's missiles in the case of the second Lebanon war (out of a total of forty-three Israeli civilians killed), the war still polarized Jews and Arabs in Israel.

Clearly, a significant improvement in Arab-Jewish relations in Israel depends on a resolution of the Israeli-Palestinian conflict. This is not to say that no progress can be made in the meantime. Some progress is certainly possible while the Israeli-Palestinian conflict continues. Much can be accomplished, for instance, in reducing economic inequalities between Jews and Arabs (chiefly by providing more government funding to Arab communities and more employment opportunities for Arab citizens). A more prosperous Arab minority is likely to have better relations with the Jewish majority and a better attitude toward the state, even if the Israeli-Palestinian conflict remains unresolved.[6] Nevertheless, major progress,

---

[5] See Eli Ashkenazi, Jack Khoury, and Liel Kyzer, "Police interrogate Islamic Movement chief Sheikh Raed Salah over role in Gaza flotilla clashes," *Ha'aretz*, June 1, 2010.

[6] It is worth noting here that positive political developments in Northern Ireland in the late 1990s, including the breakthrough "Good Friday" agreement, occurred in the context of a positive economic situation in the province.

especially involving the kind of political changes we believe to be necessary, are highly unlikely to occur before a resolution of the Israeli-Palestinian conflict.

The dilemma is that whereas the external Israeli-Palestinian conflict must be resolved in order to satisfactorily deal with the internal Arab-Jewish conflict, the internal conflict makes it harder to resolve the external conflict. There are, of course, many issues that bedevil an Israeli-Palestinian peace agreement. Such an agreement would be difficult to achieve even if Israel had no Palestinian citizens. But the presence of a large, nationalistically conscious, and politically mobilized Palestinian minority inside Israel definitely adds another complicating factor to an already complex set of issues. Specifically, it makes it all the more difficult for the PA to agree to Israel's demand that it formally recognize Israel as a Jewish state in return for Israel's acceptance of a Palestinian state. Whatever the motives behind this demand (which has been made by both the Olmert and Netanyahu governments), it has now become a condition for Israeli acquiescence to and recognition of a future Palestinian state. In other words, if Palestinians in the West Bank want to achieve statehood, they must first accept Israel as a Jewish state (this doesn't apply to Palestinians living in Gaza under Hamas rule, who are currently excluded from the peace process). How, one wonders, will they do this while Palestinians inside Israel loudly reject it as a Jewish state and want it to become "a state for all its citizens"? This would amount to a betrayal of their co-nationals inside Israel.

For this reason alone, the PA is unlikely to agree to explicitly recognize Israel as a Jewish state in the framework of an Israeli-Palestinian final status agreement. Hence, if the Israeli government continues to insist that a peace agreement establishing a Palestinian state also recognizes Israel as a Jewish state, it will be very difficult, if not impossible, to reach such an agreement. The only way in which the PA would probably consent to recognize Israel as a Jewish state would be if Israel agreed to recognize its Palestinian citizens as a national minority and significantly improve their status in the country – something that we have advocated in this book. Thus, without directly addressing the status of the Palestinian minority in Israel, a peace agreement between Israel and the PA is, at best, a long shot.

Whereas the current Israeli demand to recognize Israel as a Jewish state makes an Israeli-Palestinian peace agreement much harder to achieve, a future Israeli demand that many Palestinian citizens of Israel instead become citizens of a Palestinian state will almost certainly be a deal-breaker. This demand, already being voiced by Foreign Minister Lieberman and others, calls for an exchange of territory in which heavily populated Palestinian areas inside Israel would come under the sovereignty of a future Palestinian state while Israel would annex some areas of West Bank territory heavily populated by Jewish settlers. This would mean that a large number of Palestinians who are currently citizens of Israel (the approximately 115,000–140,000 Palestinian residents of the region known as the Triangle) would become citizens of the new state of Palestine and would no longer be Israeli citizens.[7] Although such a "land swap" has not yet become an official Israeli demand in the context of Israeli-Palestinian peace negotiations,[8] it could well become one in the future. If it does, there is almost no chance that the PA will ever agree to it, given the strong opposition it faces from Palestinians in Israel, including from the vast majority of those living in the areas concerned.[9] However much they support the establishment of a Palestinian state, few Palestinian citizens of Israel actually wish to live in it, even if they didn't have to leave their homes and land. The reason for their reluctance to join a future Palestinian state is not hard to fathom – they do not want to give up the higher standard of living they have grown accustomed to in Israel to live in what would undoubtedly be a much less developed state. Thus, were Israel to re-draw its borders and revoke the Israeli citizenship of masses of Palestinians against their will, this would not only be unethical and illegal, it would also almost certainly create more conflict and instability.

[7] Eetta Prince-Gibson, "Land (Swap) for Peace?" *The Jerusalem Post*, November 8, 2007; Ilene Prusher, "Israelis ponder a land swap," *Christian Science Monitor*, April 5, 2006. The best known advocate of this has been Avigdor Lieberman, see, for instance, Greg Myre, "New Voice on Right in Israeli Cabinet Is Likely to Be Loud," *The New York Times*, October 24, 2006; Mazal Mualem, "Lieberman blasts Arab MKs, pulls party out of government," *Ha'aretz*, January 16, 2008. Then Prime Minister Sharon also considered a "population swap," see a BBC news report on Tuesday, February 3, 2004, http://news.bbc.co.uk/1/hi/world/middle_east/3455561.stm

[8] The idea has, however, been raised by Israeli officials on numerous occasions in private during the final status negotiations conducted by the Olmert government and the Palestinian Authority following the American-sponsored Annapolis summit in November 2007 (according to a Palestinian participant in these negotiations in an off-the-record conversation with the author).

[9] In an opinion poll conducted in November 2007, 72.1 percent of Palestinian citizens were opposed to the annexation of towns and villages in the Triangle to the Palestinian Authority in exchange for the annexation of West Bank settlement blocs to Israel. Mada Al-Carmel, the Arab Center for Applied Social Research, http://www.mada-research.org/archive/sru12.htm

## Internal Peace and External Peace

Although ending the Israeli-Palestinian conflict is a prerequisite for a positive transformation of Arab-Jewish relations in Israel, it will not by itself bring about such a transformation. On the contrary, it may well worsen these relations. In the unlikely event that Israel and the PA sign a peace agreement dealing with all the so-called final status issues (namely, the demarcation of borders, the status of Jerusalem, the future of Israeli settlements, water rights, and the resolution of the refugee issue) while ignoring the issue of the Palestinian minority in Israel (as the Oslo Accords did), this could actually exacerbate the conflict within Israel between the Jewish majority and the Palestinian minority.

In the wake of a peace agreement, Israel's Palestinian minority can be expected to intensify their demands for major changes within Israel, because they will not want to be left out and ignored. Though Palestinian citizens of Israel will undoubtedly enthusiastically support an Israeli-Palestinian peace agreement and jubilantly welcome the establishment of a Palestinian state in the Occupied Territories, they will still have their own problems to solve inside Israel. What's more, once the external Israeli-Palestinian conflict is over, they will be less patient and more insistent that their demands be addressed because the conflict will no longer dominate the public agenda or be used as an excuse to defer responding to their demands. Thus, Palestinians in Israel will want and expect (justifiably so) much more attention from Israeli governments (and possibly from the international community) than they have received until now. If unfulfilled, such an expectation could raise their frustration to a dangerously high level, increasing the chances of a violent outburst.

This scenario is by no means far-fetched. There is every reason to believe that while the Palestinian minority will become more assertive in demanding a major improvement in their status within Israel following an Israeli-Palestinian peace agreement, Israel's Jewish majority will be even less accommodating than it is now. Many, probably most, Israeli Jews will believe that they have made enough "concessions" to the Palestinians and will adamantly refuse to make any more. In the words of the Israeli writer David Grossman: "It is difficult to imagine that Israel will, after withdrawing from the occupied territories – a withdrawal that is liable to produce a trauma when Jewish settlements in the West Bank and Gaza Strip are evacuated, creating a deep and violent rift in the Israeli social fabric – find within itself the necessary strength, and generosity, and sense of security, to grant its Palestinian minority equal rights, and even some of its national demands."[10]

Israel's Jewish majority will be especially opposed to what it might regard as compromising on anything concerning the Jewish character of the state. After all, the primary rationale for the two-state solution in the minds of many Israeli Jews is that it secures Israel's existence as a Jewish state. Israel's withdrawal from occupied Palestinian territories has long been domestically "sold" to the Israeli-Jewish public as necessary to maintain Israel's future as a Jewish and democratic state, and it is this belief that underpins a lot of Israeli-Jewish support for such a territorial withdrawal. If this withdrawal eventually takes place, and Israeli Jews are then asked by Palestinians in Israel to agree to anything that could be perceived as undermining the "Jewishness" of the state, they are likely to adamantly reject this. Why give up (strategically, historically, and religiously) valuable territory and undergo the trauma of a withdrawal and probable evacuation of Jewish settlers for the sake of Israel's identity as a Jewish and democratic state, Israeli Jews will no doubt ask, only to then compromise this identity to appease Arabs in Israel? If "Israeli Arabs" want to be Palestinian and have collective rights and their national aspirations satisfied, then many Israeli Jews (and their political representatives) are likely to argue that they should just move to the new Palestinian state. Indeed, this is already what some right-wing and even centrist Israeli-Jewish politicians have been saying.[11]

The argument that Palestinian citizens of Israel should live in a Palestinian state, not a Jewish one, is now mostly heard from the Radical Right. Traditionally concerned with ensuring their dream of a "Greater Israel" – involving Jewish sovereignty over the entire historic Land of Israel (*Eretz Yisrael Ha'Shlema*) stretching from the Jordan River to the Mediterranean – in recent years, the Radical Right in Israel have become increasingly focused on the "problem" of Israel's Arab minority. Their solution to this "problem" is to encourage Arabs to emigrate, or simply expel them. Thus, the Radical Right has begun to shift its focus from an exclusive concern with the Land of Israel to a concern over having a purely "Jewish Israel," one that is basically devoid of Arabs. This is likely to become the sole focus of the Radical Right after an Israeli withdrawal

---

[10] David Grossman, *Sleeping on a Wire: Conversations with Palestinians in Israel* (New York: Picador, 2003), 333.

[11] Neta Sela, "Livni: Palestinian state – solution for Israeli Arabs as well," *Ynet*, November 18, 2007; "Livni: National aspirations of Israel's Arabs can be met by Palestinian homeland," *Ha'aretz*, December 11, 2008.

from the West Bank. Having lost the struggle over the Land of Israel, they will channel all their energies into a struggle against the Arab minority with the goal of creating an ethnically and religiously pure Israel. In doing so, they will almost certainly try to stoke Arab-Jewish tension in the country, as they have done in the past.[12]

To make matters worse, extremist Jewish settlers relocating after an Israeli withdrawal from the West Bank may move into Arab or "mixed" towns inside Israel. This has in fact already been happening since Israel's disengagement from Gaza in 2005. Former Gaza settlers have moved into mixed towns such as Acre, Jaffa, Ramle, and Lod and have established Orthodox religious seminaries within or close to Arab neighborhoods.[13] In the case of Acre, a significant number of Jewish settlers, some of them political extremists, moved there after being evacuated from Gaza.[14] This influx negatively affected the already delicate relations between Jewish and Arab residents of Acre and contributed to the tensions that led to the Arab-Jewish rioting and violence in the town that broke out in October 2008.[15]

A future flood of West Bank Jewish settlers into Arab areas inside Israel could potentially have disastrous consequences for Arab-Jewish coexistence. Angry and embittered by having to leave their homes and communities in the West Bank, and accustomed to extremely hostile relations with Palestinians, these former settlers could, inadvertently or not, fuel Arab-Jewish tension in Israel and spark violent confrontations. Not only would this undermine peace and stability within Israel, it could also

---

[12] In March 2009, for example, a group of radical rightists led by Baruch Marzel, a Hebron settler and disciple of the late Rabbi Meir Kahane, marched in the Arab town of Umm al-Fahm, provoking rioting by some Arab youth (see Dina Kraft, "Rioting in Umm el-Fahm highlights tension," *JTA News*, March 24, 2009). According to Ali Haider, the co-executive director of Sikkuy, this incident demonstrates the risk of future violence. He fears that extreme nationalist Jews could try to provoke Palestinian citizens into violence. Authors' interview with Ali Haider, June 29, 2009, Ramat Aviv.

[13] A religious Zionist *yeshiva* was recently founded in Ajami, a predominantly Arab part of Jaffa, south of Tel Aviv (see Eli Senyor, "Jaffa: Yeshiva to be built in heart of Arab neighborhood," *Ynet*, September 24, 2008). The presence of Orthodox Jews, some of them West Bank settlers, in the neighborhood has created tensions with the local Arab community. Authors' interview with Ibrahim Abu-Shindi, founder and executive director of the Arab-Jewish Community Center in Jaffa, June 28, 2009, Jaffa.

[14] Young religious Zionist Jews started moving to Acre years earlier after the building of a large yeshiva in the town (the largest in the north of Israel) in 1997.

[15] The Mossawa Center, "Akka: City on the Front," December 2008, 5. In its detailed report on the Acre riots, the Mossawa Center ominously warns that: "The situation in Akka is an early-warning signal of a potentially explosive country-wide conflict between Arabs and Jews." Ibid., 8.

undermine peace and stability between Israel and a future Palestinian state. Large-scale Arab-Jewish violence within Israel might well drag in the government of Palestine and possibly jeopardize an Israeli-Palestinian peace agreement.

Contrary to popular expectations, therefore, Arab-Jewish relations in Israel could actually deteriorate further following an Israeli-Palestinian peace agreement and the establishment of a Palestinian state. What does this mean then for the present peace process and for the possibility of achieving peace and reconciliation? It means that the peace process in its present form is inadequate, and that even if a final status agreement is signed it will not bring about lasting peace between Israeli Jews and Palestinians. A stable and sustainable peace requires a comprehensive resolution of the Palestinian problem, inside and outside Israel. That is, it requires internal peace (peace between Jews and Palestinians in Israel) and external peace (peace between Jews and Palestinians outside Israel). Only by addressing the Palestinian problem in its entirety can such peace be achieved. This has not yet been done, as the current peace process (initiated by the Obama administration) and its failed and short-lived predecessors (the Oslo peace process, the Road Map for Peace, the Annapolis process, etc.) all avoid dealing with the issue of the Palestinian minority in Israel. This is a serious mistake that must be rectified.

Although it may be unrealistic and overly ambitious to add the issue of the Palestinian minority to the international diplomatic agenda at the present time, there must at the very least be a greater awareness within the international community and in the United States in particular (because of its leading role in the peace process and its close alliance with Israel) that this is indeed an important issue that must be addressed sooner rather than later. Although it is ultimately up to Israel to deal with the increasingly problematic relationship between its Jewish majority and its Palestinian minority, the international community led by the United States can and should emphasize to Israeli leaders the need to constructively and energetically tackle this issue as part of its quest for peace with the Palestinian nation. Simply put, the resolution of both Israel's internal and external conflicts must be promoted simultaneously.

Many people wrongly believe that the Palestinian problem is basically limited to Israel's occupation of Palestinian territories – the West Bank, Gaza Strip, and East Jerusalem. According to this widespread view, the Palestinian problem dates back to Israel's conquest of these territories in the war of 1967. However, the Palestinian problem did not begin in 1967 (though it was greatly exacerbated in that year); it really began in 1948 with the displacement of hundreds of thousands of Palestinians from what became the State of Israel and the sudden transformation of those who remained from being a majority to a minority in the country. Whatever view one takes as to the justification of Israel's establishment (for us, it is justified), the fact remains that Palestinians have suffered greatly as a result. Recognizing this suffering and rectifying it to some extent – while not negating Jewish national rights – is the fundamental criterion for bringing about peace and reconciliation between Jews and Palestinians. To do this, one has to address both the internal and external dimensions of the Palestinian problem – internally, the status and rights of the Palestinian minority in Israel and externally, the future of the Occupied Territories and Palestinian refugees in the Diaspora. Hence, the issue of Israel's Palestinian minority needs to be incorporated into our thinking about solving the Palestinian problem. Establishing a Palestinian state is necessary but not sufficient. Only by ending the occupation and transforming Israel internally can the Palestinian problem be fully resolved. This is what a comprehensive solution really entails.

Unfortunately, we do not believe that a comprehensive resolution of the Palestinian problem is likely to happen in the foreseeable future. There are many reasons for this, chief among them the fact that the Palestinians are too politically divided at present and the current Israeli government too hard-line. At most, a weak, geographically fragmented, nominal Palestinian "state" may be established. Rather than peace, conflict is likely to continue between Israel and Palestinians in the territories, as well as within Israel between Jews and Arabs. The great danger with this is that these conflicts may eventually merge. Until now, the campaigns of Palestinians in Israel and Palestinians in the Occupied Territories have remained separate and distinct, with the former seeking equality and the latter statehood.[16] If neither is successful, however, they may well unite and both demand the so-called one-state solution. Thus, if Palestinians in the territories abandon their demand for an independent state and instead demand equal rights within Israel, Palestinians in Israel could easily join them in demanding a single bi-national state covering the entire territory of Israel/Palestine.

As long as the occupation continues and the Palestinian minority in Israel is completely marginalized, the chances of this happening – a

---

[16] Oren Yiftachel, *Ethnocracy: Land & Identity Politics in Israel/Palestine*. (Philadelphia: University of Pennsylvania Press, 2006), 186.

"nightmare" scenario for Israel – steadily increase.[17] There are already signs of growing support for the one-state solution among Palestinians in the territories,[18] and although most Palestinian citizens of Israel are currently opposed to this,[19] some prominent ones have voiced support for it.[20] One thing is certain – there is absolutely no way Israeli Jews will accept a one-state solution. They will staunchly resist this, even at the cost of war. If Palestinians in the territories and in Israel push for a one-state solution, therefore, the outcome will probably be a lot of bloodshed.

In this book, we offer a solution that is aimed at preventing violence and avoiding a disastrous escalation of the conflict. Our solution, like any viable possible solution, is based on mutual compromise. It accepts the fact that there are two nations in Israel/Palestine and within Israel itself, it acknowledges the national rights of both these nations, and it seeks a just and practical way of satisfying these rights. The Jews have a right to national self-determination in Israel (but not hegemony); the Palestinians have a right to national self-determination in a Palestinian state, and those members of the Palestinian nation who are citizens of Israel have a right to recognition as a national minority, cultural autonomy, and full individual equality. Anything less than this will not bring peace and reconciliation. We can only hope this will be enough.

---

[17] Authors' interview with Hassan Jabareen, general director of Adalah, June 24, 2009, Haifa.

[18] In a recent poll (in April 2010), 34 percent of Palestinians in the West Bank and Gaza supported the one-state solution, compared to 44 percent who favored the two-state solution (a year earlier, in June 2009, only 21 percent supported the one-state solution, and 55 percent supported the two-state solution). Jerusalem Media and Communication Centre, "Poll: One-state solution gains ground," April 21, 2010, http://www.jmcc.org/news.aspx?id=759

[19] In a 2004 survey, two-thirds of Arabs in Israel were opposed to the call for a Palestinian state in all of Palestine instead of Israel. Sammy Smooha, *Index of Arab-Jewish Relations in Israel 2004* (Haifa: The Jewish-Arab Center, University of Haifa; Jerusalem: The Citizens' Accord Forum between Jews and Arabs in Israel; Tel Aviv: Friedrich Ebert Stiftung, 2005), 58.

[20] Such as Jamal Zahalka, co-founder of the Balad party and its leader since Azmi Bishara's departure from Israel (see Yair Ettinger, "'I am willing to treat the Jews with full equality,'" *Ha'aretz*, November 21, 2002).

# Bibliography

Abu-Baker, Khawla. "Social and Educational Welfare Policy in the Arab Sector in Israel." *Israel Affairs* 9, issues 1–2 (2003): 68–96.

Abu-Lughod, Ibrahim. *The Transformation of Palestine: Essays on the Origin and Development of the Arab-Israeli Conflict*. Evanston, IL: Northwestern University Press, 1971.

Abunimah, Ali. *One Country: A Bold Proposal to End the Israeli-Palestinian Impasse*. New York: Metropolitan Books, 2006.

Abu-Saad, Ismael. "State-Controlled Education and Identity Formation Among the Palestinian Arab Minority in Israel." *American Behavioral Scientist* 49, 8 (2006), 1085–1100.

Adalah: The Legal Center for Arab Minority Rights in Israel. "The Democratic Constitution." (2007): 1–19. http://www.adalah.org/eng/democratic_constitution-e.pdf.

Agha, Hussein, and Robert Malley. "The two-state solution doesn't solve anything." *The New York Times*, August 11, 2009.

Aklaev, Airat. *Democratizing and Ethnic Peace: Patterns of Ethnopolitical Crisis Management in Post-Soviet Settings*. Aldershot, UK: Ashgate, 1999.

Al-Haj, Majid. "The Arab Internal Refugees in Israel: The Emergence of a Minority within the Minority." *Immigrants and Minorities* 2, 1 (1988): 149–165.

   *Education, Empowerment, and Control: The Case of the Arabs in Israel*. Albany: SUNY Press, 1995.

   "An Illusion of Belonging: Reactions of the Arab Population to Rabin's Assassination." In Yoram Peri, ed., *The Assassination of Yitzhak Rabin*. Stanford, CA: Stanford University Press, 2000, 163–174.

   "The Political Culture of the 1990's Immigrants from the Former Soviet Union in Israel and Their Views Toward the Indigenous Arab Minority: A Case of Ethnocratic Multiculturalism." *Journal of Ethnic and Migration Studies* 30, 4 (2004): 681–696.

Allon, Yigal. *A Curtain of Sand*. Tel Aviv: Ha'kibbutz Ha'meuchad (Hebrew), 1969.

Alon, Gideon, and Jack Khoury. "Government okays affirmative action for minority groups." *Ha'aretz*, December 3, 2006.

Alpher, Joseph. *Settlements and Borders*. Tel Aviv: Jaffee Center for Strategic Studies, Tel Aviv University, 1994.

Amara, Muhammad. "The Collective Identity of the Arabs in Israel in an Era of Peace." *Israel Affairs* 9, 1–2 (2003): 249–262.

"Israeli Palestinians and the Palestinian Authority." *Middle East Review of International Affairs* 4, no. 1 (2009): 38–44.

Amara, Muhammad, and Izhak Schnell. "Identity Repertoires Among Arabs in Israel." *Journal of Ethnic and Migration Studies* 30, 1 (2004): 175–193.

Arens, Moshe. "Allegiance by choice," *Ha'aretz*, August 3, 2010.

"Israel's biggest challenge: Integrating its Arab minority." *Ha'aretz*, April 11, 2010.

Arian, Asher. *Israeli Public Opinion on National Security 2003, Memorandum no. 67*, Tel Aviv: Jaffee Center for Strategic Studies, Tel Aviv University, October 2003.

*Israeli Public Opinion on National Security*. Tel Aviv: Jaffee Center for Strategic Studies, Tel Aviv University, 2004.

*Security Threatened: Surveying Israeli Opinion on Peace and War*. Cambridge: Cambridge University Press, 1995.

Arian, Asher, Nir Atmor, and Yael Hadar, eds. *Auditing Israeli Democracy 2006*. Jerusalem: The Israel Democracy Institute, 2006.

Arian, Asher, Shlomit Barnea, and Parzit Ben-Nun. *The 2004 Israeli Democracy Index*. Jerusalem: The Israel Democracy Institute, 2004.

Aronoff, Myron, and Pierre M. Atlas. "The Peace Process and Competing Challenges to the Dominant Zionist Discourse." In Ilan Peleg, ed., *The Middle East Peace Process: Interdisciplinary Perspectives*. Albany: SUNY Press, 1998, 131–158.

Ashkenazi, Eli, and Jack Khoury. "Poll: 68% of Jews would refuse to live in same building as an Arab." *Ha'aretz*, August 22, 2006.

Ashkenazi, Eli, Jack Khoury, and Liel Kyzer. "Police interrogate Islamic Movement chief Sheikh Raed Salah over role in Gaza flotilla clashes." *Ha'aretz*, June 1, 2010.

Atrash, Aas, and Sarah Ozacky-Lazar. "A Survey of Political and National Attitudes of the Arabs in Israel." October–November 2002 (Givat Haviva: The Institute for Peace Research), cited in The Mossawa Center, "The Palestinian Arab Minority and the 2009 Israeli Elections."

Avishai, Bernard. *The Hebrew Republic: How Secular Democracy and Global Enterprise will Bring Israel Peace at Last*. Orlando, FL: Harcourt, 2008.

Avnery, Uri. "Israel's Declaration of Independence: Squaring the Circle among the Contradictions in the Declaration of Independence Is That Between a 'Jewish State' and a 'Democratic State.'" *Palestine-Israel Journal* 5, 2 (1998). http://www.pij.org/details.php?id=206.

Awawda, Bachar, and Alla Heider. "Index of Racism for 2006: Racism against Israeli Arabs – Citizens of the State of Israel." The Center against Racism, April 2007. http://www.noracism.org/arabic/data/publications/index2006.doc.

Azoulay, Yuval. "Number of Israeli Arab national service volunteers doubles." *Ha'aretz*, December 20, 2007.

Baker, Pauline H. "Conflict Resolution versus Democratic Governance: Divergent Paths to Peace?" In Chester A. Crocker and Fen Osler Hampson, with Pamela Aall, eds., *Managing Global Chaos*. Washington, DC: USIP Press, 1996, 563–571.

Barak-Erez, Dafna, ed. *Jewish and Democratic State*. Tel Aviv: Tel Aviv University Press (Hebrew), 1996.

Bar'el, Zvi. "'What are Israeli Arabs? Are they Jewish?'" *Ha'aretz*, May 25, 2004.

Barnett, Michael, ed. *Israel in a Comparative Perspective: Challenging the Conventional Wisdom*. Albany, NY: SUNY Press, 1996.

Bar-On, Dan. "Israeli Society between the Culture of Death and the Culture of Life." *Israel Studies* 2, 2 (2003): 88–112.

Barry, Brian. *Culture and Equality: An Egalitarian Critique of Multiculturalism*. Cambridge, MA: Harvard University Press, 2001.

"Review Article: Political Accommodation and Consociational Democracy." *British Journal of Political Science* 5, 4 (1975): 477–505.

Bar-Tal, Daniel and Yona Teichman. *Stereotypes and Prejudice in Conflict: Representations of Arabs in Israeli Jewish Society*. Cambridge: Cambridge University Press, 2005.

Barzilai, Gad, and Ilan Peleg. "Israel and Future Borders: Assessment of a Dynamic Process." *Journal of Peace Research* 31, 1 (1994): 49–63.

Basok, Motti. "The state gave more to settlements, less to development towns and the least to Arab towns." *The Marker* supplement, *Ha'aretz*. February 13, 2006.

Basta, Lidja R., and Thomas Fleiner, eds. *Federalism and Multiethnic States: The Case of Switzerland*. Fribourgs, Switzerland: Institut du Federalisme, 1996.

Beeri-Sulitzeanu, Amnon. "A different kind of service," *Ha'aretz*, August 13, 2010.

Ben-Meir, Yehuda, and Dafna Shaked. *The People Speak: Israeli Public Opinion on National Security 2005–2007*. The Institute for National Security Studies Memorandum No. 90, 2007.

Benn, Aluf. "Israel's Arab citizens: A hidden economic treasure." *Ha'aretz*, July 23, 2009.

"Israel to release up to 400 Palestinian prisoners ahead of Summit." *Ha'aretz*, November 12, 2007.

"Obama's new vision of Jewish State guarantees rights of Israeli Arabs." *Ha'aretz*, June 8, 2010.

Benn, Aluf, and Gideon Alon. "Netanyahu: Israel's Arabs are the real demographic threat." *Ha'aretz*, December 18, 2003.

Benvenisti, Meron. "Threats of the future vision." *Ha'aretz*, December 17, 2006.

"United we stand." *Ha'aretz*, January 29, 2010.

Benziman, Uzi. "Azmi Bishara as an example." *Ha'aretz*, April 11, 2007.

*Shel Mi Ha'aretz Hazot? Massa Lenisuach Amana Yehudit-Arvit be'Israel* (Whose Land Is It? A Quest for a Jewish-Arab Compact in Israel). Jerusalem: Israel Democracy Institute, 2006.

Bilsky, Leora. "'Speaking through the Mask': Israeli Arabs and the Changing Faces of Israeli Citizenship." *Middle East Law and Governance* 1, 2 (2009): 166–209.

Bishara, Azmi. "Reflections on October 2000: A Landmark in Jewish-Arab Relations in Israel." *Journal of Palestine Studies* 30, 3 (2001): 54–67.

"The Question of the Palestinian Minority in Israel." *Theory and Criticism* 3, 1 (1993): 7–20.

"Why Israel is after me." *Los Angeles Times*, May 3, 2007.

Bligh, Alexander. "Israeli Arab Members of the 15th Knesset: Between Israeli Citizenship and Their Palestinian National Identity." In Alexander Bligh, ed. *The Israeli Palestinians: An Arab Minority in the Jewish State.* London: Routledge, 2003, 3–15.

*The Israeli Palestinians: An Arab Minority in the Jewish State.* New York: Routledge, 2003.

Bocock, Robert. *Hegemony.* West Sussex: Tavistock Publications, 1986.

Bogdanor, Vernon. "Devolution: Decentralization or Disintegration?" *The Political Quarterly* 70, 2 (1999): 185–194.

Bonime-Blanc, Andrea. *Spain's Transition to Democracy: The Politics of Constitution Making.* Boulder, CO: Westview Press, 1987.

Bradbury, Jonathan and James Mitchell. "Devolution: Stability, Uncertainty and Crisis." *Parliamentary Affairs* 55, 2 (2002): 299–316.

Breton, Raymond. "The Production and Allocation of Symbolic Resources: An Analysis of the Linguistic and Ethnocultural Fields in Canada." *Canadian Review of Sociology and Anthropology* 21, (1984): 123–140.

Brom, Shlomo. "From Rejection to Acceptance: Israeli National Security Thinking and Palestinian Statehood." *United States Institute of Peace Special Report* 177, 2007.

Brubaker, Rogers. *Nationalism Reframed: Nationhood and the National Question in the New Europe.* New York: Cambridge University Press, 1996.

Byman, Daniel and Stephen Van Evera. "Why They Fight: Hypotheses on the Causes of Contemporary Deadly Conflict." *Security Studies* 7, 3 (1998): 1–50.

Campbell, Donald T. *Ethnocentrism.* New York: Wiley, 1972.

Canetti-Nisim, Daphna, Gal Ariely, and Eran Halperin. "Life, Pocketbook, or Culture: The Role of Perceived Security Threats in Promoting Exclusionist Political Attitudes toward Minorities in Israel." *Political Research Quarterly* 61, 1 90–103.

Cannon, Gordon E. "Consociationalism vs. Control: Canada as a Case Study," *Western Political Quarterly* 35, vol. 1 (2008): 50–64.

Carmi, Na'ama. "The Nationality and Entry into Israel Case before the Supreme Court of Israel." *Israel Studies Forum* Vol. 22, No. 1 (2007): 26–53.

Cash, John D. "The Dilemmas of Political Transformation in Northern Ireland." *Pacifica Review* 10, vol. 3 (1998): 227–234.

Chadda, Maya. "Between Consociationalism and Control: Sri Lanka." In Ulrich Schneckener and Stefan Wolff, eds., *Managing and Settling Ethnic Conflicts.* New York: Palgrave, 2004, 94–114.

Chernichovsky, Dov and Jon Anson. "The Jewish–Arab Divide in Life Expectancy in Israel." *Economics & Human Biology* 3, 1 (2005): 123–137.

Cincotta, Richard and Eric Kaufmann. "The Changing Face of Israel." *Foreign Policy Online Edition*, 2009. http://www.foreignpolicy.com/articles/2009/05/31/the_changing_face_of_israel

Coakley, John. "Approaches to the Resolution of Ethnic Conflict: The Strategy of Non-Territorial Autonomy." *International Political Science Review* 15, 3 (1994): 217–314.

"The Resolution of Ethnic Conflict: Toward a Typology." *International Political Science Review* 13, 4 (1992): 343–368.

The Territorial Management of Ethnic Conflict. London: Frank Cass, 1993.

Cohen, Asher, and Bernard Susser. "From Accommodation to Decision: The Transformation of Israel's Religio-Political Life." *Journal of State and Church* 38, 4 (1996): 817–839.

*Israel and the Politics of Jewish Identity: The Secular-Religious Impasse.* Baltimore: Johns Hopkins University Press, 2000.

Cohen, Hillel. *Good Arabs: The Israeli Security Agencies and the Israeli Arabs: 1948–1967.* Berkeley, CA: University of California Press, 2010.

"The Internal Refugees in the State of Israel: Israeli Citizens, Palestinian Refugees." *Palestine-Israel Journal* 9, no. 2 (2002).

The Present Absentees: The Palestinian Refugees in Israel Since 1948. Jerusalem: Van Leer Institute (Hebrew), 2000.

Cook, Jonathan. "Arabs left on the wrong side of the tracks in Israel." *The National*, April 6, 2009.

"I want to be a full Israeli citizen." *The National*, February 24, 2009.

"Israel bars Arab parties from election." *The National*, January 14, 2009.

"Israel to drop Arabic names." *The National*, July 17, 2009.

"Israel's Arab students are crossing to Jordan." *The National*, April 9, 2009.

"Minister calls for housing partition." *The National*, July 6, 2009.

de Quetteville, Harry. "Jews and Arabs can never live together, says Israel's vice PM." *The Sunday Telegraph*, November 5, 2006.

De Villiers, Bertus. "Foreword." In Bertus De Villiers, ed., *Evaluating Federal Systems*. Netherlands: Martinus Nijhoff Publishers, 1994.

DeVotta, Neil. "From Ethnic Outbidding to Ethnic Conflict: The Institutional Bases for Sri Lanka's Separatist War." *Nations and Nationalism* 11, 1 (2005): 141–159.

Don-Yehiya, Eliezer. "Mamlachtiut and Judaism in Ben-Gurion Thought and Policy," *Ha'Tzionut* 14, 1(1998): 51–88.

*Religion and Political Accommodation in Israel.* Jerusalem: The Floersheimer Institute for Policy Studies, 1999.

Dowty, Alan. "Emergency Powers in Israel: The Devaluation of Crisis." In Shao-chuan Leng, ed., *Coping with Crises: How Governments Deal with Emergencies.* Lanham, MD: University Press of America and the White Burkett Miller Center of Public Affairs, University of Virginia, 1990, 1–43.

"The First Decade: Building a Civic State." In Ilan Troen and Noah Lucas. *Israel: the First Decade of Independence.* Albany: SUNY Press, 1995, 31–50.

"Is Israel Democratic? Substance and Semantics in the 'Ethnic Democracy' Debate." *Israel Studies* 4, 2 (1999): 1–14.

*Israel/Palestine*. Cambridge: Polity, 2005.

*The Jewish State: A Century Later*. Berkeley, CA: University of California Press, 1998.

Eglash, Ruth. "Israel's population at 2010 is 7.5m." *The Jerusalem Post*, December 30, 2009.

Eldar, Akiva. "The Arab boycott." *Ha'aretz*, February 29, 2008.

"Let's hear it for the Haiders." *Ha'aretz*, November 12, 2006.

Ellingwood, Ken. "Israeli Arabs split over National Service Plan." *Los Angeles Times*, January 2, 2008. http://www.latimes.com/news/nationworld/world/la-fg-service2jan02,1,4215318.story?ctrack=1&cset=true.

Ethan, Bronner. "After 60 Years, Arabs in Israel are outsiders." *The New York Times*, May 7, 2008.

Ettinger, Yair. "Extremism isn't growing, but fear is." *Ha'aretz*, May 24, 2004.

"I am willing to treat the Jews with full equality." *Ha'aretz*, November 21, 2002.

"PM's Arab adviser urges mandatory flag waving and loyalty oaths." *Ha'aretz*, November 5, 2003.

"To boycott or not to boycott." *Ha'aretz*, January 26, 2003.

Etzioni, Amitai. "Minorities and the National Ethos." *Politics* 29, 2 (2009): 100–110.

Eyadat, Fadi. "Israeli Arabs have no choice but to build illegally." *Ha'aretz*, July 29, 2010.

Ezrahi, Yaron. "Democratic Politics and Culture in Modern Israel: Recent Trends." In Ehud Sprinzak and Larry Diamond, eds., *Israeli Democracy under Stress*. Boulder, CO: Lynne Rienner Publishers, 1993, 256–257.

Farah, Mounir. "Education, Empowerment, and Control: The Case of the Arabs in Israel." *The Middle East Journal* 53, 4 (1999): 649–660.

Feldman, Avigdor. "The Democratic State versus the Jewish State: A Void without Places, Time without Continuity." In Defna Barak-Erez, ed., *A Jewish and Democratic State*, Tel Aviv: Tel Aviv University School of Law, 263–273 (Hebrew), 1996.

Feldman, Yotam. "Lieberman's anti-Arab ideology wins over Israel's teens." *Ha'aretz*, February 2, 2009.

Fendel, Hillel. "GSS: Israeli Arabs Are Existential Danger to Israel." *Israel National News*, November 12, 2007.

Firro, Kais. "Reshaping Druze Particularism in Israel." *Journal of Palestine Studies* 30, 3 (2001): 40–53.

Fleiner, Thomas. "Recent Developments in Swiss Federalism." *Publius* 32, 2 (1992): 97–123.

Forman, David J. "Israel part II: The reality – Israeli Arabs." *The Jerusalem Post*, February 12, 2010.

Fossas, Enric. "National Plurality and Equality." In Ferran Requejo ed. *Democracy and National Pluralism*. New York: Routledge, 2001, 64–83.

Frantzman, Seth. "The failure of Israel's Arab MKs." *The Jerusalem Post*, February 16, 2010.

Friedman, Ron. "Employers reluctant to hire Ethiopians, Haredim and Arabs, study shows." *The Jerusalem Post*, November 9, 2009.

Frisch, Hillel. "Israel and its Arab Citizens." *Israel Affairs* 11, 1 (2005): 207–222.
"Israel's Arab Parties." In Robert O. Freedman, ed., *Contemporary Israel: Domestic Politics, Foreign Policy, and Security Challenges.* Boulder, CO: Westview Press, 2008, 115–133.
Galili, Lily. "A Jewish Demographic State." *Journal of Palestine Studies* 32, 1 (2002): 90–93.
Gallie, W. B. "Essentially Contested Concepts." In Max Black, ed., *The Importance of Language.* Englewood Cliffs, NJ: Prentice-Hall, 1962, 121–146.
Gans, Chaim. *A Just Zionism: On the Morality of the Jewish State.* Oxford: Oxford University Press, 2008.
Gavison, Ruth. *Israel as Jewish and Democratic State: Tensions and Opportunities.* Jerusalem: Van Leer Institute, 1999.
"Jewish and Democratic? A Rejoinder to the 'Ethnic Democracy' Debate." *Israel Studies* 4, 1 (1999): 44–72.
Ghai, Jash, ed. *Autonomy and Ethnicity: Negotiating Competing Claims in Multiethnic States.* Cambridge & New York: Cambridge University Press, 2000.
Ghanem, As'ad. "The Bi-National State Solution." *Israel Studies* 14, 2 (2009): 120–133.
*The Palestinian-Arab minority in Israel, 1948–2000.* Albany: SUNY Press, 2001.
"The Palestinian Arabs in Israel and Their Relation to the State of Israel." In National Committee for the Heads of the Arab Local Authorities in Israel, *The Future Vision of the Palestinian Arabs in Israel,* 2006.
"The Palestinian Minority in Israel: The 'Challenge' of the Jewish State and its Implications." *Third World Quarterly* 21, 1 (2000): 87–104.
"State and Minority in Israel: The Case if Ethnic State and the Predicament of Its Minority." *Ethnic and Racial Studies* 21, 3 (1998): 428–448.
"Zionism and Anti-Zionism in Israel: Jews and Arabs in Conflict Over the Nature of the State." In Ephraim Nimni, ed., *The Challenge of Post-Zionism: Alternatives to Israeli Fundamentalist Politics.* London: Zed Books, 2003, 98–115.
Ghanem, As'ad, and Muhannad Mustafa. "The Palestinians in Israel and the 2006 Knesset Elections: Political and Ideological Implications of Election Boycott." *Holy Land Studies* 6, 1 (2007): 51–73.
Ghanem, As'ad, and Sarah Ozacky-Lazar. "The Status of the Palestinians in Israel in an Era of Peace: Part of the Problem, but not Part of the Solution," *Israel Affairs* 9 (1) and 9 (2), (2003): 263–89.
Gitelman, Zvi. *Immigration and Identity: The Resettlement and Impact of Soviet Immigrants on Israeli Politics and Society.* Los Angeles: The David and Susan Wilstein Institute of Jewish Policy Studies, 1995.
Golan, Avirama. "Forcing Arabs to study Zionism is no solution." *Ha'aretz,* June 18, 2009.
"Where the 'alliance of blood' has led." *Ha'aretz,* February 17, 2005.
Golan-Agnon, Daphna. "Separate but Not Equal: Discrimination Against Palestinian Arab Students in Israel." *American Behavioral Scientist* 49, no. 8 (2006): 1080–1100.

Goldenberg, Suzanne. "Hated and Feted." *The Guardian*, March 23, 2002.

Goldhaber, Ravit. "A Spatio-Perceptual Segregation Model: A Case Study of Jewish and Arab Experiences in Jaffa, Israel." *Urban Geography* 28, 6 (2007): 578–603.

Goldstein, Evan. "Does Israel have an Immigrant Problem?" *Foreign Policy*. January 25, 2010.

Gordon, Evelyn. "'Kassaming' coexistence." *The Jerusalem Post* (Online Edition), May 23, 2007.

Gorenberg, Gershom. "Is Israel a Democracy?" *The American Prospect*, December 4, 2009, 13–15.

Grossman, David. *Sleeping on a Wire: Conversations with Palestinians in Israel*. New York: Picador, 2003.

*The Yellow Wind*. New York: Farrar, Straus, and Giroux, 1988.

Guelke, Adrian. "Ethnic Rights and Majority Rule: The Case of South Africa." *International Political Science Review* 13, 4 (1992): 415–432.

*Rethinking the Rise and Fall of Apartheid*. New York: Palgrave Macmillan, 2005.

Gurr, Ted Robert. *Minorities at Risk: A Global View of Ethnopolitical Conflicts*. Herndon, VA: USIP Press, 1997.

*Peoples versus States: Minorities at Risk in the New Century*. Washington, DC: United States Institute of Peace Press, 2000.

*Ha'aretz*. "Full text of Netanyahu's foreign policy speech at Bar Ilan." June 14, 2009.

*Ha'aretz*. "Israel moves closer to banning mourning of its independence." May 24, 2009.

*Ha'aretz*. "Netanyahu: Lieberman campaign against Israeli Arabs is 'legitimate.'" February 6, 2009.

*Ha'aretz*. "The official summation of the Or Commission report." September 1, 2003. http://www.Ha'aretz.com/hasen/pages/ShArt.jhtml?itemNo=335594.

Habib, Jack, Judith King, Assaf Ben Shoham, Abraham Wolde-Tsadick, and Karen Lasky. "Labour Market and Socio-Economic Outcomes of the Arab-Israeli Population." *OECD Social, Employment and Migration Working Papers No. 102* (March 18, 2010): 14.

Halkin, Hillel. "The Jewish State and its Arabs." *Commentary* 30, 127 (2009): 30–37.

Halperin, Eran. "Group-based Hatred in Intractable Conflict in Israel." *Journal of Conflict Resolution* 52, 5 (2008): 713–736.

"Heightened by Failure to Ping Domain Resources in a New Society: Terror, Resource Gains and Ethnic Intolerance." *Journal of Ethnic and Migration Studies* 35, 6 (2009): 997–1014.

Halperin, Eran, D. Canetti-Nisim, E. S. Hobfoll, and J. R. Johnson. "Heightened by failure to gain resources in a new society: Terror, resource gains and ethnic intolerance." *Journal of Ethnic and Migration Studies* (2007): 997–1014.

Halperin, Orly. "Jerusalem Takes a Fresh Look at Maligned Vision for Arab Equality." *Forward*, March 2, 2007, 6–11.

Hammer, Joshua. "I'm a Realist." *The New York Review of Books*, March 25, 2010.

Harel, Amos. "Two Israeli Arabs arrested on suspicion of planning attacks." *Ha'aretz*, May 10, 2010.

Harel-Shalev, Ayelet. "The Status of Minority Languages in Deeply Divided Societies: Urdu in India and Arabic in Israel – A Comparative Perspective." *Israel Studies Forum* 21, 2 (2006): 28–57.

Hassan, Ghattib. "Lieberman and the Arab Citizens of Israel." *Bitterlemons.org* 14, April 6, 2009.

Hazareesingh, Sudir, ed. *The Jacobin Legacy in Modern France: Essays in Honor of Vincent Wright*. Oxford and New York: Oxford University Press, 2002.

Henrard, Kristin. "Post Apartheid South Africa: Transformation and Reconciliation." *World Affairs* 166, 1 (2003): 37–55.

Hintjens, Helen M. "Explaining the 1994 Genocide in Rwanda." *The Journal of Modern African Studies* 37, 2 (1999): 241–286.

Hooghe, Liesbet. "Belgium: From Regionalism to Federalism." In John Coakley ed., *The Territorial Management of Ethnic Conflict*. London: Frank Cass, 1993, 44–68.

Horowitz, Dan, and Moshe Lissak. *Trouble in Utopia*. Albany, NY: SUNY Press, 1990.

Horowitz, Donald L. *Ethnic Groups in Conflict*. Berkeley: University of California, 1985.

"Making Moderation Pay." In Joseph Monteville ed., *Conflict and Peacemaking in Multiethnic Societies*. Lanham, MD: Lexington Books, 1991, 451–476.

Human Rights Watch. "Land and Housing Rights Violations in Israel's Unrecognized Bedouin Villages." March 30, 2008. http://www.hrw.org/en/node/62284/section/1.

International Crisis Group. "Identity Crisis: Israel and its Arab Citizens." *Middle East Report* 25, 1 (March 2004): 2–15.

Israel Democracy Institute. "2007 Israeli Democracy Index: Cohesiveness in a Divided Society." June, www.idi.org.il.

Israel's National Insurance Institute, Miri Endeweld, Alex Fruman, Netanela Barkali, and Daniel Gottlieb. *2008 Poverty and Social Gaps Annual Report*. Jerusalem: National Insurance Institute, Research and Planning Administration, 2009, www.btl.gov.il.

Izenberg, Dan. "Cabinet backs bill to register NGOs funded by foreign states." *The Jerusalem Post*, February 15, 2010.

Jabareen, Yousef. "Arab Minority's Vision is Foremost about Opportunity." *Forward.com*, April 13, 2007.

"Constitution Building and Equality in Deeply-Divided Societies: The Case of the Palestinian Arab Minority in Israel." *Wisconsin International Law Journal* 26, 2 (2008): 345–401.

"An Equal Constitution for All? On a Constitution and Collective Rights for Arab Citizens in Israel." Haifa: Mossawa Center: The Advocacy Center for Arab Citizens in Israel (2007): 1–80. http://www.mossawacenter.org/files/files/File/An%20Equal%20Constitution%20For%20All.pdf.

"Law and Education: Critical Perspectives on Arab Palestinian Education in Israel." *American Behavioral Scientist* 49, no. 8 (2006): 1052–1074.

"Who's afraid of educated Arabs?" *Ha'aretz*, July 24, 2009.

Jacob, Abel. "Trends in Israel's Public Opinion on Issues Related to the Arab-Israeli Conflict 1967–1972." *The Jewish Journal of Sociology* 16 (December, 1974): 187–208.

Jamal, Amal. "The Ambiguities of Minorities Patriotism: Love for Homeland versus State among Palestinian Citizens of Israel." *Nationalism and Ethnic Politics* 10, (2004): 433–471.

"Collective Rights for Indigenous Minorities: Theoretical and Normative Aspects." In Elie Rekhess and Sarah Osacky-Lazar eds. *The Status of the Arab Minority in the Jewish Nation State*. Tel Aviv: Tel Aviv University Press, 2005, 27–44.

"The Contradictions of State-Minority Relations in Israel: The Search for Clarifications." *Constellations* 16, 3 (2009): 493–508.

"The Counter-Hegemonic Role of Civil Society: Palestinian-Arab NGOs in Israel." *Citizenship Studies* 12, 3 (2008): 283–306.

"Nationalizing States and the Constitution of 'Hollow Citizenship': Israel and its Palestinian Citizens." *Ethnopolitics* 6, 4 (2007): 471–493.

"Strategies of Minority Struggle for Equality in Ethnic States: Arab Politics in Israel." *Citizenship Studies* 11, 3 (2007): 263–282.

Jerusalem Media and Communication Centre. "Poll: One-state solution gains ground." http://www.jmcc.org/news.aspx?id=759, April 21, 2010.

*Jerusalem Post*. "Poll finds former Soviet olim less tolerant of Arabs than native Israelis." August 3, 2009.

Jiryis, Sabri. *The Arabs in Israel*. New York and London: Monthly Review Press, 1976.

Jones, Rachel Leah. "Ayn Hawd and the Unrecognized Villages." *Journal of Palestinian Studies* 31, 1 (2001): 39–49.

JTA, The Global News Service of the Jewish People. "Druze protest funding discrimination." June 21, 2009.

"Israeli Jews Favor 'Palestine' for Arabs." April 1, 2008.

"Israelis want Jewish prime minister." July 6, 2007.

"Mosque Wears Israeli Colors." April 7, 2009.

Judt, Tony. "Israel: The Alternative." *The New York Review of Books*, October 23, 2003.

Kanaaneh, Rhoda Ann. *Surrounded: Palestinian Soldiers in the Israeli Military*. Stanford, CA: Stanford University Press, 2009.

Kaplan, Avi, Ismael Abu-Sa' ad, and Yossi Yonah. "Jewish–Arab Relations in Israel: Perceptions, Emotions, and Attitudes of University Students of Education." *Intercultural Education* 12, 3 (2001): 289–307.

Karayanni, M. Michael. "The Separate Nature of the Religious Accommodations for the Palestinian-Arab Minority in Israel." *Northwestern Journal of International Human Rights* 5, 1 (2006): 41–71.

Karayanni, Michael Mousa. "Multiculture Me No More! On Multicultural Qualifications and the Palestinian-Arab Minority of Israel." *Diogenes* 54, 3 (2007): 39–58.

Kashti, Or. "Poll: Half of Israeli high schoolers oppose equal rights for Arabs." *Ha'aretz*, March 12, 2010.

"Poll: Majority of Israel's Jews back gag on rights groups." *Ha'aretz*, May 7, 2010.

Katz, Yossi. "Status and Rights of the Arab Minority in the Nascent Jewish State." *Middle Eastern Studies* 33, 3 (1997): 568–590.

Kaufman, Ilana. *Arab National Communism in the Jewish State.* Gainesville, FL: University Press of Florida, 1997.

"Ethnic Affirmation or Ethnic Manipulation: The Case of the Druze in Israel." *Nationalism and Ethnic Politics* 9, 4 (2004), 53–82.

"Jews and Arabs in the State of Israel: Is There a Basis for a Unified Civic Identity?" *Israel Affairs* 9 (1) and 9 (2), (2003): 227–48.

Kearney, R. N. "Ethnic Conflict and the Tamil Separatist Movement in Sri Lanka." *Asian Survey* 25, 9 (1985): 898–917.

Kedar, Alexander. "A First Step in a Difficult & Sensitive Road: Preliminary Observations on Quaadan v. Katzir." *Israel Studies Forum* 16, 1 (2000): 3–11.

Keinon, Herb. "FM: Tibi is more dangerous than Hamas." *Jerusalem Post*, August 5, 2009.

Kershner, Isabel. "Gaza war gives bigger lift to Israel's right than to those in power." *The New York Times*, January 26, 2009.

"Israeli rights groups view themselves as under siege." *The New York Times*, April 5, 2010.

"Noted Arab citizens call on Israel to shed Jewish identity." *The New York Times*, February 8, 2007.

"Together apart." *The Jerusalem Post*, January 22, 2007.

Khoury, Jack. "Israeli Arabs warn against dangers of 'racist legislation.'" *Ha'aretz*, May 30, 2009.

Khoury, Jack, and Yair Yagna. "Police destroy dozens of buildings in unrecognized Bedouin village in Negev." *Ha'aretz*, July 28, 2010.

Kimmerling, Baruch. "Between the Primordial and the Civil Definitions of the Collective Identity: *Eretz Israel* or the State of Israel?" In Cohen, Erik, Moshe Lissak, and Uri Almagor, eds., *Comparative Social Dynamics: Essays in Honor of S.N. Eisenstadt.* Boulder, CO: Westview Press, 1985, 262–283.

*Zionism and Territory: The Socioterritorial Dimensions of Zionist Politics.* Berkeley, CA: University of California Press, 1983.

Kimmerling, Baruch, and Joel S. Migdal. *The Palestinian People: A History.* Cambridge, MA: Harvard University Press, 2003.

Kivisto, Peter. *Multiculturalism in a Global Society.* Oxford and Malden, MA: Blackwell Publishing, 2002.

Knesset. "The Declaration of the Establishment of the State of Israel." http://www.knesset.gov.il/docs/eng/megilat_eng.htm, May 14, 1948.

Kook, Rebecca B. "Between Uniqueness and Exclusion: The Politics of Identity in Israel." In Michael Barnett, ed., *Israel in Comparative Perspective.* Albany, NY: SUNY Press, 1996, 199–226.

*The Logic of Democratic Exclusion: African Americans in the United States and Palestinian Citizens in Israel.* Lanham, MA: Lexington Books, 2003.

Kop, Yaakov, and Robert E. Litan. *Sticking Together: The Israeli Experiment in Pluralism.* Washington, DC: Brookings Institution Press, 2002.

Kraft, Dina. "Arabs Plan to Boycott 60th Celebrations." *JTA*, April 3, 2008.

"Israeli bills aimed at limiting dissent spark fierce debate." *JTA*, June 2, 2009.

"Rioting in Umm el-Fahm highlights tension." *JTA*, March 24, 2009.

"U.S. Jews boosting Arab employment in Israel." *JTA*, May 18, 2009.

Kretzmer, David. *The Legal Status of the Arabs in Israel.* Boulder, CO: Westview Press, 1990.

Kymlicka, Will. *Finding Our Way: Rethinking Ethnocultural Relations in Canada.* Oxford: Oxford University Press, 1998.

"The Impact of Group Rights on Fear and Trust: A Response to Offe." *Hagar* 3, 1 (2002): 19–36.

"The Internationalization of Minority Rights." *International Journal of Constitutional Law* 6, 1 (2008): 1–32.

*Multicultural Citizenship: A Liberal Theory of Minority Rights.* Oxford: Oxford University Press, 1995.

*Multicultural Odysseys: Navigating the New International Politics of Diversity.* New York: Oxford University Press, 2007.

Laczko, Leslie L. "Canada's Pluralism in Comparative Perspective." *Ethnic and Racial Studies* 17, 1 (1994): 20–41.

Laor, Nechama, Noa Alpent Leffler, and Havi Inbar-Lankri. "The Absent and Present at Peak Viewing Time – Follow-up Study." http://www.rashut2.org.il/editor.

Landau, Jacob M. *The Arab Minority in Israel, 1967–1991: Political Aspects.* Oxford: Clarendon Press, 1993.

Lapid, Yossef. "A State within a State." *Ma'ariv*, December 6, 2006.

Lapidoth, Ruth. *Autonomy: Flexible Solutions to Ethnic Conflicts.* Washington, DC: United States Institute for Peace, 1996.

Laponce, Jean. *Languages and Their Territories.* Toronto: University of Toronto Press, 1987.

Lappin, Yaakov. "National-religious housing project puts Jaffa coexistence at risk, Tel Aviv municipality says." *The Jerusalem Post*, June 18, 2009.

Laqueur, Walter Z. and Barry Rubin, eds. *The Israel-Arab Reader: A Documentary History of the Middle East Conflict*, 4th ed. New York: Penguin Books, 1984.

Lenaerts, Koen. "Constitutionalism and the Many Faces of Federalism." *American Journal of Comparative Law* 38, 1 (1996): 205–263.

Lesch, Ann M., and Dan Tachigi. *Origins and Development of the Arab-Israeli Conflict.* Hartford: Greenwood, 1998.

Levy, Gal. "From Subjects to Citizens: On Educational Reforms and the Demarcation of the 'Israeli-Arabs.'" *Citizenship Studies* 9, 3 (2005): 271–291.

Levy, Gideon. "Kahane won." *Ha'aretz*, February 8, 2009.

Liebman, Charles S. "Religion and Democracy in Israel." In Shlomo A. Deshen, Charles S. Liebman, Moshe Shokeid, eds., *Israeli Judaism: The Sociology of Religion in Israel.* New Brunswick, NJ: Transaction Publishers, 1995, 350–367.

Lijphart, Arend. *Democracies: Patterns of Majoritarian and Consensus Government in Twenty-One Countries.* New Haven: Yale University Press, 1984.

*Democracy in Plural Societies: A Comparative Exploration.* New Haven: Yale University Press, 1997.

Linz, Juan, and Alfred Stepan. *Problems of Democratic Transition and Consolidation*. Baltimore: Johns Hopkins University, 1996.

Lis, Jonathan. "Israel arrests 700 people, mostly Arabs, in protests against IDF Gaza op." *Ha'aretz*, January 12, 2009.

"Salah calls for 'intifada' against Temple Mount excavation." *Ha'aretz*, February 17, 2007.

Louer, Laurence. *To Be an Arab in Israel*. New York: Columbia University Press, 2007.

Lustick, Ian. "Abandoning the Iron Wall: Israel and 'The Middle Eastern Muck.'" *Middle East Policy* 15, 3 (2008): 30–56.

*Arabs in the Jewish State: Israel's Control of a National Minority*. Austin, TX: University of Texas Press, 1980.

"Israel as a Non-Arab State: The Political Implications of Mass Immigration of Non-Jews." *Middle East Journal* 53, 3 (1999): 417–433.

"Zionism and the State of Israel: Regime Objective and the Arab Minority in the First Years of Statehood." *Middle Eastern Studies* 16, 1 (1980): 127–156.

Mackey, Eva. *The House of Difference: Cultural Politics and National Identity in Canada*. New York: Routledge, 1999.

Mada al-Carmel: The Center for Applied Social Research. "The Haifa Declaration," Mada al-Carmel (2007): 1–19. http://www.mada-research. org/archive/haifaenglish.pdf.

Makover, Sari. "Danger: No Border Ahead," *Ma'ariv*, February 21, 2002.

Margalit, Dan. "A democracy on the defensive." *Ha'aretz*, October 5, 2000.

Masalha, Nur. "Collective Memory, Indigenous Resistance and the Struggle for Return: Palestinians inside Israel Six Decades after the Nakba." *Jadal* 3, 1 (2009). http://www.mada-research.org/publications/PDF/Jadal_May09_Eng.pdf.

Mazie, Steven V. "Importing Liberalism: Brown v. Board of Education in the Israeli Context." *Polity* 36, 3 (2004): 389–211.

McCarthy, Rory. "Wanted, for Crimes against the State." *The Guardian*, July 24, 2007.

McGarry, John. "'Democracy' in Northern Ireland: Experiments in Self-Rule from the Protestant Ascendancy to the Good Friday Agreement." *Nation & Nationalism* 8, 4 (2002): 451–474.

McGarry, John, and Brendan O'Leary eds. *The Politics of Ethnic Conflict Regulation*. London and New York: Routledge, 1993.

Medding, Peter. *The Founding of Israeli Democracy, 1949–1967*. Oxford and New York: Oxford University Press, 1990.

Meranda, Amnon. "'Softened' Nakba law passes 1st reading." *Ynet*, March 16, 2010.

Migdal, Joel S. *Through the Lens of Israel: Explorations in State and Society*. Albany: SUNY Press, 2001.

Migdal, S. Joel. "Whose State Is it, Anyway? Exclusion and the Construction of Graduated Citizenship in Israel." *Israel Studies Forum* 21, 2 (2006): 3–27.

Miller, David. *On Nationality*. Oxford: Clarendon Press, 1995.

Misra, Amatendu. "Politics of the Hindu Right: Emergence and Growth of the Bharatiya Janata Party." *Politics, Administration and Change* 32, 2 (1999): 36–55.

Mitnick, Joshua. "Israeli Cabinet to Consider Loyalty Oath for Citizens – Including Arabs." *The Christian Science Monitor,* May 27, 2009.

Moran, Dominic. "Israel's State-Druze Rift." *International Relations and Security Network.* November 6, 2007. http://www.isn.ethz.ch/isn/CurrentAffairs/SecurityWatch/Detail/?ots591=4888CAA0-B3DB-1461-98B9-E20E7B9C13D4&lng=en&id=53699.

Moreno, Luis. *The Federalization of Spain.* London: Frank Cass, 2001.

Morris, Benny. *The Birth of the Palestinian Refugee Problem, 1947–1949.* New York: Cambridge University Press, 2004.

   *Israel's Border Wars, 1949–1956 Arab Infiltration, Israeli Retaliation, and the Countdown to the Suez War.* Oxford: Clarendon Press, 1993.

   *Righteous Victims: A History of the Zionist-Arab Conflict 1881–2001.* New York: Knopf, 2001.

Mouffe, Chantal. "Which Public Sphere for a Democratic Society?" *Theoria* 99 (2002): 55–65.

Mualem, Mazal. "Lieberman blast Arabs MKs, pulls party out of government." *Ha'aretz,* January 16, 2008.

Myre, Greg. "New voice on right in Israeli cabinet is likely to be loud." *The New York Times,* October 24, 2006.

Naffa', Hisham. "The Palestinians in Israel and Operation Cast Lead: A View from Haifa." *Journal of Palestine Studies* 38, no. 3 (2009): 54–63.

Nahshoni, Kobi. "Poll: Most Israelis see themselves as Jewish first, Israeli second." *Ynet,* May 2008.

National Committee for the Heads of the Arab Local Authorities in Israel. *The Future Vision of the Palestinian Arabs in Israel.* 2006: 1–40.

Negbi, Moshe. *Above the Law: The Crisis of the Rule of Law in Israel.* Tel Aviv: Am Oved, 1987.

Negev Coexistence Forum for Civil Equality. *The Bedouin-Arabs in the Negev-Naqab Desert in Israel.* 2009, 3–4.

Neumann, Iver B. "Self and Other in International Relations." *European Journal of International Relations* 2, 2 (1996): 166–201.

Neumann, Iver B., and Jennifer M. Welsh. "The Other in European Self-Definition: An Addendum to the Literature on International Society." *Review of International Studies* 17, 4 (1991): 327–348.

Nimni, Ephraim. *The Challenge of Post-Zionism: Alternatives to Israeli Fundamentalist Politics.* London: Zed Books, 2003.

Nir, Ori. "Israeli Arab alienation intensifies." *Ha'aretz,* May 21, 2001.

   "Not by hummus and za'atar alone." *Ha'aretz,* October 13, 2000.

Nissan, Mordechai. *The Jewish State and the Arab Problem.* Tel Aviv: Mas, 1986.

OECD. *Labour Market and Social Policy Review of Israel – 2010.* Organization for Economic Cooperation and Development, Paris, France, 2010. http://www.oecd.org/els/israel2010.

Offe, Claus. "Homogeneity and Constitutional Democracy: Coping with Identity Conflicts through Group Rights." *Journal of Political Philosophy* 6, 2 (1998): 113–141.

   "Political Liberalism, Group Rights, and the Politics of Fear and Trust." *Hagar* 3, 1 (2002): 3–17.

O'Leary, Brendan. "The Nature of the British-Irish Agreement." *New Left Review* 233 (1999): 66–96.

"The Protection of Human Rights under the Belfast Agreement." *Political Quarterly* 72, 3 (2001): 353–365.

Or, Theodor. "A Year to the State Investigative Commission on the October 2000 Events." (Translated from Hebrew by Judy Krausz), The Moshe Dayan Center for Middle Eastern and African Studies, 2004.

Or Commission report. *Ha'aretz*, September 21, 2003. http://www.Ha'aretz.com/hasen/pages/ShArt.jhtml?itemNo=335594.

Pappe, Ilan. *A History of Modern Palestine: One Land, Two People*. New York: Cambridge, 2004.

"An Uneasy Coexistence: Arabs and Jews in the First Decade of Statehood." In Ilan Troen and Noah Lucas, eds., *Israel: The First Decade of Independence*. Albany, NY: SUNY Press, 1995, 617–658.

Patten, Alan. "Liberal Citizenship in Multiethnic Societies." In Alain-G. Gagnon and James Tully, eds. *Multinational Democracies*. New York: Cambridge University Press, 2001.

Payes, Shany. "Palestinian NGOs in Israel: A Campaign for Civic Equality in a Non-Civic State." *Israel Studies* 8, 1 (2003): 60–90.

Pedahzur, Ami, and Yael Yishai. "Hatred by Hated People: Xenophobia in Israel." *Studies in Conflict & Terrorism* 22 (1999): 101–117.

Peled, Alisa. *Debating Islam in the Jewish State: The Development of Policy toward Islamic Institutions in Israel*. Albany: SUNY Press, 2001.

Peled, Yoav. "Citizenship." In Uri Ram and Nitza Berkovitch, eds., *In/Equality*, Beer-Sheva: Ben-Gurion University of the Negev Press, 2006, 31–37.

"Citizenship Betrayed: Israel's Emerging Immigration and Citizenship Regime." *Theoretical Inquiries in Law* 8, 2 (2007): 333–358.

"Ethnic Democracy and the Legal Construction of Citizenship: Arab Citizens of the Jewish State." *The American Political Science Review* 86, 1 (1992): 432–443.

"The Evolution of Israeli Citizenship: An Overview." *Citizenship Studies* 12, 3 (2008): 335–345.

"The Or Commission and Palestinian Citizenship in Israel." *Citizenship Studies*, 9, 1 (2005): 89–105.

"Strangers in Utopia: The Civic Status of the Palestinians in Israel." *Teoria U'Vikoret* 3 (1993): 21–35.

Peled, Yoav, and Doron Navot. "Ethnic Democracy Revisited: On the State of Democracy in the Jewish State." *Israel Studies Forum* 20, 1 (2005): 3–27.

Peleg, Ilan. *Democratizing the Hegemonic State: Political Transformation in the Age of Identity*. Cambridge: Cambridge University Press, 2007.

"Israel as a Liberal Democracy: Civil Rights in the Jewish State." In Laurie Z. Eisenberg and Neil Caplan, eds., *Review Essays in Israel Studies: Books on Israel, Vol. V* (2000): 63–80.

"Israel between Democratic Universalism & Particularist Judaism: Challenging a Sacred Formula." *Report to the Oxford Centre for Hebrew & Jewish Studies* (2002–2003): 5–20.

"Israel's Constitutional Order and Kulturkampf: The Role of Ben-Gurion."
  *Israel Studies* 3, 1 (1998): 230–250.
"Jewish-Palestinian Relations in Israel: From Hegemony to Equality."
  *International Journal of Politics, Culture and Society* 17, 3 (2004): 415–37.
"Otherness and Israel's Arab Dilemma." In Laurence J. Silberstein and Robert
  L. Cohn, eds., *The Other in Jewish Thought and History.* New York: New
  York University Press, 1994, 258–280.
Peleg, Ilan, and Dov Waxman. "Losing Control? A Comparison of Majority-
  Minority Relations in Israel and Turkey." *Nationalism and Ethnic Politics*
  13, 3 (2007): 431–463.
Peres, Yochanan. "Ethnic Relations in Israel." *The American Journal of Sociology*
  76, 6 (1971): 1021–1047.
Peretz, Don. "Early State Policy toward the Arab-Population, 1948–1955." In
  Laurence J. Silberstein, ed. *New Perspectives on Israeli History: The Early
  Years of the State.* New York: New York University Press, 1991, 82–102.
Pinko, Noam. *Zionism and the Roads Not Taken: Rawidowicz, Kaplan, Kohn.*
  Bloomington: Indiana University Press, 2010.
Pittinsky, L. Todd, Jennifer J. Ratcliff, and Laura A. Maruskin. "Coexistence in
  Israel, A National Study." Center for Public Leadership, Harvard Kennedy
  School, Harvard University, Cambridge, MA, 2008, 1–17.
Prince-Gibson, Eetta. "Land (Swap) for peace?" *The Jerusalem Post*, November
  8, 2007.
Prusher, Ilene. "In Israel, Jews and Arabs aim to bridge 'independence' and 'catas-
  trophe' narratives." *The Christian Science Monitor*, April 29, 2009.
"Israelis ponder a land swap." *Christian Science Monitor*, April 5, 2006.
Rabinowitz, Dan. "Israel and Palestinian Refugees: Postpragmatic Reflections
  on Historical Narratives, Closure, Transnational Justice, and Palestinian
  Refugees' Right to Refuse." In Barbara Rose Johnstone and Susan Slyomovics,
  eds., *Waging war and Making Peace: Reparations and Human Rights.* Walnut
  Creek, CA: Left Coast Press, 2009, 225–240.
Rabinowitz, Dan, and Khawla Abu-Baker. *Coffins on Our Shoulders: The
  Experience of the Palestinian Citizens of Israel.* Berkeley: The University of
  California Press, 2005.
Rabinowitz, Dan, and Khawla Abu Baker. *The Stand Tall Generation: The
  Palestinian Citizens of Israel Today.* Jerusalem: Keter (Hebrew), 2002.
Rabinowitz, Dan, As'ad Ghanem, and Oren Yiftachel, eds. *After the Rift: New
  Directions for Government Policy towards the Arab Population in Israel.*
  An emergency report by an inter-university research team submitted to Mr.
  Ehud Barak, prime minister of Israel, 2000.
Ravid, Barak. "Higher Arab monitoring committee tells gov't to dismiss
  Lieberman." *Ha'aretz*, November 8, 2007.
"Meridor: Loyalty oath will only make Israeli Arabs more extreme." *Ha'aretz*,
  July 19, 2010.
Rawls, John. *A Theory of Justice.* Cambridge, MA: Belknap Press of Harvard
  University Press, 1971.
Reider, Dmitry. "Who Is Afraid of the One-State Solution?" *Foreign Affairs*,
  March 31, 2010.

Rekhess, Elie. "The Arabs of Israel After Oslo: Localization of the National Struggle," *Israel Studies* 7, 3 (2002): 1–44.

"The Evolvement of an Arab-Palestinian National Minority in Israel," *Israel Studies* 12, 3 (2007): 1–28.

*The Future Vision of the Palestinian-Arabs in Israel*. Tel Aviv Notes, The Moshe Dayan Center for Middle Eastern and African Studies, Tel Aviv University, 2006.

"Initial Israeli Policy Guidelines toward the Arab Minority, 1948–1949." In Laurence Silberstein ed., *New Perspectives on Israeli History: The Early Years of the State*. New York: New York University Press, 1991, 103–119.

"In the Shadow of National Conflict: Inter-Group Attitudes and Images of Arab and Jews in Israel." *TriQuarterly* 131, 1 (Winter 2007): 206–236.

"Israel and its Arab Citizens – Taking Stock." Tel Aviv Notes, The Moshe Dayan Center for Middle Eastern and African Studies, Tel Aviv University, 2007.

"No balm in Galilee." *The Jerusalem Post*, November 27, 2007.

Rekhess, Elie, and Sarah Osacky-Lazar, eds. 2005. *The Status of the Arab Minority in the Jewish Nation State*. Tel Aviv University: Moshe Dayan Center for Middle Eastern and African Studies.

*Reuters*. "Israel's Lieberman and controversial comments."April 1, 2009. http://www.reuters.com/article/worldNews/idUSTRE52U3FU20090401.

Rivlin, Reuven. "Arabs integral part of Israel." *The Jerusalem Post*, August 4, 2009.

Roffe-Ofir, Sharon. "40% of Israeli Arabs: Holocaust never happened." *Ynet*, May 17, 2009.

"Breach of trust: Where are Israeli Arabs headed?" *Ynet*, November 3, 2008.

"Israeli Arab leader: Don't treat us like enemies." *Ynet*, January 14, 2010.

"Peres acknowledges discrimination in employment of Arabs." *Ynet*, January 13, 2010.

"Rift between Israel, Druze growing." *Ynet*, January 18, 2008.

Ronen, Gil, and Arutz Sheva. "IDF Preparing Troops to Fight Arab Fifth Column in Wartime." May 5, 2009. http://www.israelnationalnews.com/News/News.aspx/131207.

Rosilio, Anat. "Absent from the discourse." *Common Ground News*, – Middle East, English Edition, July 9, 2009.

Rosmer, Tilde. "The Islamic Movement in the Jewish State." In Khaled Hroub, ed. *Political Islam: Context versus Ideology*. London: Saqi Books, 2010.

Rothchild, Donald, and Victor Olurunsola, eds. *State vs. Ethnic Claims: African Policy Dilemmas*. Boulder, CO: Westview Press, 1986, 240–241.

Rouhana, Nadim, ed. *Attitudes of Palestinians in Israel on Key Political and Social Issues: Survey Research Results*. Haifa: Mada al-Carmel, 2007.

"Israel and its Arab Citizens: Predicaments in the Relationship between Ethnic States and Ethnonational Minorities." *Third World Quarterly* 19, 2 (1998): 277–296.

"Israel's Palestinians Speak Out." http://www.mada-research.org, December, 2007.

*Palestinian Citizens in an Ethnic Jewish State: Identities in Conflict*. New Haven, CT: Yale University Press, 1997.

"The Political Transformation of the Palestinians in Israel: From Acquiescence to Challenge." *Journal of Palestine Studies* 18, 3 (1998): 38–59.

Rouhana, Nadim, and As'ad Ghanem. "The Crisis of Minorities in Ethnic States: The Case of Palestinian Citizens in Israel." *International Journal of Middle East Studies* 30, 3 (1998): 321–346.

Rouhana, Nadim, and Nimer Soultany. "Redrawing the Boundaries of Citizenship: Israel's New Hegemony." *Journal of Palestine Studies* 33, 1 (2003): 5–22.

Rubinstein, Amnon. "And the Left is silent." *Ma'ariv*. January 5, 2007.

Russell, Peter H. "The Politics of Mega-Constitutional Change: Lessons for Canada." In Bertus de Villers, ed. *Evaluating Federal Systems*. Dordrecht: Juta & Co., 1994.

Sa'di, Ahmad. "Beyond the Pale? Avigdor Lieberman and Demographic Racism in Israel." *Holy Land Studies* 8, 2 (2009): 143–158.

"Catastrophe, Memory and Identity: Al-Nakbah as a Component of Palestinian Identity." *Israel Studies* 7, 2 (2002): 175–198.

"Minority Resistance to State Control: Towards a Re-analysis of Palestinian Political Activity in Israel." *Social Identities* 2, 3 (1996): 395–412.

Saban, Ilan. "After the Storm? The Israeli Supreme Court and the Arab-Palestinian Minority in the Aftermath of October 2000." *Israel Affairs* 14, 4 (2008): 623–639.

"Appropriate Representation of Minorities: Canada's Two Types Structure and the Arab-Palestinian Minority in Israel." *Penn State International Law Review* 24, 3 (2003): 563–594.

"Minority Rights in Deeply Divided Societies: A Framework for Analysis and the Case of the Arab-Palestinian Minority in Israel." *New York University Journal of International Law and Politics* 36, 4 (2004): 885–1003.

Sabbagh-Khoury, Areej. "The Palestinians in Israel: Historical, Social and Political Background." http:// www.mada-research.org, 2009.

Safran, William. "Non-separatist Policies Regarding Ethnic Minorities: Positive Approaches & Ambiguous Consequences." *International Political Science Review* 15, 1 (1994): 61–80.

Said, Edward. *Orientalism*. London: Penguin, 1995.

Sandel, Michael. *Liberalism and the Limits of Justice*. New York: Cambridge University Press, 1982.

Saouli, Adham. "Arab Political Organizations within the Israeli State." *The Journal of Social, Political and Economic Studies* 26, 2 (2001): 443–460.

Sartori, Giovanni. "Political Development and Political Engineering." *Public Policy* 17 (1968): 261–298.

"Understanding Pluralism." *Journal of Democracy* 8, 4 (1997): 58–69.

Schechla, Joseph. "The Invisible People Come to Light: Israel's 'Internally Displaced' and 'Unrecognized Villages.'" *Journal of Palestine Studies* 31, 1 (2001): 20–31.

Schiff, Ze'ev. "Self-inflicted injury." *Ha'aretz*, January 26, 2007.

Schmid, Carol L. *The Politics of Language: Conflict, Identity, and Cultural Pluralism in Comparative Perspective*. Oxford: Oxford University Press, 2001.

Schnapper, Dominique. "The Concept of 'Dominant Ethnicity' in the Case of France." In Eric P. Kaufmann, ed., *Rethinking Ethnicity: Majority Groups and Dominant Minorities*. New York: Routledge, 2004, 102–115.

Schneider, Howard. "Coastal Israeli city offers glimpse into deep-seated divide: Plan to house Jews in Arab sector of Jaffa seen as threat to coexistence." *The Washington Post*, May 26, 2009.

Segev, Tom. *1949: The First Israelis*. New York: Free Press, 1986.

Sela, Neta. "Livni: National aspirations of Israel's Arabs can be met by Palestinian homeland." *Ha'aretz*, December 11, 2008.

"Livni: Palestinian state – solution for Israeli Arabs as well." *Ynet*, November 18, 2007.

Selig, Abe. "Sa'ar drops 'Nakba' from Arab textbooks." *The Jerusalem Post*, August 30, 2009.

Senyor, Eli. "Jaffa: Yeshiva to be built in heart of Arab neighborhood." *Ynet*, September 24, 2008.

Shafir, Gershon, and Yoav Peled. *Being Israeli: The Dynamics of Multiple Citizenship*. Cambridge: Cambridge University Press, 2002.

Shaked, Ronny. "Arab MK: Israel 'robbery of century.'" *Ynet*, December 18, 2005.

Shalev, Michael. "Jewish Organized Labor and the Palestinians: A Study of State/Society Relations in Israel" in Baruch Kimmerling, ed., *The Israeli State and Society: Boundaries and Frontiers*. Albany: SUNY Press, 1989.

Shalit, David. "Even Menachem begin was opposed." *Ha'aretz*, August 30, 1996.

Shalom, Zaki. *Policy in the Shadow of Controversy: The Routine Security Policy of Israel, 1949–1956*. Tel Aviv: Ministry Of Defense Publishing, 1996.

Shamir, Michal, and Tammy Sagiv-Schifter. "Conflict, Identity, and Tolerance: Israel and the Al-Aqsa Intifada." *Political Psychology* 27, no. 4 (2006): 569–596.

Shamir, Shimon. "The Arabs in Israel – Two Years after the Or Commission Report." Tel Aviv University, Konrad Adenauer Program for Jewish-Arab Cooperation, 2006.

"The Historical Perspective: Introductory Notes." *Skirot* Tel Aviv: Shiloach Center (Hebrew), 1976.

Shamir, Shlomo, and Jack Khoury. "U.S. Jewish community's new mission: Equality between Israeli Jews and Arabs." *Ha'aretz*, May 9, 2008.

Shapira, Anita. *Israeli Identity in Transition*. New York: Praeger, 2004.

Shapiro, Yonathan. *Politicians as a Hegemonic Class: The Case of Israel*. Tel Aviv: Sifriat Poalim, 1996.

"Where had Liberalism Disappeared in Israel." *Zmanim* (Winter 1996): 92–101.

Shavit, Ari. "A leader is waiting for a signal." *Ha'aretz*, March 22, 2002.

"Survival of the fittest? An interview with Benny Morris." *Ha'aretz*, January 9, 2004.

Shavit, Uriya. "Talk is cheap." *Ha'aretz*, October 20, 2000.

Sheffer, Gabriel. "Sharett's 'Line', Struggles, and Legacy." In Ilan Troen and Noah Lucas eds., *Israel: The First Decade of Independence*. Albany: SUNY Press, 1995, 143–169.

Sheleg, Yair. "The demographics point to a binational state." *Ha'aretz*, May 27, 2004.

Shenhav, Yehuda. *The Time of the Green Line*. Hakibbutz: Hameuchad, 2010.

Shihadeh, Mtanes. *Poverty as Policy*. Haifa: Mada al-Carmel, 2004.

Shlaim, Avi. *The Iron Wall: Israel and the Arab World*. New York: Norton, 2001.

Shragai, Nadav. "Knesset okays initial bill to outlaw denial of 'Jewish state.'" *Ha'aretz*, May 26, 2009.

Sikkuy: The Association for the Advancement of Civic Equality in Israel. http://www.sikkuy.org.il/english/home.html.

Simon, Rita, and Jean Landis. "Trends in Public Support for Civil Liberties and Due Process in Israeli Society." *Social Science Quarterly* 71, 1 (1990): 93–104.

Sisk, Timothy. *Power Sharing and International Mediation in Ethnic Conflicts*. Washington, DC: US Institute of Peace, 1996.

Smith, Rogers M. "The 'American Creed' and the American Identity: The Limits of Liberal Citizenship in the United States." *Western Political Quarterly* 41, 2 (1988): 225–251.

Smooha, Sammy. "Arab-Jewish Relations in Israel: A Deeply Divided Society." In Anita Shapira, ed., *Israeli Identity in Transition*, 54–70. Westport, CT: Praeger Publishers, 2004.

"The Arab Minority in Israel: Radicalization or Politicization?" *Studies in Contemporary Jewry* 5 (1989): 59–88.

*Arabs and Jews in Israel Vol.1: Conflicting and Shared Attitudes in a Divided Society*. Boulder, CO: Westview Press, 1989.

*Arabs and Jews in Israel Vol. 2: Change and Continuity in Mutual Intolerance*. Boulder, CO: Westview Press, 1992.

"Are the Palestinian Arabs in Israel Radicalizing?" *Bitterlemons*. June 24, 2004. http://www.bitterlemonsinternational.org/previous.php?opt=1&id=45#182.

"Civic Service for Arabs in Israel: Findings of Attitude Survey of the Arab Public and Leadership in Fall 2007." The Jewish-Arab Center, University of Haifa, 2008.

"Control of Minorities in Israel and Northern Ireland." *Comparative Studies in Society and History* 22, 2 (1980): 256–280.

"Ethnic Democracy: Israel as an Archetype." *Israel Studies* 2, 2 (1997): 198–241.

"Existing and Alternative Policies toward the Arab in Israel." *Magamot* 26, 1 (1971): 14–41.

*Index of Arab-Jewish Relations in Israel 2004*. Haifa: The Jewish-Arab Center, University of Haifa; Jerusalem: The Citizens' Accord Forum between Jews and Arabs in Israel; Tel Aviv: Friedrich Ebert Stiftung, 2005.

"Jewish and Arab Ethnocentrism in Israel." *Ethnic and Racial Studies* 10, 1 (1987): 1–26.

"Minority Status in an Ethnic Democracy: The Status of the Arab Minority in Israel." *Ethnic & Racial Studies* 13, 3 (1990): 389–413.

"The Model of Ethnic Democracy: Israel as a Jewish and Democratic State." *Nations and Nationalism* 8, 4 (2002): 475–503.

Summary of Index of Arab-Jewish Relations, 2006.

"Types of Democracy & Modes of Conflict Management in Ethnically Divided Societies." *Nations & Nationalism* 8, 4 (2002): 423–431.

Smooha, Sammy, and Uriel Abulof. "Interview about the Vision Documents with Uriel Abulof." *Eretz Acheret* 39, 2007, 34–36.

Smooha, Sammy, and Theodor Hanf. "The Diverse Mode of Conflict-Regulation in Deeply Divided Societies." *International Journal of Comparative Sociology* 33, 1 (1992): 26–47.

Snyder, Jack. *From Voting to Violence: Democratization and National Conflict.* New York: Norton, 2000.

Sofer, Sasson. *Begin: An Anatomy of Leadership.* Oxford: Blackwell, 1988.

Somfalvi, Attila. "Lieberman defends PR, slams opposition." *Ynet,* June 6, 2010.

Spinner, Jeff. *The Boundaries of Citizenship: Race, Ethnicity and Nationality in the Liberal State.* Baltimore: Johns Hopkins University, 1994.

"Unoriginal Sin: Zionism and Democratic Exclusion in Comparative Perspective." *Israel Studies Forum* 18, 1 (2002): 26–56.

Stern, Yoav. "Arab education panel sets up extra-ministerial oversight body." *Ha'aretz,* December 7, 2007.

"Ben-Eliezer: Continued neglect of Israeli Arabs may spark 'Internal Intifada.'" *Ha'aretz,* September 9, 2007.

"Israeli Arab leaders: A Palestinian state is not the solution for us." *Ha'aretz,* December 4, 2007.

"Israeli Arabs' 'Haifa Declaration' urges Israel to own up to Nakba responsibility." *Ha'aretz,* May 15, 2007.

"Majadele: New Arab city will bolster our sense of belonging." *Ha'aretz,* February 12, 2008.

"Opposition to national service in Israel's Arab sector is bitter," *Ha'aretz,* August 4, 2008.

"National service to accept only half of its Israeli Arab applicants." *Ha'aretz,* May 13, 2009.

"Poll: 75% of Israeli Arabs support Jewish, democratic constitution." *Ha'aretz,* April 29, 2007.

Sternhell, Ze'ev. *Nation-Building and Nationalism: Nationalism and Socialism in the Israeli Labor Movement, 1904–1940.* Tel Aviv: Tel Aviv University Press, 1995.

*Nation-Building or Model Society: Nationalism and Socialism in the Israeli Labor Movement, 1904–1940.* Tel Aviv: Tel Aviv University Press (Hebrew), 1995.

Strum, Philippa. "The Road Not Taken: Constitutional Non-Decision Making in 1948–1950 and Its Impact on Civil Liberties in the Israeli Political Culture." In Ilan Troen and Noah Lucas, eds., *Israel: The First Decade of Independence.* Albany, NY: SUNY Press, 1995, 83–104.

Sumner, William G. *Folkways.* Boston, MA: Ginn, 1906.

Susser, Leslie. "Fanning the Flames of Discontent." *The Jerusalem Report,* July 6, 2009.

"'Land Day' March Highlights Israeli Arabs' Dilemmas." *The Jewish Journal,* April 6, 2010.

"National Service Seeks Arab Volunteers." *The Jerusalem Report,* April 28, 2008.

Tal, Avraham. "This means war." *Ha'aretz*, December 9, 2006.

Tamar, Karin Schafferman. "Arab Identity in a Jewish and Democratic State." *The Israeli Democracy Institute*, 2008.

"Participation, Abstention and Boycott: Trends in Arab Voter Turnout in Israeli Elections." *The Israeli Democracy Institute*, 2009.

Tamir, Yael. *Liberal Nationalism*. Princeton, NJ: Princeton University Press, 1993.

Taras, Raymond C., and Rajat Ganguly. *Understanding Ethnic Conflict: The International Dimension*. New York: Longman, 2008.

Taylor, Charles. *Multiculturalism and the Politics of Recognition*. Princeton, NJ: Princeton University Press, 1992.

"The Politics of Recognition." In Amy Gutman, ed., *Multiculturalism: Examining the Politics of Recognition*. Princeton, NJ: Princeton University Press, 1992, 25–73.

Tessler, Mark, and Audra K. Grant. "Israel's Arab Citizens: the Continuing Struggle." *Annals of the American Academy of Political and Social Science* 555, 1 (1998): 97–113.

Teveth, Shabtai. *Ben-Gurion and the Palestinian Arabs from Peace to War*. New York: Oxford University Press, 1985.

The Abraham Fund Initiatives. "Governmental Responsibility for Social Inclusion and Jewish-Arab Equality in Israel." Herzliya Conference, 2008.

The Association for Civil Rights in Israel (ACRI). "The State of Human Rights in Israel and the Occupied Territories 2007 Report." 2007.

*The Jerusalem Post*. "28% of Israel's Arabs deny Holocaust." March 18, 2007.

"Arabs shouldn't live with Jews, Shas minister says." July 3, 2009.

*The Jerusalem Post*. "Druse, Circassians protest in Jerusalem." June 21, 2009.

"Israeli Arabs struggle with burgeoning identity crisis." January 14, 2007.

The Konrad Adenauer Program for Jewish-Arab Cooperation. "The Arabs in Israel – Three Years after the Or Commission Report." Lecture by Judge Hashim Khatib, 2006.

*The Future Vision of the Palestinian Arabs in Israel*. The Moshe Dayan Center for Middle Eastern and African Studies, Tel Aviv University, 2007, 1–19.

The Mossawa Center. "Akko: City on the Front." The Mossawa Center, Haifa, Israel, December 2008.

"The Palestinian Arab Citizens of Israel: Status, Opportunities and Challenges for an Israeli-Palestinian Peace." The Mossawa Center, Haifa, Israel, June, 2006.

"The Palestinian Arab Minority and the 2009 Israeli Elections." The Mossawa Center, Haifa, Israel, March 2009.

The National Committee for the Heads of Arab Local Authorities in Israel. *The Future Vision of the Palestinian Arabs in Israel*. Nazareth: Al Woroud, 2006.

The Reut Institute. "Democratic Constitution of Adalah." 2007.

The Reut Institute. "Integrating Israel's Arab Citizens into the ISRAEL 15 Vision." (2009): 1–9.

"Internationalization of the Issue of Israeli Arabs." June 14, 2005. http://reut-institute.org/Publication.aspx?PublicationId=535.

The White House, Office of the Press Secretary. "Remarks by the President to the United Nations General Assembly." September 23, 2009.

Towns, Ann (Reviewer). "Multicultural Odysseys: Navigating the New International Politics of Diversity." By Will Kymlicka (New York: Oxford University Press, 2007), *Ethics & International Affairs* 23, 1 (2009): 69–71.

Urian, Dan, and Efraim Karsh, ed. *In Search of Identity: Jewish Aspects in Israeli Culture*. Portland, OR: Frank Cass, 1999.

Van der Berghe, A. C. "Protection of Ethnic Minorities: A Critical Appraisal." In R. G. Wirsing, ed. *Protection of Ethnic Minorities: Comparative Analysis*. Oxford: Pergamon Press, 1981, 343–355.

Waxman, Dov. "From Controversy to Consensus: Cultural Conflict and the Israeli Debate over Territorial Withdrawal." *Israel Studies* 13, 2 (2008): 73–96.

*The Pursuit of Peace and the Crisis of Israeli Identity: Defending/Defining the Nation*. New York: Palgrave Macmillan, 2006.

Waxman, Dov, and Ilan Peleg. "Neither Ethnocracy Nor Bi-Nationalism: In Search Of The Middle Ground," *Israel Studies Forum* 23, 3 (2008): 55–73.

Weiler-Polak, Dana. "Poll: Half of Israelis feel those born elsewhere can't be 'true Israelis.'" *Ha'aretz*, August 3, 2009.

Weiss, Philip, and Adam Horowitz. "Loyalty and Democracy in Lieberman's Israel: Interviews with Israeli Knesset Members Alex Miller and Ahmad Tibi." *TPM Café*, June 8, 2009. http://tpmcafe.talkingpointsmemo.com/2009/06/08/loyalty_and_democracy_in_liebermans_israel_intervi/.

Wolfsfeld, Gadi, Avraham, A., and Issam Abu Rayah. "When Prophesy Always Fails: Israeli Press Coverage of the Arab Minority Land Day protests." *Political Communication*, 17, 2 (2000): 115–131.

Yael, Hadar, and Himeyn-Raisch Naomi. "Who Are We? National Identity in the State of Israel." *The Israeli Democracy Institute*, 2008.

Yakobson, Alexander, and Amnon Rubinstein. *Israel and the Family of Nations: The Jewish Nation-State and Human Rights*. New York: Routledge, 2009.

Yanai, Natan. "Ben-Gurion Concept of Mamlachtiut and the Forming Reality of the State of Israel." *Jewish Political Studies Review* 1, 2 (1989): 159–191.

"The Citizen as Pioneer: Ben-Gurion's Concept of Citizenship." *Israel Studies* 1, 1 (1996): 127–143.

Yehoshua, A. B. "Israeli state." *Ha'aretz*, June 19, 2009.

Yiftachel, Oren. "Between Nation and State: 'Fractured' Regionalism among Palestinian-Arabs in Israel." *Political Geography* 18, 3 (1999): 285–308.

"'Creeping Apartheid' in Israel-Palestine." *Middle East Report* 39, 253 (2009): 7–15.

"The Ethnic Democracy Model and Its Applicability to the Case of Israel." *Ethnic and Racial Studies* 15, 1 (1992): 125–137.

"'Ethnocracy' and Its Discontents: Minorities, Protests, and Israeli Polity." *Critical Inquiry* 26, 4 (2000): 725–756.

*Ethnocracy: Land & Identity Politics in Israel/Palestine*. Philadelphia, PA: University of Pennsylvania Press, 2006.

"Ghetto Citizenship: Palestinian Arabs in Israel." In Nadim Rouhana & A. Sasagh, eds., *Israel and the Palestinians: Key Terms*, Haifa: Mada Center for Applied Research (2009), 56–661.

"The Shrinking Space of Citizenship: Ethnocratic Politics in Israel." *Middle East Report* 32, 2 (2002): 38–42.

"Voting for Apartheid: The 2009 Israeli Elections." *Journal of Palestine Studies* 38, 3 (2009): 1–15.

Yiftachel, Oren, and Alexander Kedar. "Landed Power: The Making of the Israeli Land Regime." *Theory and Criticism* 16, 1 (2000): 67–100.

Yiftachel, Oren, Rassem Khamaissi, and Sandy Kedar. "Land and Planning." In Dan Rabinowitz, As'ad Ghanem, and Oren Yiftachel, eds. *After the Rift: New Directions for Government Policy towards the Arab Population in Israel.* 2000.

Yiftachel, Oren, and Michaly D. Segal. "Jews and Druze in Israel: State Control and Ethnic Resistance." *Ethnic and Racial Studies* 21, no. 3 (1998): 476–506.

Yonah, Yossi. "Israel as a Multicultural Democracy: Challenges and Obstacles." *Israel Affairs* 1 (2005).

Young, Iris Marion. *Justice and the Politics of Difference.* Princeton, NJ: Princeton University Press, 1990.

Zakaria, Fareed. *The Future of Freedom: Illiberal Democracy at Home and Abroad.* New York: Norton, 2003.

"Israel's Biggest Danger." *Newsweek* 153 (8), February 23, 2009.

"The Rise of Illiberal Democracy." *Foreign Affairs* 76, 6 (1997): 22–43.

Zureik, Elia. "Being Palestinian in Israel." *Journal of Palestine Studies* 30, 3 (2001): 88–96.

*The Palestinians in Israel: A Study in Internal Colonialism.* London: Routledge and Kegan Paul, 1979.

# Index